Claus en Kaan Building

As I begin writing these words, the images of the architecture of Claus en Kaan are fresh in my mind, images I've been gazing at in a carefully edited book in which the intensity of the colour bespeaks its authors' ambition to present the works documented in it as faithfully as possible.* Terse, clean surfaces; blue and red walls; neat paving; glossy roofs; delineated plinths; precise windows, generous doors, and so on. Once the material used for building is defined, the constituent elements are encrusted in it without fuss, being installed in the overall whole, now with freedom, now by emphasizing the order with provocative boldness. Thus it is that in the architecture of Claus en Kaan we encounter facades in which the diversity of window spaces – in terms of their measurements and proportions – makes us think of the architectures of the interwar avant-gardes. At the same time there are other facades in which the regular disposition of the spaces puts us in mind of the influence the Italian Tendenza architects had on 1970s European architecture. Generally speaking, we can say that the architecture of Claus en Kaan is thought of in volumetric terms, in relation to the solid form that will become a building – houses, schools, hospitals, factories – once the elements are accommodated within it. There is in all the built work of Claus en Kaan a rejection of rhetoric that would lead us to conclude that they possess the puritan, contented distance of those who understand that it is not essential to enlist the help of the superfluous. Nothing in their work is unnecessary; it contains only what is right and necessary. Expression is reduced to the mere presence of materials and elements, without the architect assuming the role of inventor that we have become so accustomed to. The intrinsic austerity is what dictates the forms. But can we really speak of forms when faced with the architecture of Claus en Kaan? In it there seems to be a deliberate forgetting of iconography – something that implies the ignoring of all arbitrary form – with such forgetting giving primacy to the syntax. Architecture as the invention of a language, or, more accurately, architecture that understands language as syntax. Architecture, then, as a continual syntactical proposition that makes of the art of building its territory. Therein, perhaps, lies the key to understanding their work.

Claus en Kaan's energy seems to be devoted to exploring the meeting of materials and elements: such a meeting must be held responsible for the aura we perceive around the architecture of Claus en Kaan.
Brickwork/prefabricated concrete frames; red/blue; wood/plastic; stone/stucco; glass/steel; joints/panels. Glossiness as opposed to roughness. Order as opposed to

chance. Volume as opposed to line. Opacity as opposed to transparency. Perhaps the most important contrast of all is the one that leads us to speak of what, in the architecture of Claus en Kaan, takes place between artifice and nature. The contrast between materials that plainly have their origin in nature and those others that make no secret of their industrial provenance is a constant in the architecture of Claus en Kaan, who appear to take pleasure in this contrast by making continual use of it in the definition of their work: through this contrast, they seem to speak of what our culture is right now, a culture increasingly dependent on technology and industry, at a time when nostalgia is shown for a way of life in which a deeper awareness of ecology enables us to speak once again of nature. It is to the continuous contrast between materials, to the uncompromising juxtaposition of elements, much more than to the form, that Claus en Kaan entrust the epiphanic apparition of the architectural experience. Confirming such a hypothesis would lead us to affirm that when forms are present in their architecture they always allude to known forms: the status of strict quotations they often have, frees the architects from any kind of formal interpretation we might seek to give to their architecture.

This way of understanding the act of building, which renders the architect's task transparent, is not, however, foreign to the culture, to the society in which it is produced. Thus the work of Claus en Kaan is for us closer to all those virtues of Dutch society that we admire from down south. The taste for detail, the pleasure taken in the domestic world, which so astonishes us in the painters of Dutch interiors, is consistently present in the architecture of Claus en Kaan. Yet it must also be said that the desire for newness, so present in recent Dutch architecture – from De Stijl through Rietveld to Rem Koolhaas – has not been lost in this architecture which seems to celebrate, or at least not to overlook, the fragmented condition of our time. Perhaps it is – at any rate for me – this potential double reading of the architecture of Claus en Kaan that makes their work so contemporary, and therefore so attractive.

Rafael Moneo

* Michel, H., *Claus en Kaan*, Amsterdam 2000

NAi Publishers

Hans Ibelings

CLAUS EN KAAN

2
Rafael Moneo

9
Hans Ibelings Hard and Soft
The work of Claus en Kaan

13
Felix Claus and Kees Kaan Being there

16
Molenerf De Ster, Utrecht

20
Office and Apartment Kaan Assurantiën, Bergen op Zoom

22
Health Centre, Rotterdam

24
Buitenveldert Depot, Amsterdam

30
Molenwijk Children's Centre, Amsterdam

34
Housing, Haarlemmerbuurt, Amsterdam

38
Clubhouse Plejadenplein, Amsterdam

40
Apartments, Landsteinerlaan, Groningen

44
Business Centre Papaverweg, Amsterdam

48
Housing, Amstelveenseweg, Amsterdam

52
Spatial Master Plan, Southwest Quadrant Nieuw Sloten, Amsterdam

56
Hoornse Heem Pensioner Apartments, Groningen

58
Police Post and Social Services District Office, Amsterdam

62
Housing, Gulden Kruis, Amsterdam

70
Ronald McDonaldhouse and Apartments, Amsterdam

74
Housing, Marvelo, Zaandam

80
Housing, Sporenburg, Amsterdam

86
Communal Amenities, Dierdonk, Helmond

88
Van Schaik Company Premises, Breukelen

90
Housing, Hoogte and Laagte Kadijk, Amsterdam

96
Switching stations, PTT Telecom, Amsterdam

98
Housing, Vier Ambachten, Spijkenisse

102
Housing, Kalenderpanden, Amsterdam

104
Taxation Department Pavilion, Haarlem

106
Reception Pavilion Zorgvlied Cemetery, Amsterdam

110
Housing, Rietlanden, Amsterdam

114
Housing, De Aker, Amsterdam

116
Housing, Eekmaat, Enschede

118
Student Housing Drienerlo, Enschede

122
Housing, Park Duijnwijk, Zandvoort

124
Sheltered Housing, Stadshagen, Zwolle

128
Draaisma House, Amsterdam

130
Housing, Beekpark, Apeldoorn

132
Housing, Zenderpark, IJsselstein

134
University of Amsterdam Deck, Amsterdam

136
Apartment Tower, Almere

140
Dutch Embassy, Maputo

144
Housing, Floriande Island 10, Haarlemmermeer

146
Urban Design, Haveneiland and Rieteilanden, Amsterdam

150
Hotel, Oostelijke Handelskade, Amsterdam

154
Netherlands Forensic Institute, Rijswijk

160
Housing, Oostelijke Handelskade, Amsterdam

162
Municipal Offices, Breda

166
National Museum of Modern Art, Rome

170
Municipal Archives, Amsterdam

174
Museum Nationaal Monument Kamp Vught, Vught

176
Town Hall, Tynaarlo

180
David Chipperfield Serious and Romantic

182
Andrea Deplazes Les extrèmes se touchent
Visiting Claus en Kaan

186
Christoph Grafe Urbane Architectures

191
Building 1988-2001

229
Biography Felix Claus and Kees Kaan, 229
Bibliography, 230
Lectures, 232
Exhibitions and prizes, 233
Staff members Claus en Kaan Architecten, 234
About the authors, 235
Picture credits, 236
Acknowledgements, 237

238
Han Michel

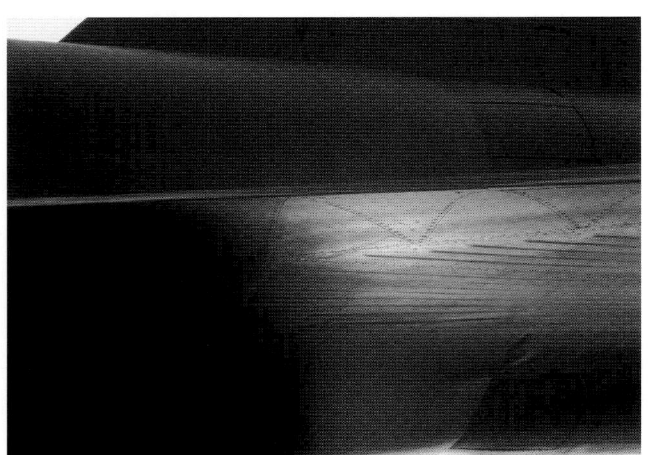

HARD AND SOFT

THE WORK OF CLAUS EN KAAN

Hans Ibelings

Building: the very soberness of the title of this book says much about the work of Claus en Kaan. It reduces architecture to what these architects see as the essence of their profession. Kees Kaan and Felix Claus once described their endeavour as the desire to breach the barrier between low practice and high theory, between architecture that serves its immediate purpose and architecture that addresses itself, over the heads of the users, to fellow-architects and critics. There is more to this than the logical conclusion that architecture must transcend humdrum functionality without succumbing to theoretical pretensions. The statement reveals two fundamentals of their work. In the first place it alludes to their quest for a normal architecture that acknowledges the richness of the profession as intellectual discipline and the meaning of building as craft. Secondly, it characterizes their method of working, which is all about breaching barriers. This is not, certainly not in their case, synonymous with abolishing differences. In the architecture of Claus en Kaan difference is generally explicitly present, even if it is at first sight often concealed by a simple outward form. The complexity of the work is revealed not in discordant confrontations of contrasts, but rather in the unproblematical marriage of two or more incompatible images or realities.

The clearest instances of such conjunctions of incongruous images are to be found in projects where morphology and typology are apparently at odds. Examples are the public works depot in Amsterdam-Buitenveldert that looks like a patio bungalow, and the factory-like housing blocks beside the river Zaan. At issue in these and other projects, is not so much the difference between appearance and reality, as the uncoupling of architectural form and programmatic content, the disentangling of the general meaning of a building for the city and the expression of the specific architectural purpose and, nearly always, the creation of a palpable distinction between inside and outside.

Architectural form is neither a product nor a representation of function in the work of Claus en Kaan. In this it deviates from both modern and post-modern determinism. Yet the form is not entirely autonomous either, even though it could be argued that there is an unarticulated parallel with Aldo Rossi's ideas on autonomous architecture. Certainly in buildings that they would term generic and that are not tied to a unique programme, the architectural form is to a large degree self-sufficient. The architecture of Claus en Kaan is not generic in the sense of having no particularity, a meaning that Rem Koolhaas and his many imitators have conferred on that word. Generic in their architecture refers to the neutral relationship between form and programme. However distinct the architectural form may be, it is not necessarily programmatically defined. The form has a rationale of its own, independent of any functional (pre-)determination, however much that function may have prompted the form in the first place. In that respect the work begs comparison with the dualistic modernism of Gordon Bunshaft who displayed a great affinity with form, material and detail, but who usually managed to deploy these powerful ingredients to produce a neutral architecture.

The lack of congruence between form and programme finds an echo in similar disparities between exterior and interior and, at the level of the street, between front and rear. In many cases these are differences of the 'stern of face, soft at heart' variety. The exterior is generally neutral, rational, hard, aloof or abstract; the interior tactile, colourful, spatial and sensuous. In the work of Claus en Kaan, hard and soft are not ranged against one another as two extremes but are inextricably bound up with one another. Severity and geniality: these two qualities characterize the entire oeuvre of Claus en Kaan. And since they often appear together, the architecture of Claus en Kaan, even at its most Spartan, is never inhumane.

The idea of two discrete worlds that exist side by side without contradicting one another also finds expression in most of the projects in which old and new are combined. As projects in historical contexts or involving the conversion of listed buildings make clear, Claus en Kaan are not in the business of paying polite lip service to what is, was or might have been. Old and new stand side by side in their architecture, crystal-clear and unmixed.

Claus en Kaan have realized several projects in the historical inner city but it is not necessarily the setting with which they have the greatest affinity, nor the one where their architecture shows to best advantage. That distinction belongs to the open, postwar housing estate and to the 'stone city' of boulevards and large housing blocks that blossomed in the nineteenth century. The Netherlands is richly endowed with the first, while the second is virtually non-existent. In the open suburban developments of the 1950s and '60s, Claus en Kaan invariably show themselves to be circumspect modernizers who treat the existing architecture and the spatial structures and features with respect. The housing projects in Groningen and Schiedam and the depot in Buitenveldert are good examples.

Also evident in the work of Claus en Kaan is a great affinity with the architecture of the stone city, with its regular street patterns and long rows of town houses. A rarity in the Netherlands, such contexts have in recent years been invented from scratch: in the housing developments at Sporenburg and Rietlanden in Amsterdam, in the houses with formal, fenced-in front gardens in Amsterdam South and De Aker, and in the spatial master plan for IJburg drawn up in collaboration with Ton Schaap and Frits van Dongen. In all these cases, the dwellings are conceived in accordance with the German tradition of the turn of the 20th century: as the material with which to build cities.

Ever since the publication of *Collage City* by Colin Rowe and Robert Slutzky, it has been customary in the architectural world to think in terms of the spatial contrast between figure and ground. In this way of thinking, the pre- and postmodern closed city and the modern, open city are diametrically opposed as positive and negative – which Rowe and Slutzky visualized rhetorically in maps where mass and space were represented by black and white. For Claus en Kaan it is not a question of choosing between positive and negative; they approach both aspects with the same strategy, one based on the primacy of the spatial plan.

There is an architectural counterpart to this in the *Leitbilder* between which the architecture of Claus en Kaan oscillates: the patio bungalow and the factory, metaphors for a relaxed modernism and a stern rationalism. They not only represent the green suburb and the stone city, but also exemplify two different architectural approaches, one geared to beauty and comfort, the other to an ascetic renunciation of aesthetics.

Although there is no way the architecture of Claus en Kaan could be seen as postmodern, their stance is nonetheless indebted to postmodernism. This is evident not only in their free use of references, such as Marcel Breuer's Whitney Museum or Mies van der Rohe's Barcelona Pavilion. It is above all evident in their broad and undogmatic interests, which range from Heinrich Tessenow to Gordon Bunshaft, from Auguste Perret to I.M. Pei. They do not see any real contradiction between modernist and classical values.

Because of this, Claus en Kaan do not belong to the category of innovators who believe that architecture should bear direct witness to cultural, social and economic change. It is not macro-phenomena such as these that stimulate them to produce a new architecture. The innovative aspect of their work lies in the way they bring together discrete worlds and ways of thinking and in so doing breathe new life into the traditions of their own discipline.

Just as Schinkel was a natural reference for Mies van der Rohe, and Mies in turn for Gordon Bunshaft, so Schinkel, Mies and Bunshaft are natural references for Claus en Kaan. In that respect they are continuing a tradition of a modern architecture that is aimed not, or not primarily, at formal or technical innovation, but at purification. Minimalist design and expression are the hallmarks of this approach, not aesthetic aims as such. Claus en Kaan's interpretation of both classic and modern architecture is one that encompasses the simplicity of the everyday, that looks not for the exceptional but for the self-evident. In the hands of architects, the self-evident inevitably acquires a certain glamour, an architectural dimension impossible to avoid. This is why the self-evidence Claus en Kaan aspire to will never be fully achieved, because they cannot pretend that they are not architects. And, paradoxically enough, in the midst of all those works by colleagues bent on making something idiosyncratic and unusual, their pursuit of a self-evident, ordinary architecture results in something personal.

The substantial body of work Claus en Kaan have realized to date reflects their consistent pursuit of an architecture in which arbitrariness has been reduced to a minimum. But the high level of consistency in their work is not solely down to their design philosophy. There is also a more prosaic explanation: the size of their portfolio. Because the practice has so many commissions and builds so much, and because it is impossible to keep on reinventing architecture time after time, the oeuvre is necessarily a succession of thematically and formally related works.

In addition, the discovery of a specific, tailor-made solution always overlaps with the most universal solution. Though the universal solution is not present in pure form in any one work, it can be distilled from the oeuvre as a whole. In *The Shape of Time: Remarks on the History of Things* (1962), the archaeologist George F. Kubler described how in every classification system, objects cluster like satellites around a non-existent ideal. Every division into categories is based on a ranking of individual objects vis à vis a notional type that embodies all the characteristics in their purest form. The real objects can be seen as smaller or larger deviations from that ideal. With many architects, coherence takes the form of a personal style that permeates every building to a greater or lesser degree. With Claus en Kaan it is much more a matter of an oeuvre that revolves around an essence that is approached more nearly with every successive project. In this respect they can be compared with oeuvre-builders like Mies van der Rohe, who arrived at the same thing every time, or Paul Schmitthenner, whose entire body of work can be characterized as an encircling of the idea of the German private house. Claus en Kaan do something similar, albeit to a less extreme degree. In their architecture they are always looking for the same thing, however different the circumstances and however different the results may be. It is always possible to discover some hint of the unifying keynote of an ideal. That ideal can by definition never be deduced from one, or even a few, buildings. Even when one considers the entire oeuvre to date, it is still not possible to identify it precisely.

The Netherlands has never known anything comparable to Palm Springs in 1960 or Berlin in 1900. Nonetheless, these two very different cities encapsulate the ideals on which the architecture of Claus en Kaan turns. Their works can be read as reflections or after-images of these models, as incomplete recollections of something that has never existed here. In that sense it is possible to detect a certain nostalgia in the work of Claus en Kaan – not so much a yearning for another age, as a mild homesickness for forms of urbanism and architecture that do not exist in the Netherlands.

This nostalgic component makes their architecture comparable to the realistic tendency in postwar architecture as described by Manfredo Tafuri in an essay ('Realismus und Architektur') for the 1984 anthology *Das Abenteuer der Ideen; Architektur und Philosophie seit der industriellen Revolution* (The Adventure of Ideas; Architecture and Philosophy since the Industrial Revolution). Tafuri categorized the late work of architects like Ridolfi and Frankl and Ludovico Quaroni as realist, seeing in their architecture a direct reflection of the available methods and means of production. Such realist architecture is directed not towards formal or technological innovation but towards the interpretation of the given circumstances, towards finding a new form for familiar images.

In an architectural culture that is besotted with the one-off shock of the new, the realism with which Claus en Kaan are building up an oeuvre that prioritizes familiarity is striking. Realism is a concept that relates to various aspects of the work of Claus en Kaan: not only to their interpretation of familiar images, but also, for example, to the detailing. For all the precision, the details are often surprisingly simple, and simple to make. But they also often resort to standard products, such as frames and doors, which are used as supplied. The pragmatism this implies should not, however, be construed as nonchalance or cynicism. What it comes down to is that Claus en Kaan accept Dutch conditions and all the restraints this entails. The culture of endless consultation and the parsimonious budgets that many of their colleagues complain of, do not faze them in the least: they manage to achieve an optimal result by not rowing against the current. After all, going with the current makes it easier to steer one's own course. It is in this sense that Claus en Kaan are pragmatists, but they are passionate pragmatists. Their enthusiasm reveals itself in the optimism with which they approach their discipline, as reflected in their credo: 'Building is an expression of optimism. This optimism is our principal motivation.'

BEING THERE

Felix Claus and Kees Kaan

What was particularly nice about the garden was that at any moment, standing in the narrow paths or amidst the bushes and trees, Chance could start to wander, never knowing whether he was ahead of or behind his previous steps. All that mattered was moving in his own time, like the growing plants.

Jerzy N. Kosinski, *Being There*, 1971

Time

In *Being There*, the gardener Chauncy Gardiner, Chance, has his own world that begins and ends at the wall of the garden he has tended since he was a child and which is also his source of knowledge. For information about what is happening outside the walls he depends on television. He has no contact with other people. Time is measured by the seasons.

Architecture is by nature slow. The time a project takes from the first contact between client and architect to the final handover is long. In some of our projects this period has stretched to as much as seven or eight years. An idea on which a project is based is often already dated before the building has been occupied, especially when that idea is derived from fashion or the latest trends. The same applies to the building programme. In many cases a space requested at the beginning for a specific use is no longer needed by the time the building is finished.

The social and architectural context within which a project comes about is subject to continuous change and it keeps on changing even after the building is finished. As such, architecture is not simply a material reflection of a complex programme for use, but is more a matter of buildings that facilitate various forms of use.

Once upon a time we pondered how to go about making architecture. Now we know that it cannot be made. All you can do is build and that building may subsequently turn into architecture. Architecture is born out of building. The physical presence and stubbornness of materials, people and time, which force us to get our hands dirty, have a decisive and profound impact on the quality of the project. Acceptance of the banal conditions of construction enables a good concept to become fit for building.

Knowledge

I don't want to be interesting, I want to be good.

Ludwig Mies van der Rohe

The will to architecture is tedious, even irritating. All that striving after originality is fatal. What would architects make if they were possessed of universal knowledge? If every architect were to be programmed with the complete history of architecture, with an encyclopaedic knowledge of everything ever conceived in architecture? Concepts can be judged purely on the basis of intelligence and utility. Knowledge renders the idle craving for originality superfluous.

In the Netherlands there exists an ideal basis for architecture without originality. Dutch consensus society is not conducive to the creativity of brilliant individuals, whether they be clients or designers. The development of our built environment is so organized that all the parties involved have a direct say in it. The architect has no special authority as creator but is primarily a professional adviser in a team made up of all concerned. The design is the outcome of a process for which the entire team is responsible.

We experience both the design and the building process as a necessary self-punishment, but it is our firm belief that the essence of each project can only be discovered in this dual process. We consequently see no reason to complain about something that is an immutable part of the society in which we work. We adapt and turn the culture of consensus to our advantage.

The lack of autonomy of the design can result in considerable latitude for the designer. Freed from the compulsion to be original, an idea can assume an infinite number of outward forms. Like beaches that change as the tide shifts the sand, like the plants in Chance's garden. The idea remains constant, the form changes. The form is not the aim, but the outcome of an action. Beauty is contingent upon the degree of care with which that action is performed.

This care implies a maximum degree of expertise, attention, concentration. The moment we reject the imperative of originality, a world opens up for us. What is needed is not the celebration of the latest technological development but intelligent use and command of it. Only through command of knowledge and technology can we liberate ourselves from them.

All this begins with acceptance of our condition, our 'being there'. We sidestep architecture as concept and simply set about making buildings and cities.

Being an architect is not about architecture, being an architect is an attitude.

**Viele sind dazu ausgebildet, ein Urteil zu fällen,
aber nur Wenigen ist es gegeben, zu machen.
Es gilt darum, die Meisterschaft zu ehren.**

Karl Friedrich Schinkel

BUILDING

001 003 006 008
MOLENERF DE STER, UTRECHT

The juxtaposition of old and new, amalgamation without interweaving, is an important motif in the transformation of a former sawmill into a mixed-use complex of day care centre, studios, practice space and offices.

The eighteenth-century wind-powered sawmill, which was in use right up until 1982, is a pastoral enclave in the middle of the city. The complex was restored by the Utrecht Department for Conservation after which the sawmill and the sheds used for drying the wood were adapted for contemporary use. The project was realized in stages and with a limited budget. An architectural firm's first real project is often a tentative quest for an authentic approach. In this case the singularity was there from the start; at most it cost rather a lot of time and paper before a definitive solution emerged from the myriad of possibilities.

The day care centre is housed in one of the former drying sheds and is slightly below ground level. The central zone is occupied over its entire length by a volume containing rooms on two levels. One of the long elevations, previously open, was closed off with corrugated sheet punctuated by five large bay windows.

The studios were inserted into the other shed as a box within a box. This solution is typical of an approach in which both old and new are accorded an autonomous existence. The new threads its way through the existing structure, but makes no allusions to it. Yet although the formal and spatial interventions make no concessions to the monument, they are so reticent that the original architecture appears untouched. 'The addition must, by way of a restrained contrast, reinforce the shell and offer a new encounter. This is accomplished by placing patently modern materials alongside the existing ones and letting them speak for themselves.'

In this forthrightness, the addition takes its cue from the architecture of the sawmill. The early industrial monument and the post-industrial conversion share a similar perspicuity and directness.

Unbuilt design for music practice space

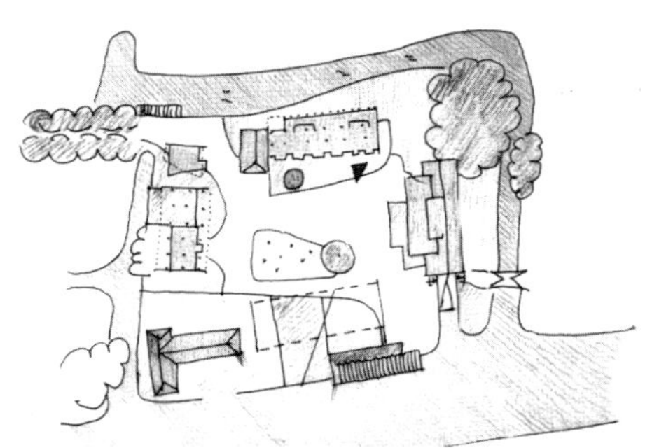

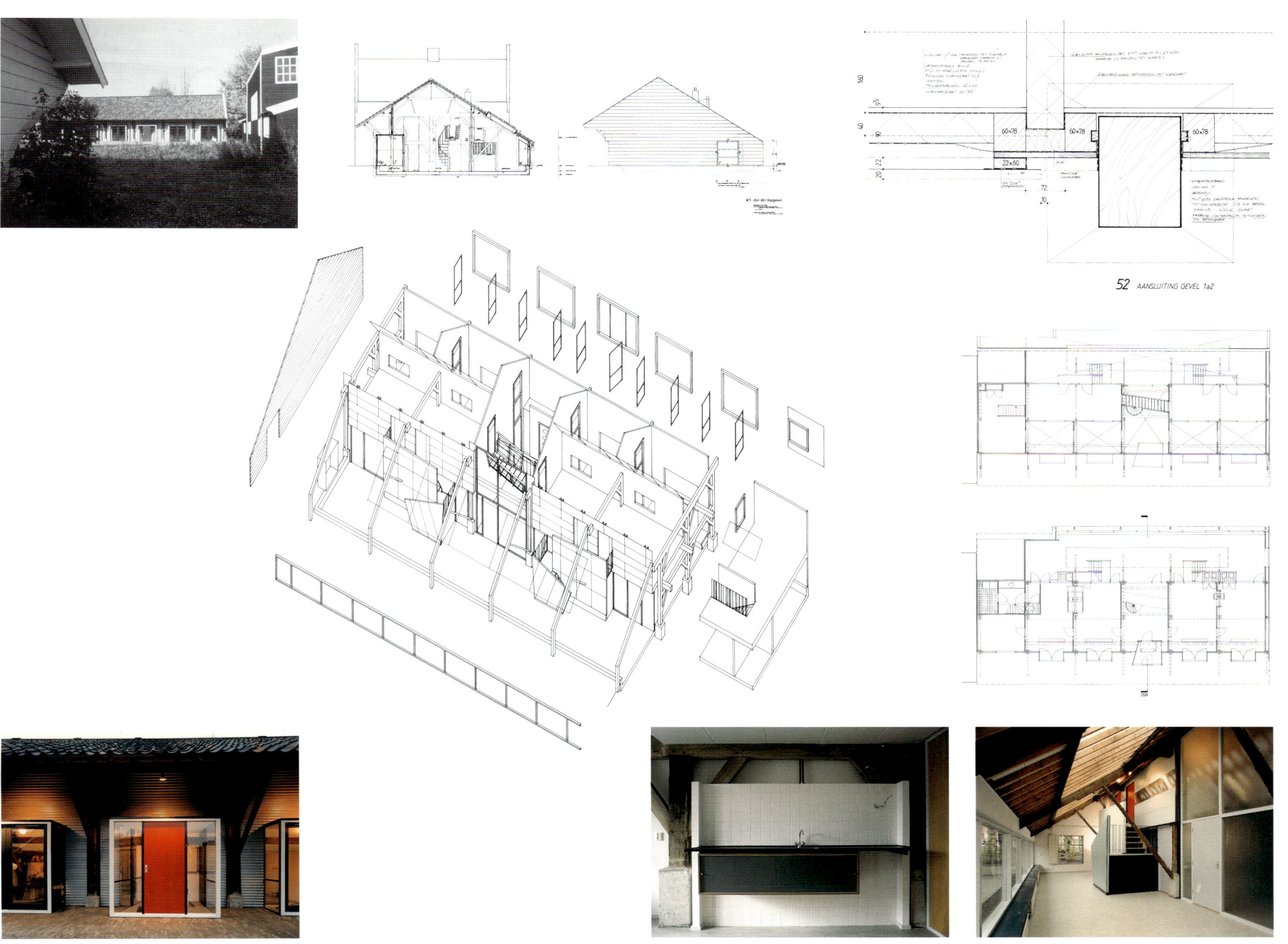
60×78
60×78
60×78
22×60
52 AANSLUITING GEVEL 1a2

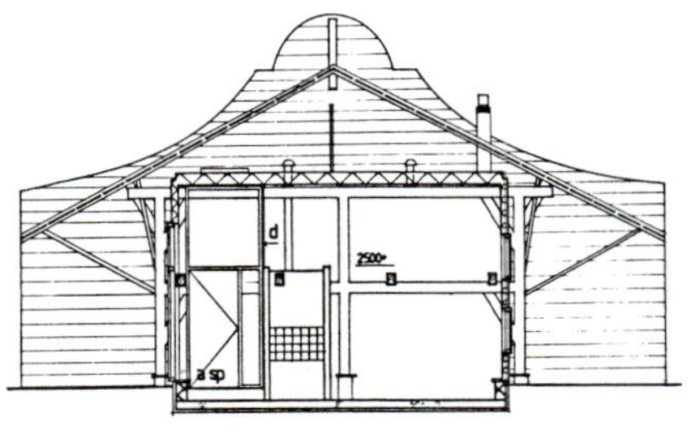

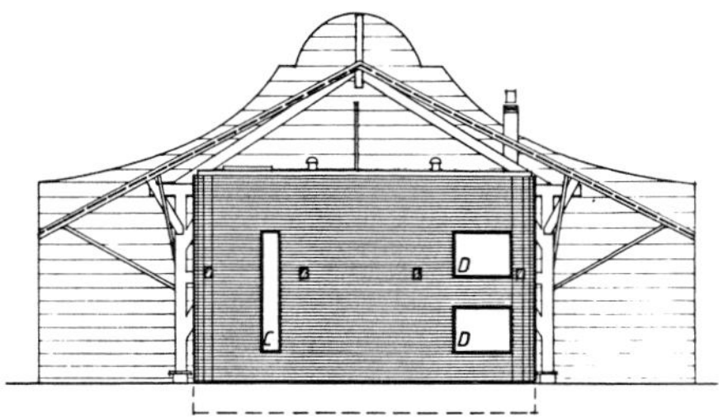
D
D
C

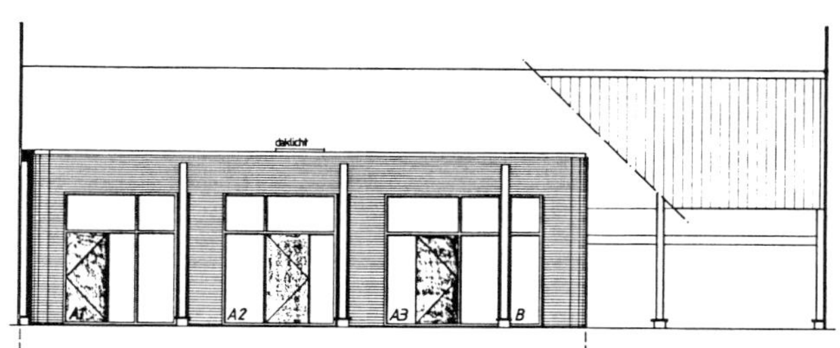
daklicht
A1
A2
A3
B

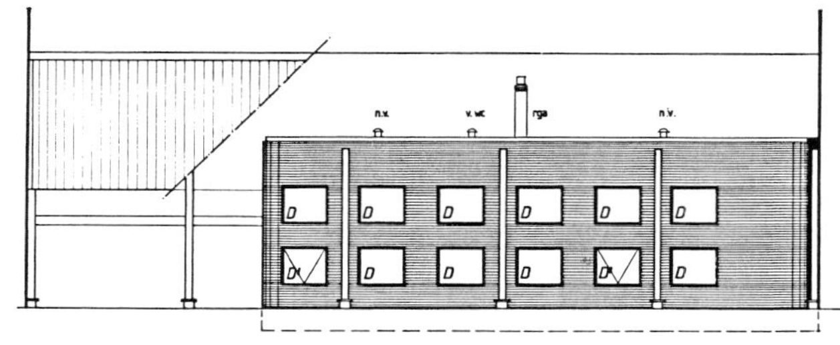
rga
D

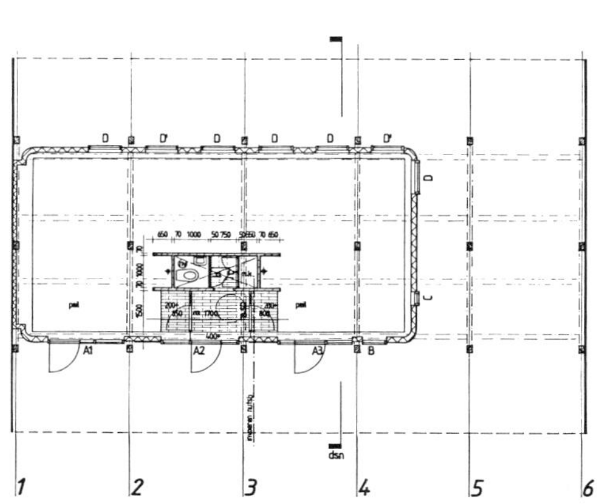
A1
A2
A3
B
1
2
3
4
5
6

005 029
OFFICE AND APARTMENT KAAN ASSURANTIËN, BERGEN OP ZOOM

A basically straightforward assignment, the conversion of two buildings located along a main road into double-width business premises with upstairs flat, has been seized on here for an exploration of the facade as separating and ordering element. The new elevation, which screens the two premises from public view, is an abstract skin whose thickness is made explicit at various points. These 'strategic details' underscore the ambiguity of the tectonic mass of the elevation and the ephemeral thinness of the facade. The building consists of two open spaces one above the other. On the ground floor the space is bisected by a wall of cupboards that separates the travel agency from the insurance office, and in the upstairs flat by a pivoted wooden wall beside the kitchen which allows the loft to be divided into a living and a study area.

There is no immediate relationship between interior and exterior. The verticality of the huge frames on the front elevation not only contradicts the horizontality of the spaces behind, but the associated displacement vis à vis the facade plane weakens still further the connection between outside and inside. The steel and glass facade sections appear merely to rest against the facade which reveals its true thickness at only a few places, such as the glass door of the insurance office where the steel frame projects ever so slightly from the facade. Such nuances are lost on motorists whizzing past at fifty kilometres an hour who see only an abstract billboard that is illuminated at night by three spotlights. The composition of the facade as executed is determined by a subtle asymmetry in the division of the surface. The chosen solution was one of many. During the design process a lot of possibilities that would have resulted in a more complex facade composition were explored and rejected. The end product would not look out of place on one of car-minded Los Angeles' many boulevards, of which the 'straatweg' is the much rarer Dutch equivalent.

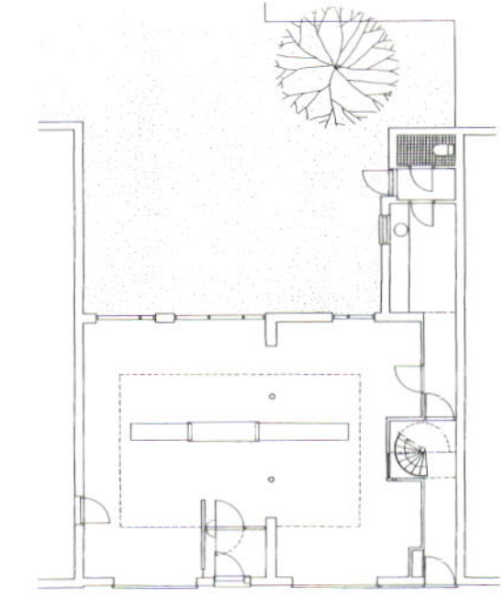

1 Garfield Avenue, Alhambra
2 Frank O'Gehry, Gehry House, Santa Monica, 1979
3 Office
4 House

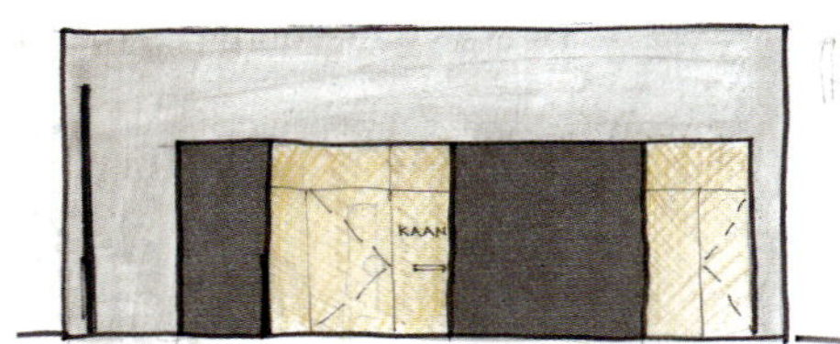

1

2

3

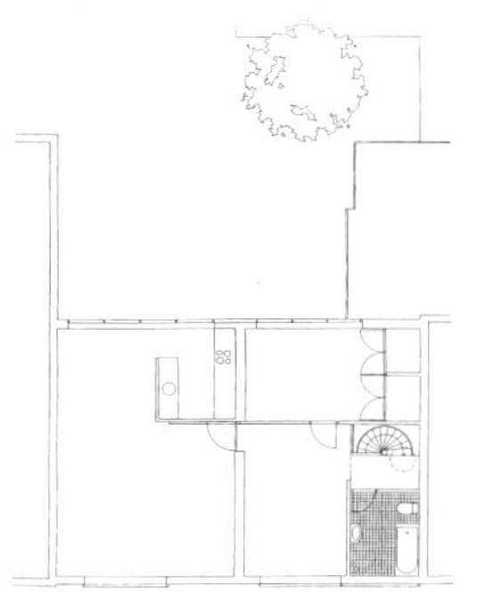

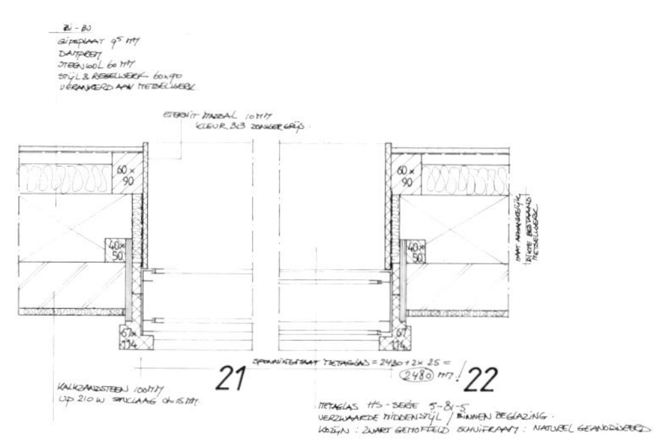

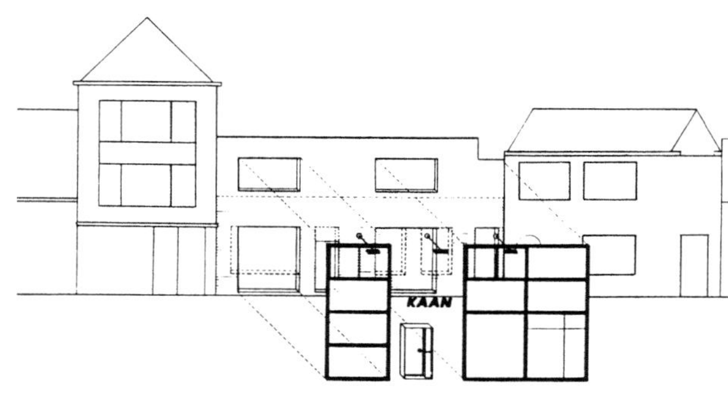

4

4

Office and Apartment Kaan Assurantiën, Bergen op Zoom

012
HEALTH CENTRE, ROTTERDAM

Two adjacent business premises on the Afrikaander housing estate in Rotterdam were knocked together to provide space for three doctor's consulting rooms, a treatment room, an office, a kitchen and a waiting room. The translucent facade of glass bricks floods the interior with light without compromising the privacy of its users. A tall, narrow corridor running from front to back is the ordering element in the interior. From the outside, the glazed elevations lend the conversion a strong sense of abstraction that is in marked contrast to the bleak social housing dating from around 1900. As in the conversion of the sawmill in Utrecht, there has been no attempt to blur the boundaries between old and new. The frames encasing the new facades separate them visually from the existing architecture. The difference in height between the two facade sections is accentuated by the thick surrounds of clear glass.

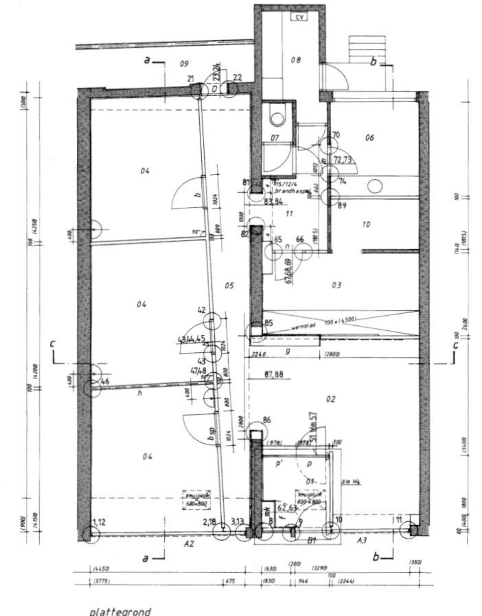

plattegrond

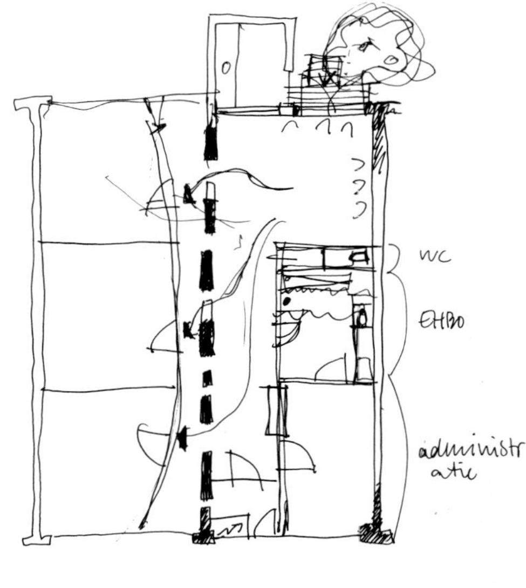

Health Centre, Rotterdam

023
BUITENVELDERT DEPOT, AMSTERDAM

The depot of the public works department of the Amsterdam borough of Buitenveldert, combines the functionality of a warehouse with the opulence of a bungalow. Function and appearance contradict one another.
The convention of utilitarian simplicity usually associated with the premises of those who maintain the public realm is breached by the generous architecture, the stylishness of the entrance with canopy, the glazed elevations and the flagstone walls. As such, the architecture imparts glamour to the workaday existence of public works employees.

The architecture is as relaxed as the music of Stan Getz, with everything falling 'coolly' into place. At the urban level, the building is an appropriate response to the modern open planning of the district, at the architectural level it alludes to the heyday of postwar modernism that was almost unknown in the Netherlands but which found expression, for example, in the 'Case Study Houses'.

The depot slots into the orthogonal pattern of freestanding objects that characterizes the postwar district of Buitenveldert. Coherence is achieved at the local level in that the long narrow building forms a screen that marks the boundary between the linear parkway and the square in front of the building.

The depot is the first in a series of 'flat boxes' by Claus en Kaan in which the programme is organized horizontally. The long corridor, which in many of these works is the organizing motif, here runs along the full 56 metres of the rear of the building. This passageway not only provides access to nearly all the workrooms and to the locker and shower rooms, but also acts as a filter between the depot and the tree-lined street. At two points along its length huge, floor-height glazed facade sections establish a connection between inside and outside.

During the design process, the search for ways of simplifying the shape and composition of the building went hand in hand with an increasing refinement of material, space and detail, in the course of which contrasts were accentuated. The depot shows Claus en Kaan at their – literally – most sensational, with a strong contrast between the tactile wall of natural stone and the huge areas of cool glass, between the massiveness of the wall and the lightness of the glass box and of the canopy resting on the wall, between the natural colours of the materials and the brightly coloured planes in the interior which are also visible from the outside through the two transparent panels. Thus is the difference between interior and exterior, between indoor and outdoor world, brought to the surface.

1

2

1 Stan Getz Plays, Verve Records, 1953
2 Erwin Broner, Can Erik, Formentera
3 Pierre Koenig, Case Study House #21, Los Angeles, 1958
4 Ludwig Mies van der Rohe, German pavilion, World's Fair, Barcelona, 1929

PARK
WERKPLAATS
PARK

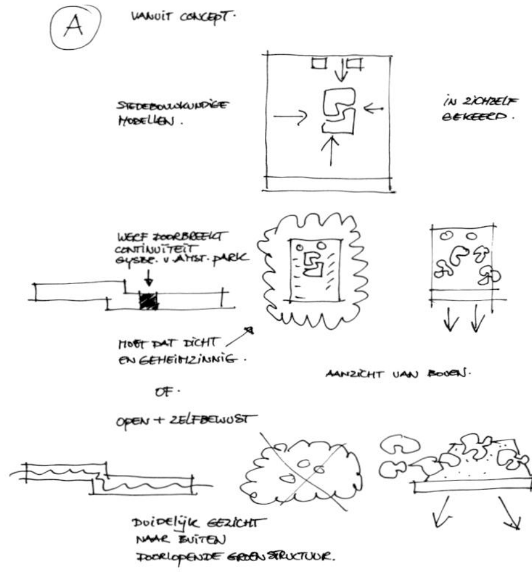

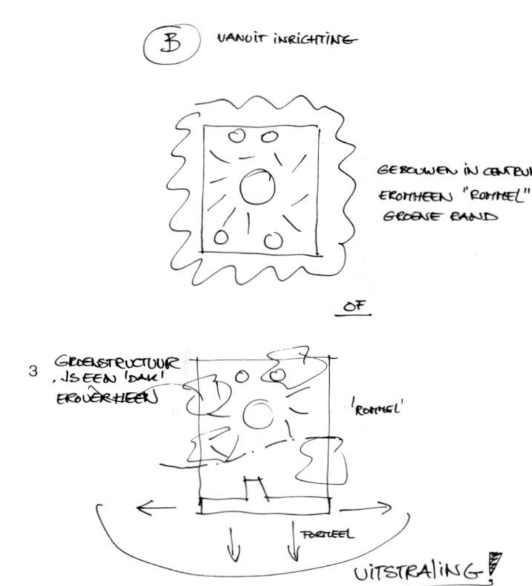

3

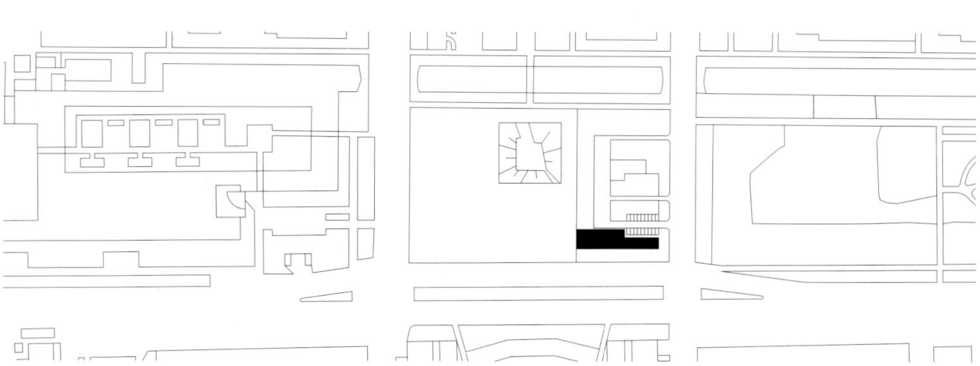

3

4

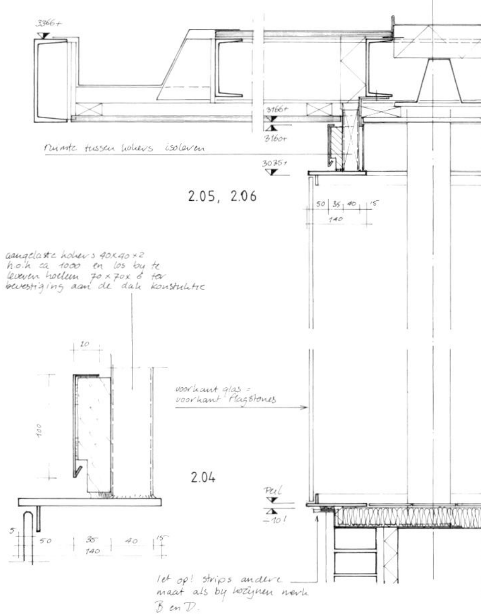
3366+
3166+
3160+
ruimte tussen kokers isoleren
3035+
2.05, 2.06
50 35 40 15
140
aangelaste kokers 40x40x2
h.o.h ca 1000 en los by te
leveren hoeken 70x70x6 ter
bevestiging aan de dak konstruktie
20
100
voorkant glas =
voorkant flagstones
2.04
Peil
-10!
5
50 35 40 15
140
let op! strips andere
maat als by kozijnen werk
B en D.

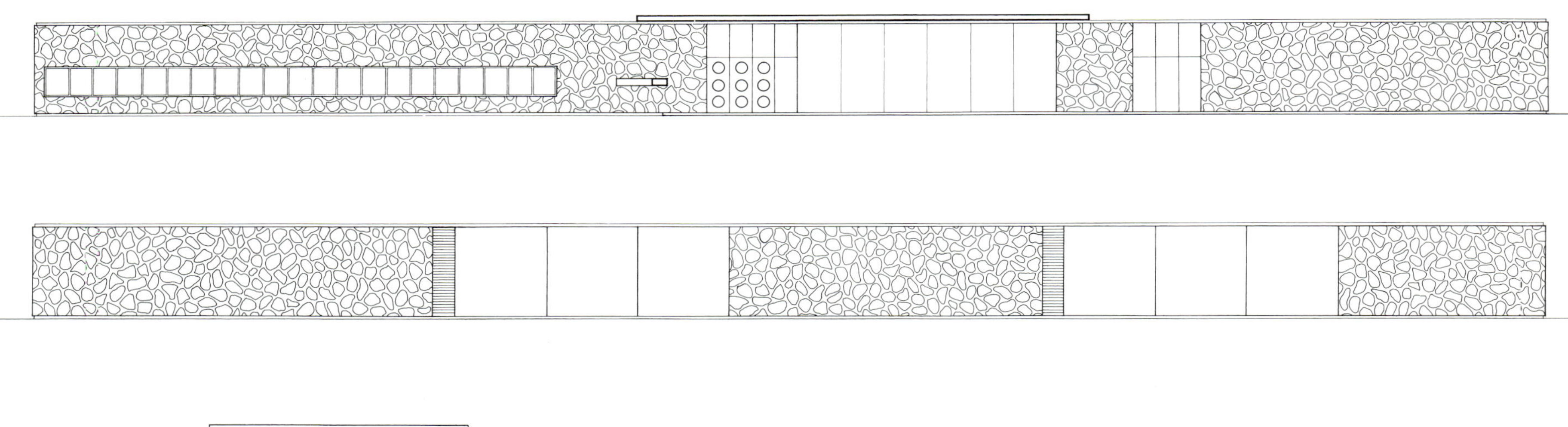

Eero Saarinen, General Motors Technical Centre, Warren, Michigan, 1948–1956

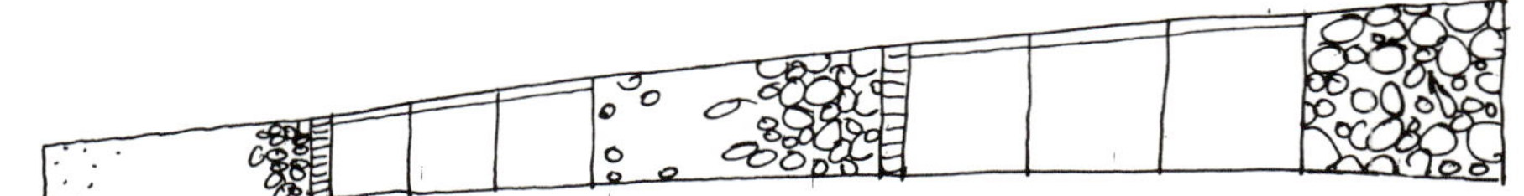

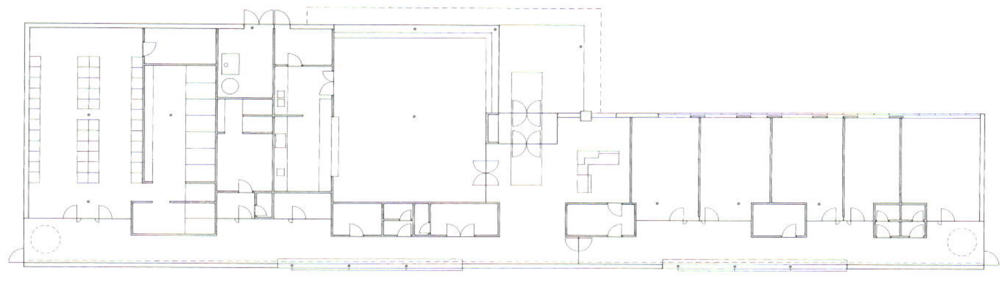

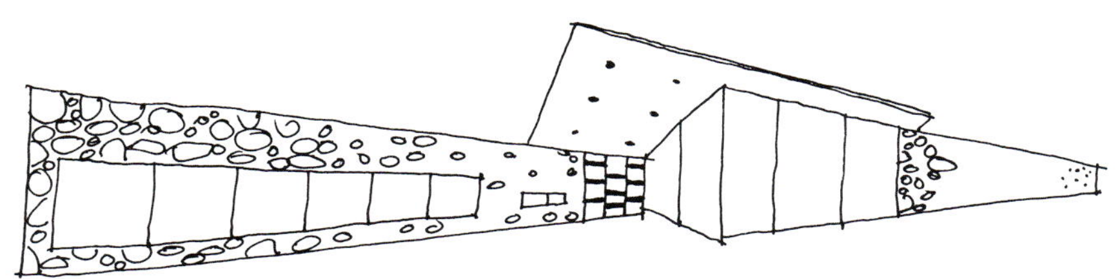

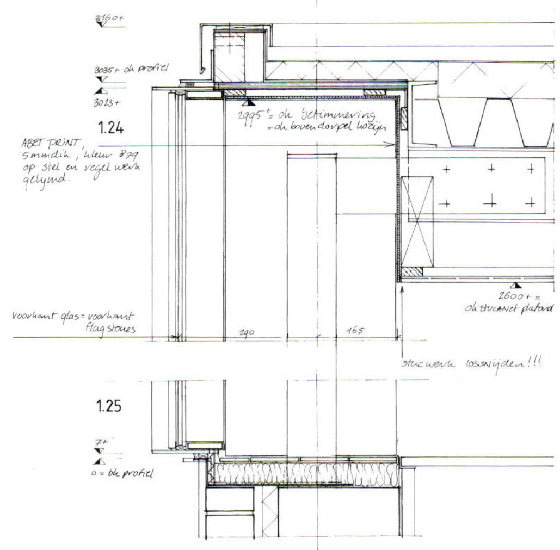
3160+
3035+ oh profiel
3023+
2995+ = oh betimmering = oh bovendorpel kozijn
1.24
ABET PRINT, 5mm dik, kleur 879 op stel en regelwerk gelijmd.
2600+ = oh stucwerk plafond
voorkant glas = voorkant flagstones
290
165
stucwerk lossnijden!!!
1.25
7+
0 = bk profiel

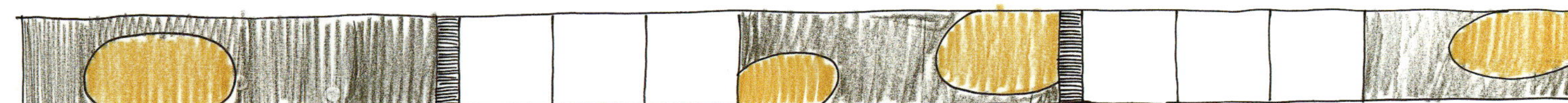

ZUIDGEVEL.

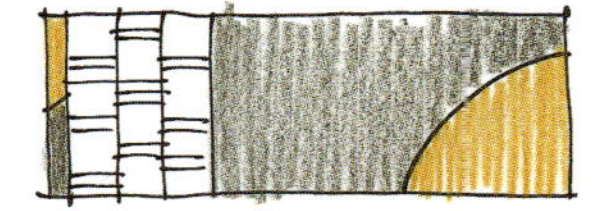

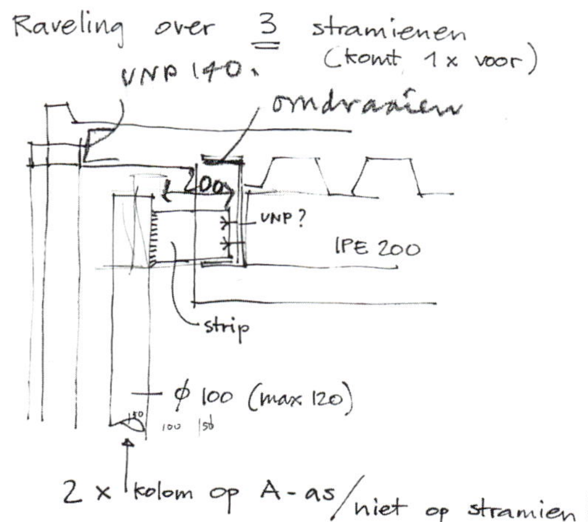

Raveling over 3 stramienen
(komt 1x voor)
UNP 140.
omdraaien
200
UNP ?
IPE 200
strip
ϕ 100 (max 120)
2 x kolom op A-as/niet op stramien!

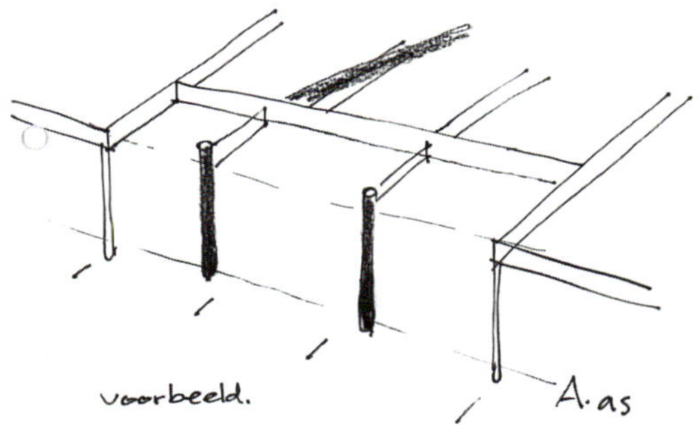

voorbeeld.
A.as

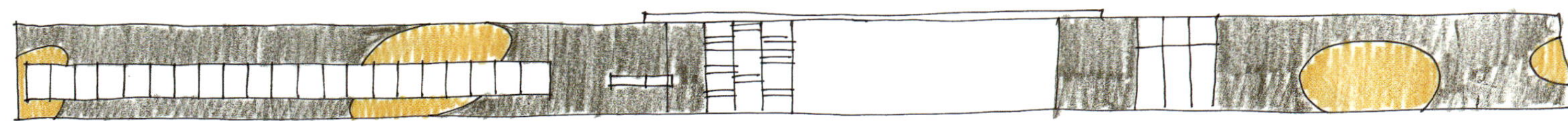

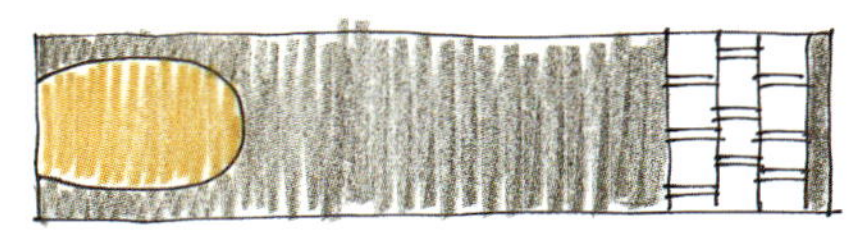

NOORDGEVEL

026 MOLENWIJK CHILDREN'S CENTRE, AMSTERDAM

The Molenwijk complex comprises a day care centre for babies and toddlers, a play room for pre-schoolers and after-school facilities for children up to the age of twelve. The building stands at the foot of tall, gallery-access flats built in the early 1960s as a dress rehearsal for the Bijlmermeer development in Amsterdam Southeast, the most famous example of large-scale modernist open planning in the Netherlands and coincidentally emblematic of the total failure of this approach. The principles applied in Bijlmermeer are found here on a smaller scale, with clusters of high-rise flats surrounded by green space.

Apart from the all-dominating high-rise, the neighbourhood also boasts a square-like space with several low school buildings that lack any clear relationship either to one another or to the blocks of flats. The children's centre serves to give these indeterminate surroundings a greater sense of cohesion.

Although the centre is strongly introverted, providing a place of shelter within the boundless space, it does not entirely repudiate the modernist openness that is so appropriate in this setting. The ambivalence is most strikingly in evidence at each end of the building where the long elevation continues in the form of freestanding walls that act as screens defining the playground. These two planes are linked, not by a solid wall but by the relatively 'soft' boundary of a vine-covered fence.

In the heart of the building is a patio. The severity of the long walls of dark concrete brick is relieved by a glazed staff room from where personnel can keep an eye on the playground, and by the wooden protrusions of the pre-schoolers' dormitories.

In this building and in many that came after it, it is possible to see the retrospective significance of the exhibition display that Mark Linnemann and Pieter Bannenberg produced for Claus en Kaan. Designed to present Molenerf, their first project, at an exhibition in the Centraal Museum in Utrecht. The display consisted of a box out of which a volume had been cut. With hindsight, this can now be seen as a model for a design approach where inside and outside, rather than being connected to each another in a congruent fashion, each represent their own world.

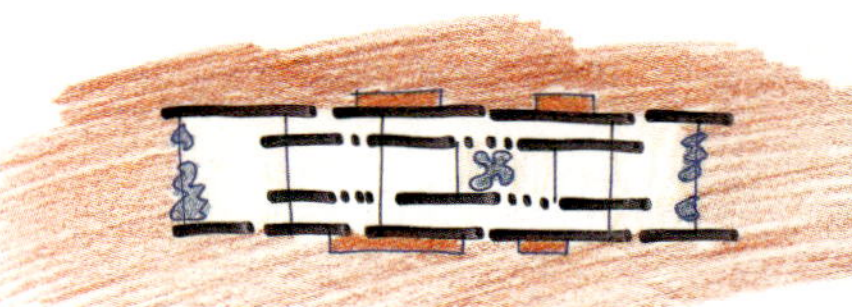

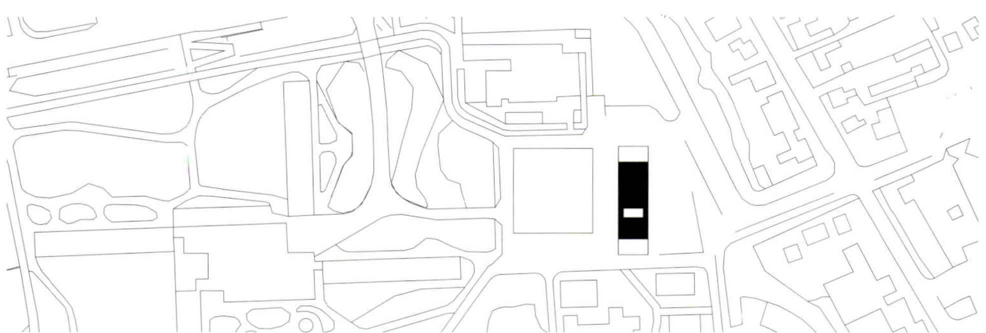

Mark Linnemann and Pieter Bannenberg,
exhibition design, Utrecht, 1994

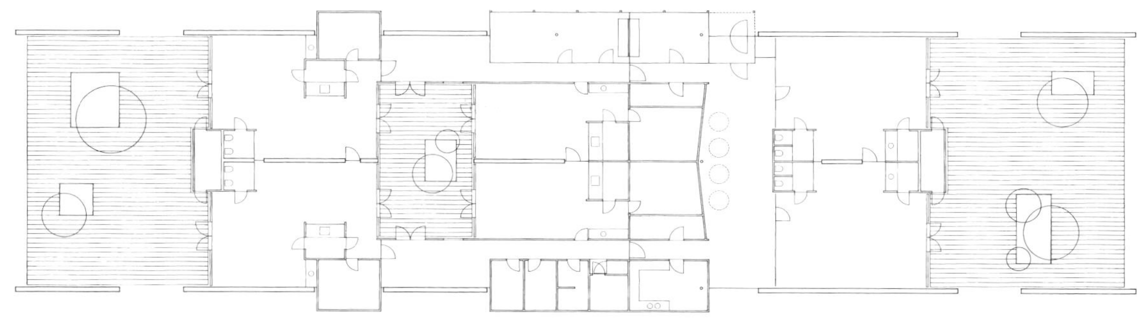

Molenwijk Children's Centre, Amsterdam

028 030 048 059 HOUSING, HAARLEMMER-BUURT, AMSTERDAM

The dense urban fabric of the Haarlemmerstraat area acts as the boundary between an old docks area and the formal urbanization of the historic canal zone. Four designs – three of which were executed – were made for this area as part of a municipal urban renewal scheme.

On Binnen Wieringerstraat, two historic monuments were combined into a single building containing three apartments. The fabric of one of the monuments was retained, the adjoining one was completely demolished and replaced by a new structure. This approach was applauded and encouraged by veteran architects H.J. Zantkuyl and Herman Knijtijzer who were involved in the project on behalf of the Netherlands Department for Conservation.

In the historic monument each storey is a clear bay containing the living room and kitchen; in the new section, the entrance, bathroom/toilet and bedroom are separated from the front elevation by a full-height hall with spiral staircase. Although the tripartite and partially frosted glass facade of the new building is totally unrelated in form and type to the context, the neutrality of the reductive abstraction ensures that it slots comfortably into its surroundings. There was even talk of emblazoning the text 'time is a good friend', designed by graphic artist Max Kisman, on the glass of the facade.

On Binnen Vissersstraat, on the site of a former cinema, the architects had wanted to restore the original alleyway structure but this idea was rejected by the city council in favour of restoration of the three existing historical buildings. The modern additions, such as the glazed connecting corridor, stand cold and hard against the historical architecture: once again there has been no attempt to downplay the distinction between old and new.

The third project carried out in this area also entails the amalgamation of an existing and a new building, with shops on the ground floor and five dwellings above, two in the old structure and three in the new building where the two top floors form a maisonette, with a void behind a huge glazed facade.

All five dwellings are reached via a corridor leading to a staircase at the back of the buildings where there is also a shed for bicycles etcetera and a small patio. This solution has since been used in a related project in another part of Amsterdam (Hoogte Kadijk). The three Haarlemmerbuurt projects are studies in compact living in which dwellings that are tiny even by Amsterdam standards offer a maximum of space thanks to the efficient, neutral layout and the minimization of circulation space.

1 Herman Knijtijzer
2 Max Kisman, design for lettering for facade on Binnenwieringerstraat, 1993

1

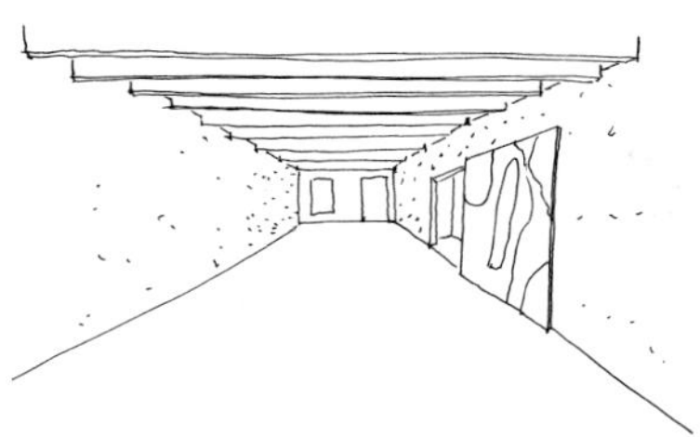

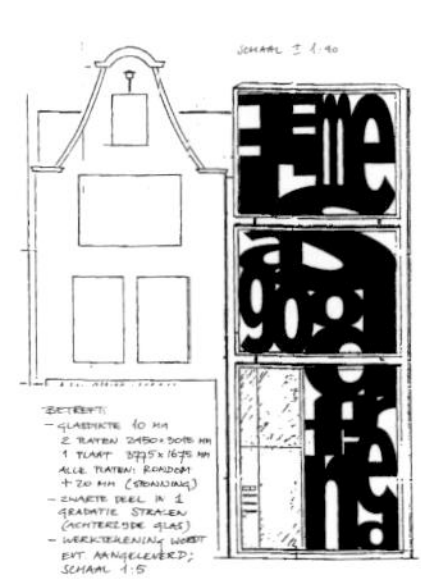

2

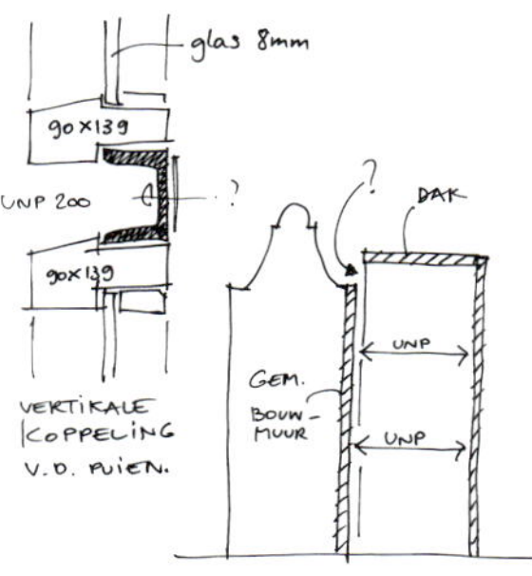

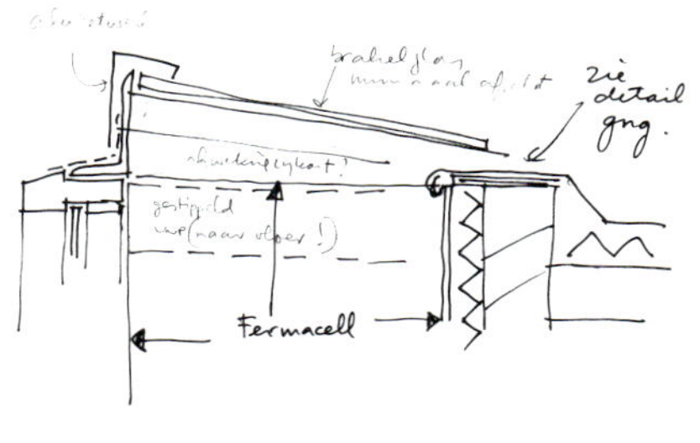

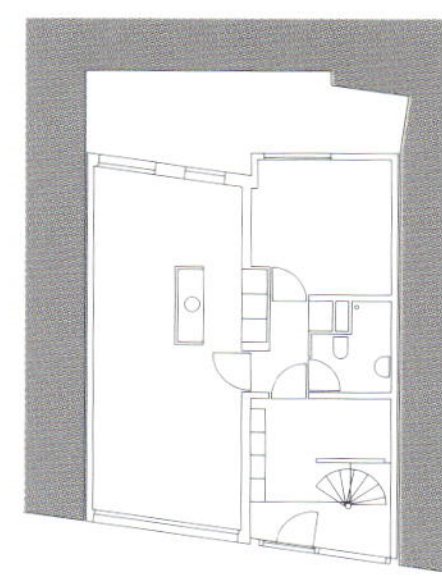

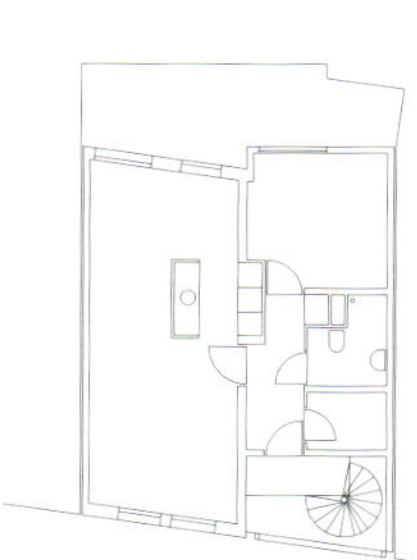

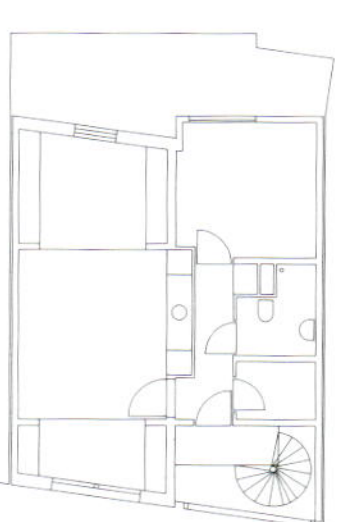

Housing, Haarlemmerbuurt, Amsterdam   Binnen Wieringerstraat

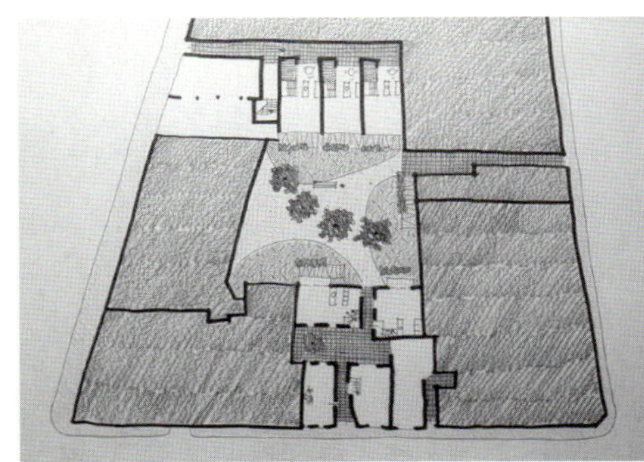

Unbuilt design for inner court, Binnen Vissersstraat

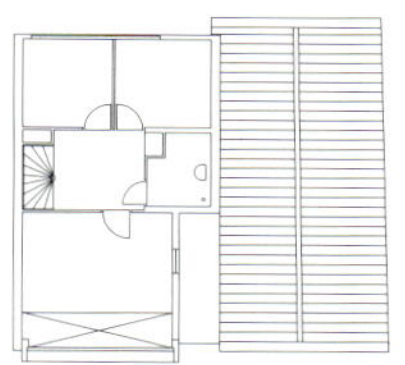
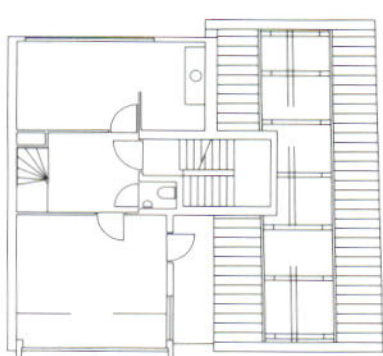
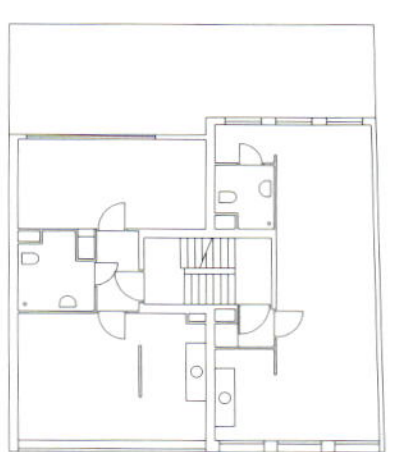
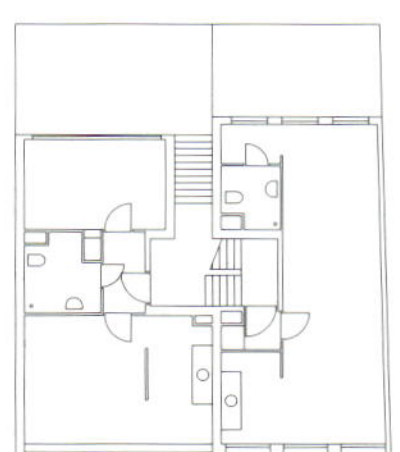
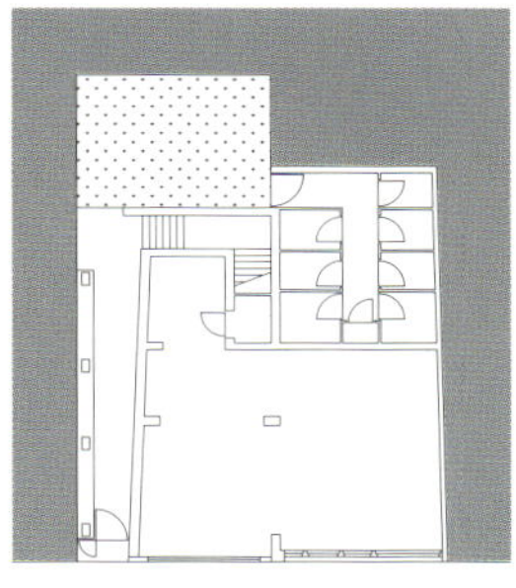

Housing, Haarlemmerbuurt, Amsterdam

Haarlemmerstraat

031 CLUBHOUSE PLEJADENPLEIN, AMSTERDAM

The clubhouse, designed for a playground association in Amsterdam North, stands in the middle of a garden suburb built in the 1910s and '20s. Owing to its location on the edge of the plot, the building – a long, low, abstract box – forms a boundary between the playground and the main public square with its church, library and community centre.

Much of the clubhouse is taken up by a party room. The building opens up on the side facing the playground. Steel grilles are available to protect the large panes of glass in this facade against vandalism when the clubhouse is not in use.

The long wall conceived as partition and screen is a recurrent theme in the practice's work. The Miesian simplicity of this architecture acquires a subtle accent here in the corner detail of the party room windows. Although the building's plainness is in stark contrast to the rustic character of the garden suburb, it is this very normality that enables it to slot smoothly into its surroundings.

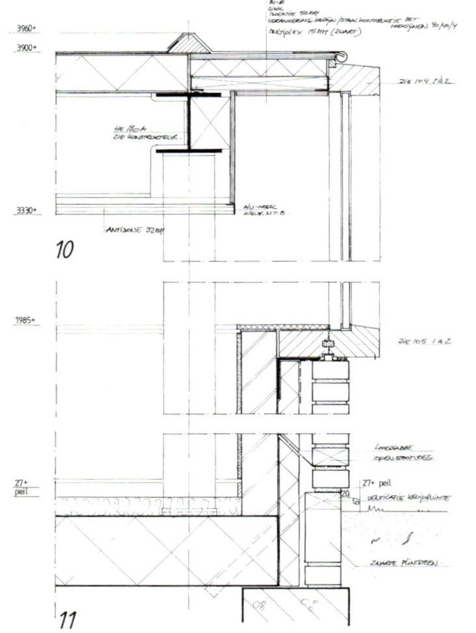

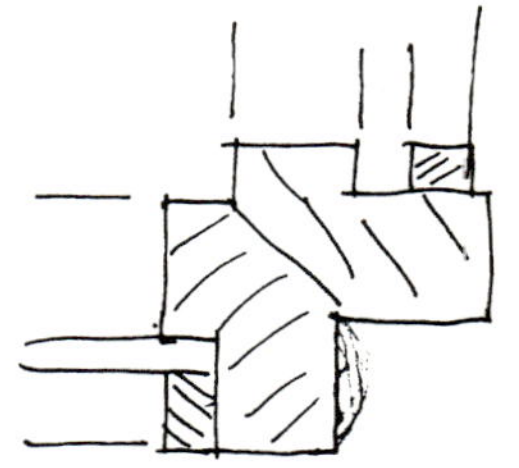

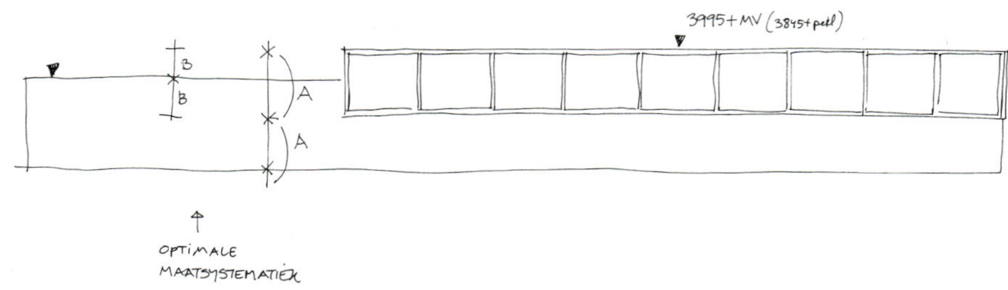

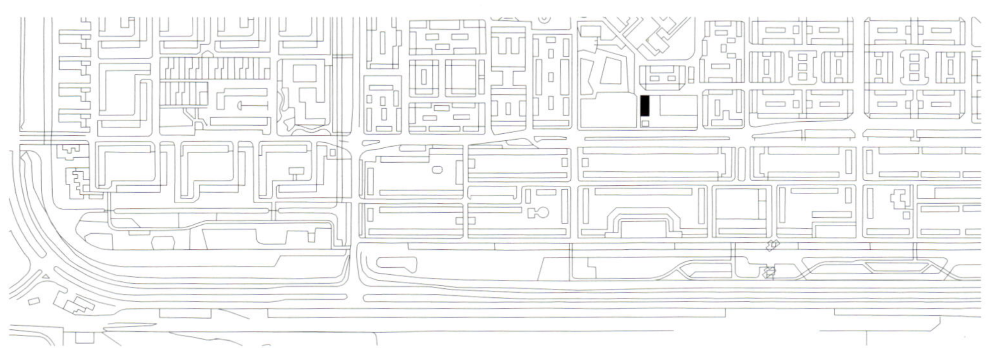

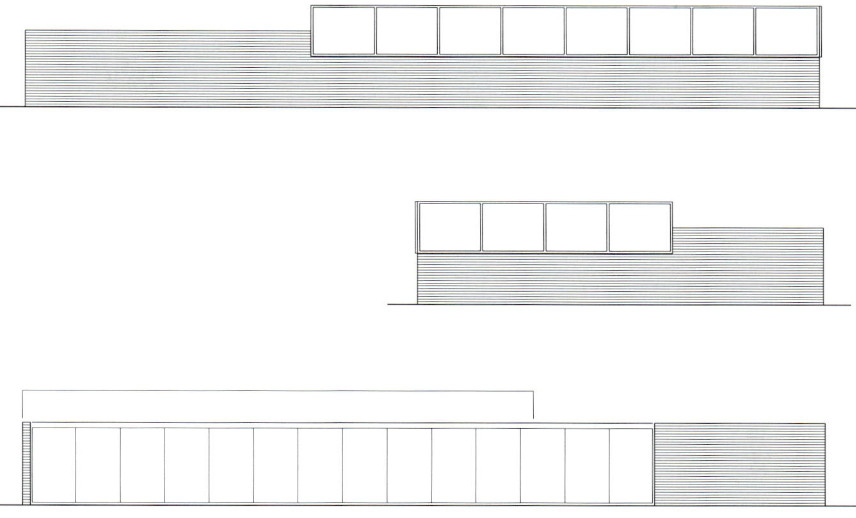

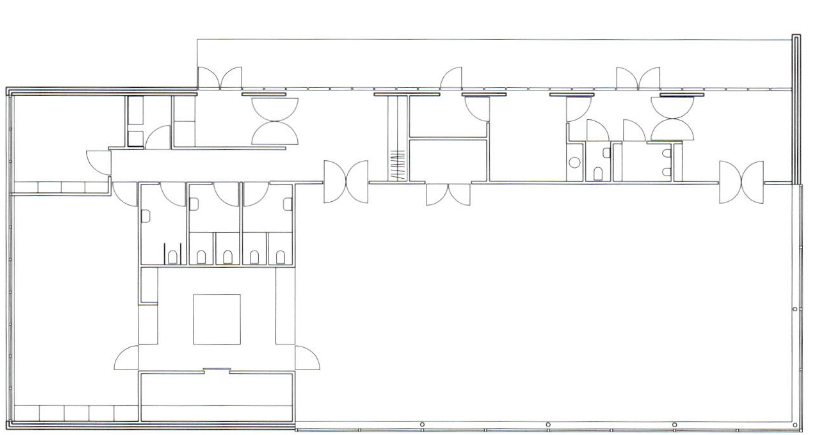

Clubhouse Plejadenplein, Amsterdam

035 036 APARTMENTS, LANDSTEINERLAAN, GRONINGEN

The demolition of an old people's home in a 1960s residential district on the southern edge of Groningen released a site suitable for new housing. Claus en Kaan managed to persuade the client and the city council that a courtyard block would compromise the structure of the district. Instead, they submitted a proposal for an open development that conforms to the existing lot structure and so respects and maintains the principles of open planning. Owing to the open layout, the modest dimensions of the new volumes and their lack of ostentation, the new architecture establishes a symbiotic relationship with its environment.

The programme – accommodation for the elderly and ground-accessed single-family dwellings – was not easy to fit into the location. By reducing the scale of the first and increasing the scale of the second, the architects were able to arrive at proportions in keeping with the context.

The 48 pensioner apartments (subsidized rental sector) are distributed over three small blocks of galleried apartments; the 24 owner-occupied dwellings for starters are grouped together in four clusters where collectivity rather than individuality is expressed by a formal front elevation and by hiding the gardens from public view.

By placing the buildings along the perimeter of the site, space was left for a central green zone. The hinge of this wedge-shaped area is formed by Coen Bekink's austere church with its Corbusian tower. One long side of the triangle is lined by four-storey blocks of galleried flats. At right angles to the other long side are the clusters of single family dwellings, which can be seen as a simplified version of the patio dwelling. Because the public space between the buildings is relatively narrow, the facades were made as abstract and the boundary between public and private as clear-cut as possible: the pensioner flats have internal verandas rather than projecting balconies, for example. Thus, the architecture serves the design of the public realm. Between the blocks of flats this space has been laid out as public rooms that can be seen as a collective extension of the dwellings. The entrances to the flats border these collective rooms and in this way, in accordance with good modernist practice, a distance is created between home and street.

For Claus en Kaan this project was their first opportunity to address the question of the relation between part and whole, individuality and collectivity. It marks the beginning of the development of their ideas about the relation between architecture (the dwelling) and spatial planning (of the residential area) in which it is not the dwelling that is the measure of things, but the formal spatial order.

Iñiguez de Onzoño and Vázquez de Castro, Poblado dirigido de Caño Roto, Madrid, 1957–1959

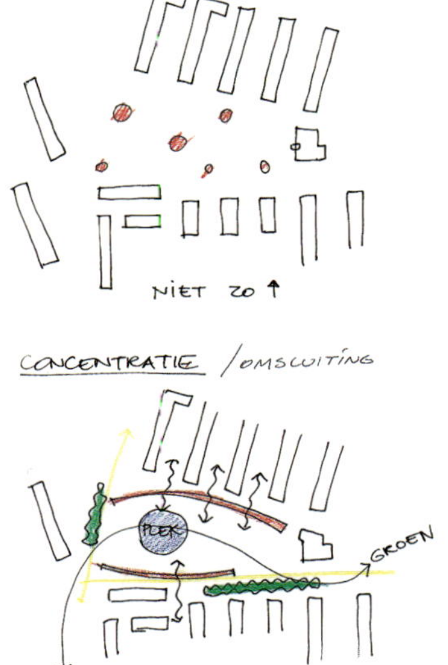

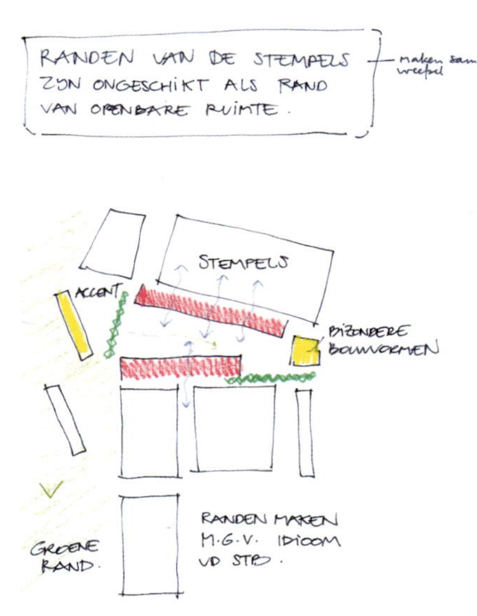

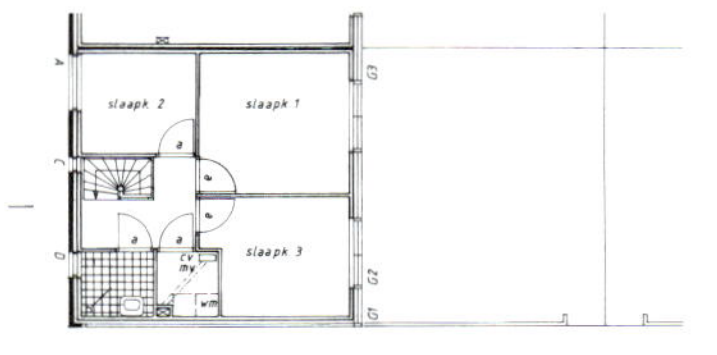

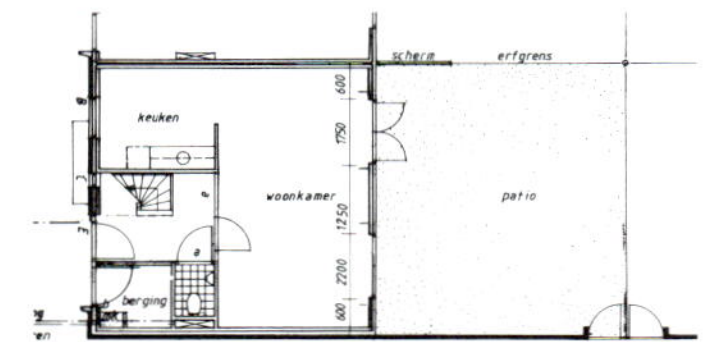

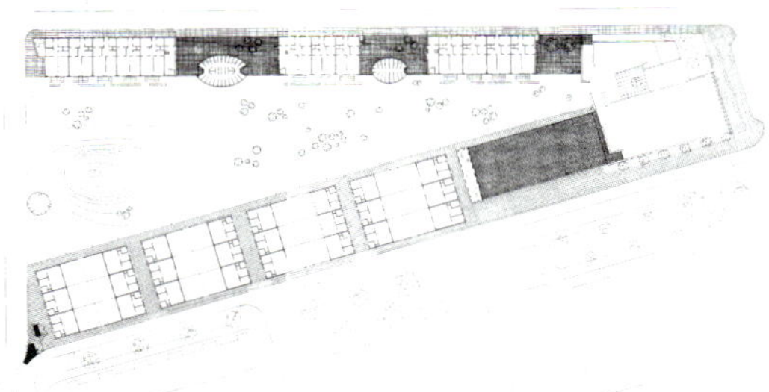

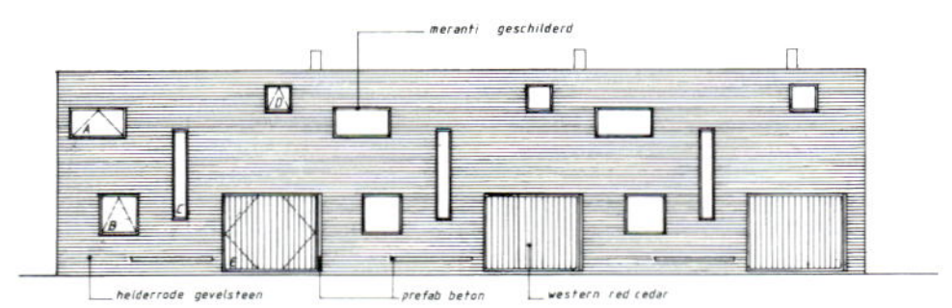

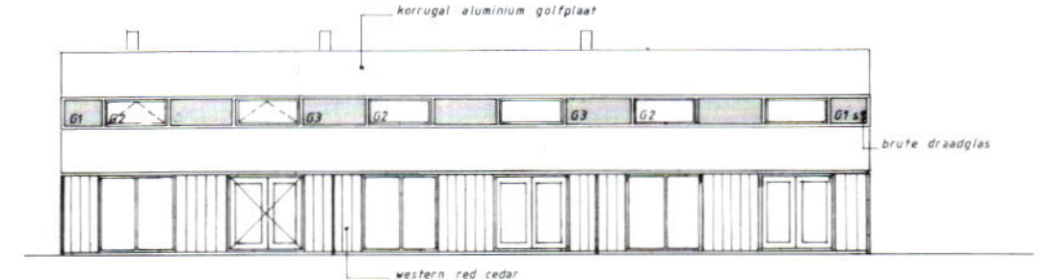

Apartments, Landsteinerlaan, Groningen

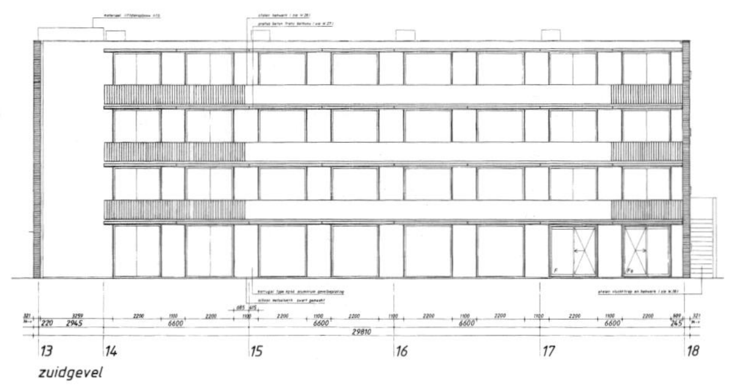
13
14
15
16
17
18
zuidgevel

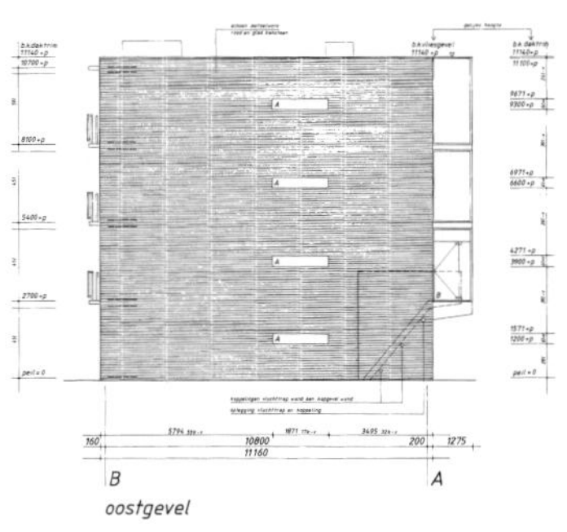
B
A
oostgevel

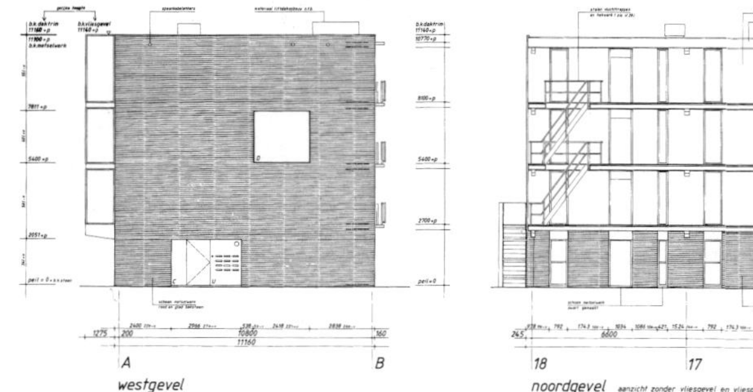
A
B
westgevel

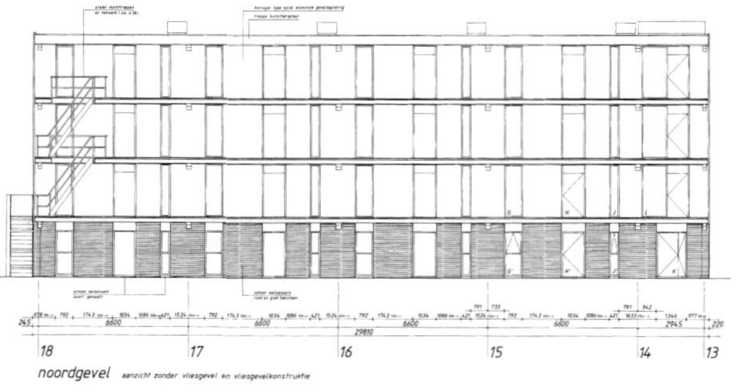
18
17
16
15
14
13
noordgevel aanzicht zonder vliesgevel en vliesgevelkonstruktie

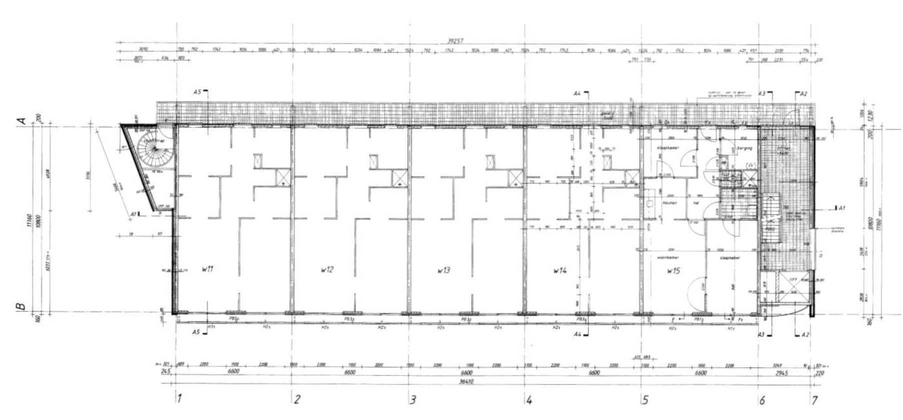
w11
w12
w13
w14
w15
1
2
3
4
5
6
7
bouwdeel A tweede verdieping

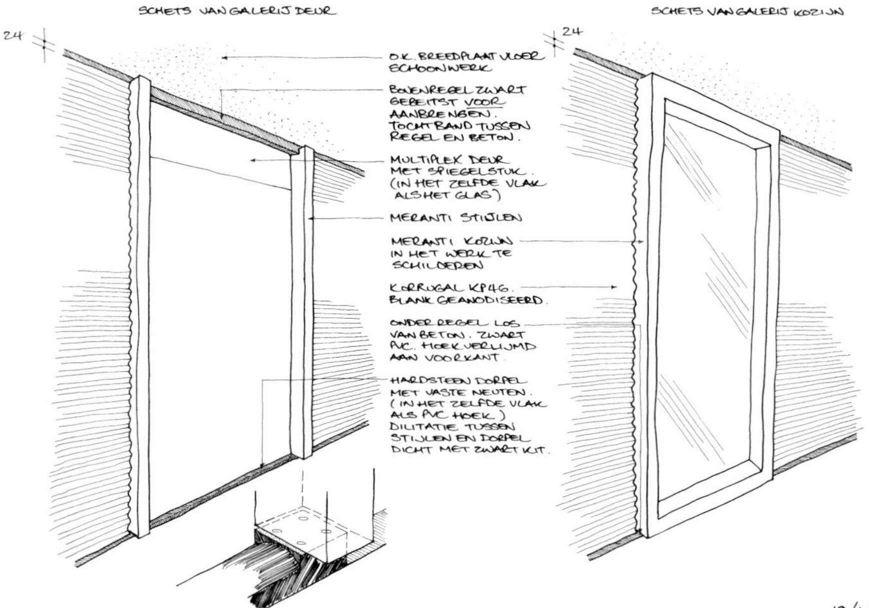
SCHETS VAN GALERIJ DEUR
SCHETS VAN GALERIJ KOZIJN
24
24
O.K. BREEDPLAAT VLOER SCHOONWERK
BOVENREGEL ZWART GEBEITST VOOR AANBRENGEN. TOCHTBAND TUSSEN REGEL EN BETON.
MULTIPLEX DEUR MET SPIEGELSTUK. (IN HET ZELFDE VLAK ALS HET GLAS)
MERANTI STIJLEN
MERANTI KOZIJN IN HET WERK TE SCHILDEREN
KORRUGAL KP46. BLANK GEANODISEERD.
ONDER REGEL LOS VAN BETON. ZWART PVC. HOEK VERLIJMD AAN VOORKANT.
HARDSTEEN DORPEL MET VASTE NEUTEN. (IN HET ZELFDE VLAK ALS PVC HOEK) DILITATIE TUSSEN STIJLEN EN DORPEL DICHT MET ZWART KIT.
19/1/93
W26.24-A

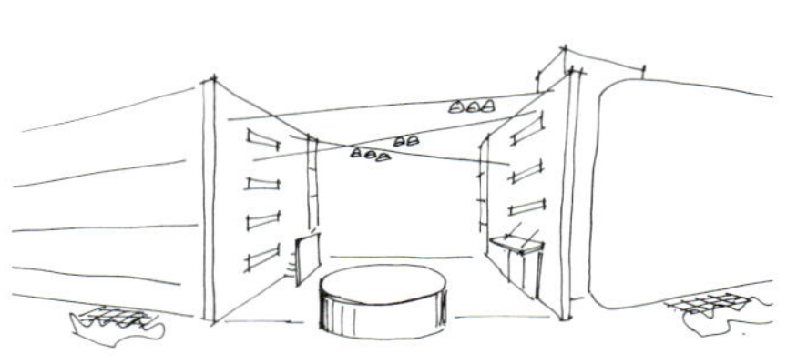
RUIMTE VORMEN/OMSLUITEN.

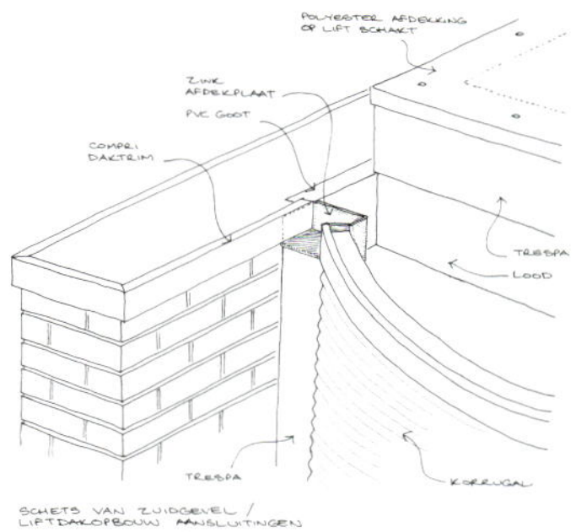
POLYESTER AFDEKKING
OP LIFT SCHACHT
ZINK
AFDEKPLAAT
PVC GOOT
COMPRI
DAKTRIM
TRESPA
LOOD
TRESPA
KORRUGAL
SCHETS VAN ZUIDGEVEL /
LIFTDAKOPBOUW AANSLUITINGEN
(DETAILS 8, 9 & 10)

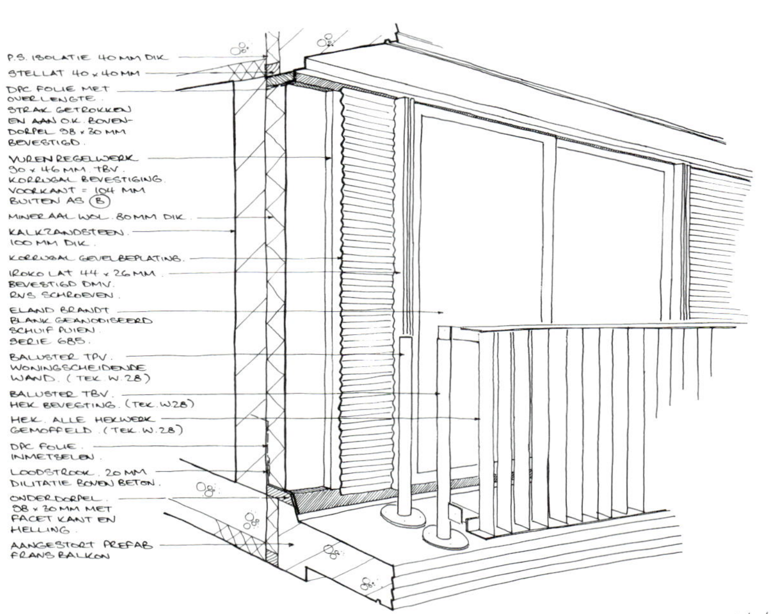
P.S. ISOLATIE 40MM DIK
STELLAT 40 x 40MM
DPC FOLIE MET
OVERLENGTE.
STRAK GETROKKEN
EN AAN O.K. BOVEN-
DORPEL 98 x 30 MM
BEVESTIGD.
VUREN REGELWERK
90 x 46 MM TBV.
KORRUGAL BEVESTIGING.
VOORKANT = 104 MM
BUITEN AS (B)
MINERAAL WOL. 80MM DIK.
KALKZANDSTEEN.
100 MM DIK.
KORRUGAL GEVELBEPLATING.
IROKO LAT 44 x 26MM.
BEVESTIGD DMV.
RVS SCHROEVEN.
ELAND BRANDT
BLANK GEANODISEERD
SCHUIF PUIEN.
SERIE 685.
BALUSTER TPV.
WONINGSCHEIDENDE
WAND. (TEK. W.28)
BALUSTER TBV.
HEK BEVESTING. (TEK. W.28)
HEK. ALLE HEKWERK
GEMOFFELD. (TEK. W.28)
DPC FOLIE.
INMETSELEN.
LOODSTROOK. 20MM
DILITATIE BOVEN BETON.
ONDERDORPEL.
98 x 30MM MET
FACET KANT EN
HELLING.
AANGESTORT PREFAB
FRANS BALKON
2/2/93
W26.04 A

042
BUSINESS CENTRE PAPAVERWEG, AMSTERDAM

The Eurotwin Business Centre is located on Papaverweg in Amsterdam North, in one of the many untidy industrial areas that abound in this part of the city. Eurotwin is a pair of mirror-image buildings, each made up of a five-storey office tower and a low-rise row of sheds. Placed like bookends at either end of a block, the two objects keep the rest of the buildings on this site together. In fact, although the architects had nothing to do with its design, their twin buildings introduce a sense of order to the area as a whole. The two objects can be construed as enlarged 'strategic details' with a strong ordering effect. Unadorned as they are, the buildings impart coherence to an environment of predominantly nondescript architecture. Compared with the blandness of this modern industrial vernacular, Claus en Kaan's simplicity possesses a minimalist distinction.

This minimalism is expressed in the reticence with which form, colour and materials have been deployed. The facades of both buildings are clad chiefly in timber which has been used to create an unpretentious but effective composition of taut boxes with finely detailed frames, corners and clearly defined boundaries between the various business premises. The formal simplicity is counterbalanced by the spatial complexity of the entrances of the two office buildings.

Although the L-shaped buildings are based on various historical examples, these are only indirectly present in a design that is free of any overt allusion to architectural history.

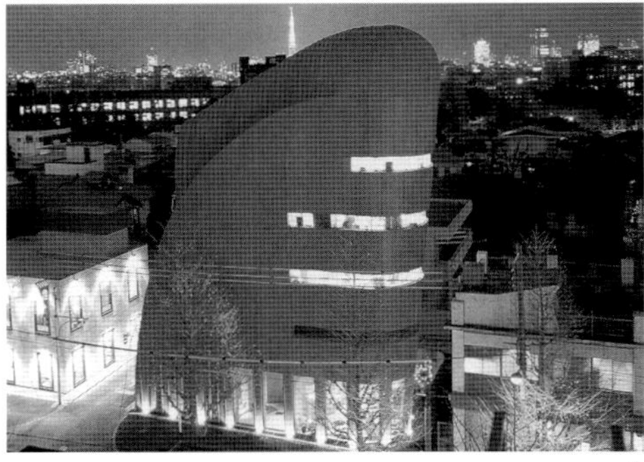

1

1 Philippe Starck, NaniNani Building, Tokyo, 1989
2 Miguel Fisac

2

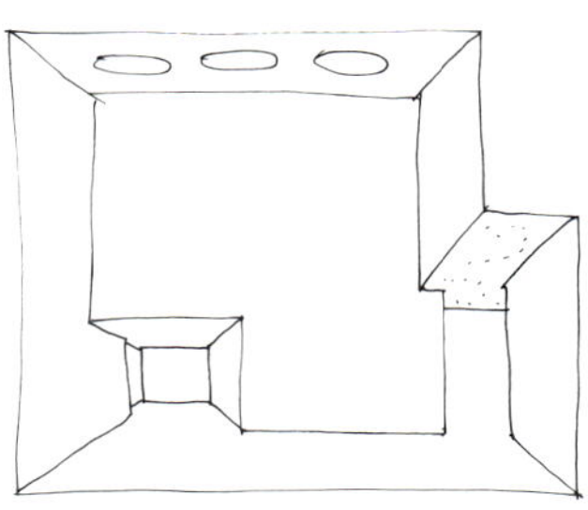

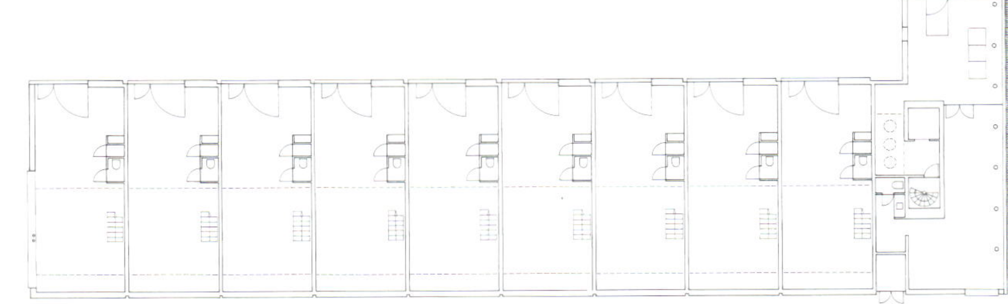

Business Centre Papaverweg, Amsterdam

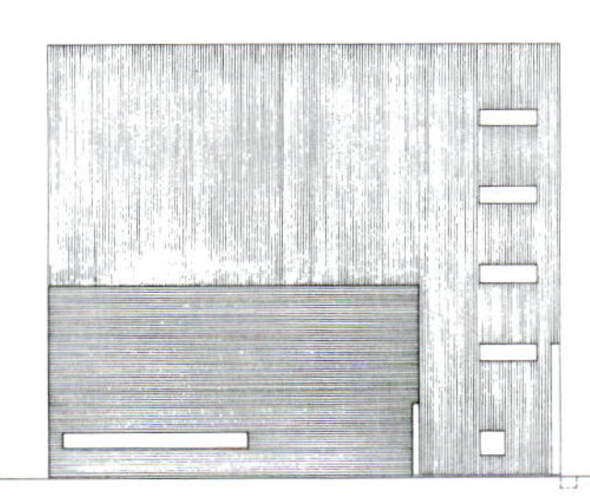

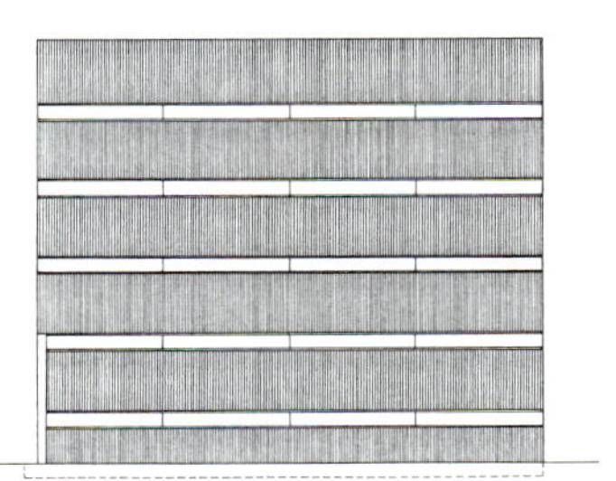

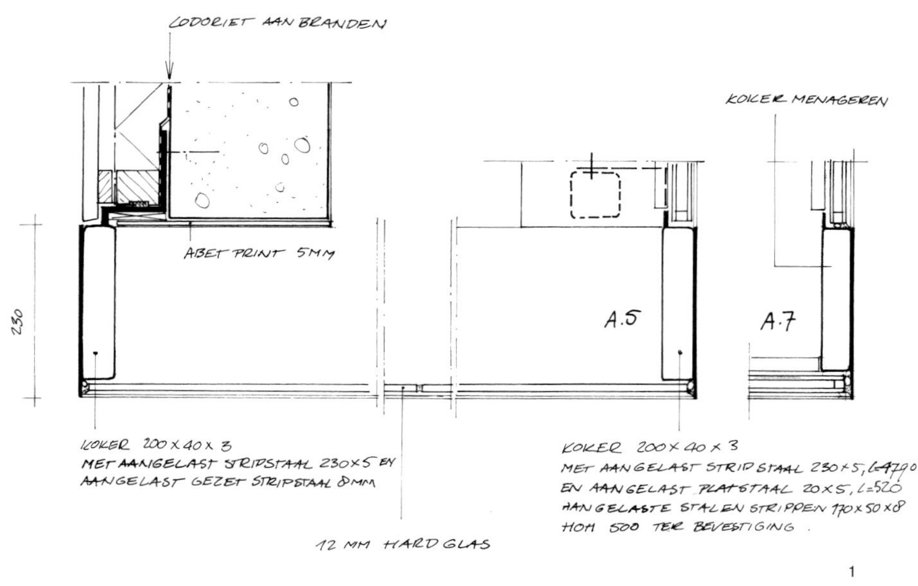

1

1 Detail entrance
2 Heinrich Tessenow, Sächsische Landesschule, Klotzsche, 1926–1927

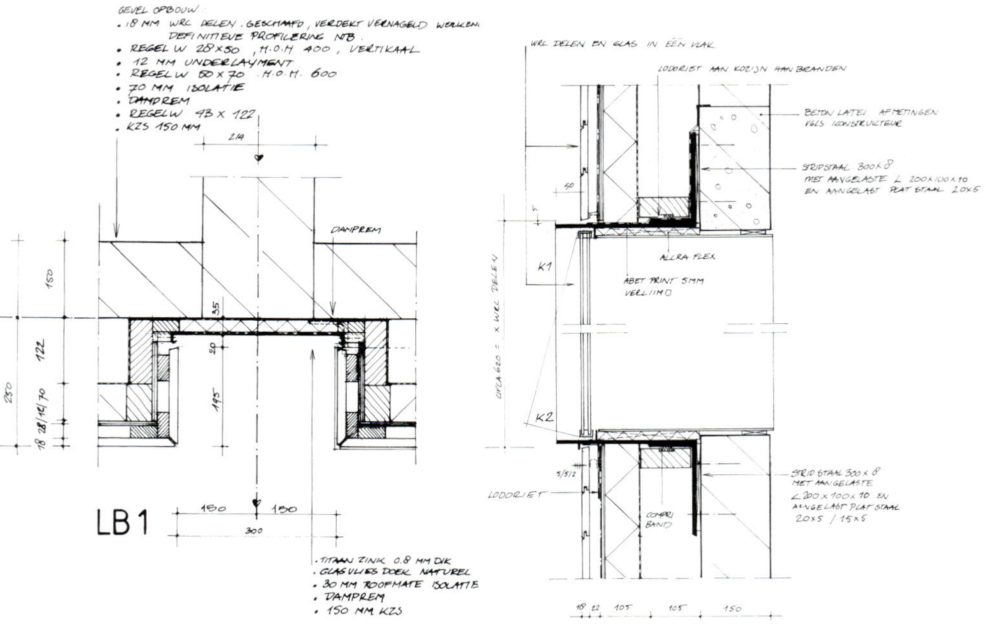
GEVEL OPBOUW:
. 18 MM WRC DELEN, GESCHAAFD, VERDEKT VERNAGELD WERKEN.
DEFINITIEVE PROFILERING NTB.
• REGELW 28x50, H.O.H 400, VERTIKAAL
• 12 MM UNDERLAYMENT
• REGELW 50x70 H.O.H. 600
• 70 MM ISOLATIE
• DAMPREM
• REGELW 43 x 122
• KZS 150 MM
DAMPREM
LB1
. TITAAN ZINK 0.8 MM DIK
. GLASVLIES DOEK NATUREL
• 30 MM ROOFMATE ISOLATIE
• DAMPREM
• 150 MM KZS
WRC DELEN EN GLAS IN EEN VLAK
LODORIET AAN KOZIJN AANBRANDEN
BETON LATEI AFMETINGEN VGLS KONSTRUKTEUR
STRIPSTAAL 300x8
MET AANGELASTE L 200x100x10
EN AANGELAST PLAT STAAL 20x5
ALLRA FLEX
ABET PRINT 5MM
K1
K2
LODORIET
COMPRI BAND
STRIP STAAL 300 x 8
MET AANGELASTE
∠200 x 100 x 10 EN
AANGELAST PLAT STAAL
20x5 / 15x5

2

7
6

045 070
HOUSING, AMSTELVEENSEWEG, AMSTERDAM

On the southern edge of Amsterdam lies the road to Amstelveen. It is slightly higher than the surrounding land and lined on either side by houses built in the nineteenth and twentieth centuries. On the city side, this modest ribbon development runs up against the large-scale structure of a university hospital, big office buildings and the orbital motorway. Claus en Kaan designed four lots of housing including townhouses along this road. Almost concurrently, though as the result of a later commission, they realized a second project in the area, a block of thirty apartments and a Ronald McDonald House offering temporary accommodation to the parents of seriously ill children admitted to the nearby hospital.

The architecture reveals a keen sense of context. The houses can be read as modern variations on the small-scale ribbon development. The front elevations of the houses are closed as a buffer against the heavy traffic. The fenced-off front yard and the entrance with its short flight of steps can be construed as a symbolic transition between public and private.

In one of the blocks of housing, which is built over a basement car park, dwellings with ground-floor office or work space are located behind a formal facade. The other three infills along the Amstelveenseweg have two faces: townhouses facing the road, drive-in houses behind. Here, too, the street elevations are closed against the passing traffic.

The quieter, 'garden side' is much more open and gives onto a strip of land providing access to the garages of the townhouses and the carports belonging to the patio houses. The latter come in two versions, one with a classic patio, the other with an internal terrace. The high density achieved by the addition of patio dwellings at the rear was one of the main reasons why this plan was chosen above other entries in what began as an invited competition.

The architecture, in which each house is distinguished by a timber-clad 'tower', emulates the staccato rhythm typical of ribbon development. The gradual transition of the street elevation in the block of home-work units and the rhythmical articulation of the individual dwellings in the three other blocks, represent a fluid adjustment to an urbanity that is becoming increasingly diffuse in this neighbourhood.

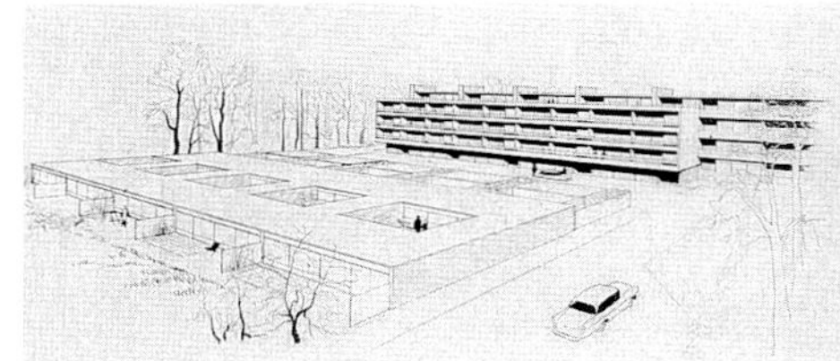

Arne Jacobsen, Bellevue Bugt, Klampenborg, Copenhagen, 1960–1961

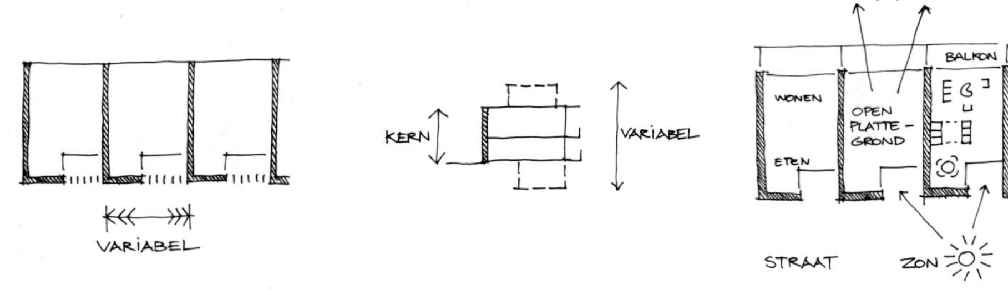

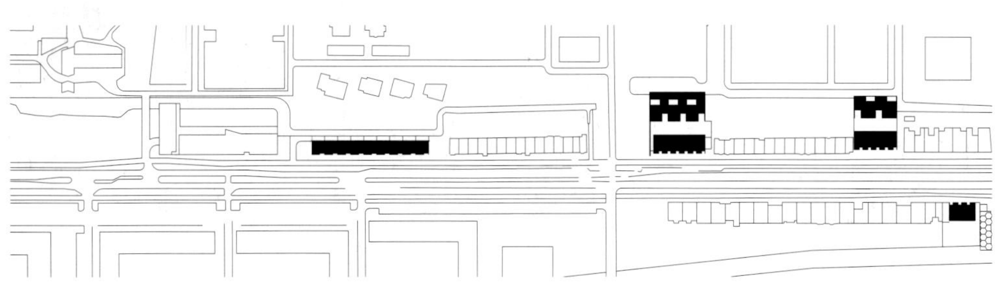

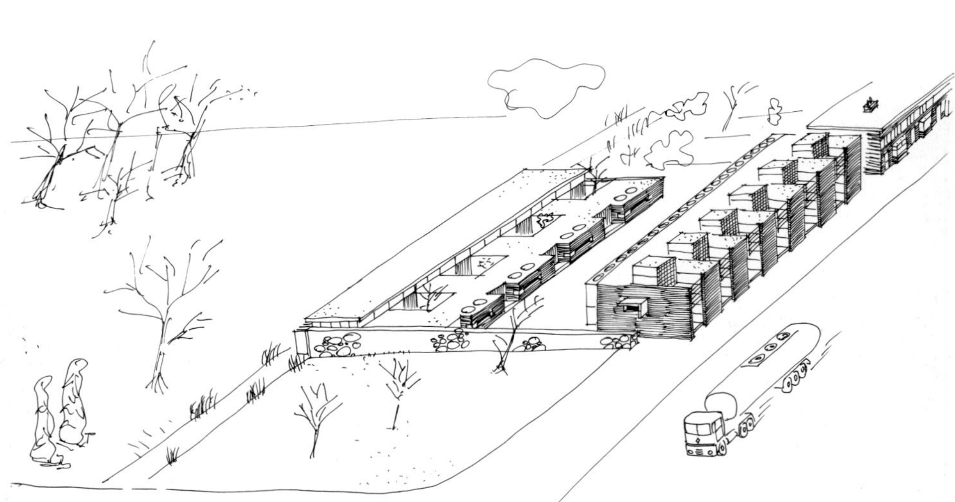

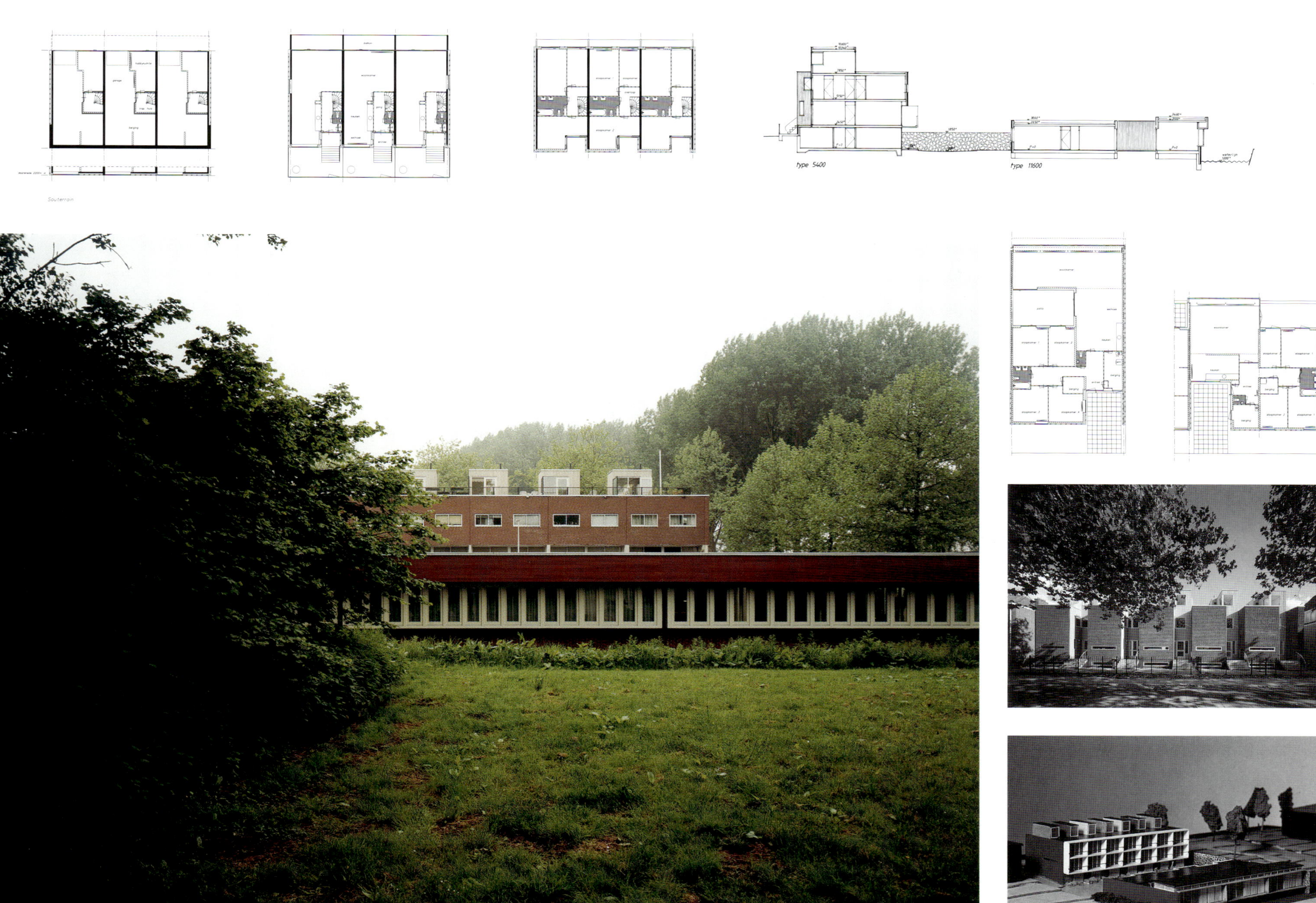

Housing, Amstelveenseweg, Amsterdam

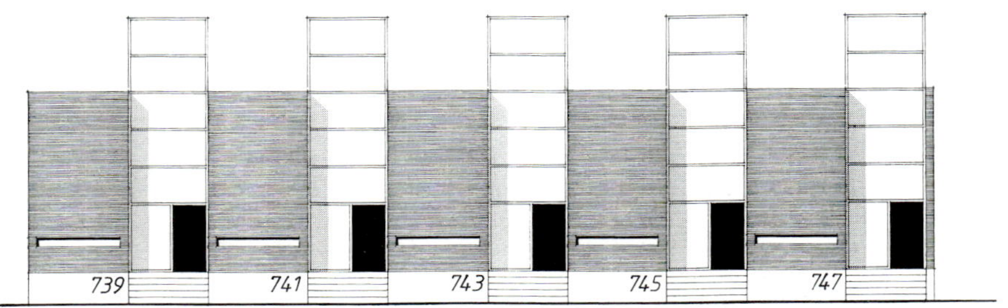
739
741
743
745
747

Housing, Amstelveenseweg, Amsterdam

051
SPATIAL MASTER PLAN, SOUTHWEST QUADRANT NIEUW SLOTEN, AMSTERDAM

Nieuw Sloten, a residential area in the southwest corner of Amsterdam, was built in phases during the 1980s and '90s. The southwest quadrant was the last section to be developed. The basic premise behind this design, which was the outcome of an invited design competition, was to provide a basis for a citified outer suburb. In this it differs crucially from the homeopathic dilutions of urbanity that characterize the other quadrants of Nieuw Sloten.

The orthogonal geometry of the plan is interrupted at only two points, for the jagged outline of a school and for a tower block shaped like a segment of a cylinder.

The plan, which consists of courtyard blocks and long rows of housing, is predicated on a differentiation rather than outright separation of public and private and entails a clear definition and design of the connections between the two realms in the tradition of Van de Broek& Bakema's work in the 1950s and '60s. At each level there is a link between urban form and housing typology rather than the other way round. Public space, and thus urban form, takes precedence over the particularity of the individual dwelling. In this respect there is an affinity with J. van Gool's celebrated Buikslotermeer housing estate (1966) in Amsterdam North. The primacy of urban space over the dwelling was one of the main reasons why the proposal encountered resistance from the Amsterdam city council: it went against the prevailing dogma that spatial form is the resultant of the house plan. Claus en Kaan's detailed urban design is, in effect, a repudiation of the modernist urban design principles that have been sacrosanct in Amsterdam ever since C. van Eesteren's period of ascendancy in the 1930s.

1

1 J. van Gool, housing scheme, Buikslotermeer, Amsterdam, 1963–1966
2 J.B. Bakema, Friendship Model

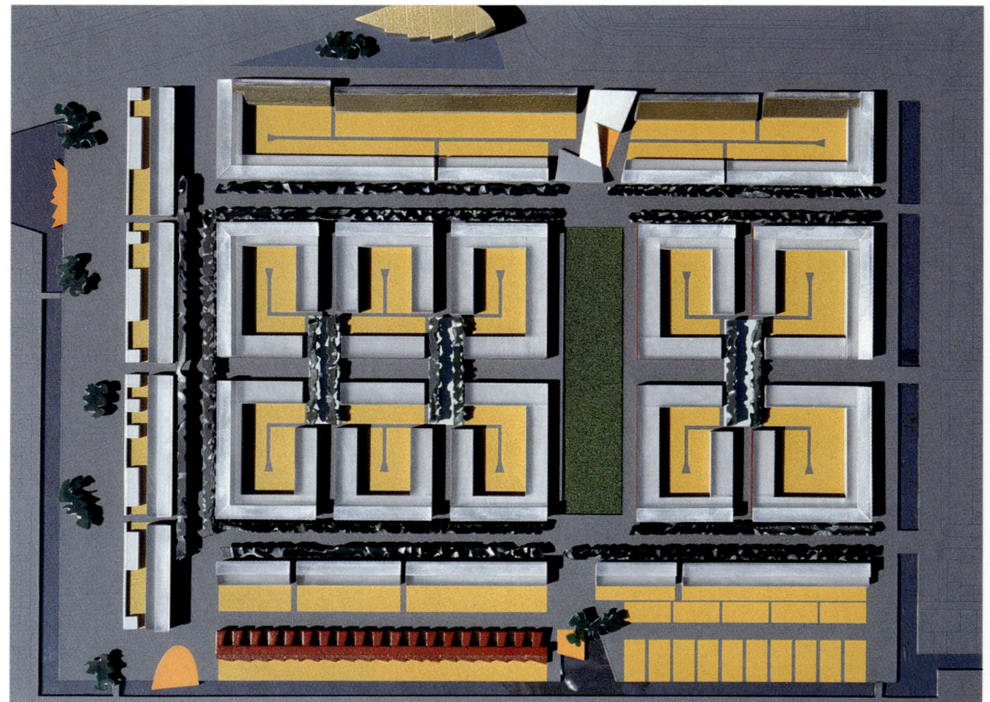

Explanation of Spatial Master Plan for Southwest Quadrant of Nieuw Sloten, Amsterdam

Felix Claus and Kees Kaan

2

Introduction

Born in the years when the CIAM principles were being applied on a large scale, we grew up in postwar suburban developments based on the spatial concept of ensembles of discrete volumes that animate the surrounding space. The planning instrument behind this, to which Team X added a more enclosing characteristic (Bakema's family group), is in our view still capable of delivering a very contemporary image for urban expansion. The abrupt return to perimeter blocks in the late 1970s may be socially explicable, but from an urban planning viewpoint it strikes us as strange.

The development parameters for Nieuw-Sloten are laid down in the original terms of reference: high density low-rise and an urban image. As Niek de Boer concludes in his book *Woonwijken Naoorlogse Stedebouw 1945–1985* (Housing Estates in Postwar Town Planning 1945–1985), there is an inherent difficulty in this combination. The urban image is determined by more factors than spatial ones alone. Yet the means at our disposal for realizing this image when designing a new area are chiefly of a spatial planning nature. Another major stumbling block is the profile. The obligatory inclusion of parking spaces precludes a street profile of urban dimensions (height=width). Urban continuity in Nieuw Sloten is potentially fairly dynamic thanks to the high-speed tram link with the centre of Amsterdam and Nieuw Sloten's location between Badhoevedorp and the Amsterdam ring road. The question is to what extent this manifests itself spatially.

Bearing these potential difficulties in mind we set ourselves the task of demonstrating the desired 'urban living' conditions. Our aim was to produce a coherent plan that, within a controlled structure, reveals a stimulating variety of spatial features as you move through it.

The theme of our design for the Southwest Quadrant is the interrelation between the spatial master plan and the architectural elaboration of this planning concept; the balance between plan, subdivision and construction. The most important means for achieving this is the relation between public and private and the associated difference in atmosphere between hard and soft.

This is not about creating the kind of artificial order or illusion of coherence that is sadly manifest in other developments, such as Carel Weeber's Venserpolder scheme in Amsterdam Southeast. The coherence we aspire to is a clear basic structure enriched by spatial differentiation and architectural detail that allows individual residents to identify not only with their own dwelling but also with the immediate surroundings. To achieve this, the architecture must be subservient to the spatial master plan (primacy of planning) and not be allowed to become autonomous.

Analysis

Nieuw Sloten is made up of quadrants, each with its own ambience, organized around a central hub located at the intersection of the main access routes that divide the district into quadrants. The spatial coherence of the district as a whole would probably have been better served if these dividing lines had run through the centre of the quadrants, rather than along their boundaries. This is particularly true of the main streets and waterways where the profile is sometimes overtly dissimilar and where it is also apparent that the single-family dwellings lack sufficient mass to define the space.

An examination of the zoning map reveals discrepancies between the spatial master plan and the built reality. The public space is often out of balance. Public-access perimeter blocks stand on a plan that conjures up a different spatial image. The existing spatial quality is nullified by views into internal courtyards, rear elevations that overlook the public area, dissimilar open corners, abrupt transitions and dissimilar street profiles (even within a single quadrant). Encouraged by the intention of the planning guidelines for the Southwest Quadrant, our plan aims to create internal coherence.

Urban image and dwelling type

Ever since the birth of modern city planning as a scientific discipline in the 1920s, row housing has been regarded as the pre-eminent urban design strategy for producing optimal housing quality. In deciding the best approach to low-rise housing, however, we feel that the most important thing is how you arrive at your decision. If the dwelling were to take precedence over everything else, the result in the Southwest Quadrant would tally with Mies's commentary on the scientific approach to architecture à la Hannes Meyer (architecture = protein X square metres): 'Stir it together, it stinks.' We, however, are

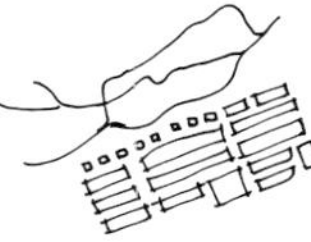

concertgebouwbuurt

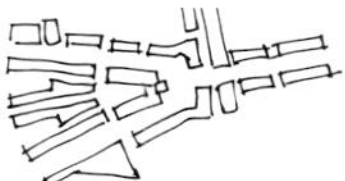

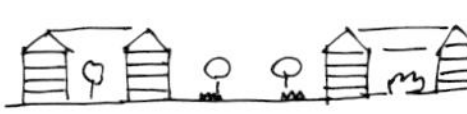

plan zuid

tuindorp oostzaan

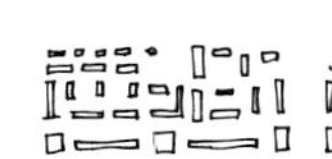

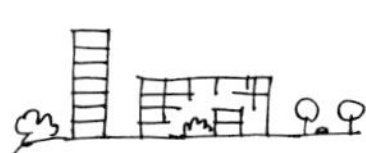

buitenveldert

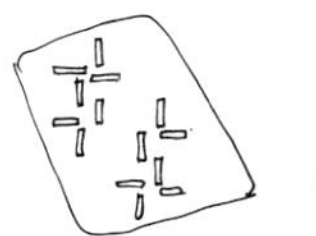

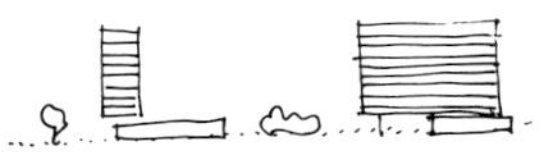

molenwijk

also concerned with public space and how this can be functionally determined, organized and bounded.

If one opts for an urban transition between street and dwelling, the block organization must be attuned to this. Our contention is that public and private should in this case only meet at the front door. A street frontage with a front door opening onto the pavement becomes ridiculous if around the corner that same pavement devolves into a garden path.

In order to be able to control the area beyond the housing plot, we abandoned the 'standard' and committed 'sacrilege' by abandoning the open subdivision with ground-accessed dwellings. We did this not because of any principled preference for the courtyard block, but for the sake of conjuring the desired urban image and being able to create differentiation in residential environments.

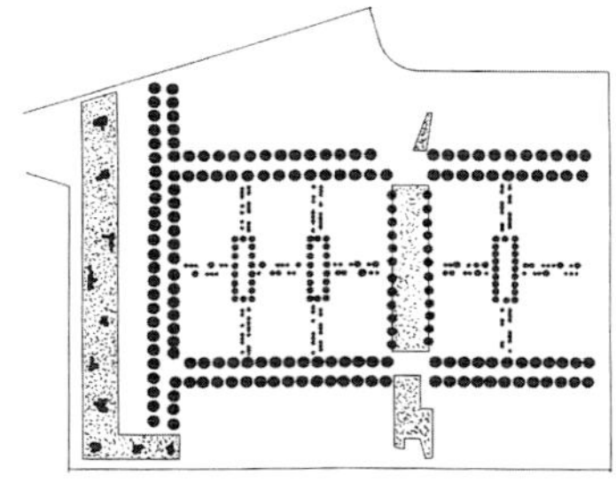

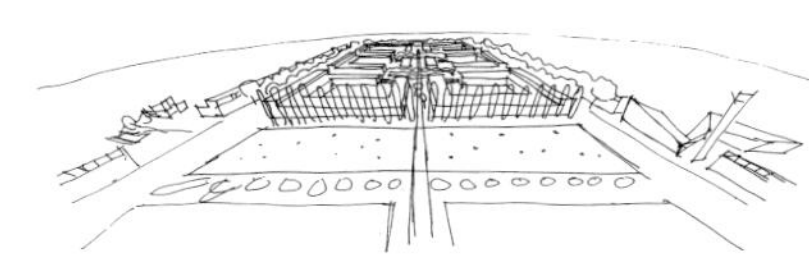

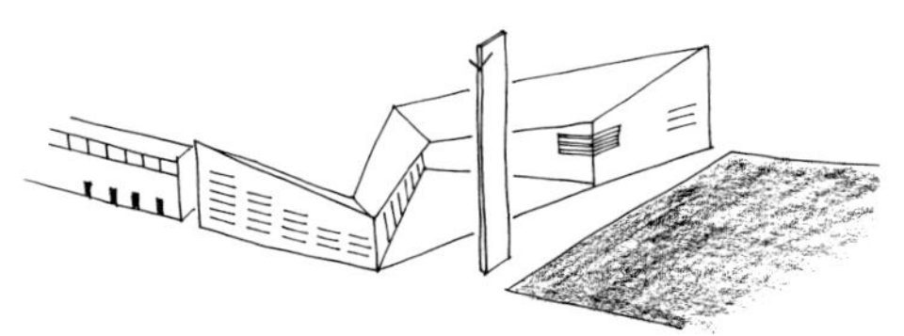

Urban master plan

The instruments for achieving the chosen planning solution are ground-accessed dwellings in a maximum of three storeys with continuous facades, organized in blocks of 45 by 62 metres. It should be emphasized that what we have in mind is not the romantic creation of urban space with a meticulous balance between the width of the street and the height of the street wall. Such profiles are rendered impossible by the need for parking spaces. The proportions of the spaces are determined by the street profile required for this in combination with buildings of two or three storeys. The desired urban vitality still has to prove itself, but for the time being Nieuw Sloten will not exude an urban atmosphere. Perhaps in thirty years' time. What remains is an image of diverse spatial features. The important thing is that this image should be able to carry the intention without any internal contradictions; it must be perfectly in accord with the desired atmosphere.

Perimeter

This endeavour is concentrated on two relationships: that between the Southwest Quadrant and the rest of Nieuw Sloten along the perimeter, and the internal relationship, or identity of the quadrant. The perimeter is made up of the clearly defined west wall, the northern boundary, the canal on the east side and the southern boundary bordered by the drainage ditch. The west and east boundaries of the quadrant will be designed by one architect which will result in a harmonious image. The presence of a trailer camp and (the most expensive) dwellings along the water's edge, will give the southern boundary an appropriately fragmented appearance. The northern boundary is currently divided among three component plans. This is unfortunate as an important transition is at stake here. We would like to propose an alternative division in which the entire northern boundary falls within a single plan. The problem of buildings that are too low to be space-forming is particularly acute on this northern edge where we propose a radical revision of the connection with the central area.

Internal

In Hans Davidson's overall plan for Nieuw Sloten there is an explicit spatial hierarchy. The intention is to make a number of clearly different spatial types: avenue, plantation, quiet street, cycle path, et cetera. Appropriate facade heights are indicated for the various spatial types. We have adhered scrupulously to this set-up and have tried to give substance to the underlying intention.

Avenue

The avenue has a broad profile with angled parking on either side between serried ranks of sturdy urban trees. The two avenues in the plan are linked to form a U. The position of the avenue in the hierarchy of the plan is emphasized by giving the avenue facades greater prominence at the intersections with north–south routes.

Green ditch

The green space-cum-sports field is below grade in order to divorce communal use of the area from the buildings lining it. Our inspiration for this arrangement is Midway Plaisance in Chicago by Frederick Law Olmsted. A plain area of grass dotted with lighting masts and bordered by closely planted poplars on top of the bank and behind that two-storey housing. In summer it can be used for football, in winter skating. The 'green ditch' is the heart of the district, skirted or crossed by all the main routes and with the school signalling its public character. The school is a modelled volume that resolves the various urban design conditions in its elevations. The schoolyard is cut out of the mass and leads, via an arcade, to the entrance to the school.

Rooms

The quiet squares are a vital link in the spatial sequence of the plan. They form the transition between public space and the private domains inside the blocks. We deliberately chose to allow the ambience of these squares to be determined by the end facades of the housing blocks: there are no distracting entrances or side gardens. The front doors are on the avenues and streets, the gardens are inside the blocks. Short paths lead to the squares which are linked by the cycle route. The squares can be regarded as rooms, as communal entrances to the gardens, as territories where communal activities take place. They act as transition, as meeting point, and they provide space. To emphasize the transition between paths and squares, the width of the north–south streets could be reduced to six metres.

Southern boundary

The most expensive, owner-occupied dwellings – staggered villas with garage – are located on a 'mews' along the southern boundary of the plan. The mews is devoid of any trace of profiling in order to emphasize the fact that this type of street falls outside the planning hierarchy.

West wall

The west wall is in fact the cornerstone of the plan. This street facade has a hybrid character, belowground a potato, aboveground a tomato. On the eastern side (the inside) it is essential that the avenue profile be continued. A 280-metre street frontage of carports opposite the three-storey canal frontage would undermine the clarity of the concept. We therefore propose a modified avenue profile with three-storey development. On the outside, the west wall marks the entrance to Nieuw Sloten and borders a strip of parkland that runs from the northern to the southern boundary. The spatial master plan makes a choice in favour of Nieuw Sloten as a whole rather than the internal coherence of the quadrant.

Wishing to qualify this choice, we found the hybrid we sought in the form of a literal west wall: inside the quadrant the 'standard' avenue frontage, and along the outside of the

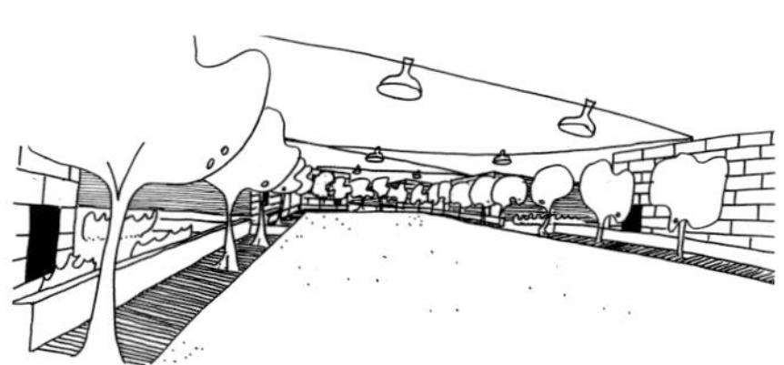

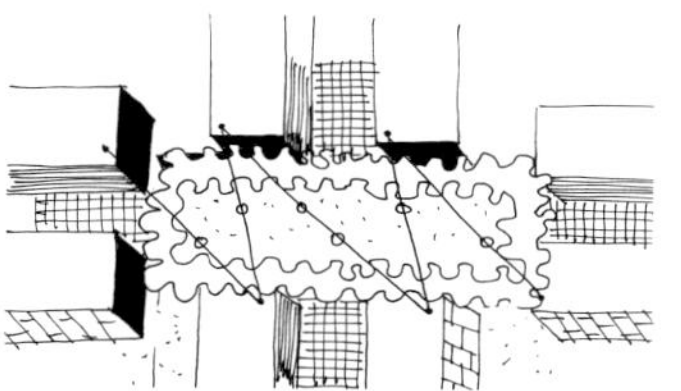

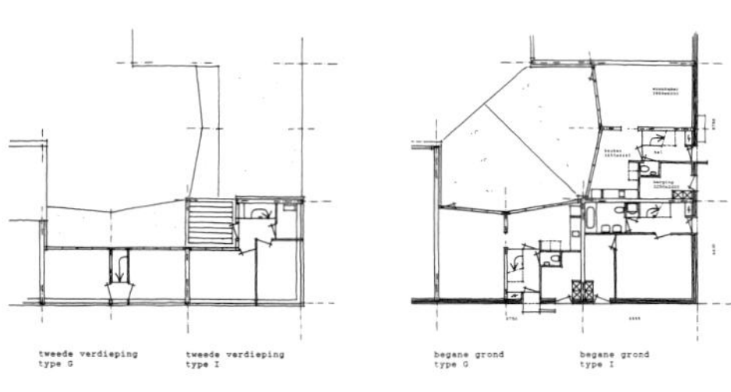

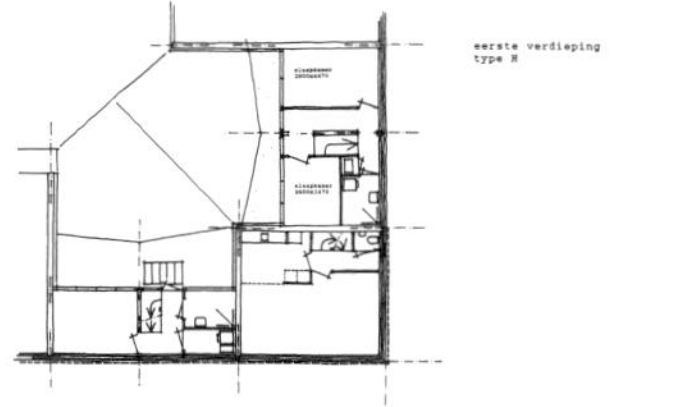

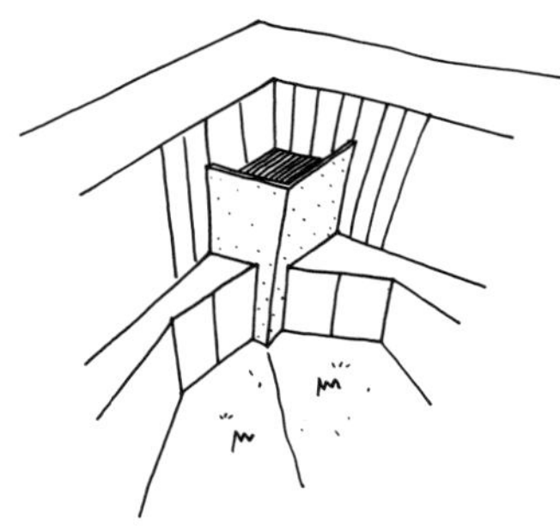

quadrant a continuous garden wall with occasional higher sections that turn it into an unmistakable front side. The rear elevation of the three-storey avenue wall forms a very strong backdrop for the differentiated garden wall. In this way we satisfy the planning requirement that this side of the quadrant be bounded by a continuous elevation, albeit in a two-stage version. The garden wall borders the strip of park with cycle path and in height forms a transition to the adjacent quadrant designed by Gunnar Daan. The rear elevation of the west wall is very abstract so that from a distance it provides the required sense of closure.

Architecture

Different spatial types require differentiated treatment of the facade and entrance. The two-storey brick body is a constant for the quadrant, progressing smoothly from northern perimeter to avenue, to streets, to green ditch and cycle path. This body turns the block into a building.
The entrance design and fenestration reflect the character of the space bordered by this body. The avenue dwellings have a formal porch, a sharp cut in the wall, marked by a vertical concrete element and a small garden bed in the pavement. In the ordinary streets, the entrances are more informal. Here the transition between inside and outside is marked with a vertical prefab concrete slab and benches that project from the wall.

Corner

One result of the decision to line the urban space with continuous facade walls is the need for a 'corner solution', a Dutch planning term that in itself implies the existence of a problem. In our view, the corner provides an opportunity for introducing a special dwelling type. No suburban two-bedroom semi, but a live/work unit perhaps, with work space on the ground floor, living space upstairs and at the rear, outdoor space in the form of a roof terrace in the inner angle of the block.

Greenery

The landscaping supports the structure of the public space. The U-shaped avenue will have a regular pattern of closely planted trees that screen the angle parking. The cycle path, which bisects the plan from east to west, will be lined by an irregular planting of small flowering trees, singly and in groups, that mitigate the linear character of the profile and turn it into a 'space' rather than a street. In the north–south streets the profile will be accentuated by hedges demarcating the area in front of the dwelling.

The rooms, where the north–south streets cross the cycle route and the internal domains are accessed, are lined by a continuous border of low-growing shrubs that are separated by an upright prefab concrete element (70 cm high) from a two-metre-wide, deep gutter. This is covered with gratings through which the trunks of closely planted plane trees grow. Lighting incorporated in the gratings illuminates the underside of the pollarded crowns, thereby lending the rooms the intimate atmosphere of a village square.
It goes without saying that the rooms are not paved, but finished with a layer of white gravel on top of a compacted layer of sand.

The green ditch is a sunken lawn intended for sport and play. The bank is green, too; the spatial demarcation takes the form of a row of poplars along the adjoining pavements flanking the ditch.

Along the eastern and western boundaries of the quadrant, the canal and the strip of park, there will be incidental plantings of park trees in groups. The water features on the southern boundary will be marked by dense, tall-growing shrubbery that screens the trailer camp.

Traffic

Motor traffic will be channelled along the U-shaped avenue that gives the quadrant its spatial structure. At one end, where the west wall meets the northern boundary, this avenue connects with the Laan van Vlaanderen; at the other end, near the canal, with the service road between the northern boundary and the block of flats. All public space parking is concentrated along the avenue, the northern boundary and the canal. While the north–south streets are accessible to motor traffic, neither they nor the rooms have any parking spaces. The southern part of the planning area – the waterside dwellings and the trailer camp – is served by streets with a 'mews' character.

For pedestrians there is an alternative network of paths that bisect the housing blocks in a north–south direction. These paths, which have been deliberately kept separate from the street structure, provide for a different, more informal experience of the plan.

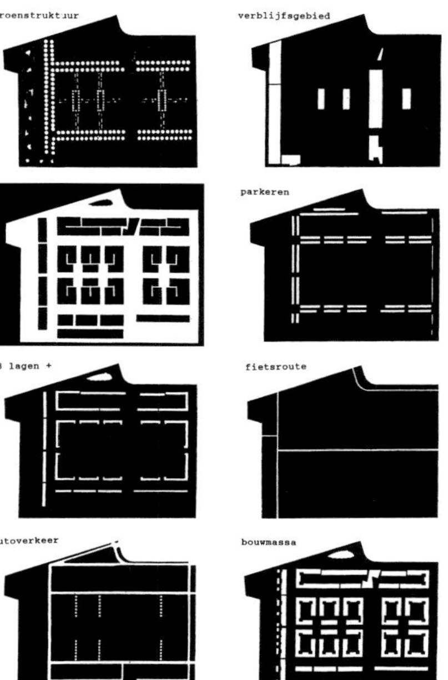

054
HOORNSE HEEM PENSIONER APARTMENTS, GRONINGEN

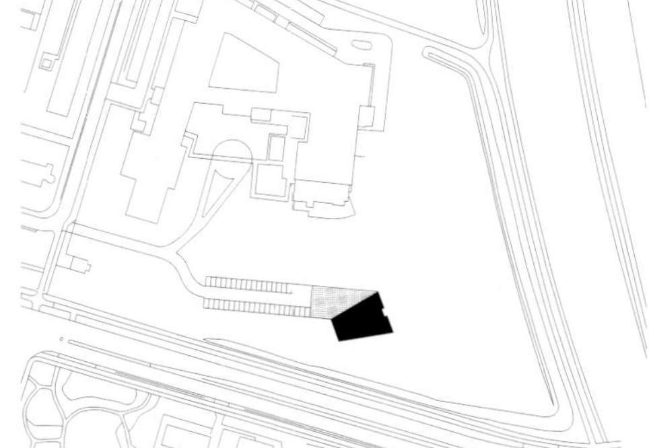

This apartment tower built next to a nursing home contains 56 flats for the elderly. The slim, fourteen-storey, wedge-shaped tower on a base containing the entrance and storage spaces, is a contemporary take on the modernist concept of the tower in the park. However, this solution was not motivated by any desire to follow the well-trodden path of light, air and space, but by a reluctance to sacrifice the green space to a rash of low-rise buildings. An incidental benefit is that the tower acts as a spatial marker for the nursing home which is located near the ring road around Groningen.

Each storey contains four apartments with a flexible floor plan that caters to changing housing needs and is also suitable for wheelchair users. Every apartment has a glazed veranda on the end elevation, a popular sheltered alternative to balconies in housing for the elderly. In this instance, the wind at higher levels also made verandas a more practical option than balconies.

On first sight, the horizontal division of the picture windows on the narrower end elevation creates confusion about the scale and the number of floors. The illusory nature of this architecture continues in the multi-coloured 'dazzle painting' on the long side elevations which, together with the crisply detailed corners of the structure, dispels any suggestion of materiality. In an oeuvre in which the tectonic character of the architecture is rarely represented in an ambiguous manner, this negation of mass is exceptional.

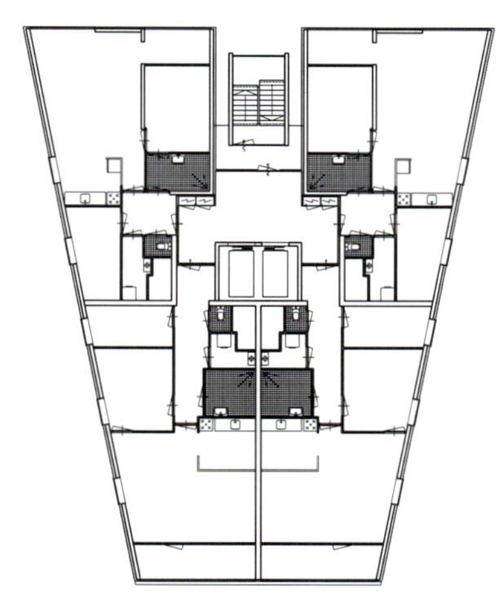

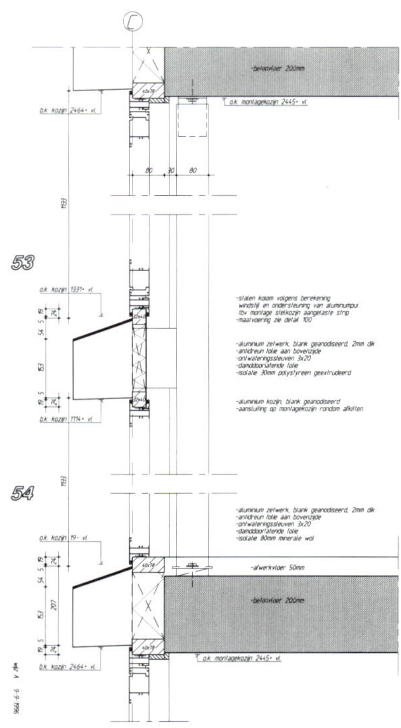

Hoornse Heem Pensioner Apartments, Groningen

057 075
POLICE POST AND SOCIAL SERVICES DISTRICT OFFICE, AMSTERDAM

This combination of neighbourhood police post and offices for the social services is a direct reflection of the complexity of the location, on the boundary between prewar Amsterdam South designed by Berlage, and the modern, postwar expansion south of Kennedylaan. Whereas in most work by Claus en Kaan a confrontation is resolved in a self-evident and self-assured form, this architecture is an unequivocal expression of two different worlds that come together here.

The programme prompted the articulation of the two separate services in two interlocking but clearly differentiated forms which mirror the two architectural worlds that touch one another at this spot. The rough, dark box, with its band of thick-framed windows, refers to the architecture of the Amsterdam School. The smooth, light box with the Breuer windows from the Whitney Museum in New York, stands for Modernism.

These two characters are united in a volume that can be read as a cut-away box in which each function is not only clearly expressed in the facades, but, because of the nature of the different activities involved, spatially separated as well. The police post is organized around an atrium while social services have their offices on the upper floor and a teahouse on the roof.

On top of all this, there is a marked difference between front and rear, with the facade on Kennedylaan forming a high front for the building which falls away to the public park at the rear.

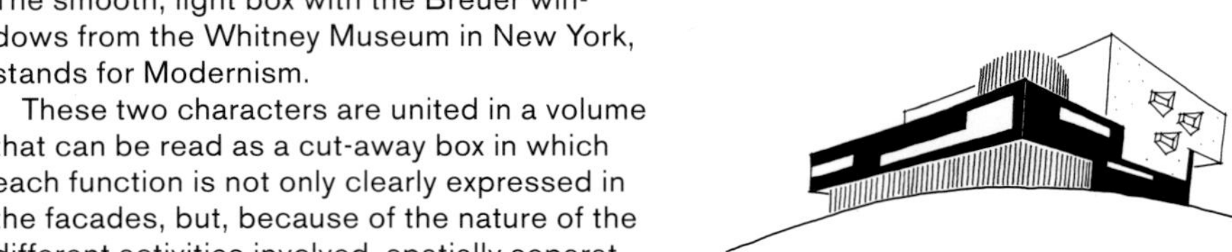

1

2

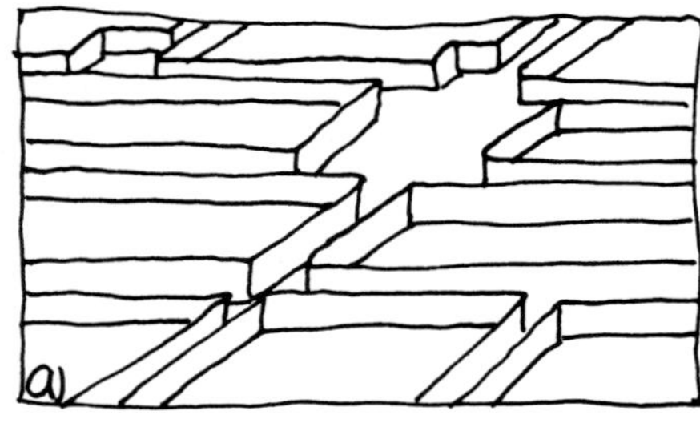

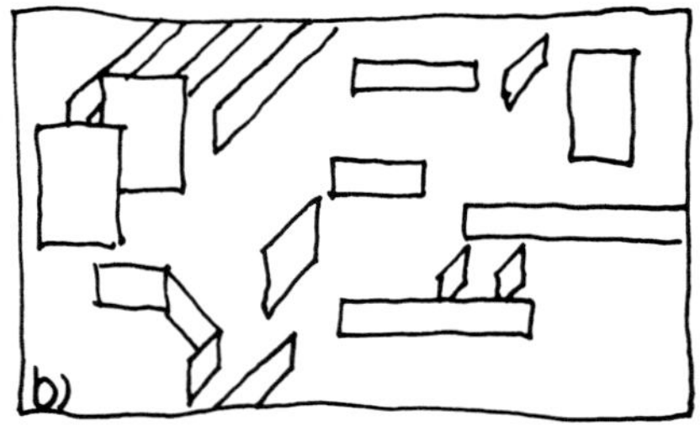

3

4

5

1 Amsterdam School housing scheme, Meerhuizenplein, Amsterdam
2 Marcel Breuer, Whitney Museum of Modern Art, New York, 1966
3 Rob Krier, the traditional city, the modern city
4 H.P. Berlage
5 Johanna Mulder and Cornelis van Eesteren

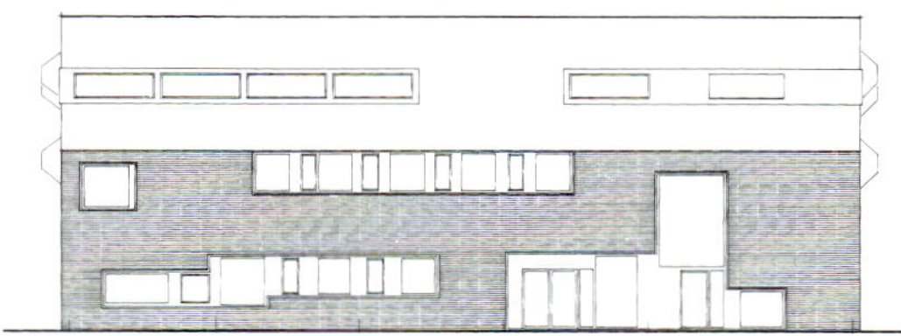

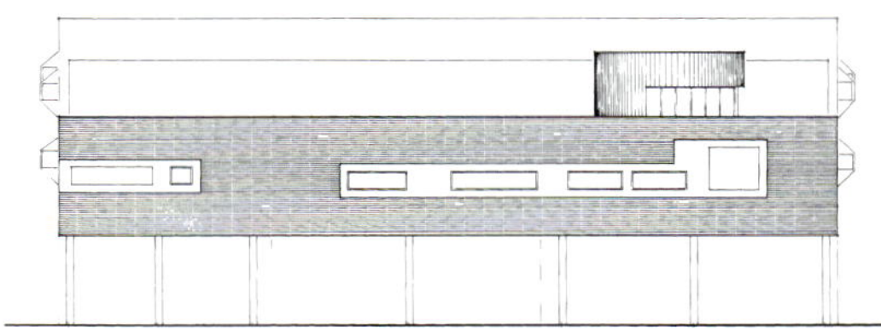

Police Post and Social Services District Office, Amsterdam

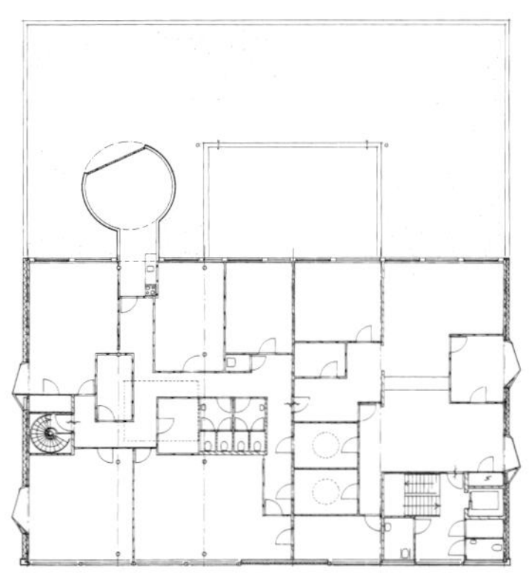

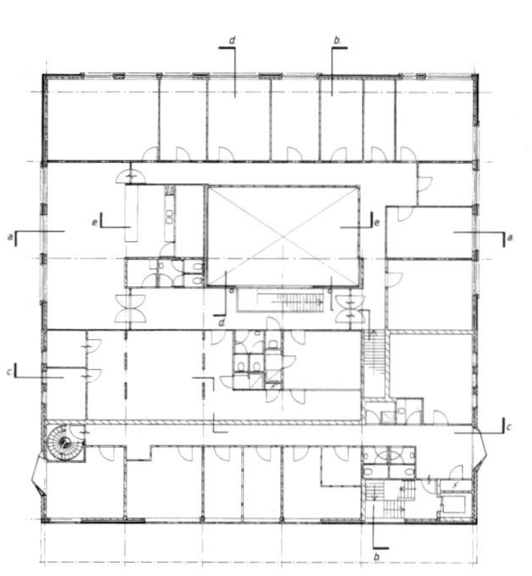

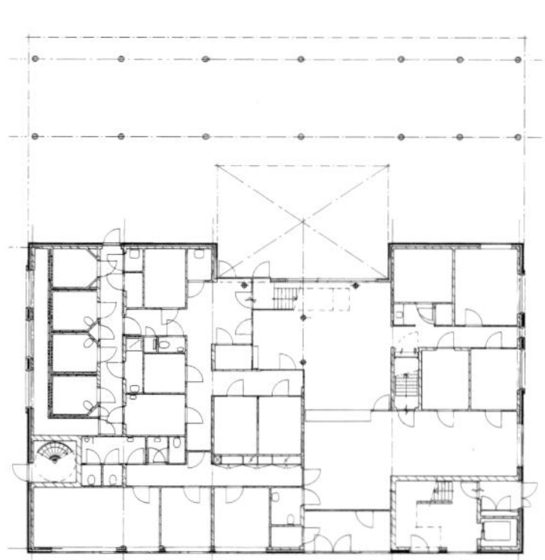

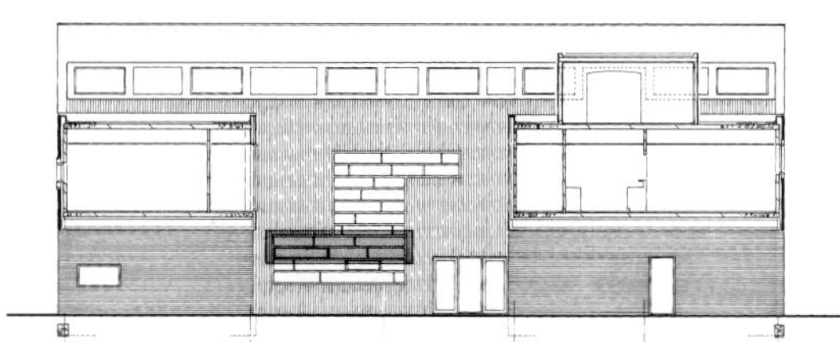

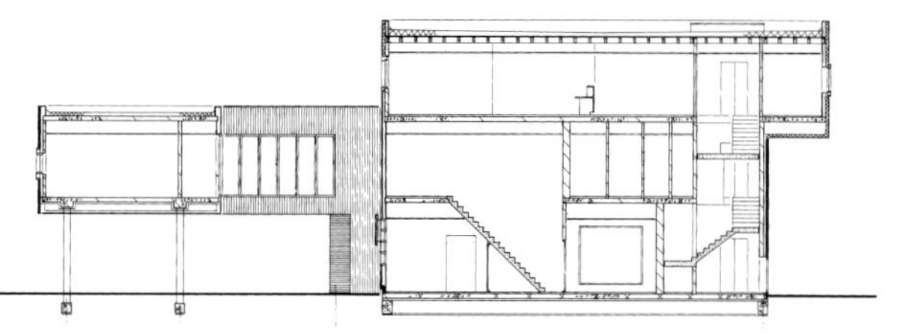

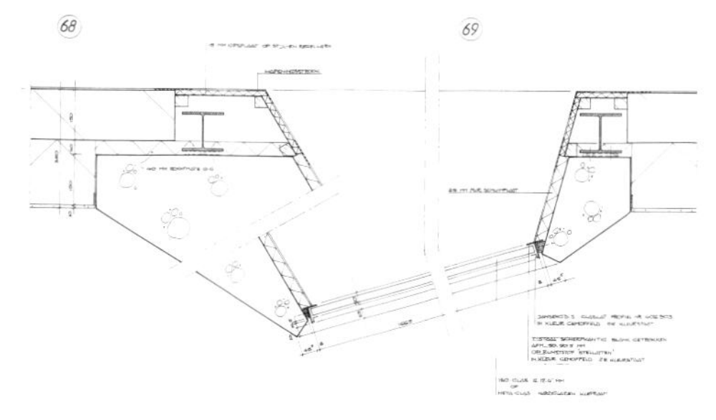

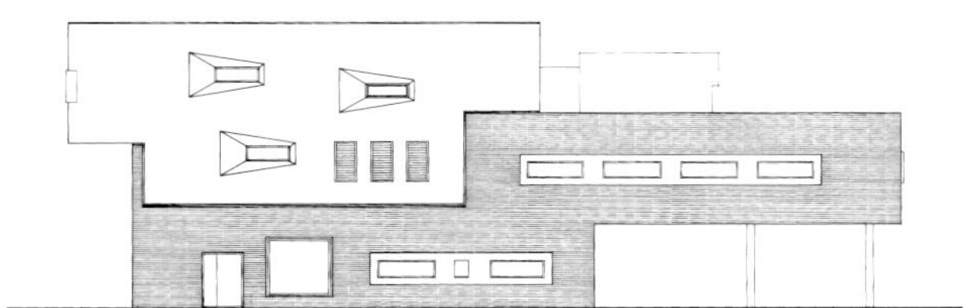

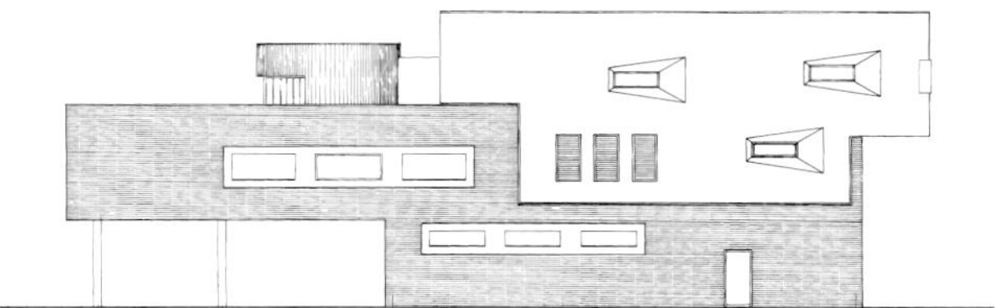

058 074 083 113
HOUSING, GULDEN KRUIS, AMSTERDAM

The Bijlmer district was developed in the 1960s southeast of Amsterdam in the former Bijlmermeer polder. It is the prime example – both famous and infamous – of large-scale modernist planning in the Netherlands. Although built as recently as the 1960s and '70s, the durability of the underlying concept proved to be short, especially since the district, for a variety of demographic and social reasons, spawned a disproportionate number of social problems. The remedy for the various shortcomings associated with living in 'towers in a park' is a return to other residential forms that mitigate the one-sidedness of the high-rise culture without immediately reverting to suburban low-rise. Claus en Kaan, in close collaboration with Donald Lambert of Kraaijvanger Urbis, who was responsible for the restructuring of Gulden Kruis, realized three housing projects, one along Bijlmerdreef, another immediately behind this, and a group of compact towers that form a boundary between Gulden Kruis and the 1970s high-rise flats in Gerenstein.

Behind the closed elevation of the dwellings along Bijlmerdreef, where the artworks by Eddy Varekamp are a contemporary take on the tradition of integrating art with architecture that existed until about the 1950s, are split-level dwellings spread over five floors (including mezzanines), topped by duplex apartments with an entresol in the void. As such, the blocks can be read as a stacking of two types that are generally built in ground-accessed form. The front elevation, with the neat garden as a buffer between public and private and the vertical progression of ever-narrower ribbon windows, has a highly formal order. By comparison, the rear elevation is more informal and open.

The so-called Pion (pawn) dwellings have an unusually free form for Claus en Kaan. Such formalism is generally found only in the odd decorative accent but here it determines the basic shape which in turn serves to emphasize the architectural and spatial autonomy of the three objects.

The Passtukken (adaptor) towers can also be construed as autonomous objects but with their neutral form and the restrained expressiveness of the detailing they are of a completely different order. The towers of eight, seven or four storeys, which are distributed between the older high-rise and the new low-rise, derive their power from their pragmatic modesty in that they do no more than play a mediatory role (hence their name) between two conflicting spatial and architectural systems.

1

2

3

4

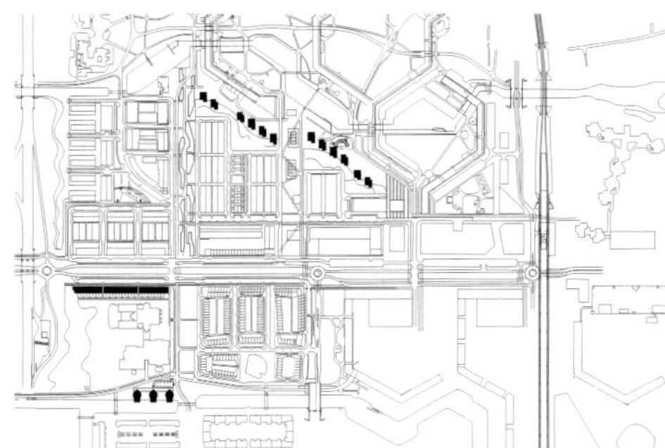

1 Dienst Stedebouw/G.S. Nassuth, Bijlmermeer, Amsterdam, 1962–1971
2 Donald Lambert, sketch of Bijlmerdreef
3 John Nash, Carlton House Terrace, London, 1827
4 Example of ground-accessed housing in the Rubensstraat, Amsterdam
5 Minervalaan, Amsterdam, 1938

5

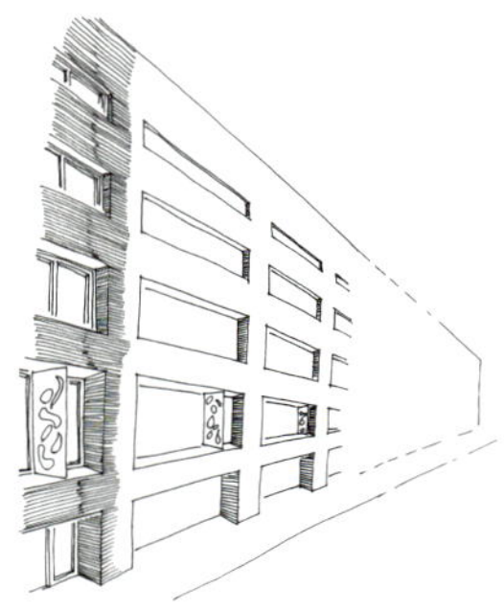

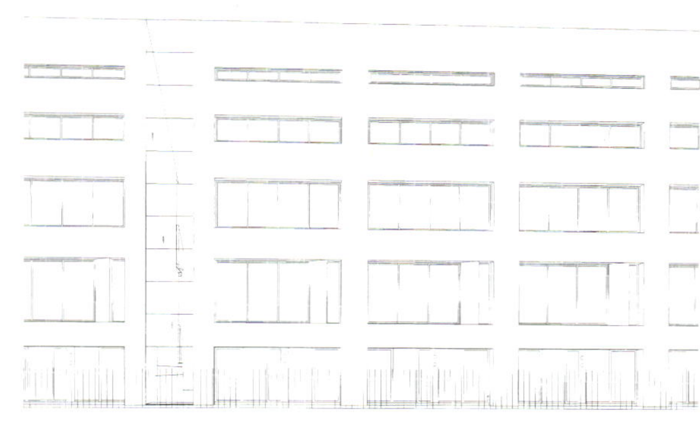

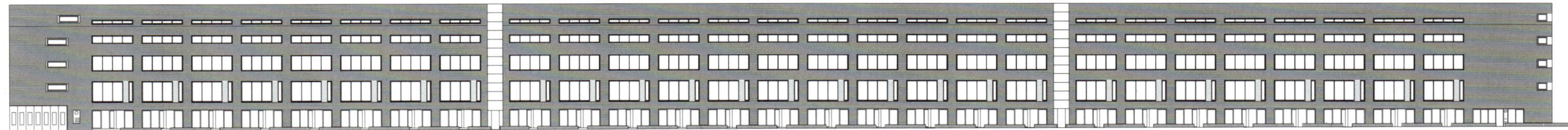

Bijlmerdreef

1 Hildo Krop at work on the facade sculpture for 1 Apollolaan
2 Eddy Varekamp, ceramic panels for 'BeBo' housing, Bijlmerdreef, Amsterdam, 1995

1

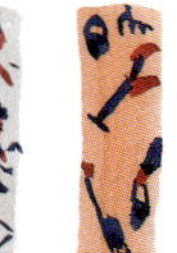

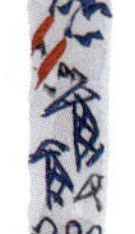

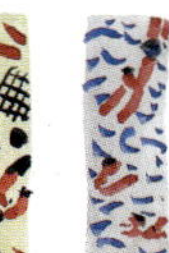

2

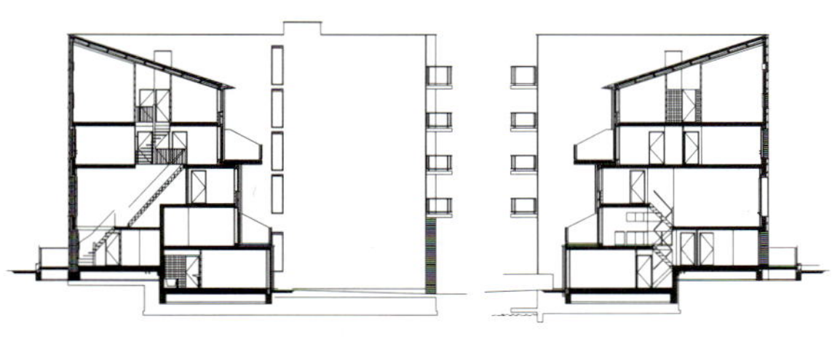
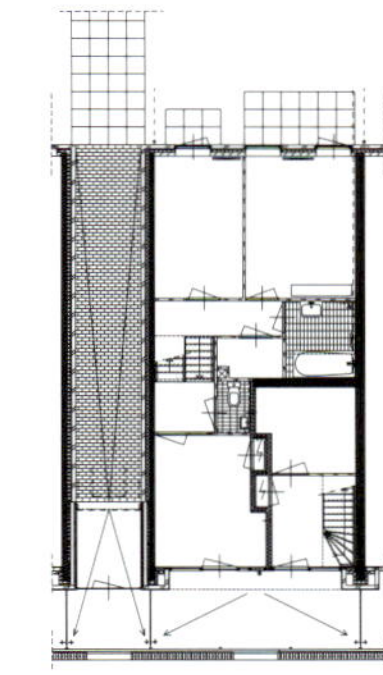
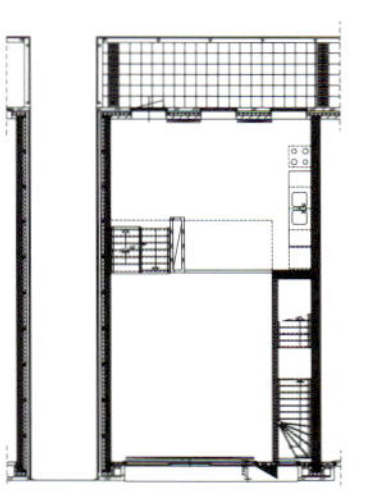
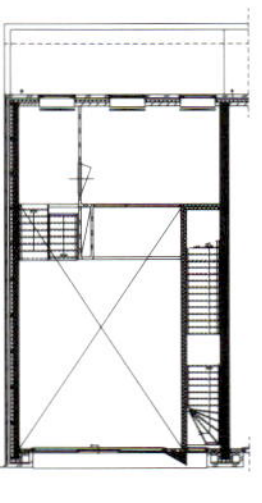
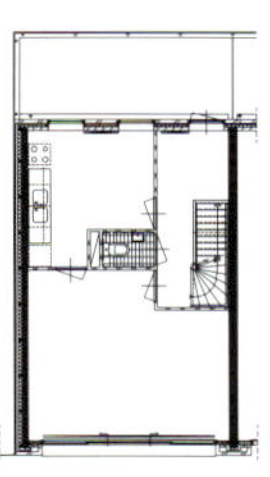
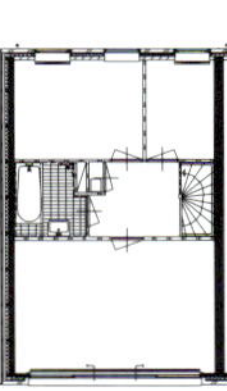

'Adaptor Blocks', Nieuw Gerenstein

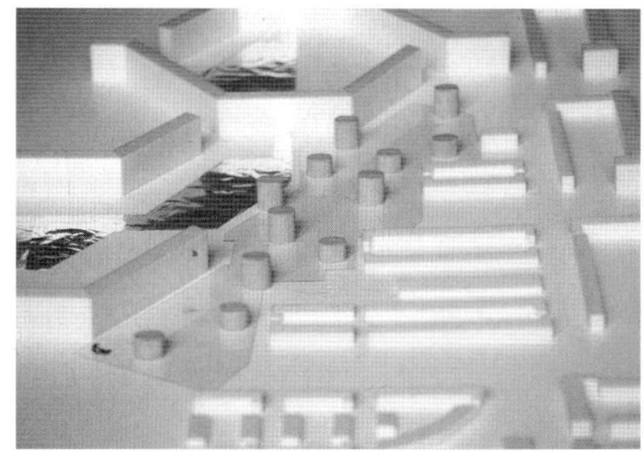

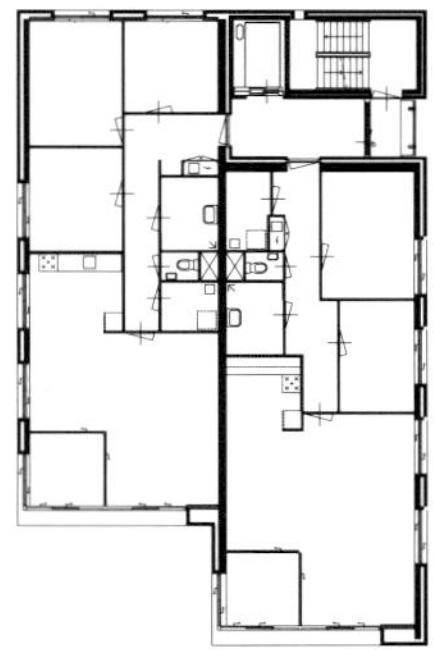

Housing, Gulden Kruis, Amsterdam

'Adaptor Blocks', Nieuw Gerenstein

‘Pawn Dwellings’

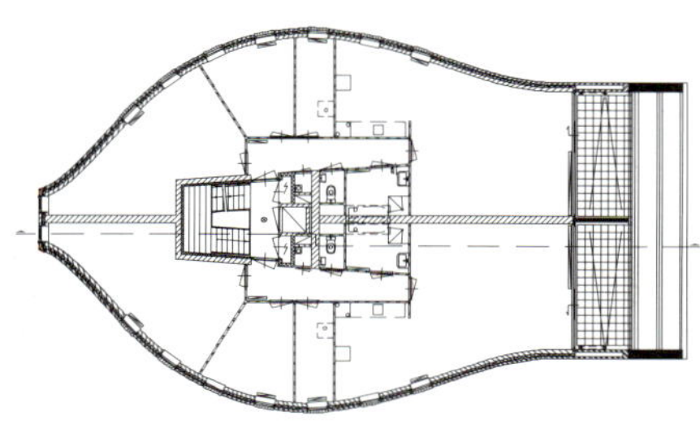
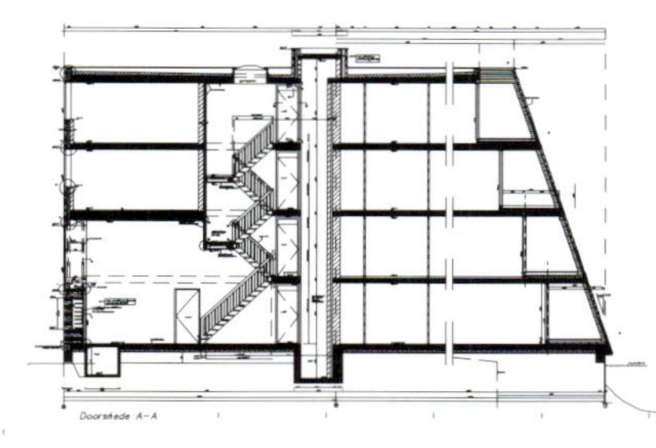

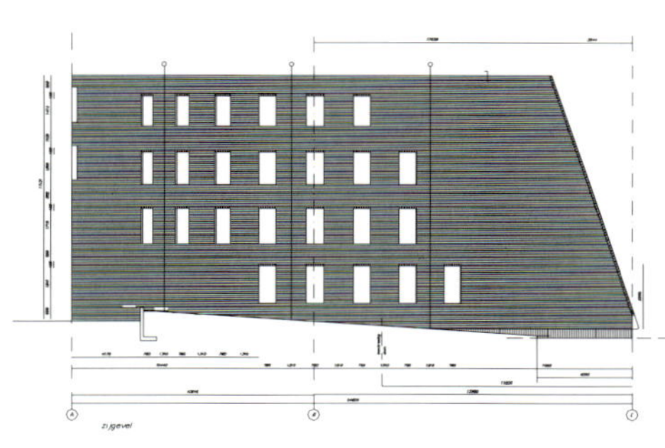
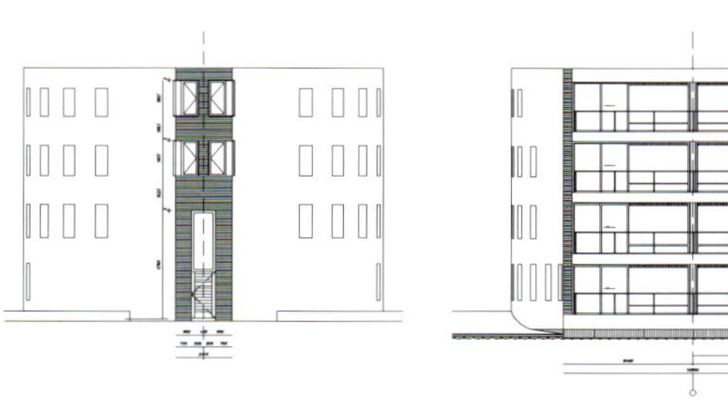

Housing, Gulden Kruis, Amsterdam

'Pawn Dwellings'

062 069
RONALD MCDONALD HOUSE AND APARTMENTS, AMSTERDAM

The block containing thirty apartments and the Ronald McDonald House is a little further along the Amstelveenseweg from the sites which were the subject of an earlier commission but which were eventually built at the same time. The L-shaped apartment block consists of a six-storey main block perpendicular to the ribbon development of Amstelveenseweg, and a lower block of three storeys atop a half-sunken parking level. The apartments are reached via galleries at the rear which is executed in dazzling white concrete. The Ronald McDonald House is a continuation of this lower section from which it is distinguished by a different fenestration.

The core of the Ronald McDonald House, a hotel-like environment, is formed by the complex communal space that is cut out of the box-shape in a large-scale version of the exhibition box by Linnemann & Bannenberg. By employing differently shaped rooms, the architects have created an intricate space that affords opportunities for both solitary retreat and informal, homely contact.

The spatial complexity of the interior is foreshadowed in the striking form of the entrance with its off-centre transom light.

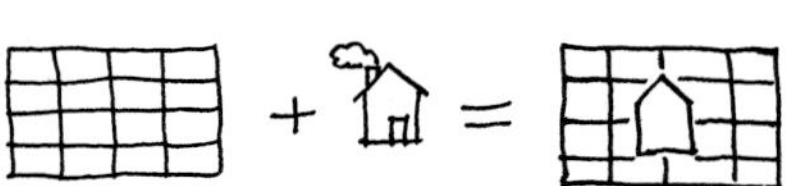

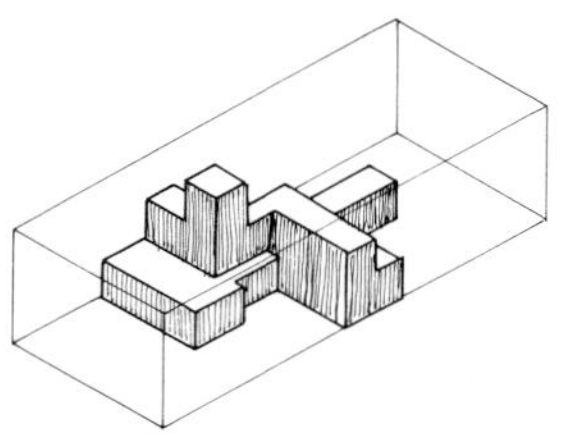

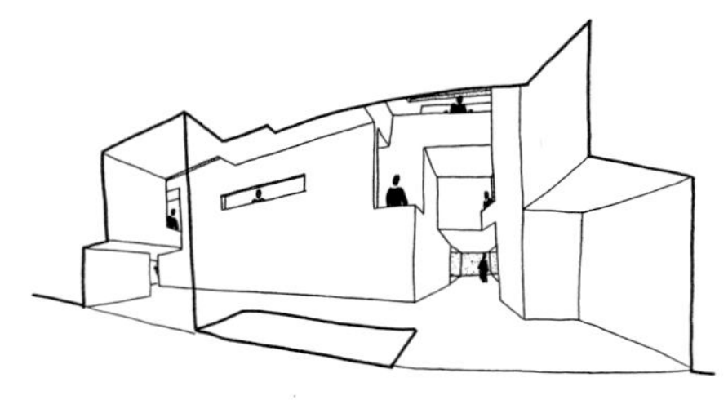

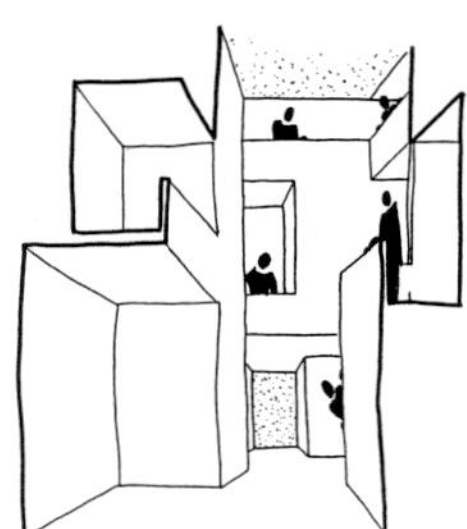

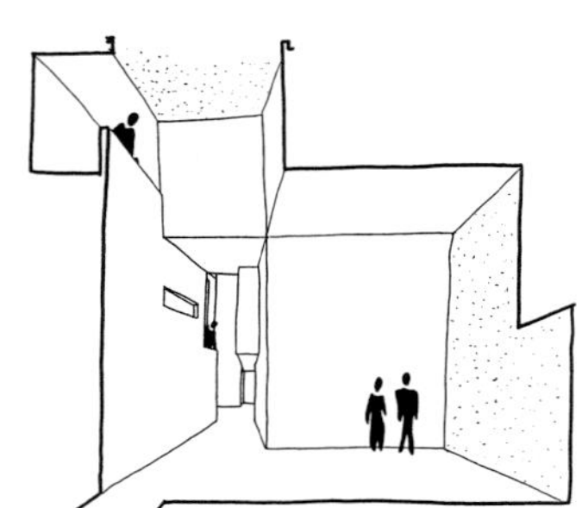

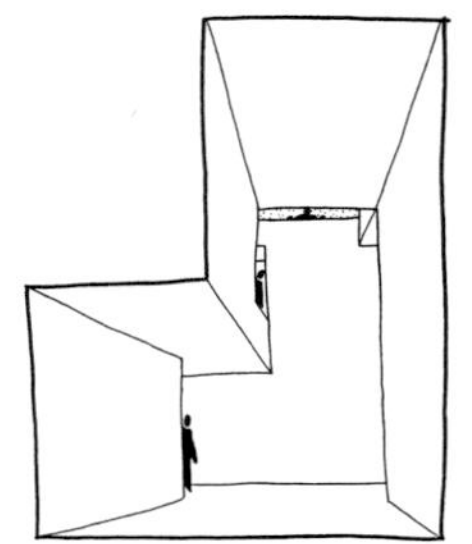

Head elevation of apartment building

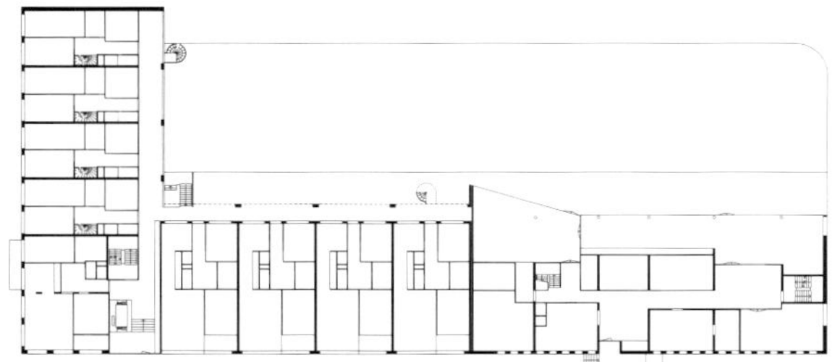

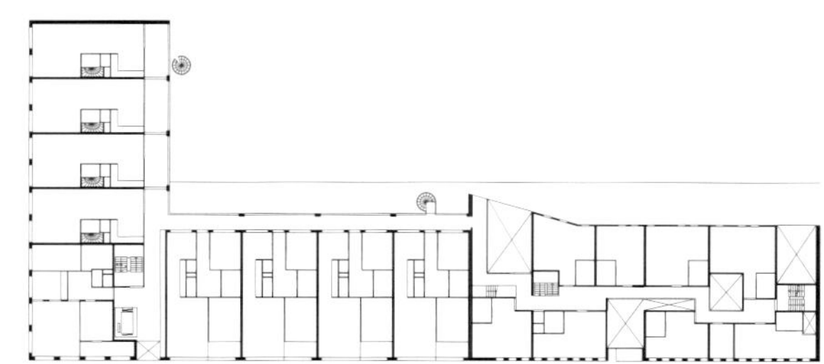

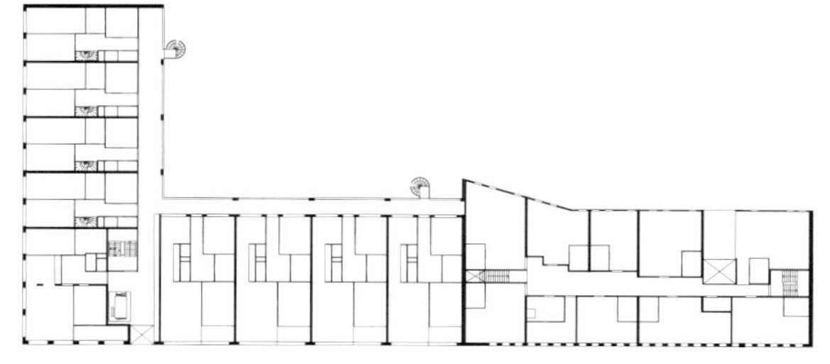

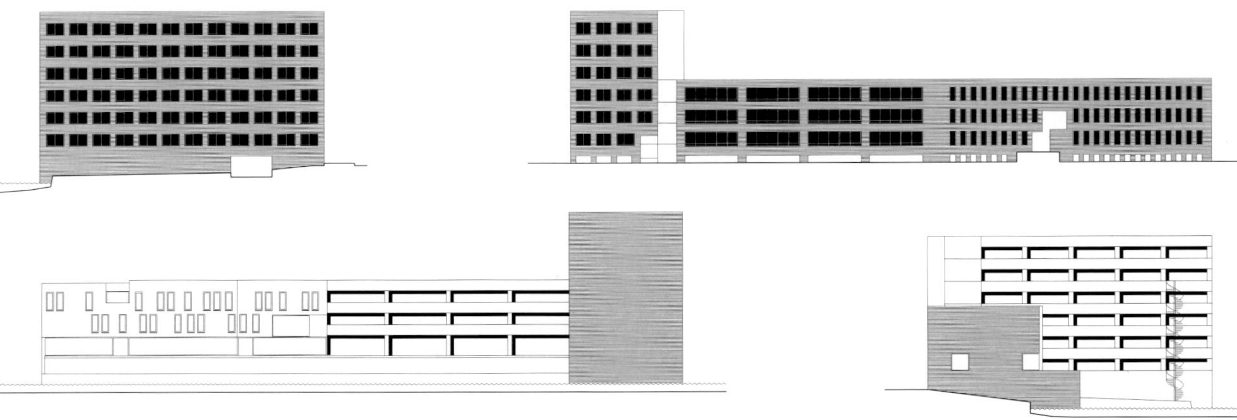

Rear elevation Ronald McDonald House and Apartment Building

Ronald McDonald House and Apartments, Amsterdam

064 HOUSING, MARVELO, ZAANDAM

1

The Marvelo site, a brownfield plot located on the river Zaan in Zaandam, was the subject of a Europan competition. The winning design by Pierre Gautier and Tania Concko has since been executed, with parts of the project being contracted out to Frank Roodbeen of Van den Oever, Zaaijer, Roodbeen & Partners, and to Claus en Kaan, who designed five of the thirteen blocks. The substantial buildings along the water are comparable in size to the factories that once stood on this riverbank location. The low-rise on the landward side forms a transition to the low development on the other side of the dike. Together the buildings make up an ensemble that in scale and expression recalls the spectacular industrial landscape of the Zaan region. It stands on a collective deck designed as a paved square, below which is a car park.

The rational uniformity that distinguishes all Claus en Kaan's larger housing projects, coincides here with the image of utilitarian simplicity that is a natural reference in this monumental industrial landscape. The big blocks are characterized by an absence of arbitrary irregularity or deliberate variation. At most the top floors, which perch on the blocks like separate rooftop units, might be regarded as manifestations of a discreet formal ambition. Because of the formal reduction, the architecture fits the notion of an industrial vernacular that persists as after-image in one's perception of this housing. Owing to the absence of balconies, the massive buildings come across not as agglomerations of
individual units, but as coherent objects.
The low-rise, with its timber-clad facades, is an abstract interpretation of the pre-industrial building method of the Zaan region.

The dialectical development of the design for building 1 was crucial for Claus en Kaan. In the first plan, the various dwelling types were arranged in clusters and each cluster was expressed on the outside of the building by means of a different facade cladding. This 'conceptual' design was followed by a second proposal to conceal the typological diversity behind a single aesthetic skin. In the third and definitive plan all idea of aestheticizing the exterior was abandoned and the building tailored in scale and outward appearance to the industrial surroundings. Using the cheapest bricks available, the architects made a surly building that radiates testiness – an architectural Lombroso type, as it were.

1 C. Lombroso, criminal types, c. 1875
2 Old situation
3 Pierre Gautier and Tania Concko, competition entry for Europan Marvelo site, Zaandam, 1991
4 Successive design stages of building 1

2

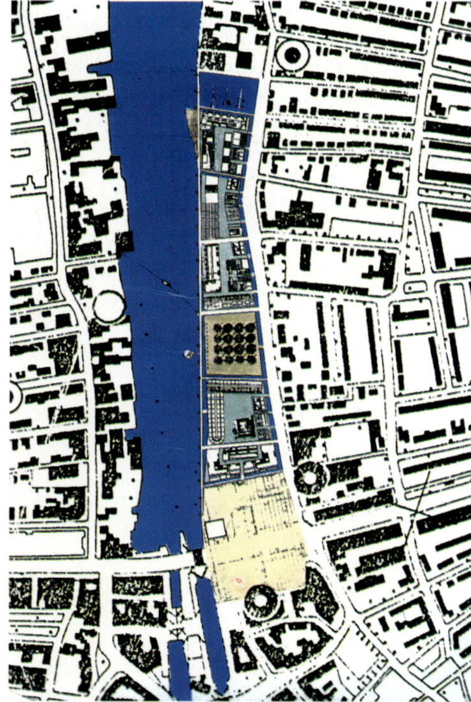

3

3

3

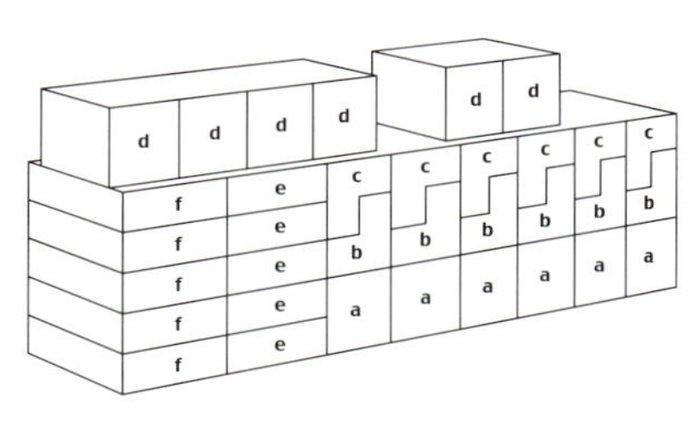

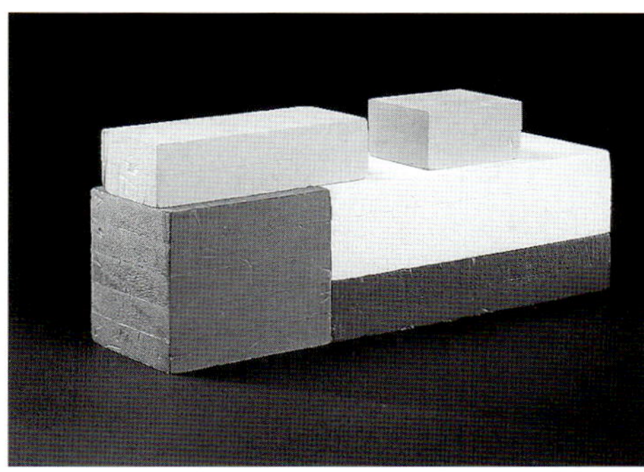

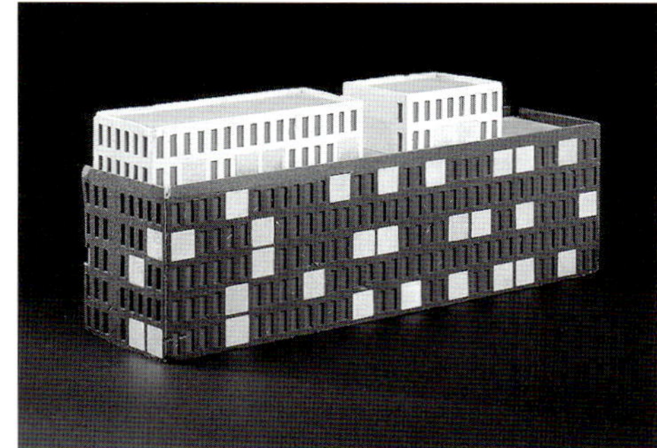

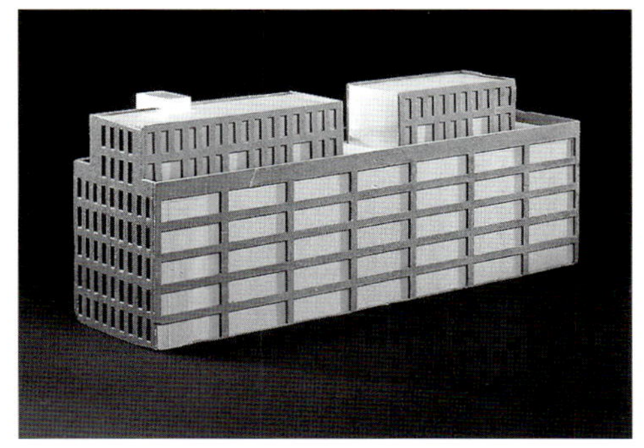

4

The Loop, Chicago

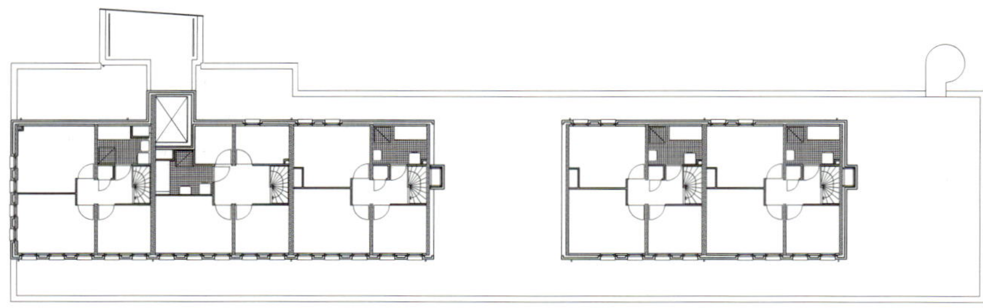
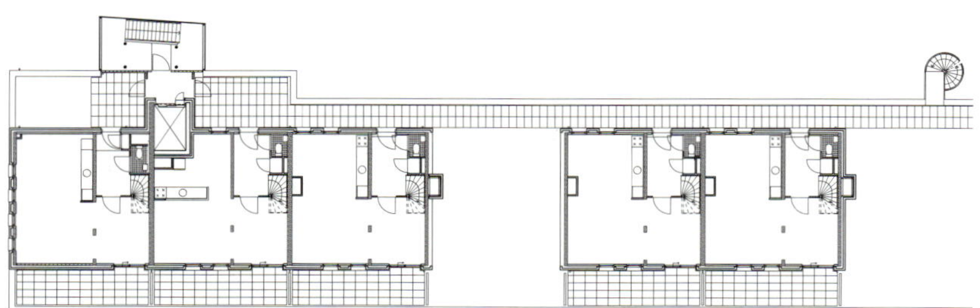

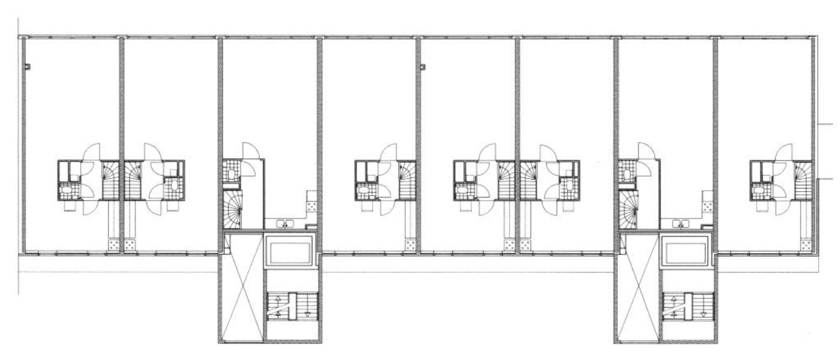

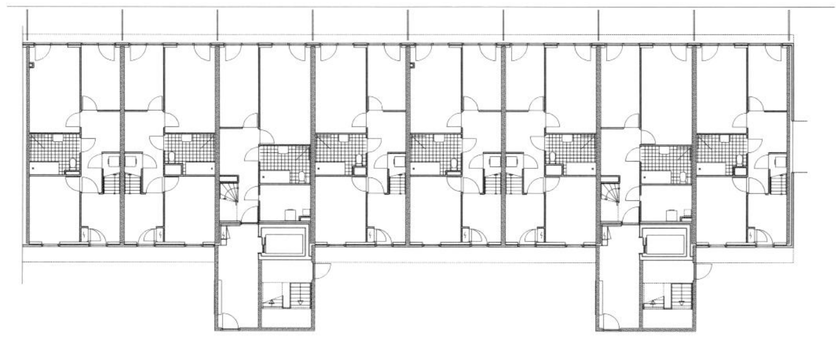

Housing, Marvelo, Zaandam

Building 5

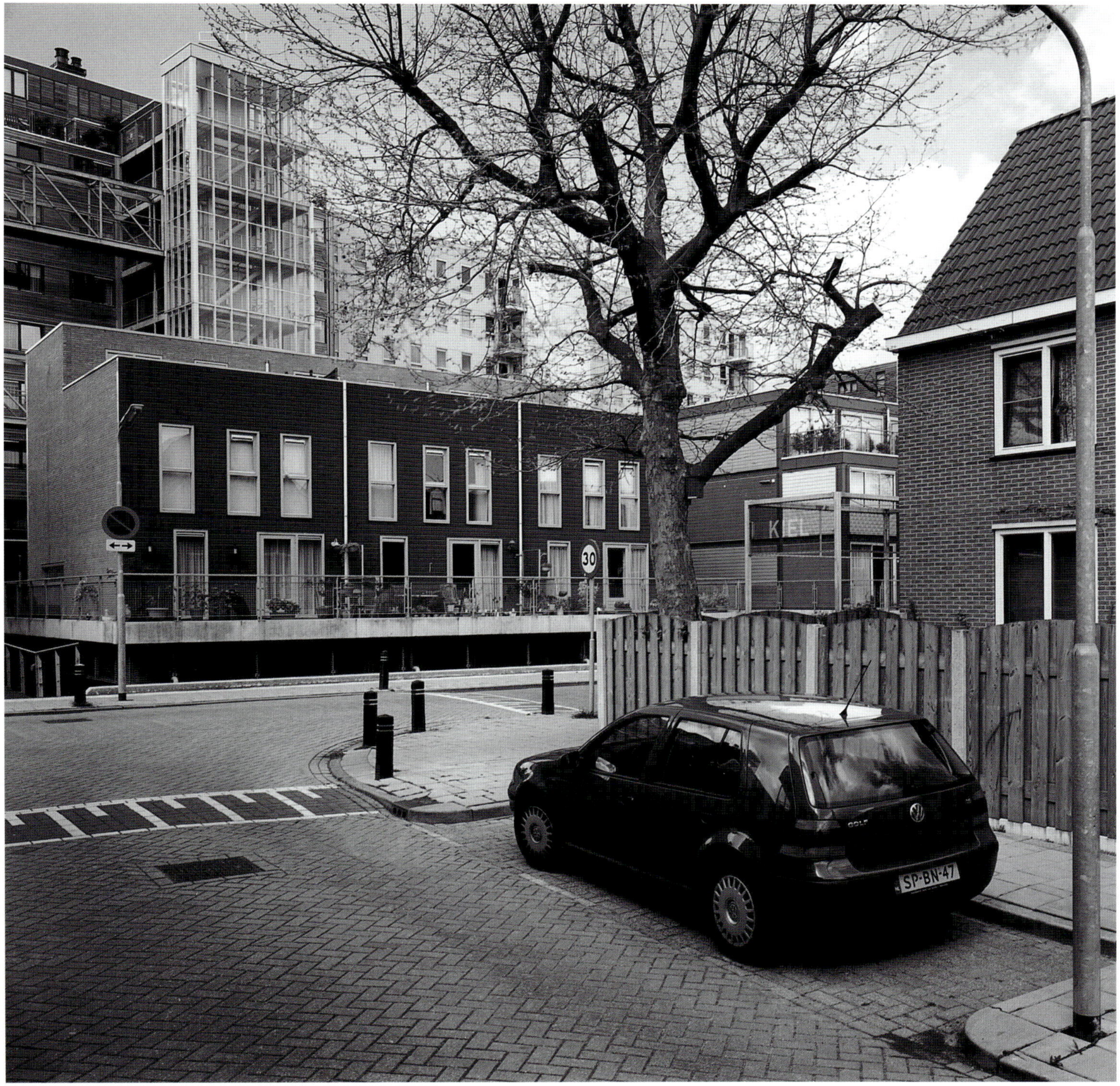

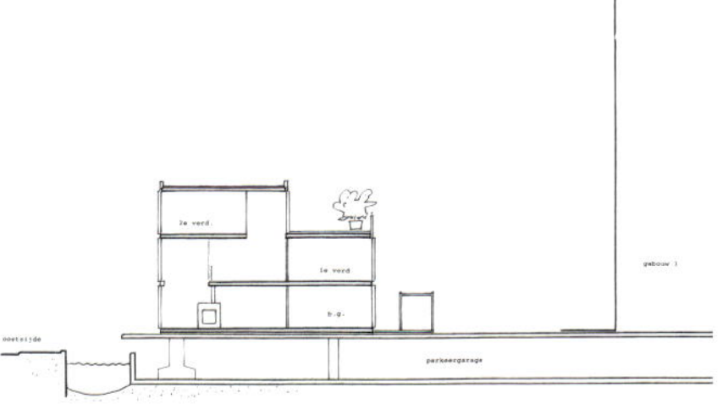

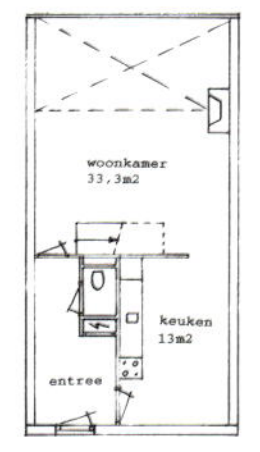
woonkamer
33,3m2
keuken
13m2
entree

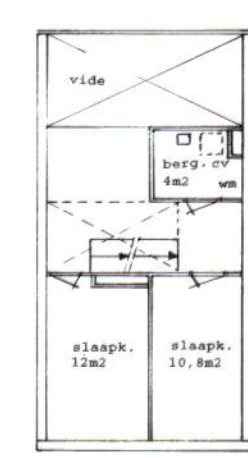
vide
berg. cv
4m2
wm
slaapk.
12m2
slaapk.
10,8m2

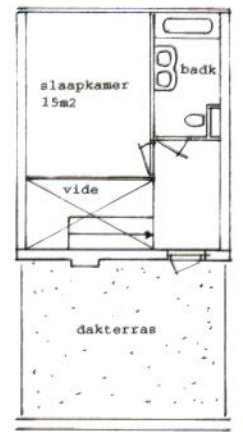
slaapkamer
15m2
badk
vide
dakterras

berging

065 098 106 109 118 HOUSING, SPORENBURG, AMSTERDAM

Robert Frank, City of London, 1951

Two peninsulas in the eastern docklands of Amsterdam, once the scene of busy harbour activities, have been redeveloped as residential areas in accordance with a master plan drawn up by West 8/Adriaan Geuze. Most of the housing on these two islands, Borneo and Sporenburg, consists of ground-accessed low-rise. Of the approximately two thousand dwellings built here, Claus en Kaan have realized 187 on 7 locations on Sporenburg. The starting point for the design was the list of requirements laid down in the brief to the effect that the dwellings should follow the contours of the plot and that within the built contour, fifty per cent of the area should be left open as outdoor space. Another requirement was that the ground floor should be 3.50 metres high. As a result, each house occupies the entire plot and has only one facade, that facing the street.

Claus en Kaan searched for an archetype suitable for the long, narrow plots laid down by the master plan. They found it in a back-to-back dwelling with two basic forms that allow for a great many variations. The design is a systematic exploration of possible differences, in which spatial configurations and front facades are combined in a variety of ways.

The separation between inside and outside, which is emphasized in nearly all of Claus en Kaan's designs, is carried to extremes here. The constellation of living rooms, voids, patios and roof terraces is impossible to fathom from the outside. As such, the architects' contribution is an impeccable realization of Geuze's desire for an image of uniform clarity, without any 'dubious semi-public zones, obstacles or front gardens. Just houses and streets.'

LOKATIE	SP - 02			SP - 07			SP - 13						SP - 15 / 16								RIET-LANDEN	
WONINGTYPE	1	2	3	1	4	5	6	7	8	9	10	11	12	13	14	15	16	17	18	19	20	21
A1		X				X		X						X	X							
A2	X			X																		
A3			X				X						X									
A4																						X
B1											X	X							X			
B2																		X				
B3																	X					
B4									X	X						X						
B5																					X	
C1					X																	
C2																				X		
GEVEL																						
PLATTEGROND																						

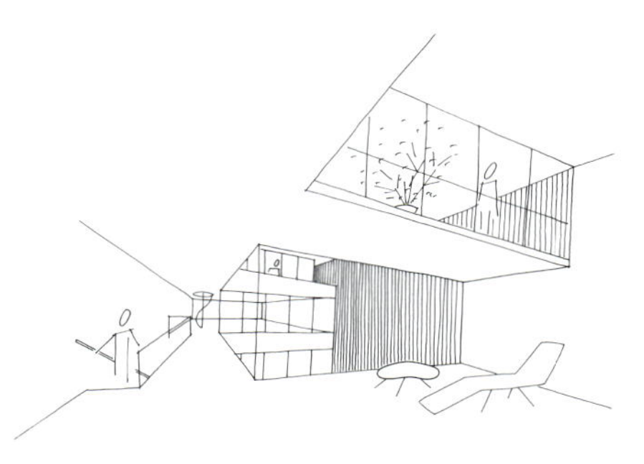

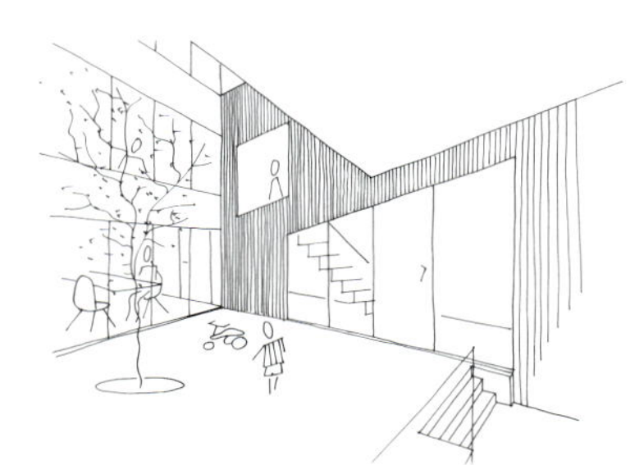

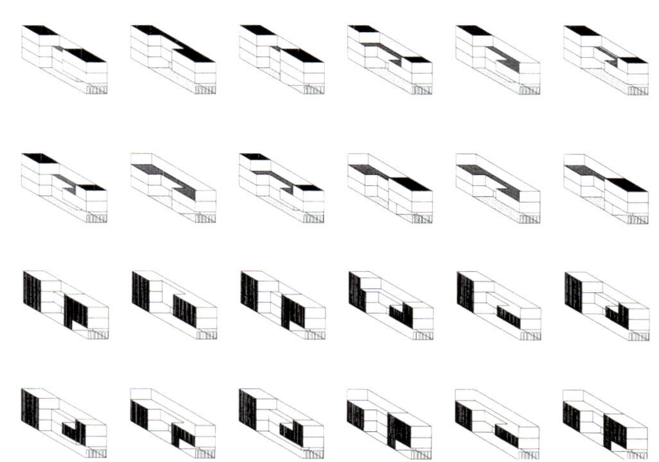

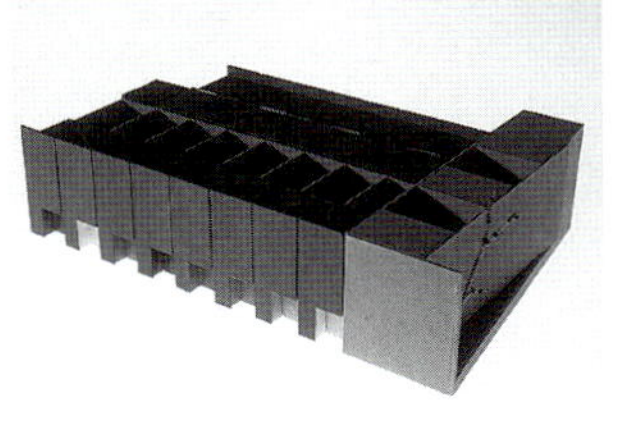

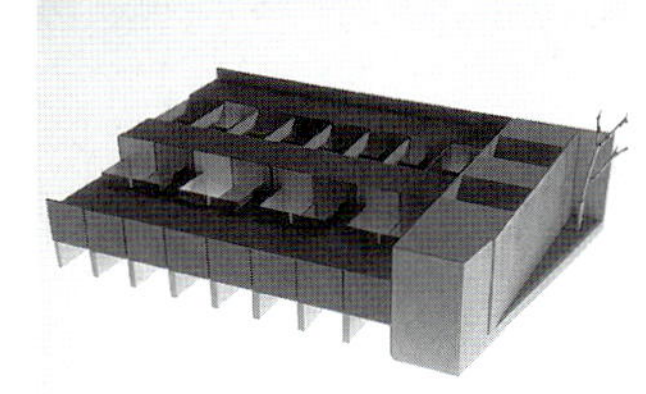

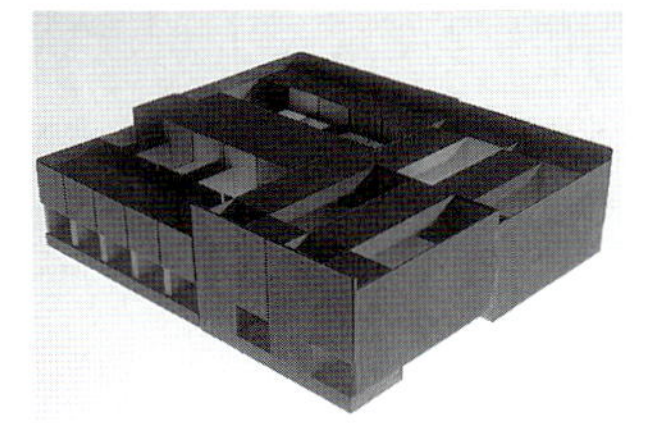

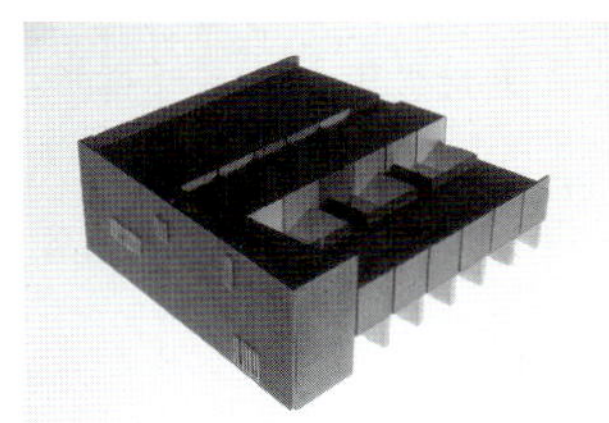

Housing, Sporenburg, Amsterdam

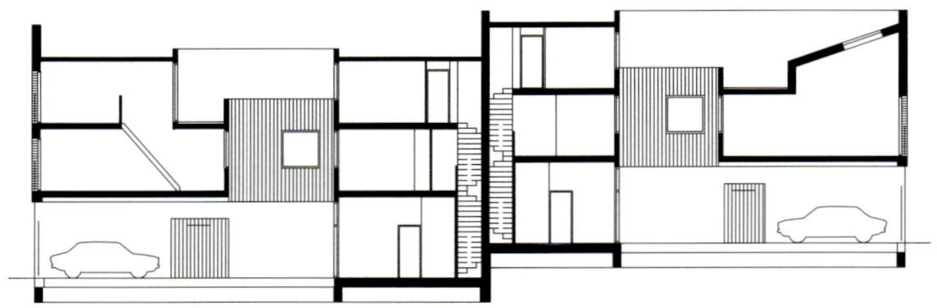

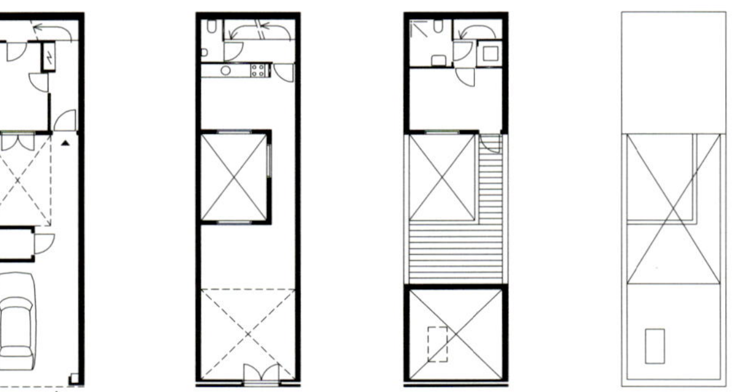

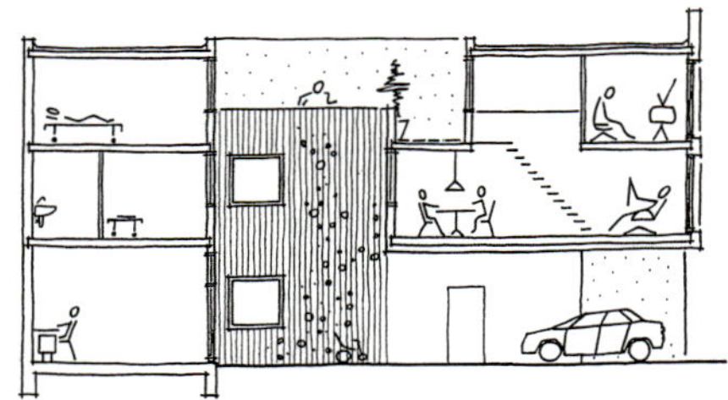

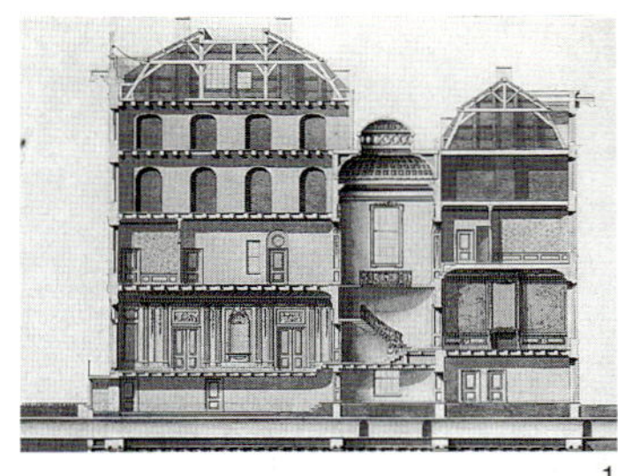

1

1 Section, Herengracht 182, Amsterdam
2 De Klerk and Van Nierop, Marriott Hotel, Amsterdam, 1973–1975

2

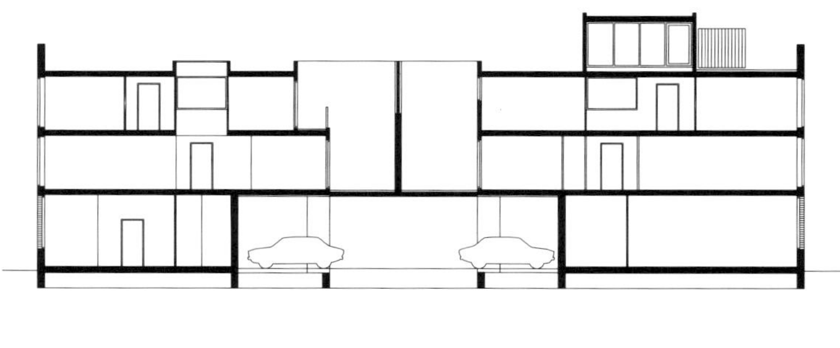

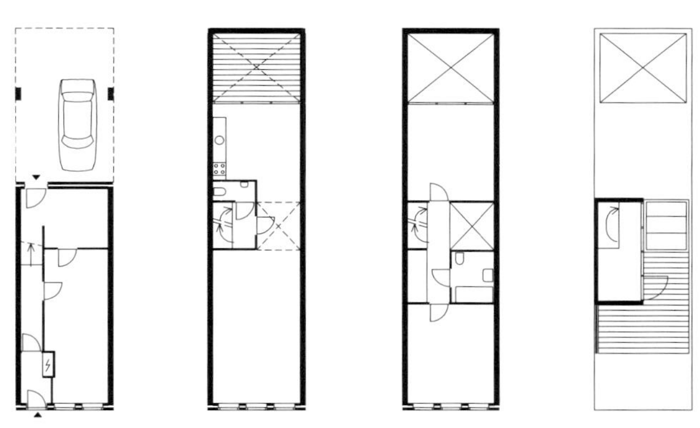

Housing, Sporenburg, Amsterdam

Housing type A1, A2 and A3

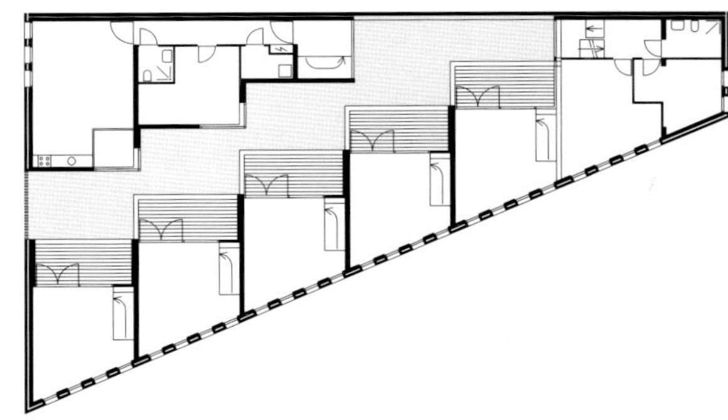

Housing type C2

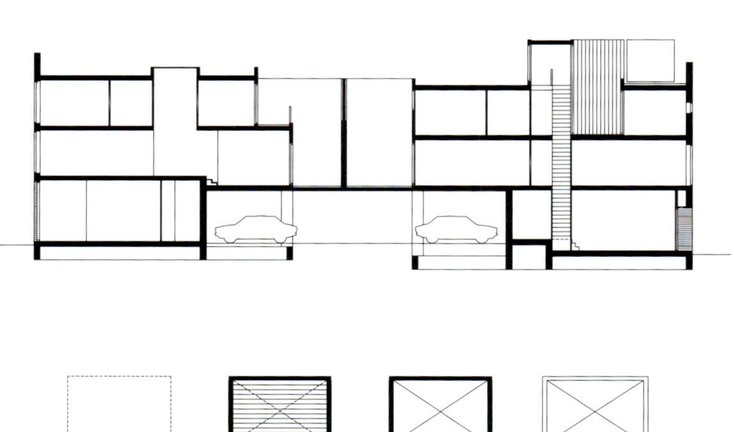

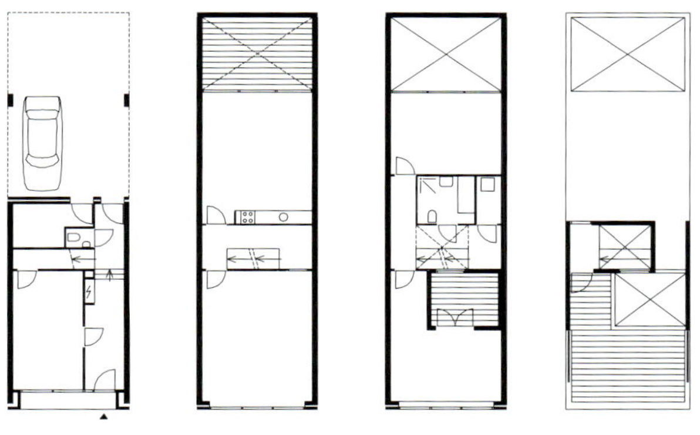

Housing, Sporenburg, Amsterdam

Housing type C2 and B3

066 COMMUNAL AMENITIES, DIERDONK, HELMOND

Dierdonk, a suburb of Helmond, is one of the earliest exponents of 'new traditionalism' with a garden village layout and houses that blatantly refer to the genteel architecture of the interwar years which was rediscovered in the 1990s as the height of style and comfort for the upper middle classes. Only the central axis running through this district eschews the nostalgic retro-philia.

In collaboration with Michael van Gessel and Fortuyn/O'Brien, Claus en Kaan produced a design for a variety of communal amenities to be located in the centre of this suburb. In a landscaped park running through the peat valley they arranged the various facilities in a cluster of free-standing object buildings that accentuate and dramatize the landscape. The two schools, a playgroup, community centre, tennis park, shops, restaurants and a few houses, together with the necessary paving for roads and parking, are accommodated in an exceptionally relaxed ensemble of structures. It was precisely because of this laid-back design that the client decided that the plan was unsuited to these surroundings: too much Palm Springs and not enough middle-of-the-road Dutch.

Although rejected by the client, the design was important for the firm's development because it entailed a different way of thinking, appropriate to this context, based not on a strict formal order for once but on a loose relationship.

2

1

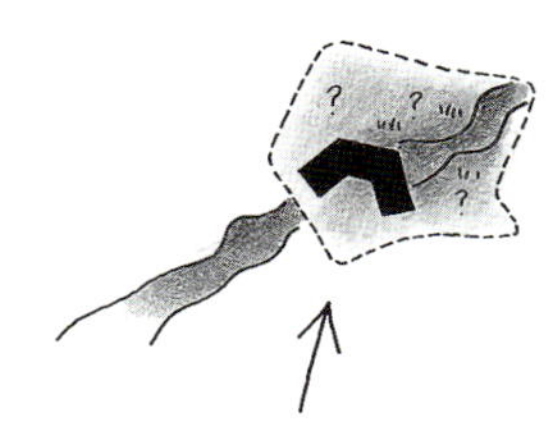

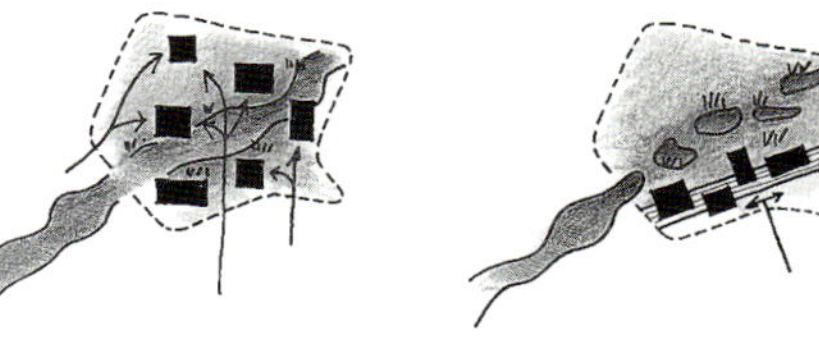

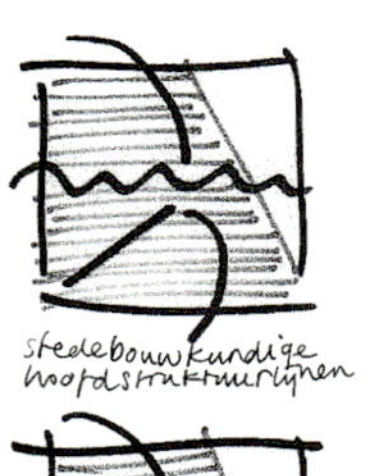

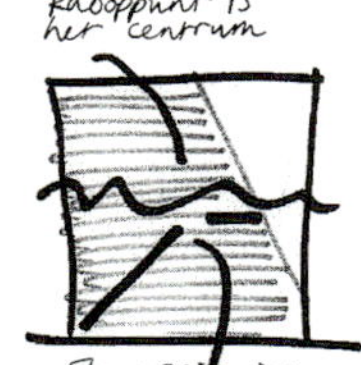

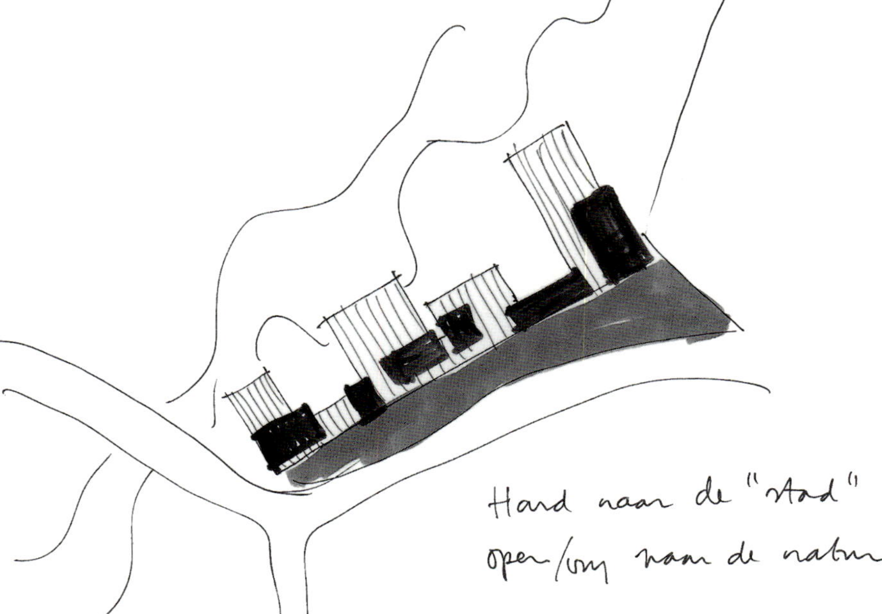

1 Elegant tailgate dining
2 Edward Hopper, People in the Sun, 1960

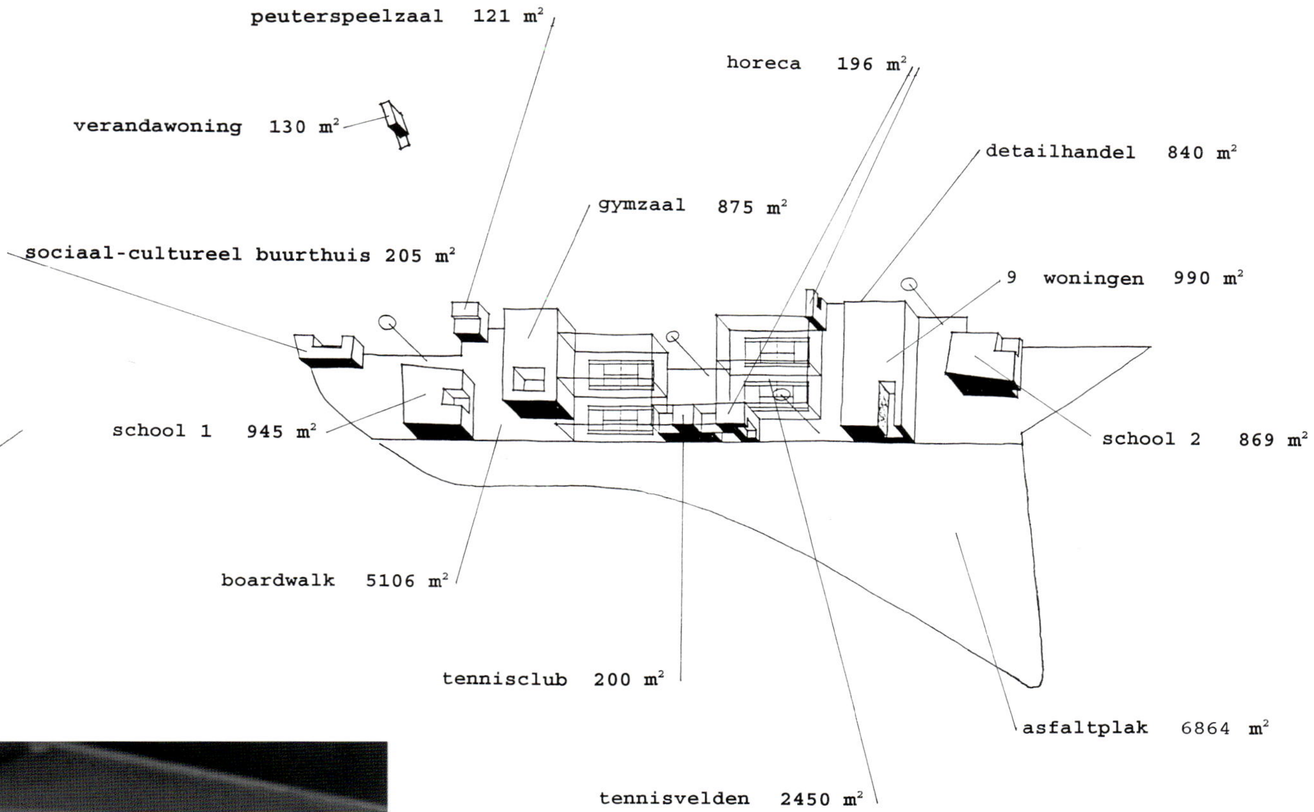

peuterspeelzaal 121 m²
horeca 196 m²
verandawoning 130 m²
detailhandel 840 m²
gymzaal 875 m²
sociaal-cultureel buurthuis 205 m²
9 woningen 990 m²
school 1 945 m²
school 2 869 m²
boardwalk 5106 m²
tennisclub 200 m²
asfaltplak 6864 m²
tennisvelden 2450 m²

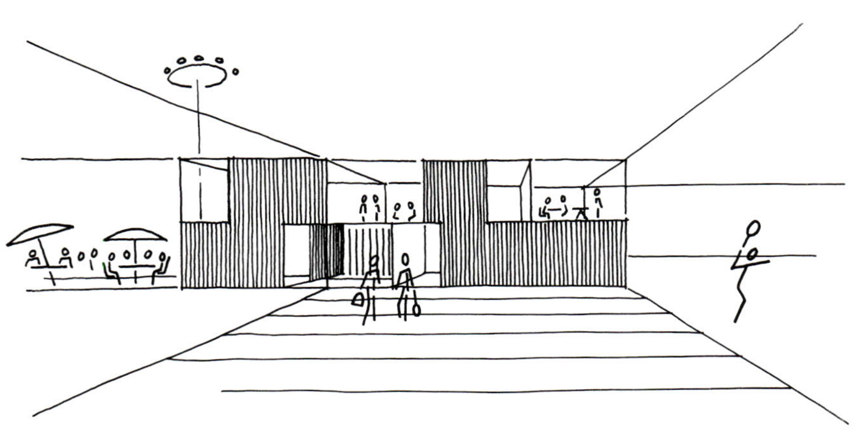

067
VAN SCHAIK COMPANY PREMISES, BREUKELEN

This company building on the outskirts of Breukelen consists of two orthogonal volumes that turn their backs on the clutter of undistinguished sheds, a school and a caravan encampment at their rear. One volume is storage, the other offices. The latter has two faces. One largely closed side fronts on to the car park where visitors leave their cars. The second face is the glazed south front which overlooks the parking lot reserved for staff and company vehicles. Behind this glass screen is a double-height gallery that gives access to the offices.

Without cars, the car park, which is laid with huge concrete paving stones, is a monumental expanse, a neutral orthogonal plaza. The two buildings bordering this plaza are a linguistic as well as a compositional ensemble. The glazed facade of the office is imprinted with the company's name, while its field of operation – bouwbedrijf (construction firm) – is picked out in relief on the concrete wall of the warehouse. The lettering incorporated into the facade ensures that the architectural order need never be disrupted by illuminated signs or neon letters. By integrating the company name into the facades, this architecture operates in two contrary directions. While the similarity to a billboard evokes an association with impermanence, the architectural 'walling-in' of the name lends this company building a permanence that is quite unusual for such an volatile and often makeshift genre.

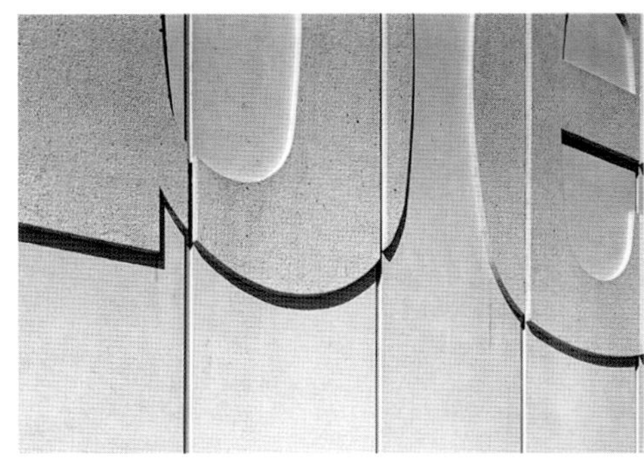

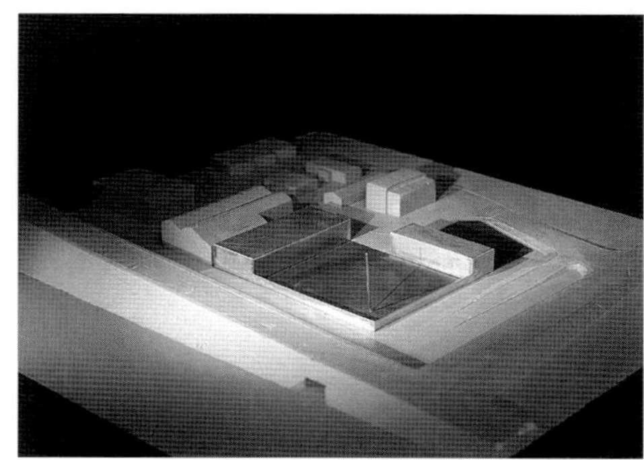

Van Schaik

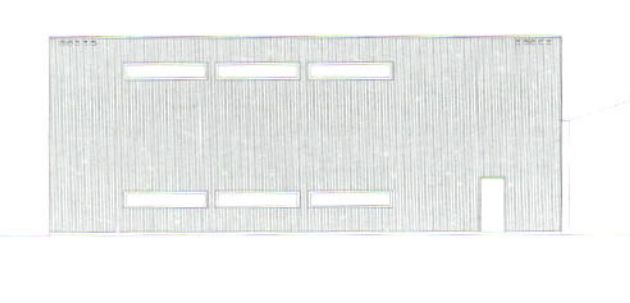
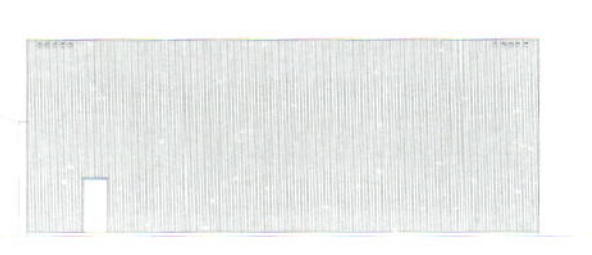
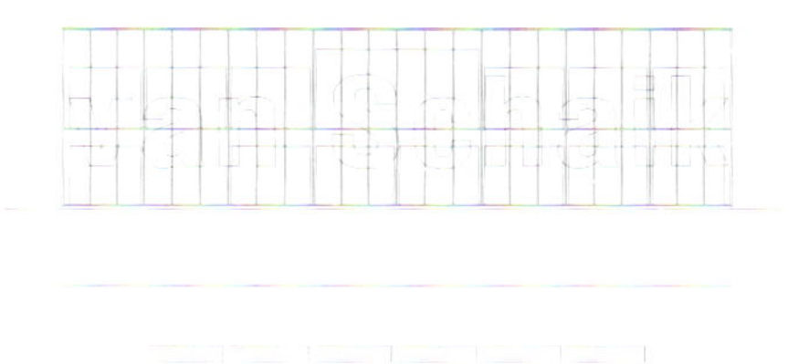

071
HOUSING, HOOGTE AND LAAGTE KADIJK, AMSTERDAM

After a commissioned study of this area, a complex surgical operation in the dense urban fabric of the Haarlemmerbuurt and a study of the possibilities for pocket-sized building sites in the heart of Amsterdam, the commission to design infills on four different lots on Hoogte and Laagte Kadijk was a logical continuation. Officially, this housing was the last urban renewal project in Amsterdam. The narrow infills on Hoogte Kadijk, in which the verticality is emphasized, conform to the rhythm of the street. On Laagte Kadijk, where any such traditional rhythm is lacking, the facades are wider. In all four projects, the dwellings have an efficient layout that recalls the floor plans of the Haarlemmerbuurt dwellings. Access is as compact as possible, with a central staircase or an entrance on the garden side that can be reached via a corridor. In all four projects, material, colour and light have been used to give the entrance a degree of individuality.

The owner-occupied dwellings on Laagte Kadijk are nearly square in plan. The subsidized rental dwellings on Hoogte Kadijk are narrow and deep: the double lot contains two loft-type dwellings per floor, the single lot two maisonettes of two and three floors respectively.

The facades refer openly to historical models. On Hoogte Kadijk the red bricks, the relief in the facade and the thickly framed transom lights introduce a dash of Amsterdam School to this architecture. In the flat, stack-bonded walls above a smooth concrete plinth on Laagte Kadijk, the only 'cosmetic details' are the hinges of the outward-opening balcony doors which stand out from the aluminium frames as functional ornamentation and an indirect reminder of Otto Wagner's Postsparkasse in Vienna. In the strict rhythm with which these doors are distributed over the facade, this architecture is more reminiscent of warehouses than of traditional housing.

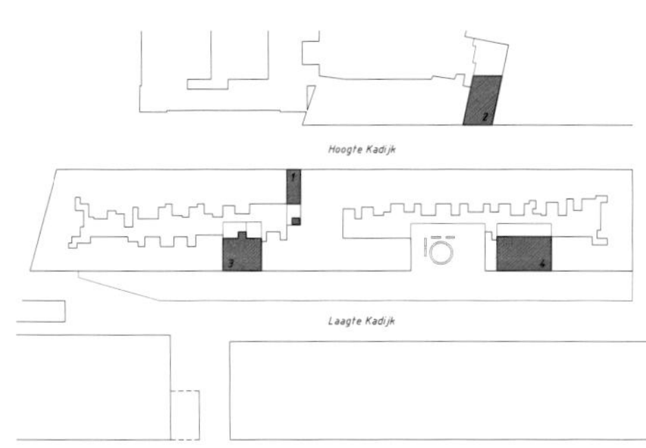

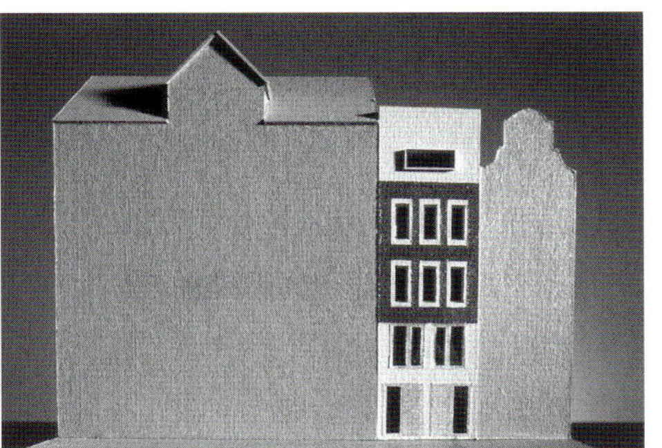

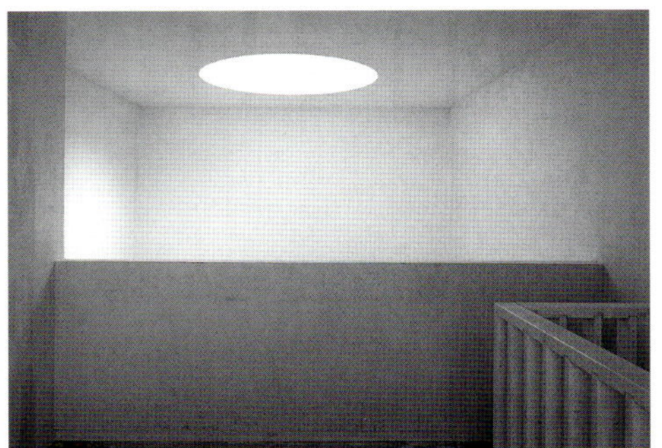

26
28

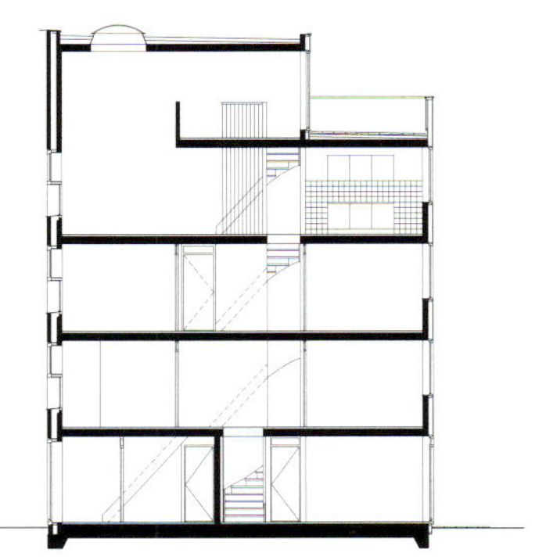

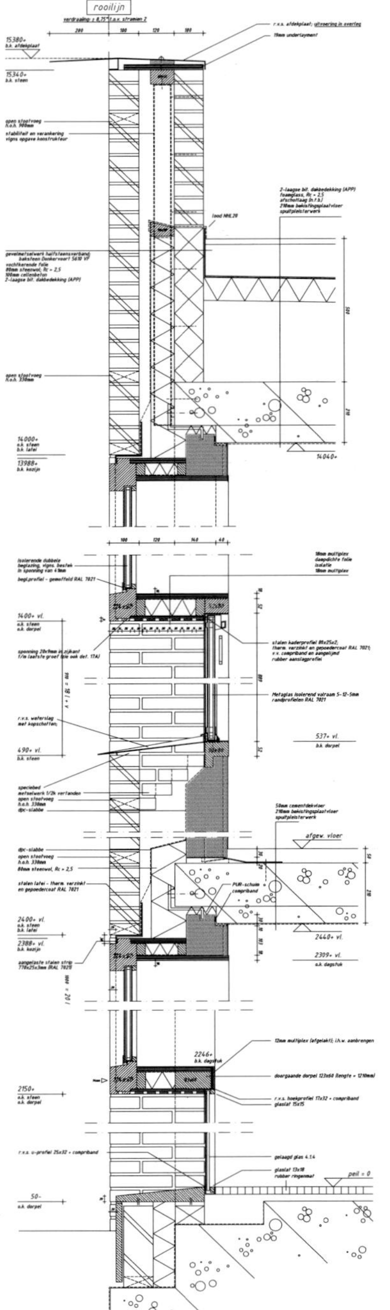
rooilijn
afgew. vloer
peil = 0

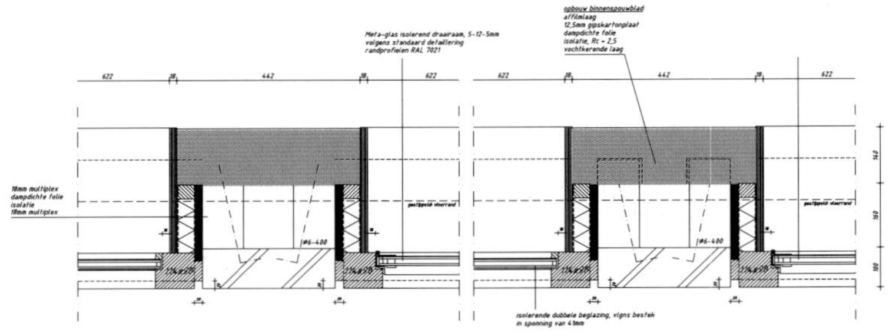

14

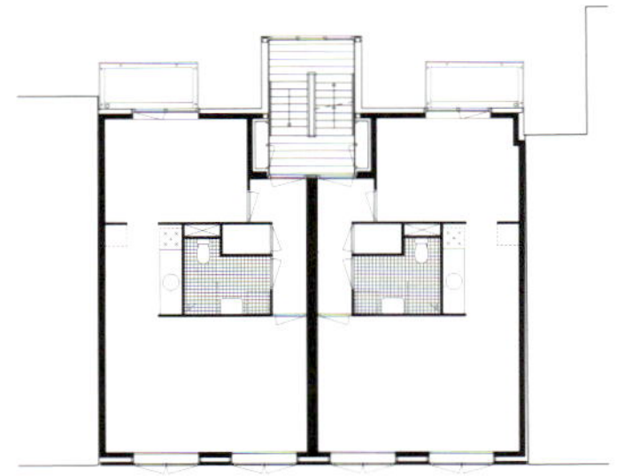

1

2

1 Richard Estes, Telephone Booths, 1968
2 Otto Wagner, Postsparkassenamt, Vienna, 1903–1910

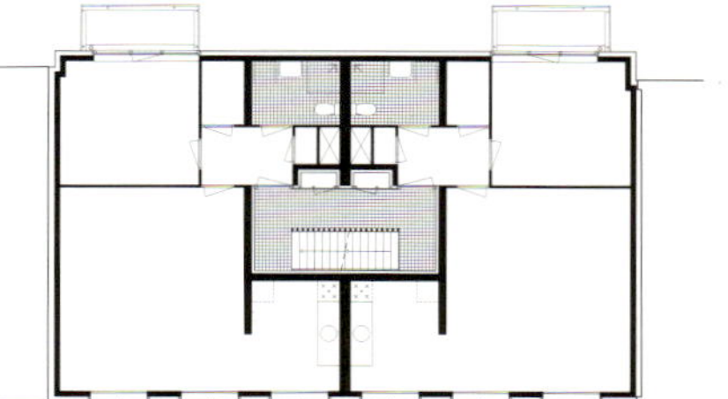

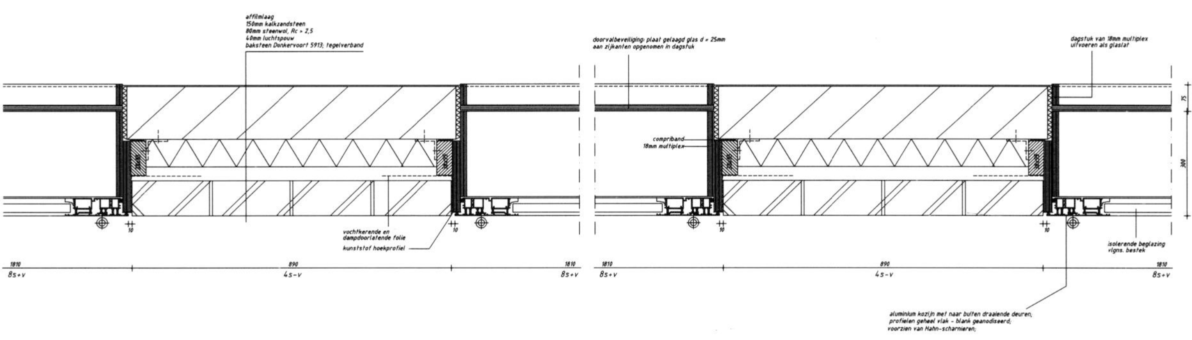

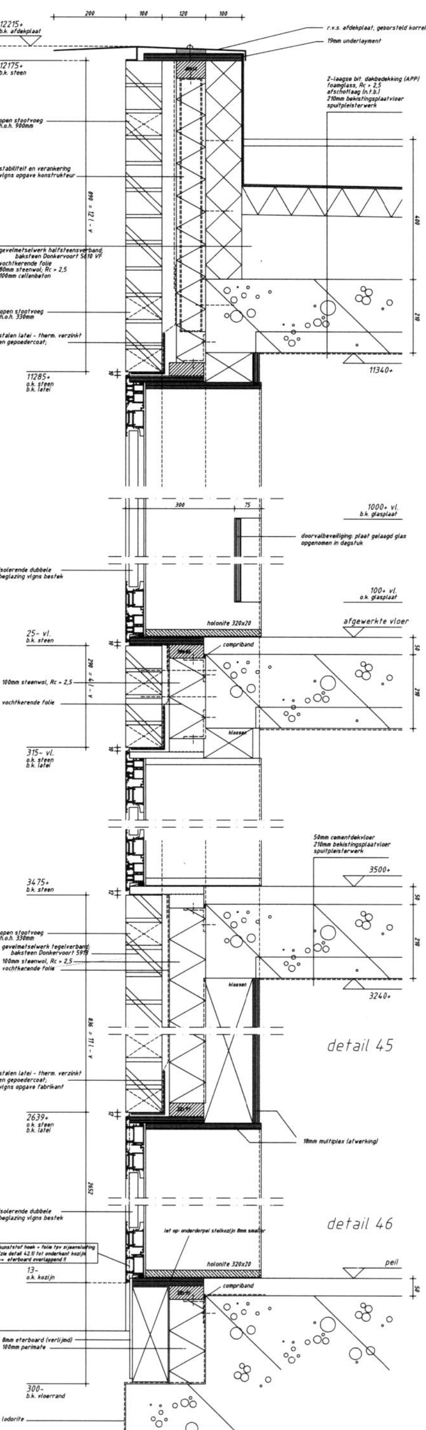
detail 45
detail 46

078
SWITCHING STATIONS, PTT TELECOM, AMSTERDAM

The switching houses for PTT Telecom's fibre optic network are box-like, free-standing objects. They encase a function that offers scant inspiration for an architectural design. Given that the locations, and thus also the context, were unknown beforehand, the only way of tackling the assignment was as an autonomous capsule, a covering for something that is of no interest to anyone. The architects did think about presenting the client with a range of containers suitable for different situations, but in the end they came up with two series of abstract boxes, an architecture as lucid as their explanation of the concept (although this suggests a more radical outcome than the one realized):

'Our proposal is a prismatic box that adheres exactly to the prescribed measurements and in so doing enhances acceptance of the building mass. The volume is dramatized by abstraction of the skin, by the effort to make something that is in fact unwanted as perfect as possible. The volume is stripped of all associative elements like roof edges, fascias, rainwater pipes and entrances. Even the materiality is suppressed. Necessity is the station's sole justification for existing. No design whatsoever can conceal this fact. This conceptual clarity calls for sophisticated detailing: clean edges, concrete of one piece – no joints, colour, texture. All details refer to the station itself.'

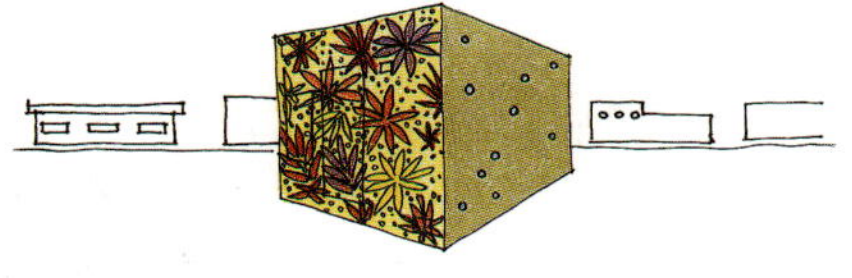

WEDEROPBOUW

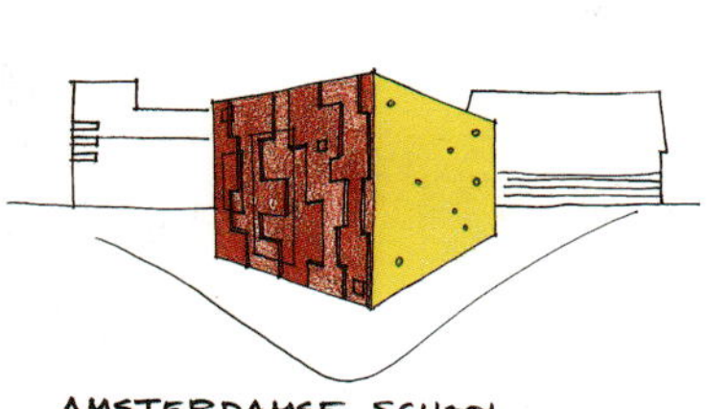

AMSTERDAMSE SCHOOL

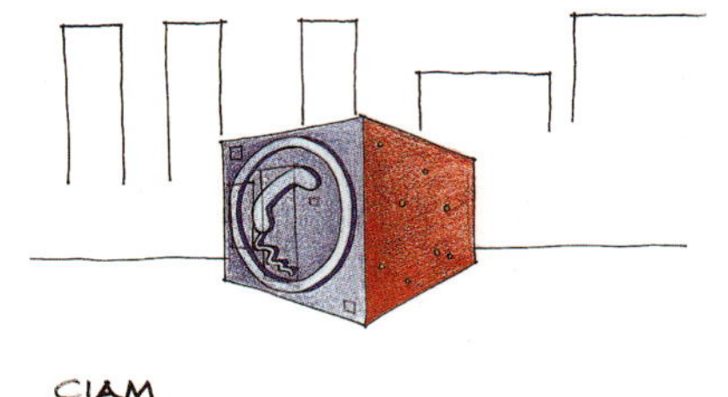

CIAM

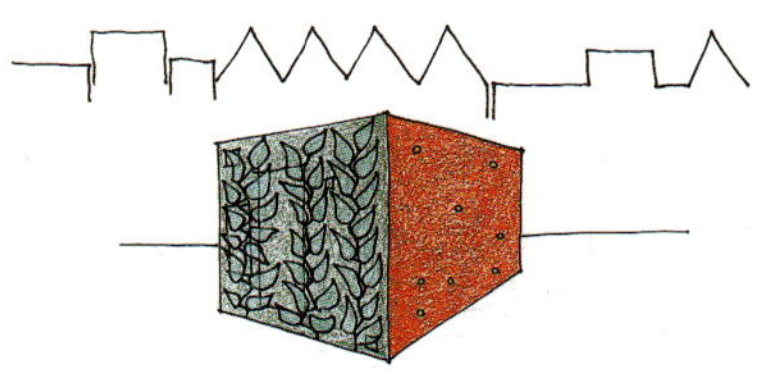

KLASSIEKE STAD

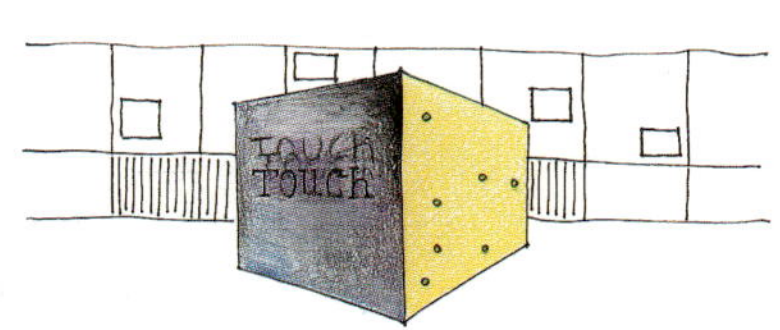

BORNEO . SPORENBURG

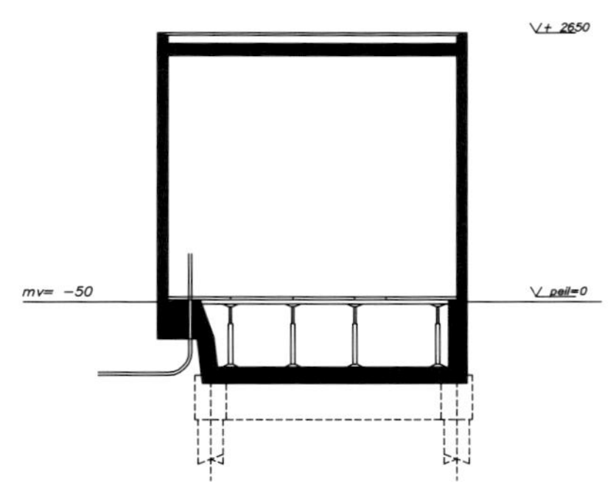

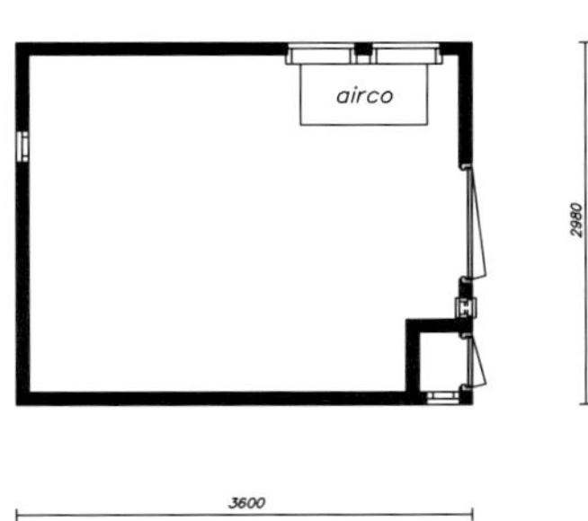

Switching stations, PTT Telecom, Amsterdam

081
HOUSING, VIER AMBACHTEN, SPIJKENISSE

Within the spatial master plan drawn up by DKV for the Vier Ambachten housing estate in Spijkenisse, Claus en Kaan designed 138 three-room pensioner dwellings that are accommodated in two gallery-access blocks of flats. Ranging in height from four to nine storeys, the two buildings form the 'back' to the main road that runs past the estate. With their L and U-shaped silhouettes, they are no commonplace slabs, but recognizable landmarks in the spacious suburban landscape. To the outside world they appear as sturdy barrier-objects, for the estate that lies behind them, they are a neutral backdrop.

The emphasis is on the overall architectural form rather than on the individual dwelling as constituent element. The glass balustrades for the internal verandas and the large glass screens that enclose the galleries to three-quarter height, accentuate the volume as a whole. The slightly undulating fronts of the dwellings and the absence of brackets supporting the floor of the gallery above, makes for spacious galleries that are more than a mere walkway.

The impression created by this architecture differs by day and by night. The glass that envelops the buildings like suit of shining armour during the day, is at night transformed into a transparent screen illuminated from behind by the lights in the galleries and the dwellings.

As so often in the architecture of Claus en Kaan, there is a clear contrast between front and rear. While the front elevation is decidedly horizontal, the rear elevation is a balance of horizontals and verticals. Relief and depth give a kind of contemporary rustic expression to the front elevation. The rear elevations are flat and neutral, in a similar fashion to the facades of the pensioner apartments in Groningen. As such, they form a detached backdrop for the low-rise neighbourhood at the foot of the two apartment buildings.

At the ends of both blocks are generous entrance lobbies with semicircular rear walls behind which lie various special functions, such as a communal recreation room.

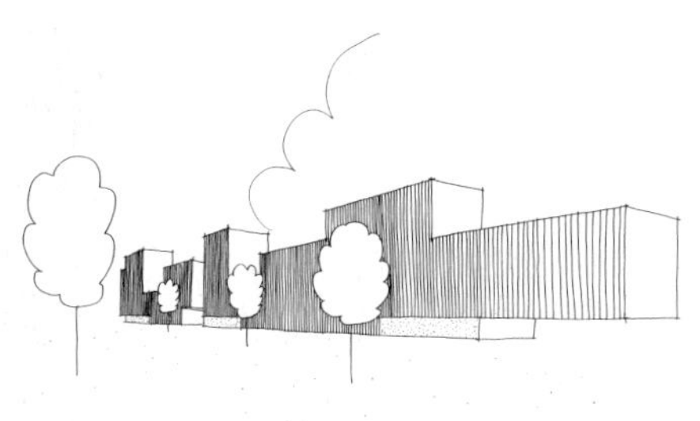

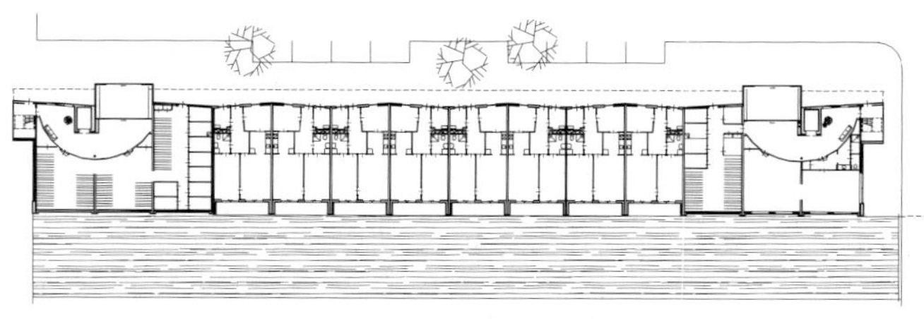

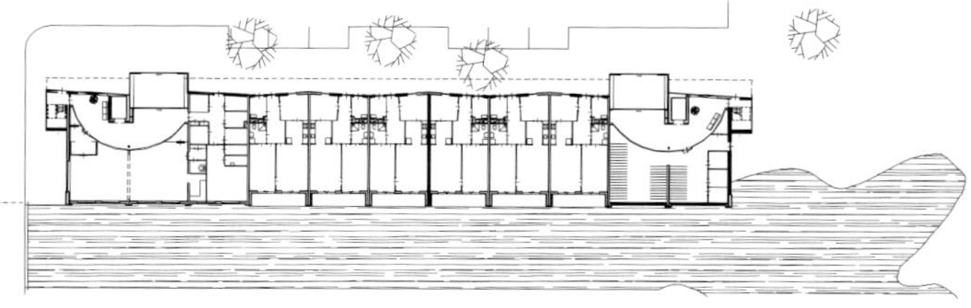

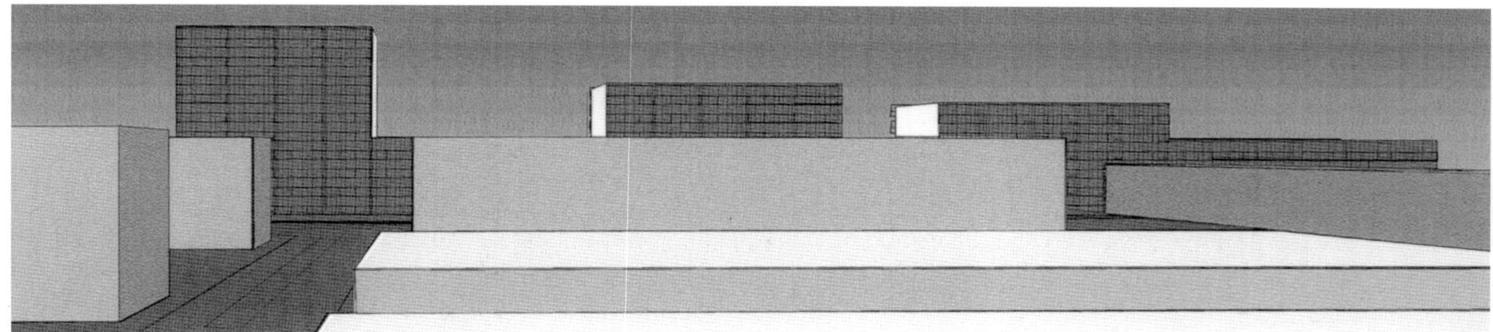

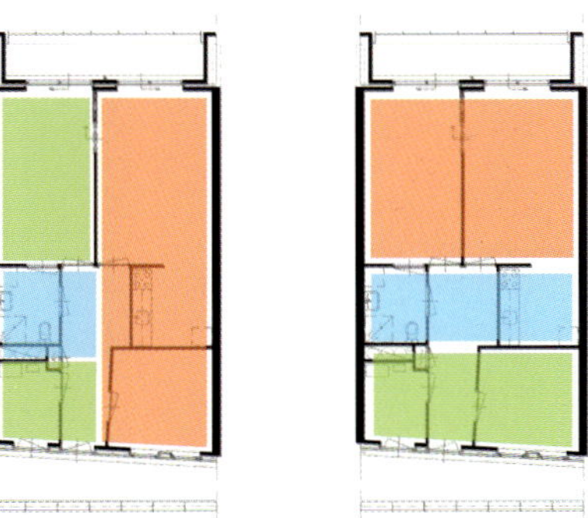

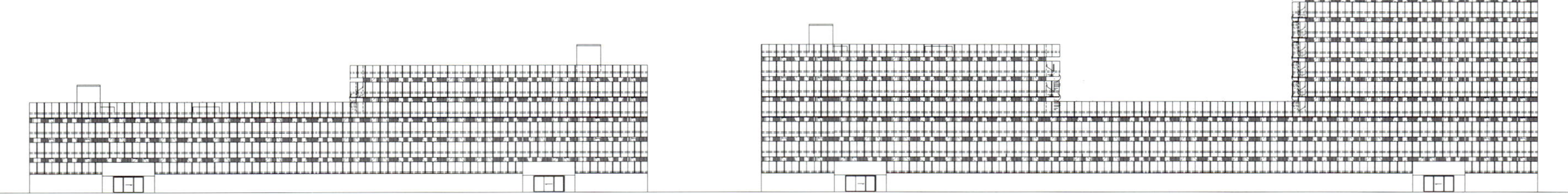

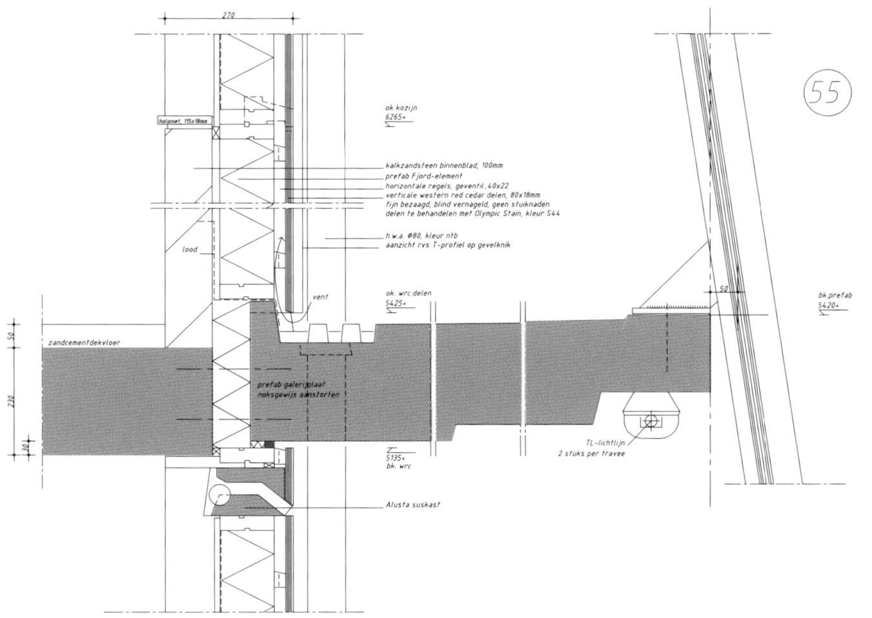
270
holoniet, 115x18mm
ok kozijn
6265+
kalkzandsteen binnenblad, 100mm
prefab Fjord-element
horizontale regels, geventil.40x22
verticale western red cedar delen, 80x18mm
fijn bezaagd, blind vernageld, geen stuiknaden
delen te behandelen met Olympic Stain, kleur S44
h.w.a. Ø80, kleur ntb
aanzicht rvs T-profiel op gevelknik
lood
vent.
ok. wrc.delen
5425+
zandcementdekvloer
50
230
30
prefab galerijplaat
noksgewijs aanstorten
5135+
bk. wrc
Alusta suskast
TL-lichtlijn
2 stuks per travee
50
bk.prefab
5420+
55

084
HOUSING, KALENDERPANDEN, AMSTERDAM

The conversion of the Kalenderpanden (Calendar Buildings) is the final piece in the transformation of the Kadijk/Entrepot quarter from a tiny industrial enclave in Amsterdam's inner city into a residential area with a scattering of 'clean' businesses. The commission entailed restoring the fabric of the twelve warehouses, which are named after the months of the year, and converting them to housing. On the north side of the complex the original facade has been left standing as a screen, but behind it the building has been cut away. Breaking the warehouses open on this side and inserting a transparent facade along the cut section, allows light to penetrate further into the deep lofts. The freed-up zone becomes an enclosed courtyard that acts as a filter between dwelling and city. The lights suspended above the courtyard form a delicate spatial boundary.

There are two types of lofts in both of which the sense of space has been maximized. The addition of large skylights allows the lofts directly below the roof to breathe. In the apartments on the floors below, the rigid orthogonality has been alleviated by allowing the two long walls to meander independently of one another so that instead of a uniform space, each loft has a different configuration. The result is a sequence of zones, comparable to the enfilade of rooms in traditional Amsterdam houses. The articulation of linear space is a motif that Claus en Kaan have used in several other designs for passages and corridors, often using colour to lend the articulation expressiveness. Here this has been left to the occupants.

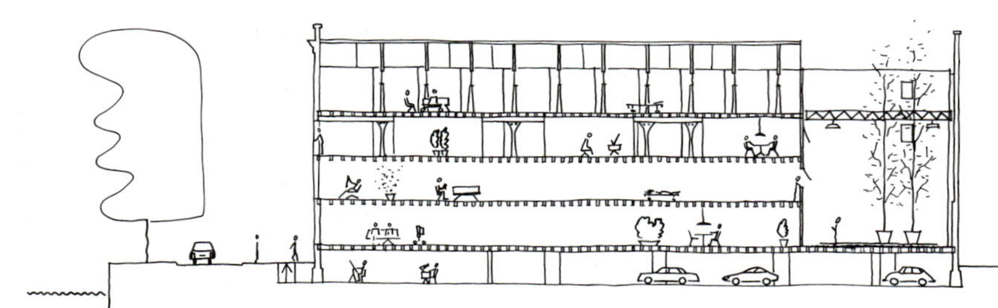

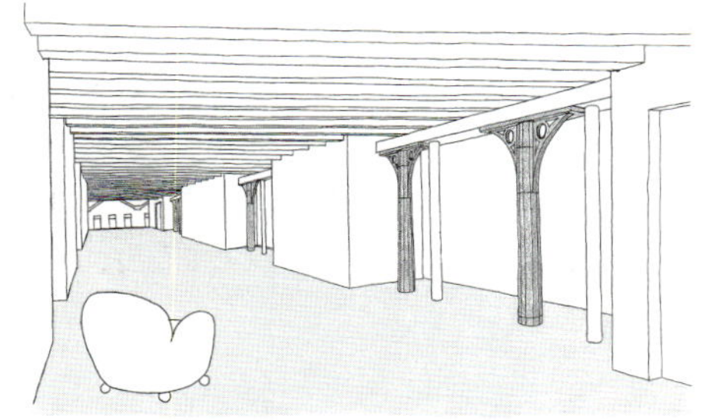

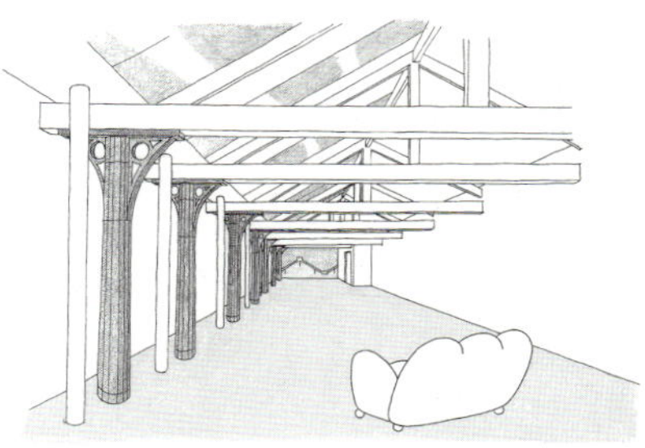

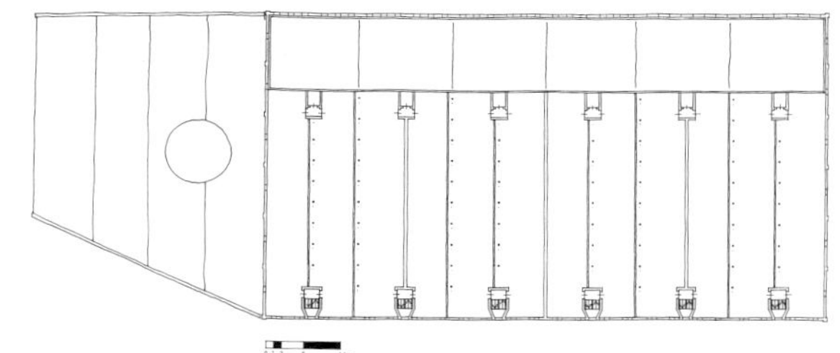

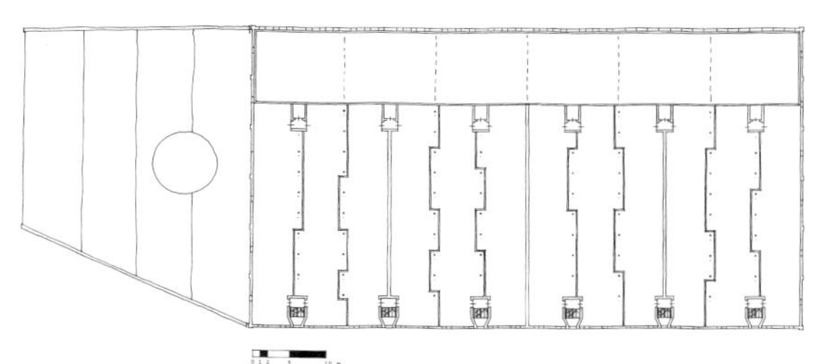

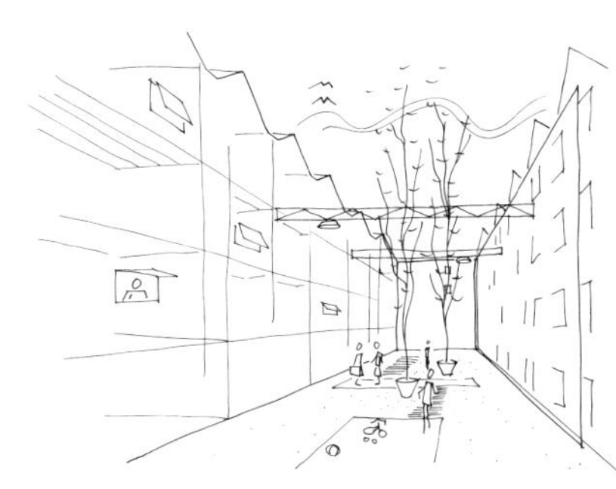

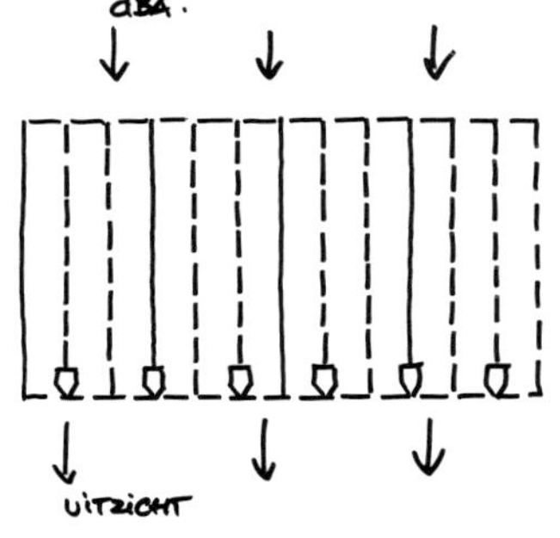

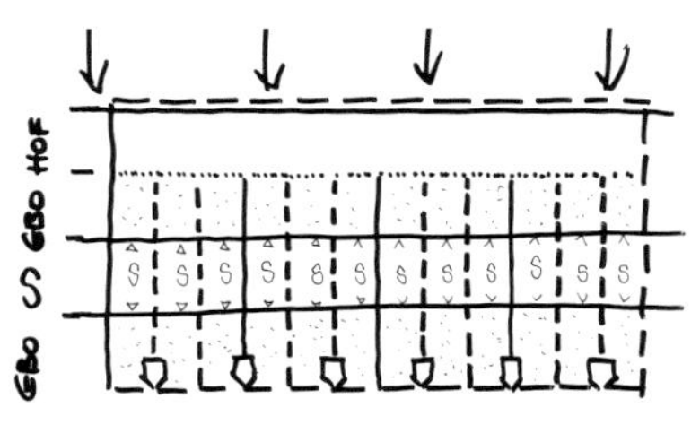

GELUIDWERING + MAXIMAAL HANDHAVEN STRUCTUUR. LEVEN BINNEN WONINGEN GBO & ONBENOEMDE (EXTRA) RUIMTE.

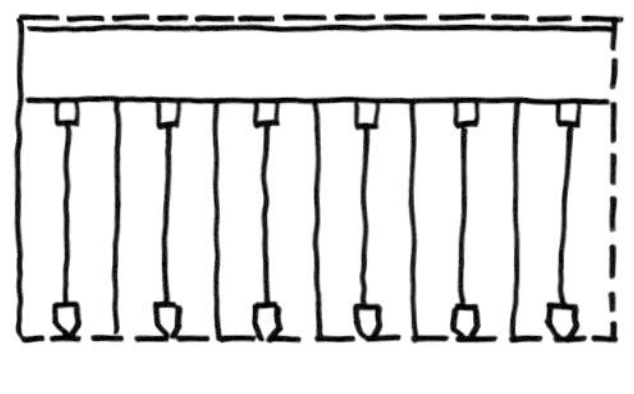

12 MAANDEN, TRAPPENHUIZEN + LIFTEN

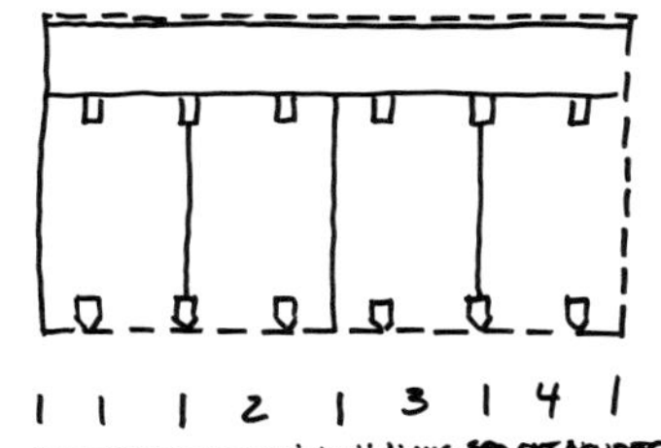

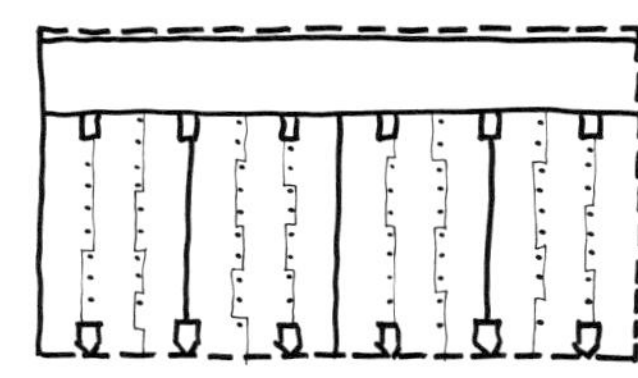

BESTAANDE STRUCTUUR & MEANDERENDE SCHEIDINGSWANDEN.

086
TAXATION DEPARTMENT PAVILION, HAARLEM

Having decided that its 1960s modernist office building, though still adequate for its internal operations, presented too hermetic a face to the outside world, the Haarlem branch of the taxation department commissioned a new entrance pavilion that would give the building greater public visibility. Despite (or perhaps because of) the service's unpopularity with large sections of the population, the new pavilion was to be inviting and open.

Thanks to the use of brick, the architecture of the pavilion designed by Claus en Kaan contrasts sharply with that of the office building behind. As such it can be read as a commentary on the building designed by A.N. Oyevaar, but a commentary that allows for communication between the two forms of architecture because it is delivered in a similar language. The basis of that language is abstraction.
In contrast to the rarefied coolness of Oyevaar, there is concrete tactility, but in form it is equally, if not more, abstract.

The massiveness of the pavilion, which appears to be one and all brick, is accentuated in several ways: by carrying the brick through as paving for the terrace at the top of the steps, by the hefty overhang and by the monochrome red ochre interior.

The monolithic character of the pavilion reinforces the autonomy of the object which, in typical Claus en Kaan fashion, permits no doubt as to the distinction between old and new.

1 Eduardo Chillida, Homenaje a Kandinsky, 1965
2 Ludwig Mies van der Rohe, detail of brick wall
3 Old and new situation

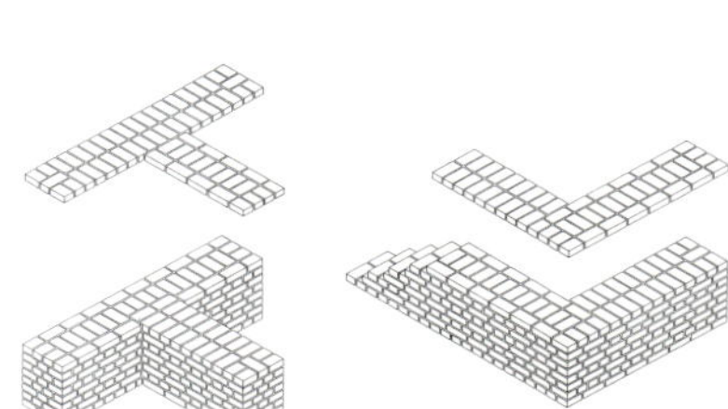

2

1

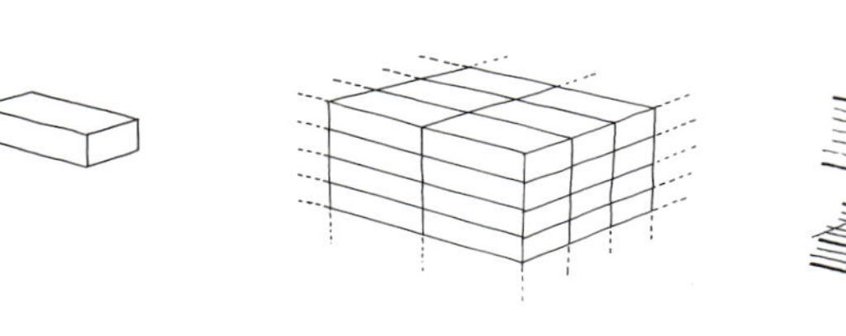

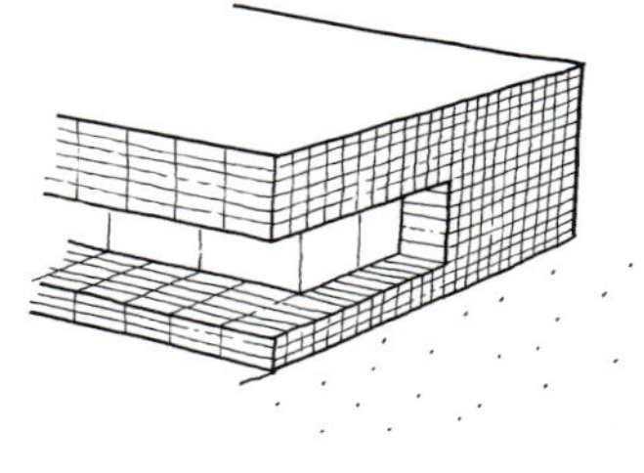

3

3

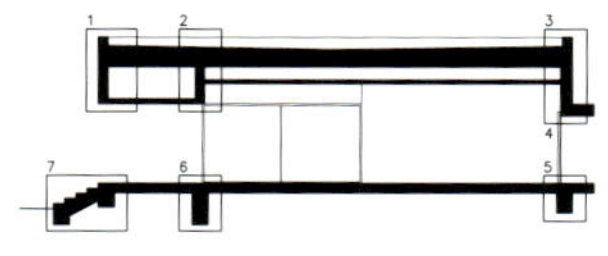
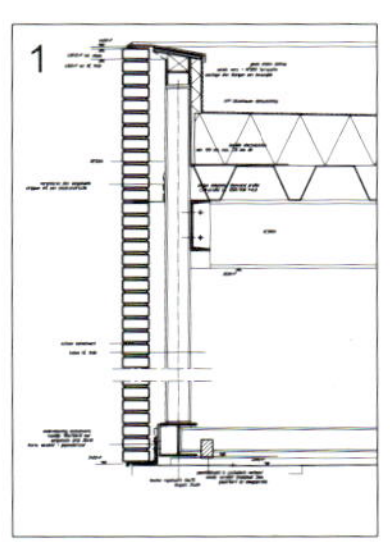
1
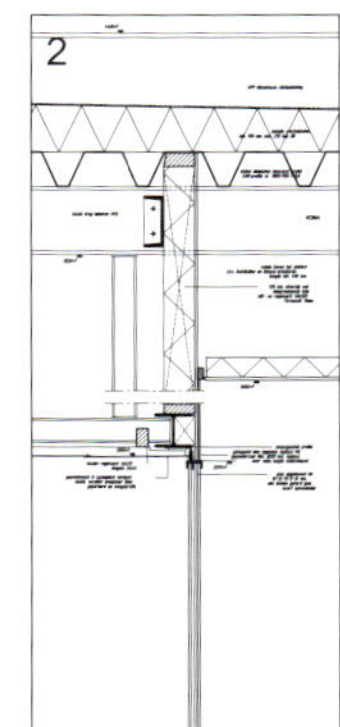
2
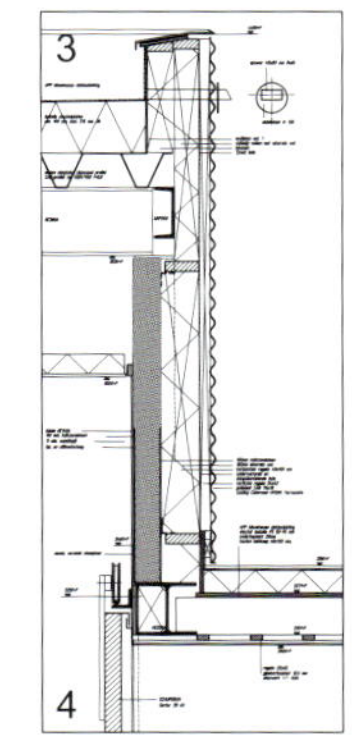
3
4
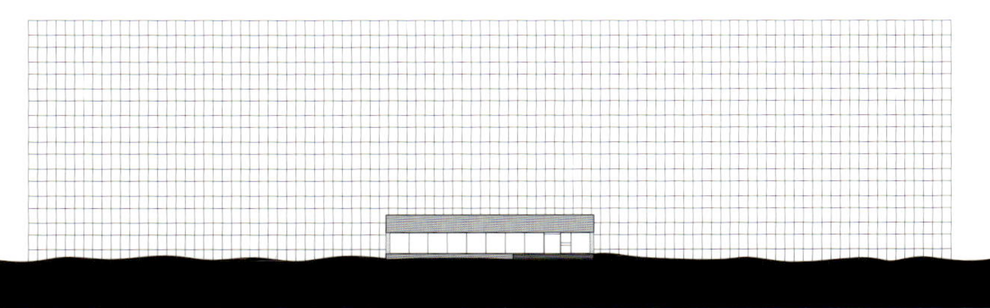
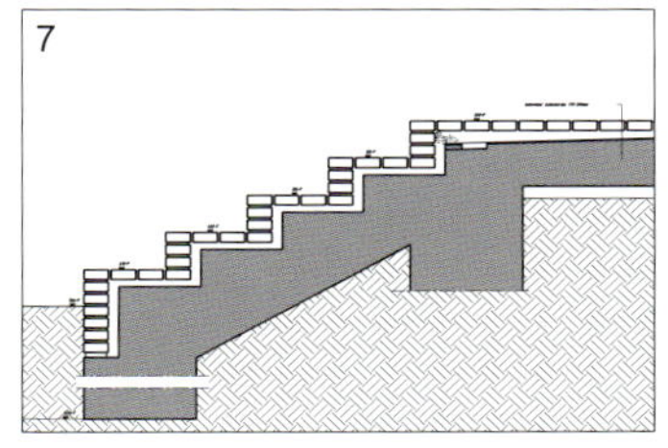
7
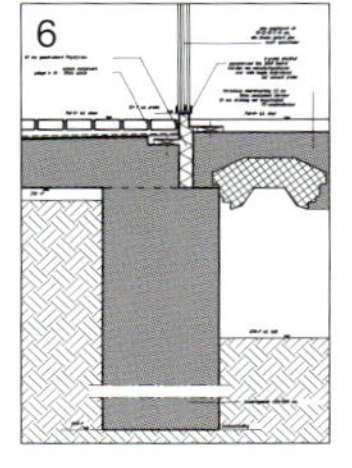
6
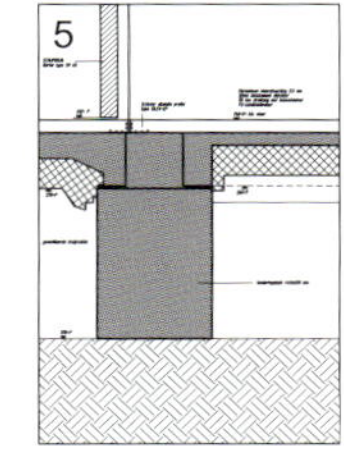
5

090 RECEPTION PAVILION ZORGVLIED CEMETERY, AMSTERDAM

The Zorgvlied reception pavilion stands next to the cemetery's funeral hall which was built in about 1930 in the curious hybrid style that was all the rage at that time: a mixture of Amsterdam School, Dudok and Functionalism. The abstract architecture of Claus en Kaan stands aloof from the expressive older building but because of the proximity a direct relationship has developed between the two buildings.

The pavilion belongs unmistakably to the same family as the entrance building for the taxation department in Haarlem, but although the form and even the function are comparable, it is the differences that are most apparent. The most striking difference lies not in the finishing of the exterior but in the siting. Whereas the Haarlem entrance pavilion stands at the top of a flight of steps, the reception room is flush with the ground, which is carpeted with white gravel.

The narrow space between the old hall and the new pavilion is defined by the latter and turned into an outdoor room. The pavilion's ceiling projects into the space in the form of a canopy while its floor is on the same level as the gravel surface outside. As such, the outdoor space becomes a logical continuation of the interior and vice versa, with only a glass skin separating the two. This self-evidence is all of a piece with Claus en Kaan's ambition to create an 'invisible architecture' here, with an atmosphere 'so positive that you would like to live there, but where there is almost nothing to be seen'. The invisibility can be interpreted as a metaphor for absence, while the positive atmosphere offers consolation, as a counterweight to loss.

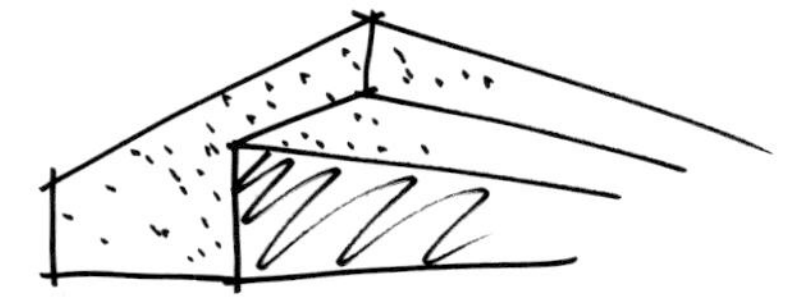

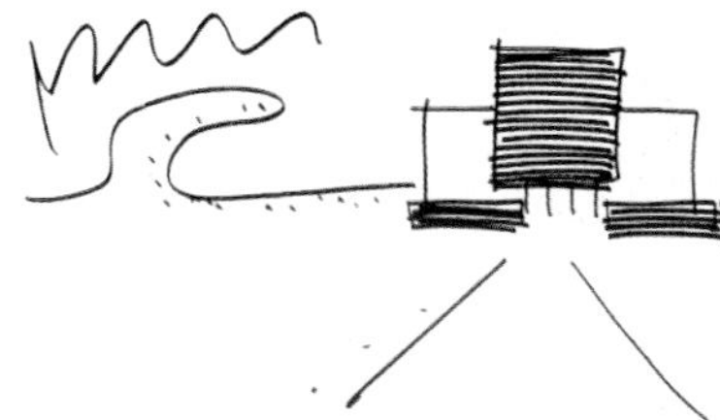

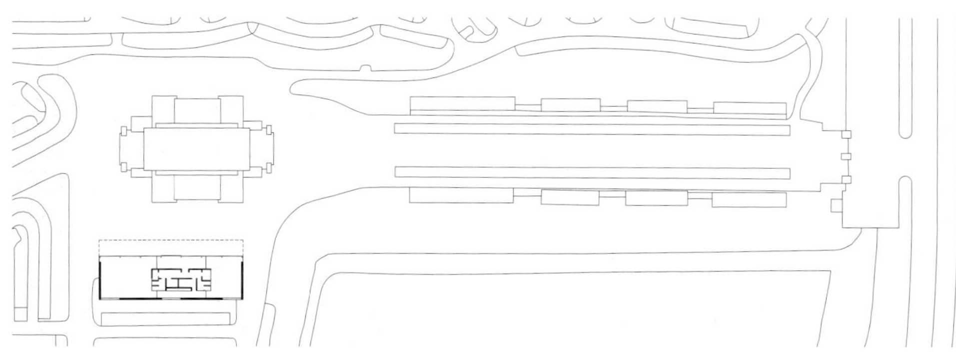

Reception Pavilion Zorgvlied Cemetery, Amsterdam

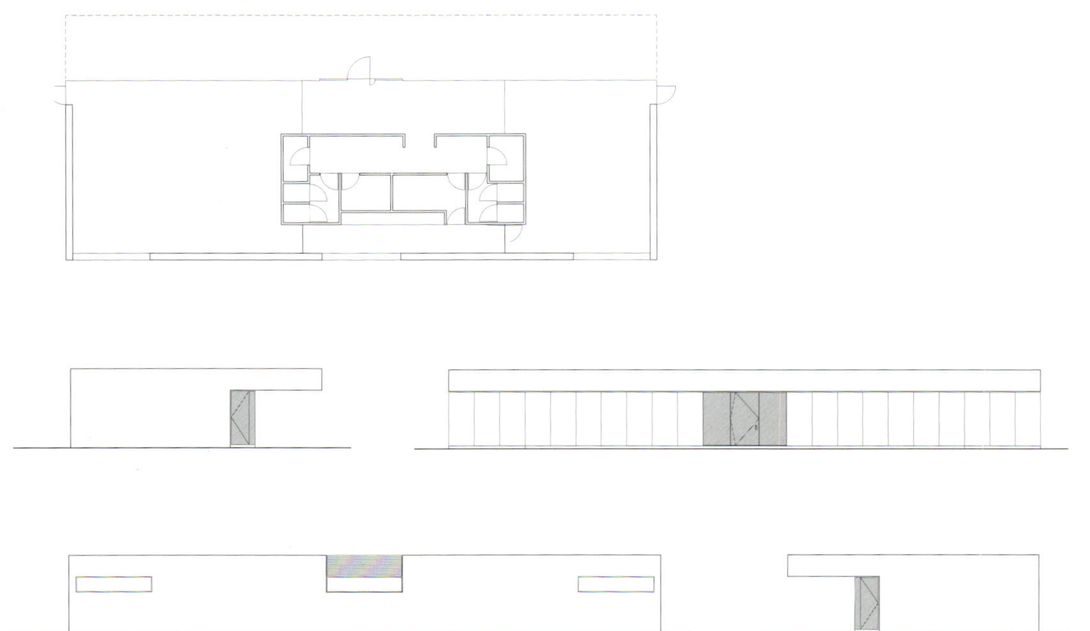

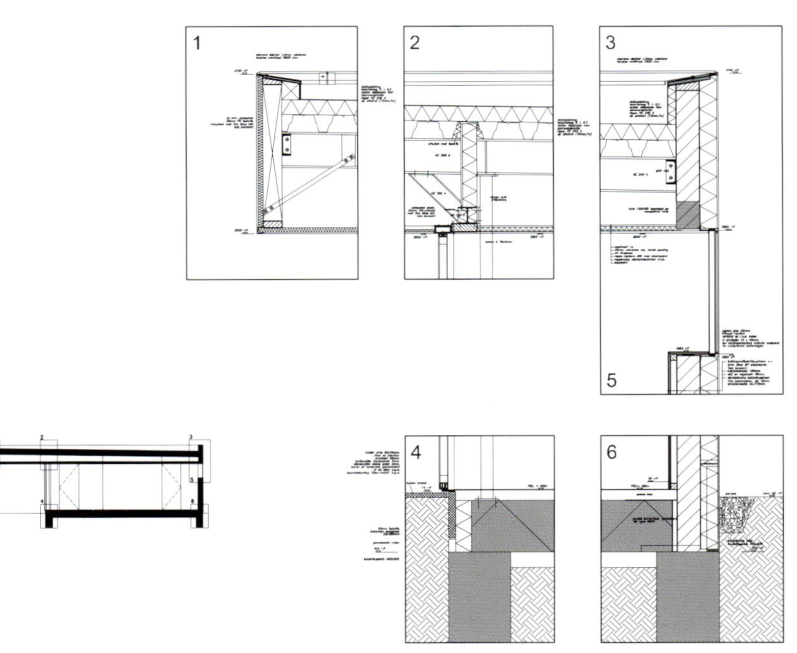

Reception Pavilion Zorgvlied Cemetery, Amsterdam

091 HOUSING, RIETLANDEN, AMSTERDAM

In this part of Rietlanden, that is separated by only the width of a road from Sporenburg, the rigid street layout of the Borneo and Sporenburg developments continues, as does the accompanying strict separation between the public space of the street and private domain of the home.

Typologically, the architecture is much more varied, with different dwellings for each price and target group category. As such, the project is an urban microcosm. The dwellings are accommodated in three blocks which together make up two rows. The facades betray little of the typological diversity or of the spatial complexity inside the individual dwellings, some of which even boast a rooftop unit. The differences in window sizes and facade composition are easily overlooked in passing. The overall impression is dictated largely by the multiplicity of windows and the reflections from the glass and the aluminium window frames that stand out from the surface of the facade. It is an impression that underscores the closeness and urban density of these blocks. The large areas of glass set up a direct relationship between dwelling and street. In their extroversion, these dwellings are the very opposite of the generally inward-looking dwellings on Borneo and Sporenburg.

The rows come to an abrupt halt at the edge of the park. Built into these largely blind head elevations is a flock-like configuration of 128 nesting boxes for swallows, an ecologically sound alternative to the egalitarian distribution among all the dwellings originally requested.

As a succession of houses, the architecture is an abstract, contemporary echo of nineteenth-century speculative building, in the course of which individual town houses were welded together into large, urban blocks. As in those days, when a window tax was still levied, some of the window openings were made and immediately filled in again. At these places the building has been tattooed with photos illustrating the area's industrial past.

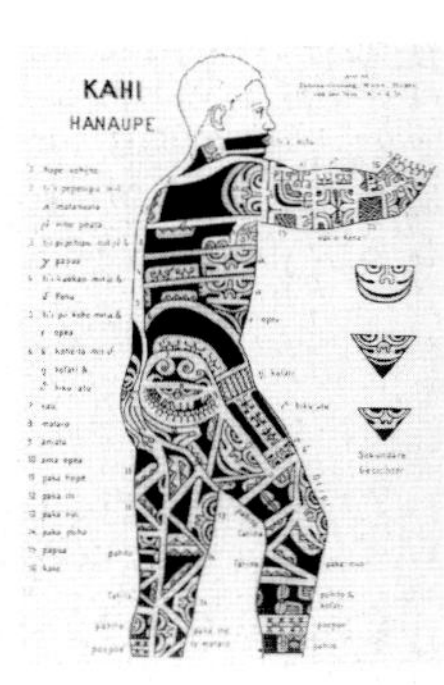

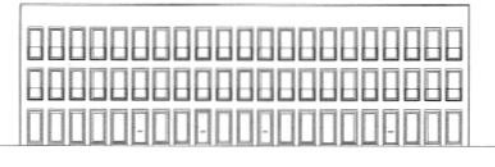

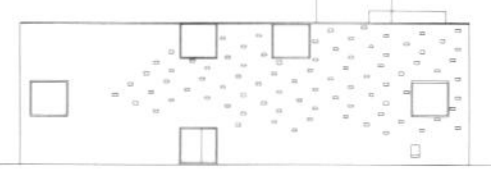

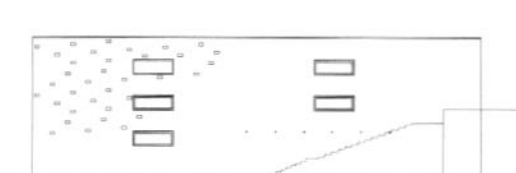

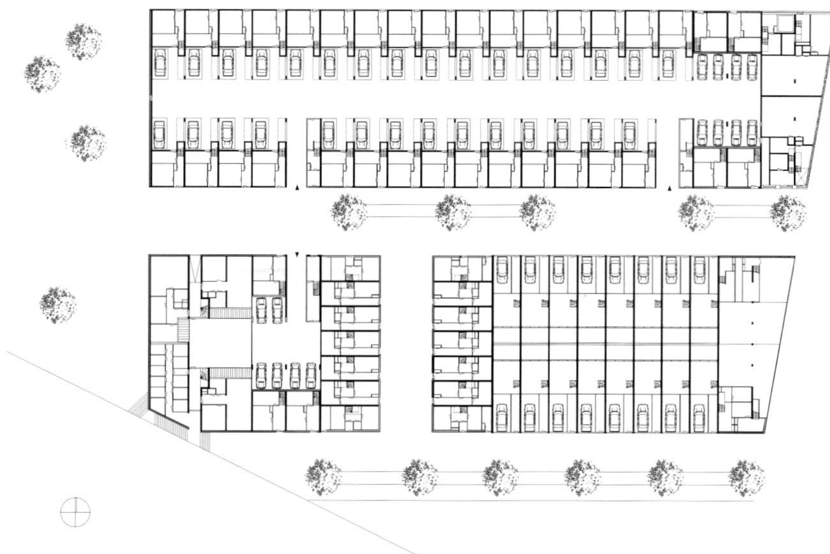

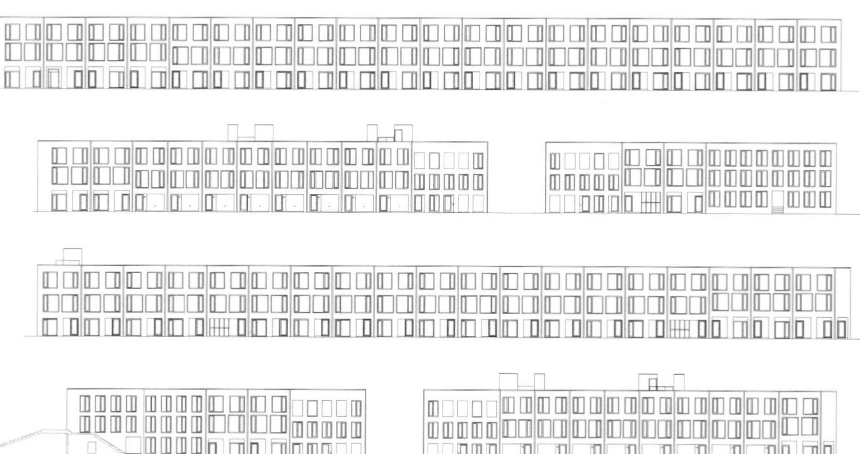

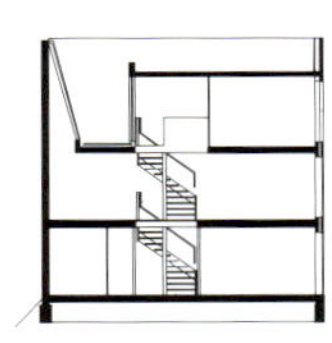

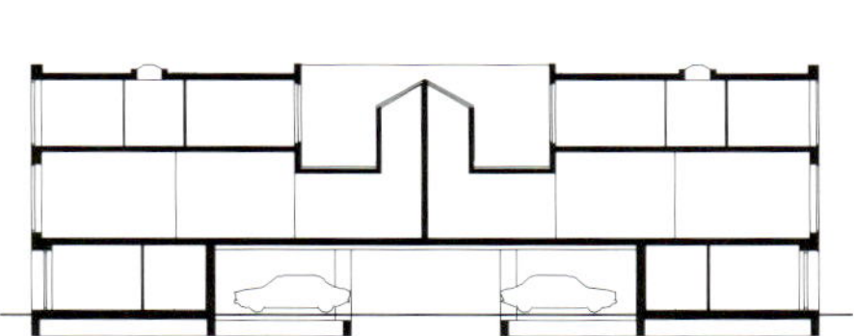
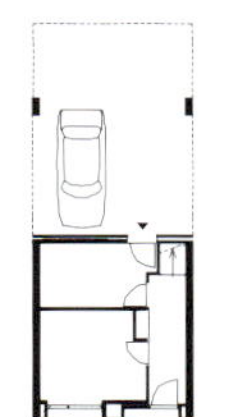

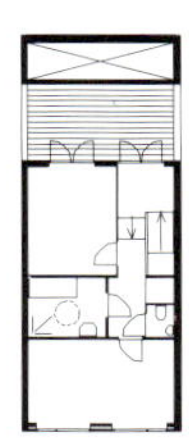
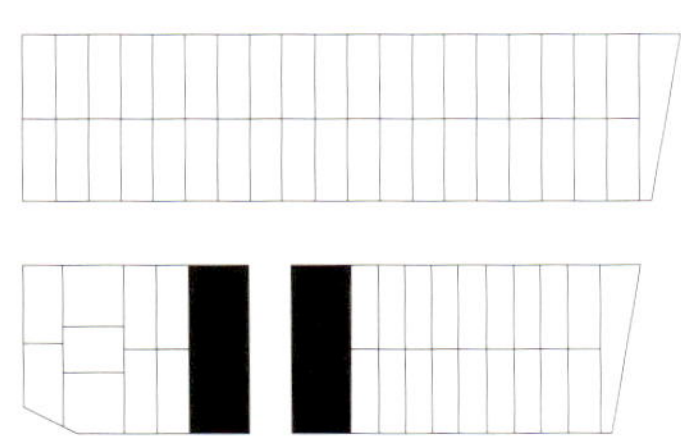

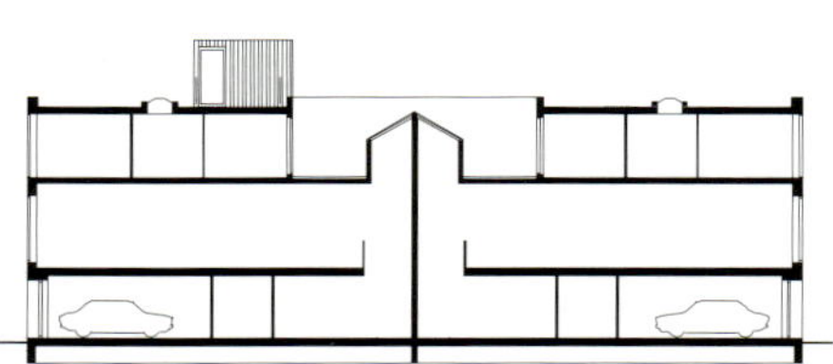
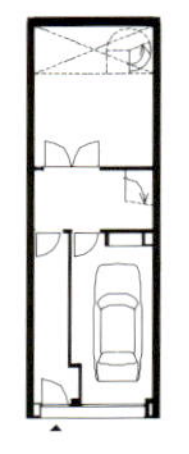
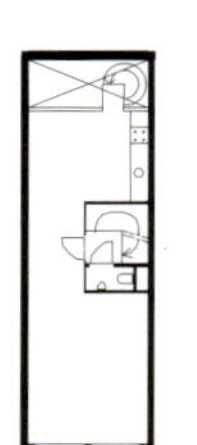
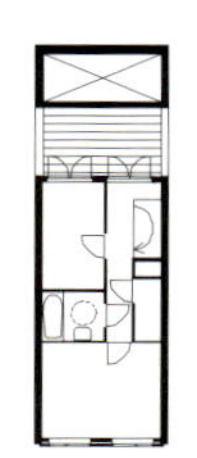
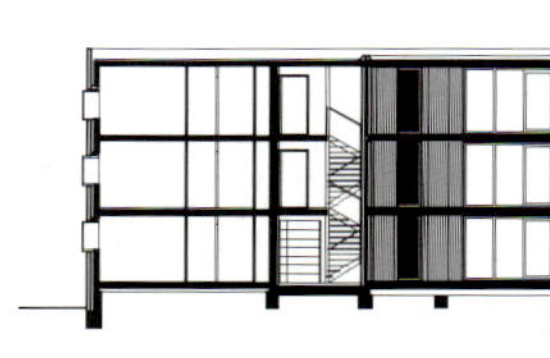
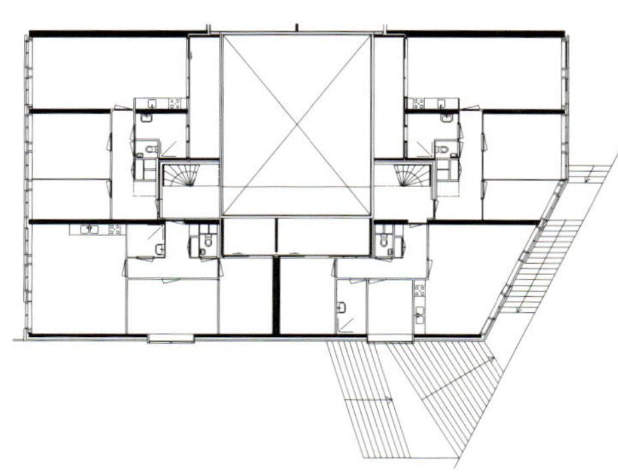
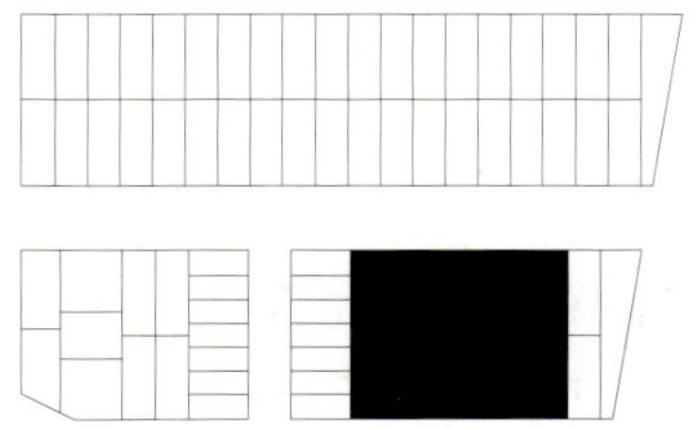

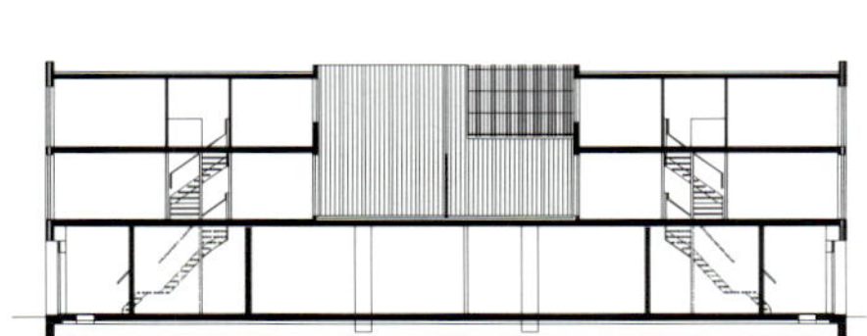
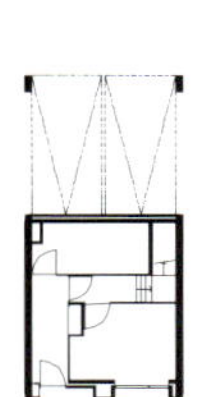
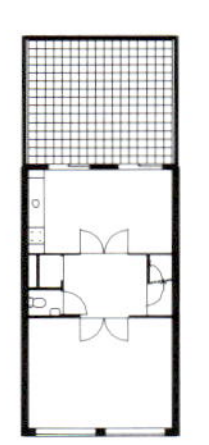
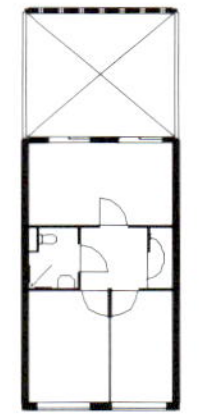
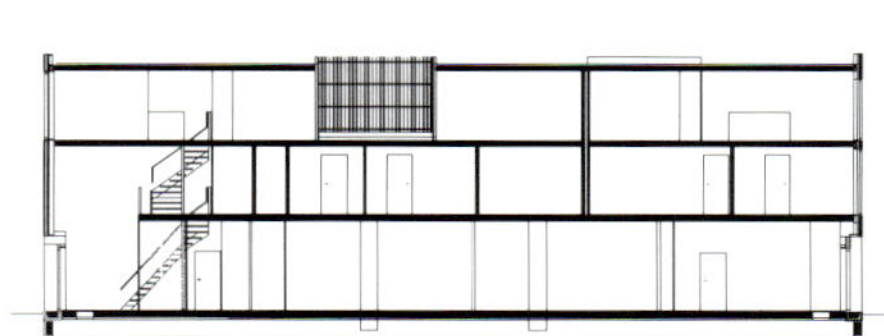
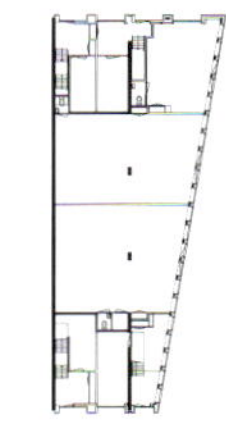
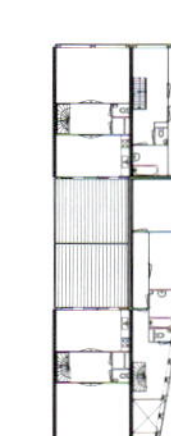
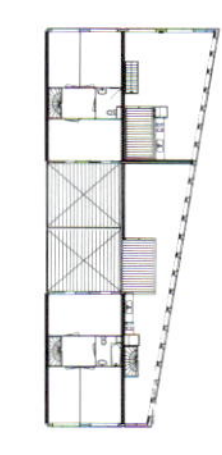
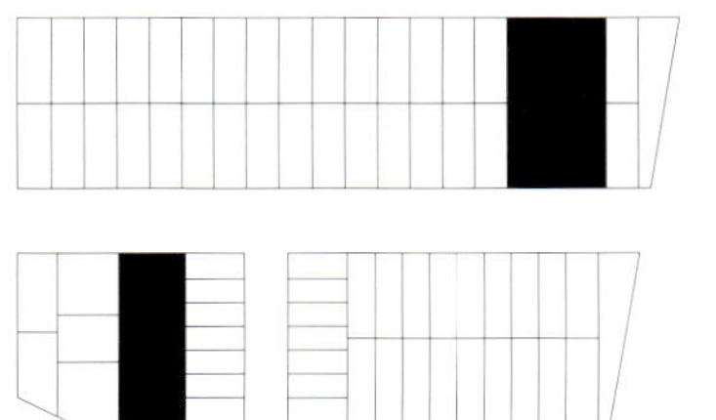

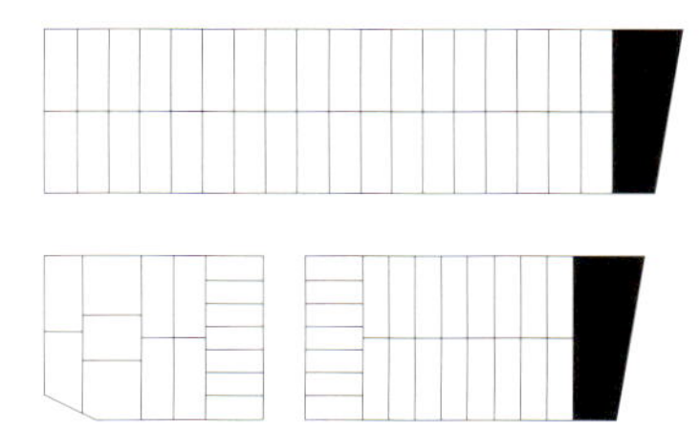

Housing, Rietlanden, Amsterdam

092 100 153 205

HOUSING, DE AKER, AMSTERDAM

In few projects by Claus en Kaan is the architecture more reductive than in the town-houses in the new De Aker housing estate on the outskirts of Amsterdam. The overall formal reduction can be construed as the after-image of an archetype. The task was to develop dwellings in which living would not be focused exclusively on the garden side, but also on the street. The bay window, the means used to achieve this end, is an abstract reflection of upper middle-class domestic architecture in the better neighbourhoods of Amsterdam. Here the whole front of the house has been turned into a bay window. The neutrality of this architecture is determined by the tautness which is revealed, for example, by the chaste, 'Rietveldian' roof edge. Whereas in the neutrality of many other Claus en Kaan projects, detachment is coupled with distinction, this is an architecture approaching zero-point – no coquettish aesthetic minimalism, rather the 'almost nothing' of Mies van der Rohe in its starkest form. The traditional image of living has been whittled down to an indivisible nucleus and in that respect this is an architecture without rhetoric: an utterly realistic interpretation of the task and no more. And in surroundings that boast a wealth of architectural and especially spatial forms, this very starkness acquires a poetic charge. Nonetheless, it is not a stern architecture any more than it is a friendly one. It is quite simply and naturally a blank decor against which daily life is played out.

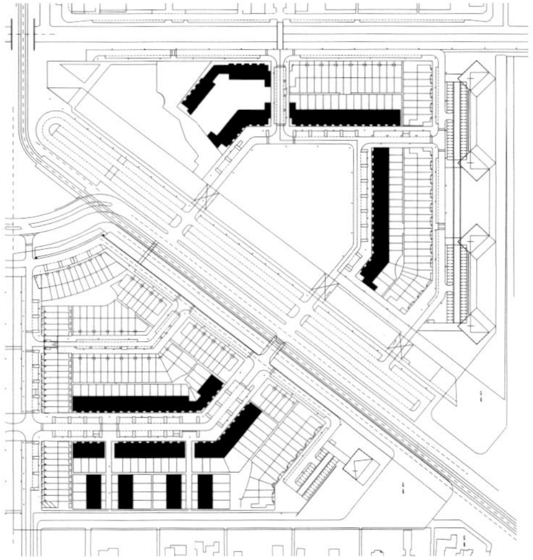

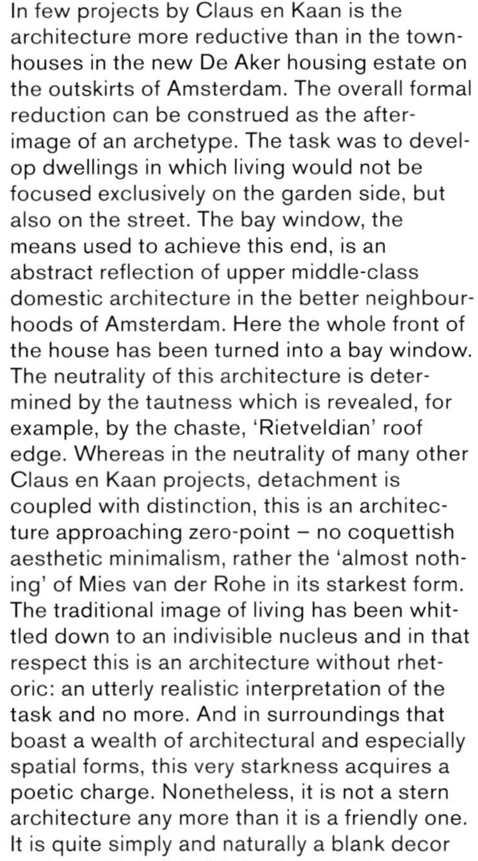

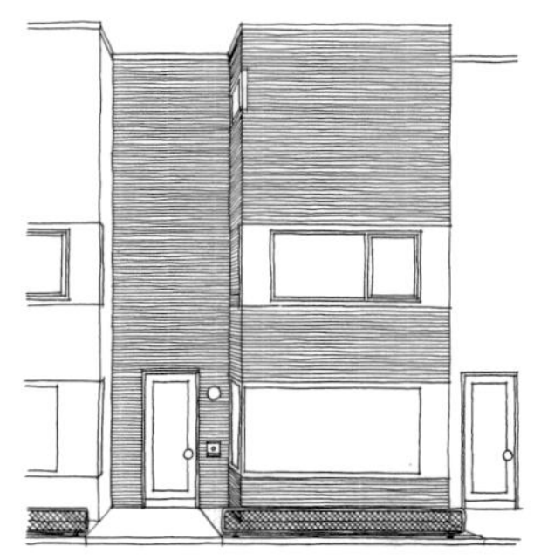

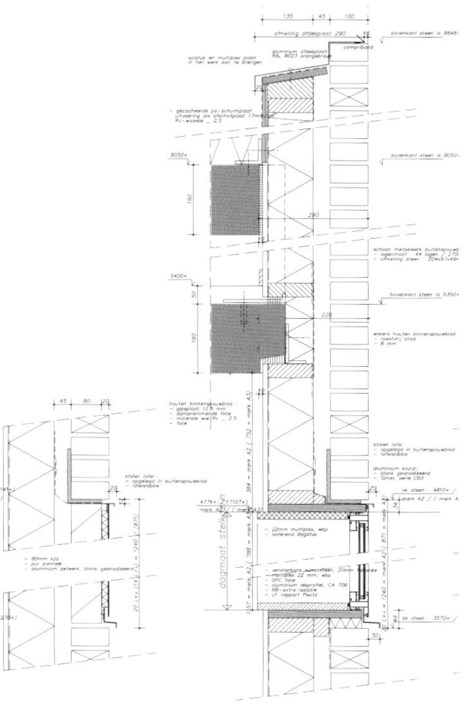

Streetscape, Jan van Eyckstraat, Amsterdam

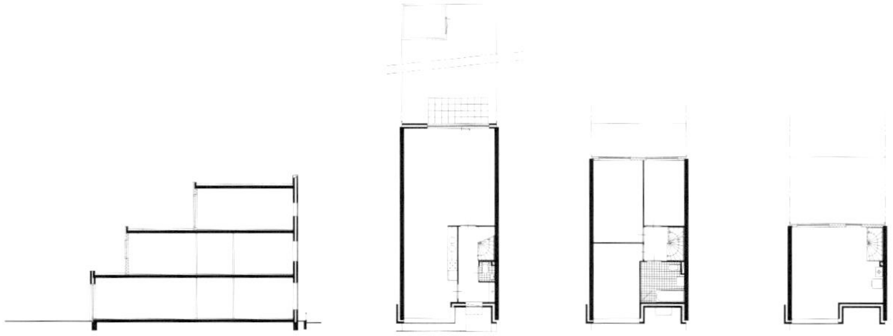

097
HOUSING, EEKMAAT, ENSCHEDE

The spatial master plan drawn up by Sjoerd Soeters for this district on the outskirts of Enschede included the block organization and a housing type developed by Soeters and referred to by him as a 'new acropolism': a house on a mound in which the bedrooms are located in the underground portion while the rest of the house stands gloriously above. Claus en Kaan were unwilling to adhere to this type and instead came up with a proposal for two housing types – a carport and a patio dwelling – within the tight subdivision imposed by Soeters. An aerial perspective of these dwellings, endlessly repeated – a commentary on and salute to Soeters's image of his new acropolism as Levittown – was one of the arguments by which Claus en Kaan succeeded in carrying the day.

The architecture of the 55 dwellings was kept simple. The architects opted for an attractive brick and concentrated on one or two 'strategic details' such as the front door and the roof edge. For the rest it is an exceptionally uncomplicated architecture.

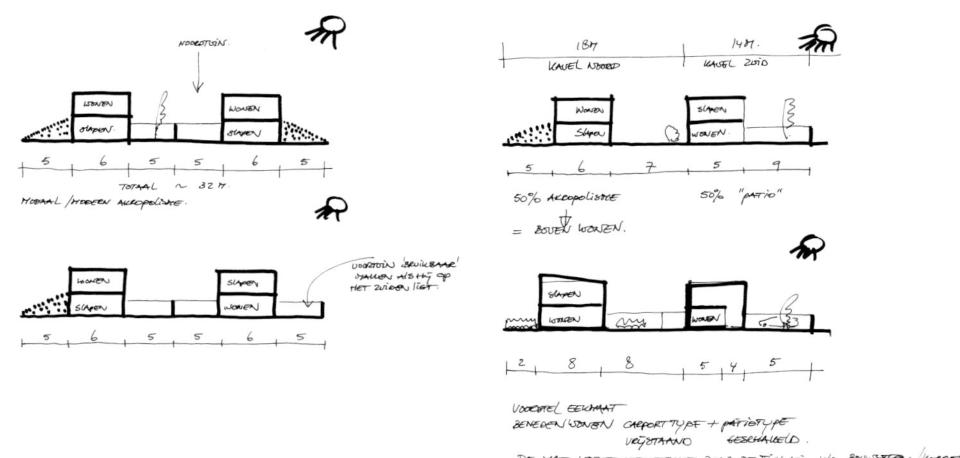

1

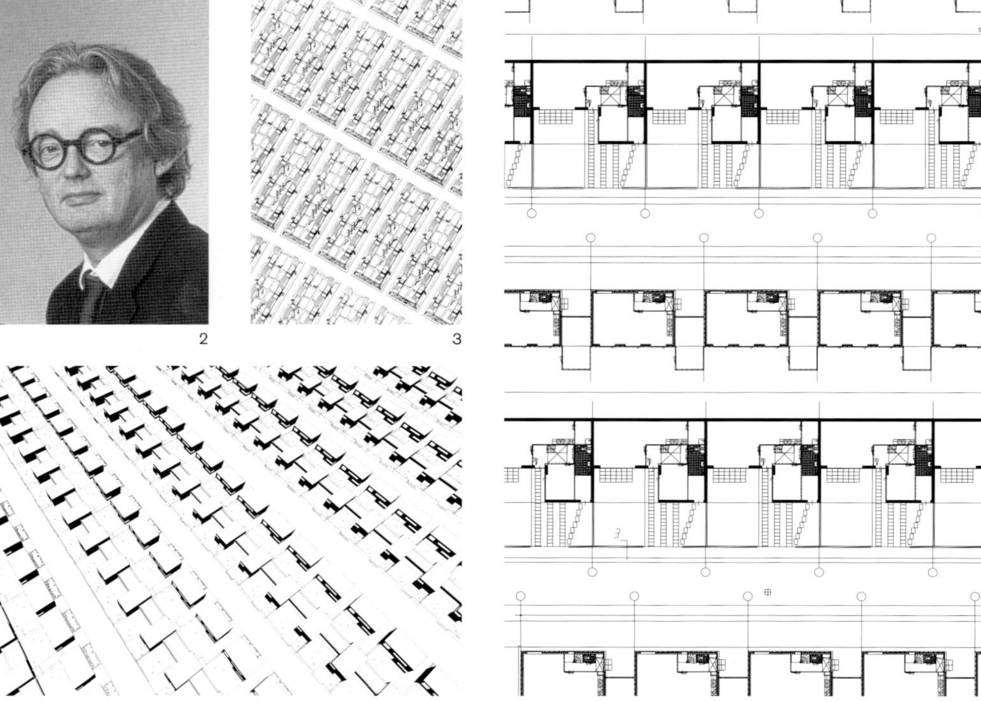

2

3

1 Levittown, Long Island, New York, 1947–1952
2 Sjoerd Soeters
3 Sjoerd Soeters, 'New Acropolism', 1983–1990

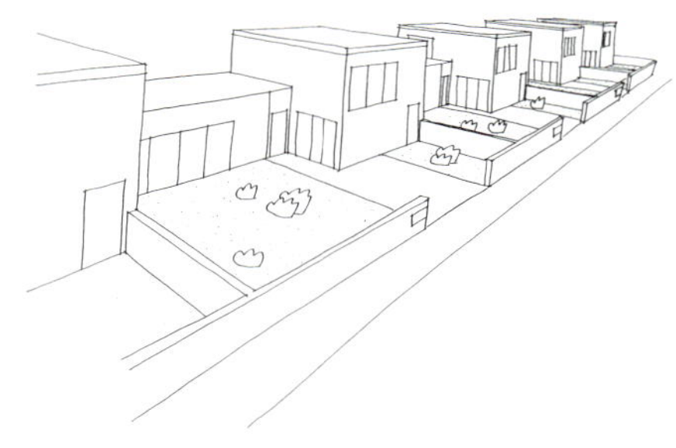
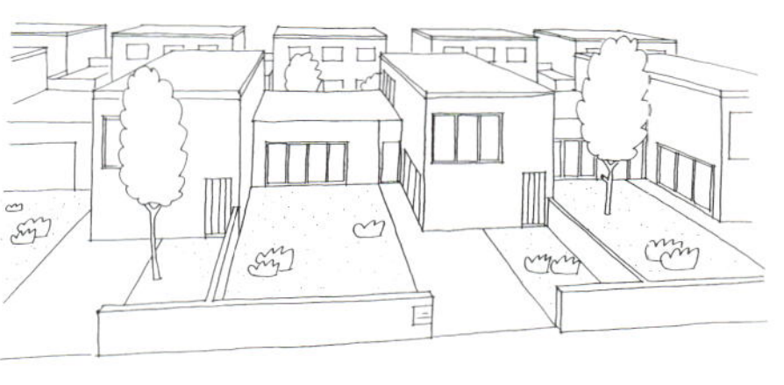

099
STUDENT HOUSING DRIENERLO, ENSCHEDE

Part of a complex of student flats built in the 1960s on the campus of the Twente University of Technology has undergone a radical renovation. In the original set-up, twenty students were housed in each block which had a communal kitchen on the ground floor. In the converted buildings each floor contains five or six student rooms plus a common room with adjoining kitchen. In the centre of each block is a spiral staircase. The front and rear elevations were moved outwards so that the students' rooms are somewhat larger than before, although they remain tiny. In stark contrast to the niggardly proportions of the living space, is the generous impression made by the complex as a whole. Structuralist illegibility has made way for a crystal-clear outward form. The deep-set vertical windows give the white-stuccoed architecture a stately air. The marble cladding of the entrance and the heavy toughened-glass entrance doors lend the very basic life of a student an uncustomary distinction. Whereas the original linked cubes gave the impression of being part of an endlessly repeatable structure, the renovated blocks convey a sense of autonomy.

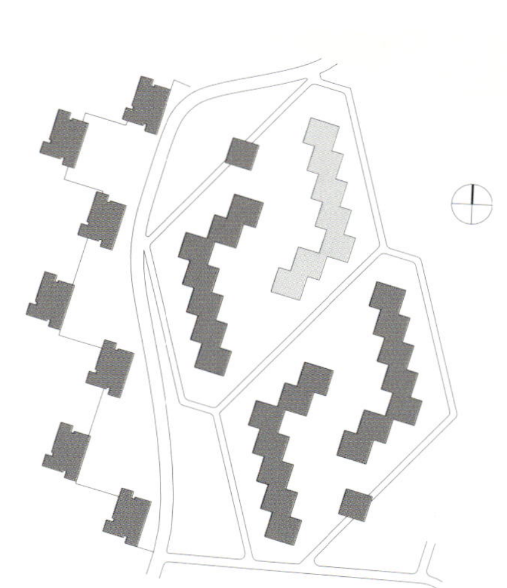

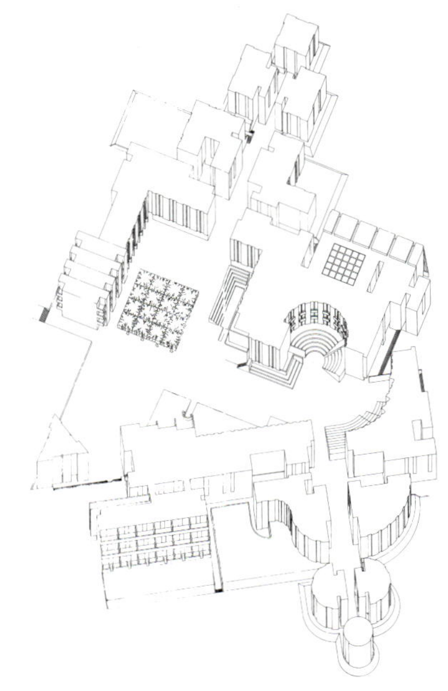

Oswald Mathias Ungers, competition design for student housing, TH Twente, Enschede, 1964

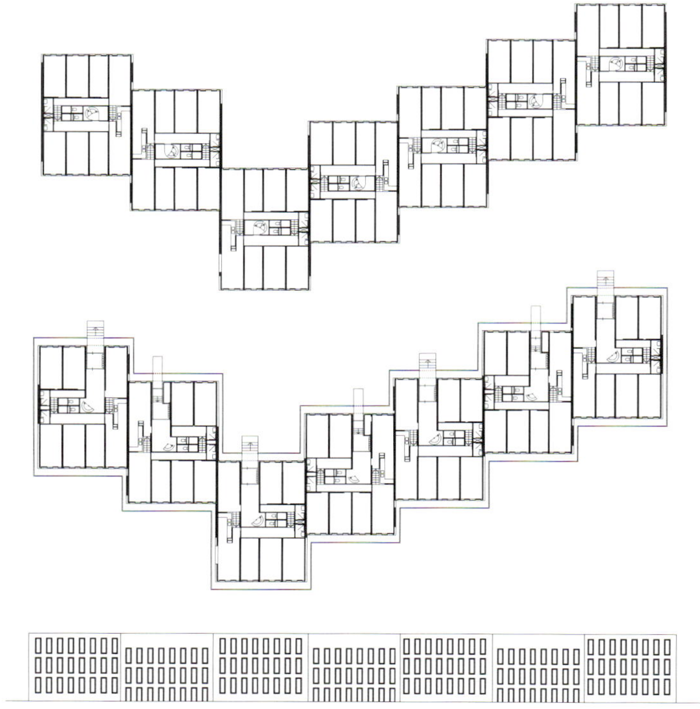

Student Housing Drienerlo, Enschede

Aquafresh

Student Housing Drienerlo, Enschede

102
HOUSING, PARK DUIJNWIJK, ZANDVOORT

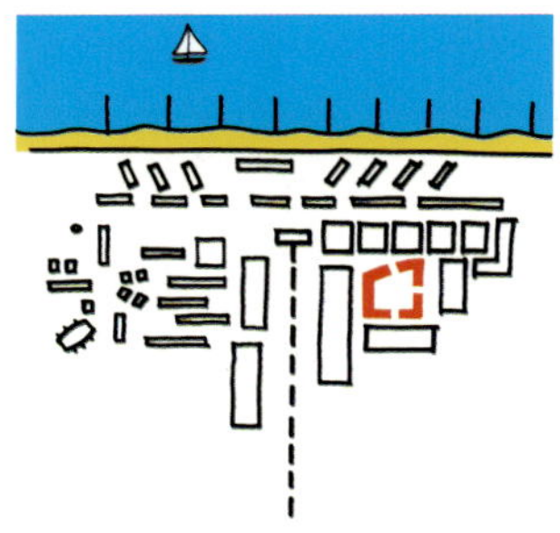

The spatial master plan for a new residential area close to the centre of the seaside resort of Zandvoort, was drawn up by Donald Lambert of Kraaijvanger Urbis. Claus en Kaan were invited to design a block with 102 dwellings in the heart of the planning area. Lambert, with whom Claus en Kaan had previously collaborated in the Gulden Kruis estate in Amsterdam Southeast, wanted the same typology of upstairs and downstairs dwellings as the blocks along the Bijlmerdreef with the addition of underground parking. The block encloses an internal courtyard with a spring-fed pond, a typical feature of the local dune landscape. The solid, four-storey block introduces a touch of urbanity into this otherwise low-rise neighbourhood, although in terms of density it already smacks of the big city in what is in effect an overgrown village. The block's facade is topped by a wide band of brick relief work, a lightly sculptural touch in the tradition of the Amsterdam School. However different in size and execution, the traditional court of pensioners' houses built by B.J.M. Stevens as part of the postwar reconstruction of Zandvoort was a point of reference for this new design: an introverted environment, focused on its own centre.

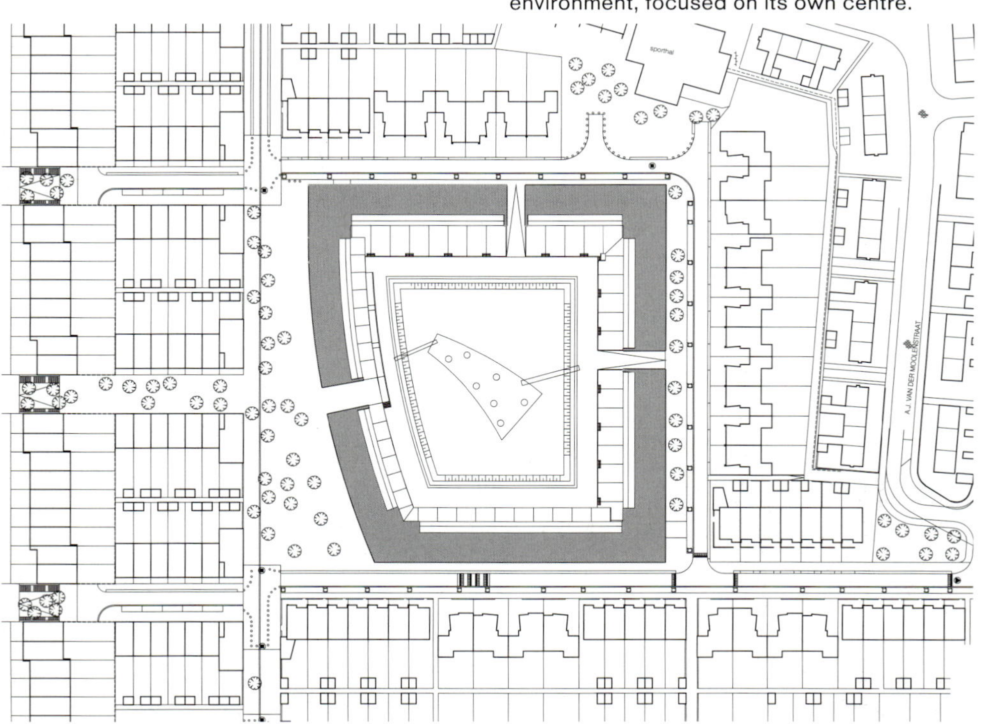

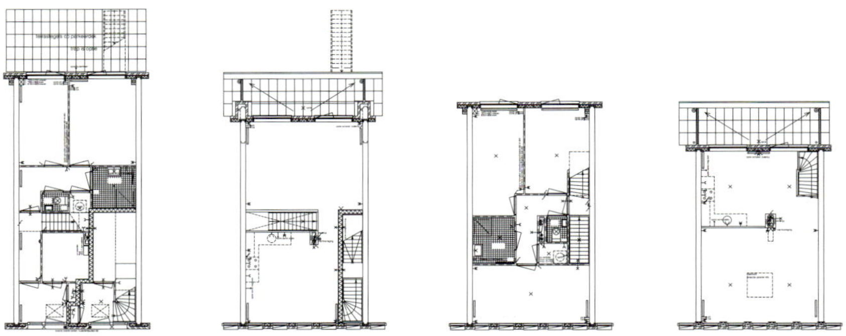

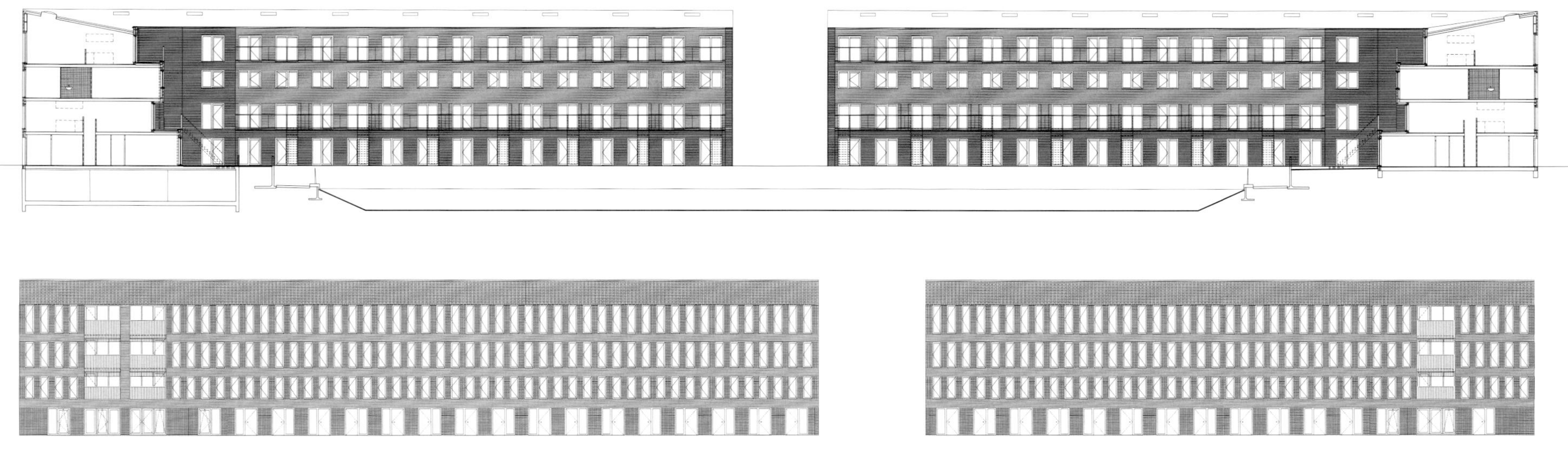

108
SHELTERED HOUSING, STADSHAGEN, ZWOLLE

This sheltered housing complex stands in the middle of Stadshagen, a new residential district being built on the outskirts of Zwolle that will eventually consist of more than eight thousand dwellings. Compared with the surrounding low-rise housing, the five-storey complex is solid and substantial. It has been designed to look as if it predates the new district: a factory converted to apartments for the elderly, say. In this it resembles Building 1 in Zaandam, which evokes the same image. The industrial-looking building in Stadshagen is a close relative of that Lombroso type, although it is more apparent here that there is a friendly nature lurking behind the gruff exterior.

The sheltered housing complex is a perfect example of the 'rough diamond with a heart of gold'. The forbidding hardness of the exterior is offset by the softness of the interior, which is the social domain of the residents. Originally, the outer facade was to have been in concrete, but for financial reasons this was changed to dark brick. The interior of the block is determined by warm shades of orange and red. Once again the original design, where a single shade of orange was used throughout, had to be modified, this time in response to protests from the future occupants. The orange was replaced by red except at places not immediately visible to the residents. The dwellings, most of which have a glazed veranda, lie along wide galleries given a spatial articulation by the staggered facades. The dwellings are distributed over two buildings which together make up one long and one short side of the block. On the corner, like a slit in the volume, is the glazed entrance lobby with stairs. The opposite corner is occupied by the chunky building containing district services. Between the two is a communal square.

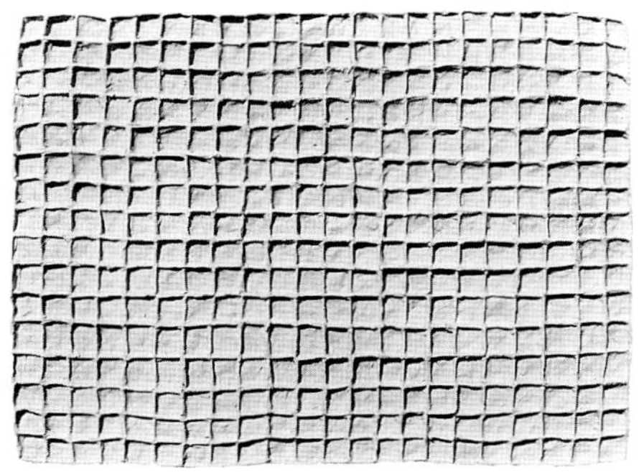
1

2

1 Jan Schoonhoven, untitled, 1960
2 Peter Celsing, Riksbank, Stockholm, 1970

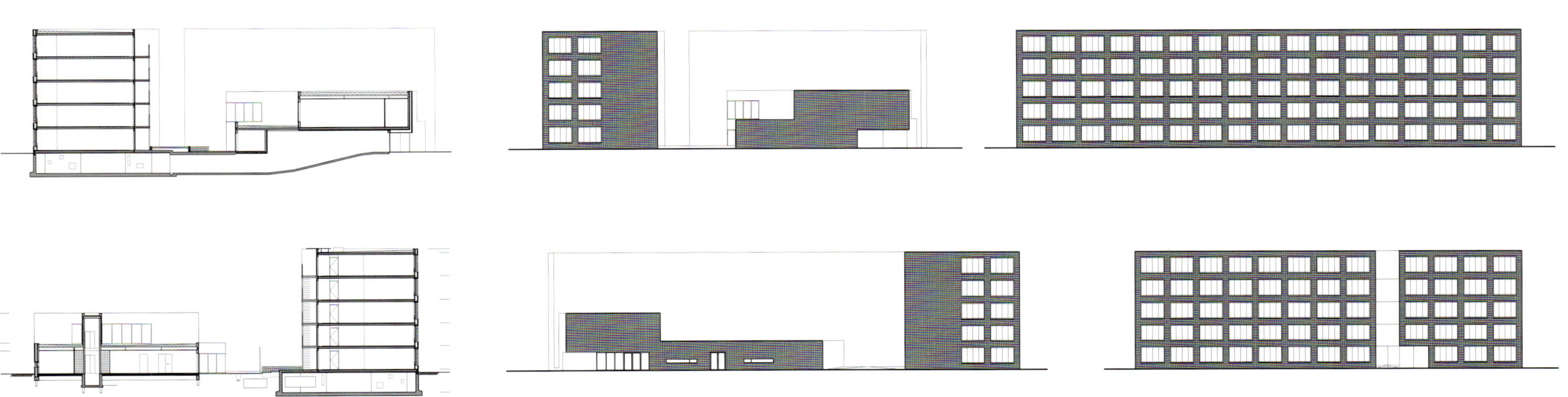

Sheltered Housing, Stadshagen, Zwolle

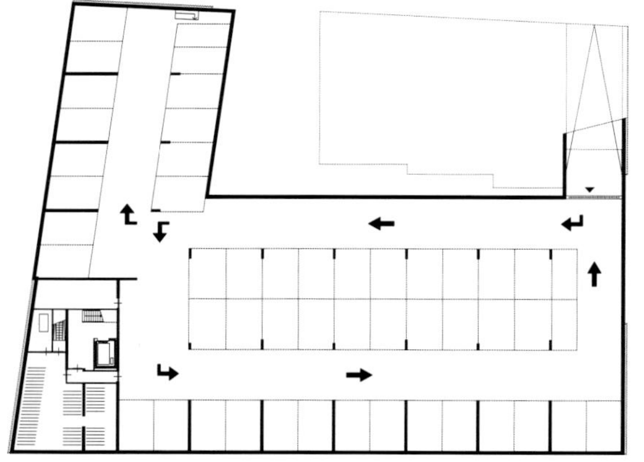

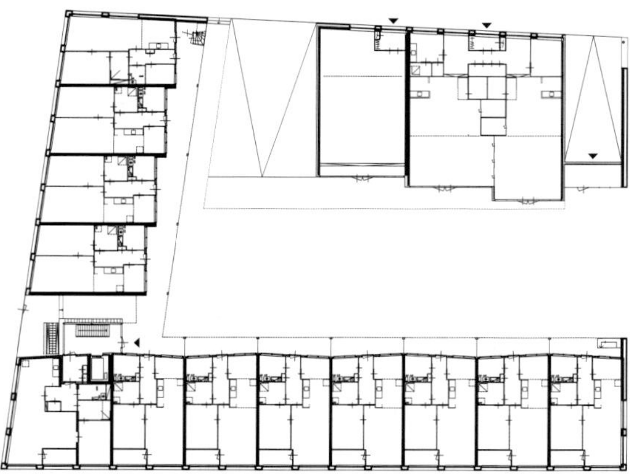

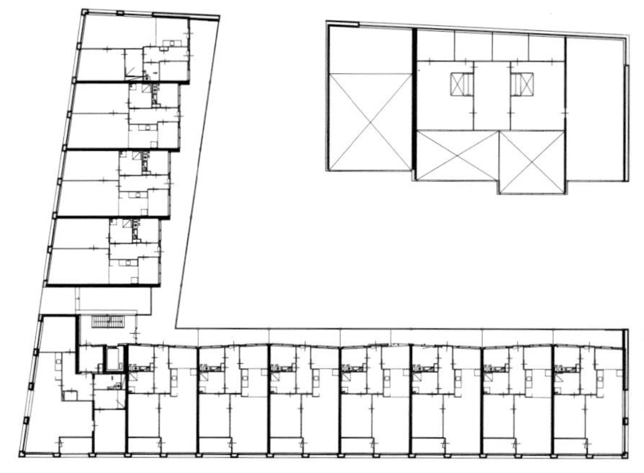

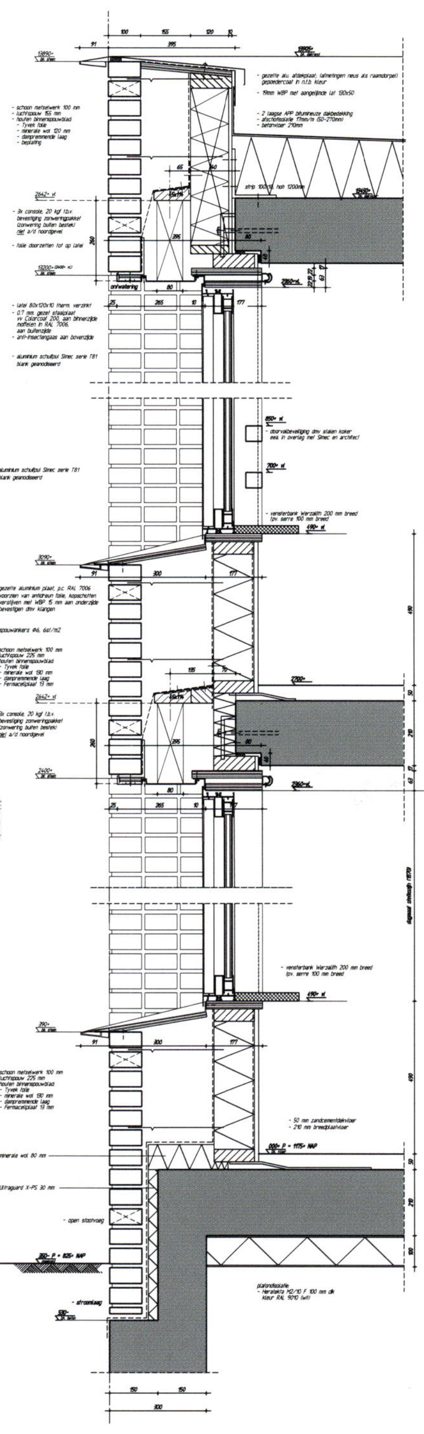

Sheltered Housing, Stadshagen, Zwolle

109 065 098 106 148
DRAAISMA HOUSE, AMSTERDAM

One of the Sporenburg projects assigned to Claus en Kaan was the design of five dwellings on one of the head elevations. The unique siting was seized on as an argument for breaking out the material straight-jacket imposed on architects throughout Borneo-Sporenburg by the area's master planners (Adriaan Geuze/West 8). The facades here are not hermetic expanses of brick interrupted only by window openings framed in unpainted wood. Although the side elevations conform to the dominant brick image, the first sign of dissidence is already evident here in the form of aluminium frames and doors. The head elevation is composed almost entirely of concrete and aluminium framed glass. This raised elevation consists of two bands of storey-high windows, the horizontality of which is offset by the vertical frame divisions.

One corner dwelling differs from the rest and has been tailored to the wishes of the occupant, a long-standing professional contact of the architects who also designed the interior. In this it is a unique project for Claus en Kaan since the practice has never taken on any other commissions for private homes. There is an enormous sense of space in the Draaisma home thanks to the five split-level floors which turn the interior into a continuum. The finishing – plasterwork, stone and parquet – is of is of an immaculacy unusual in Dutch house construction.

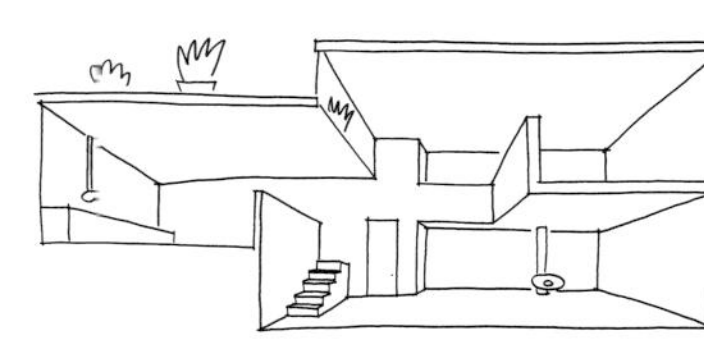

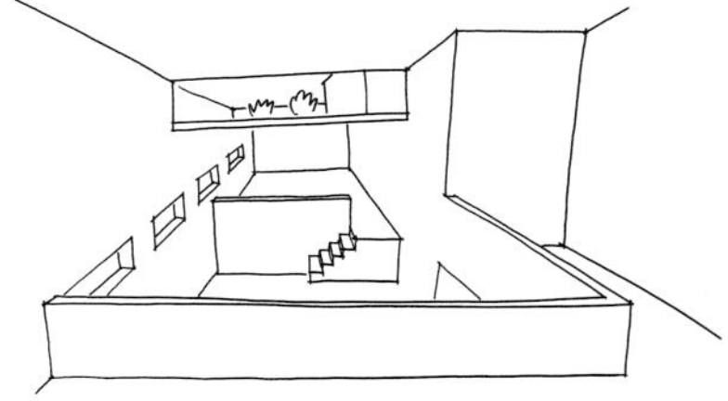

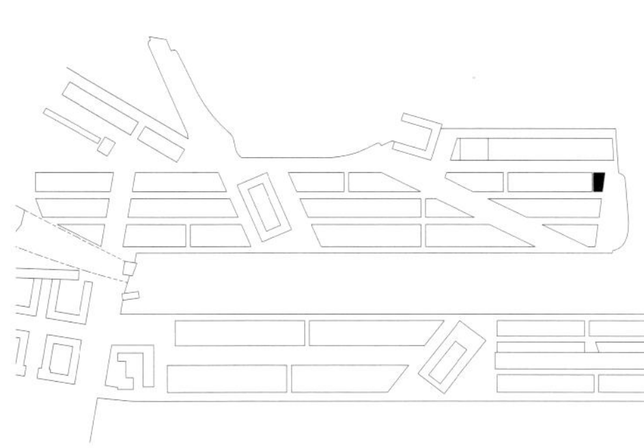

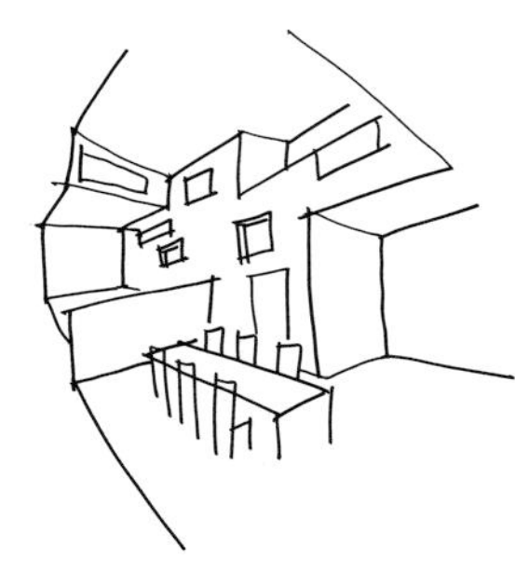

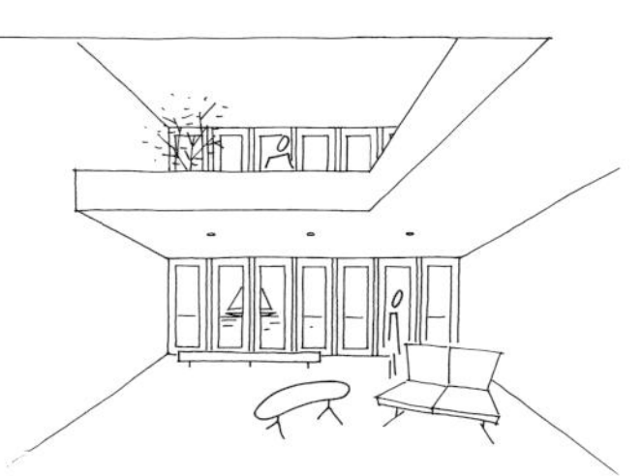

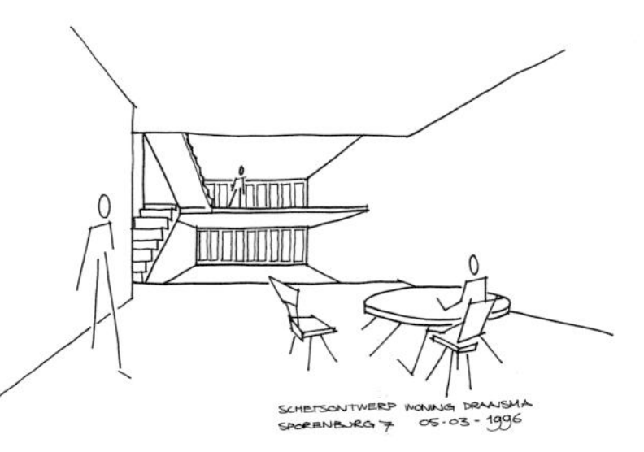

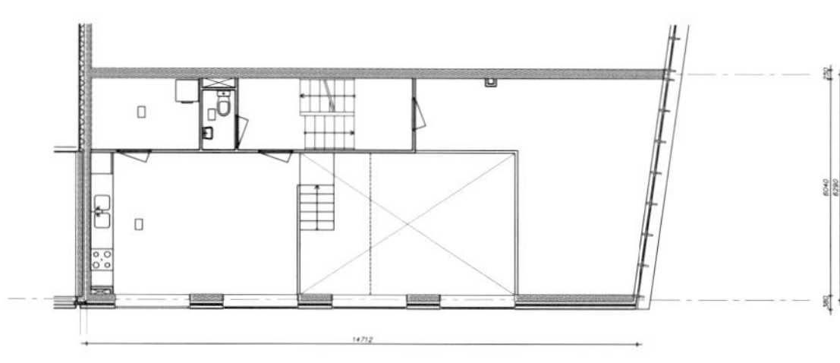

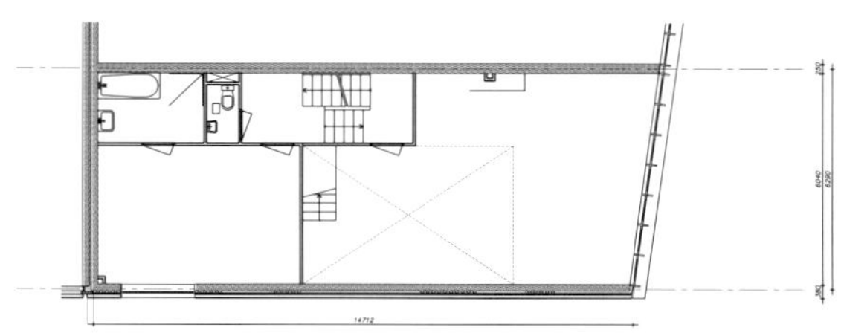

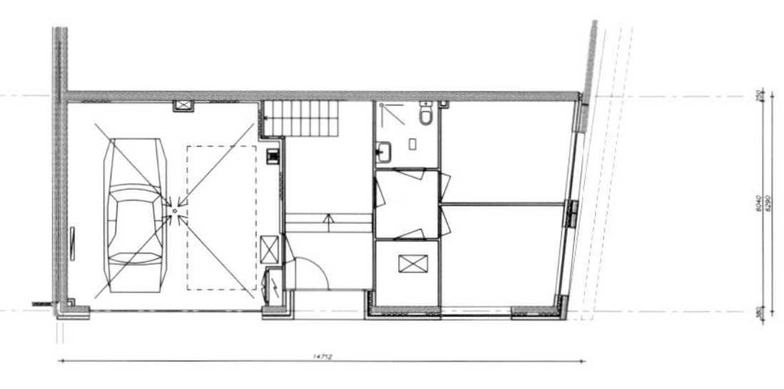

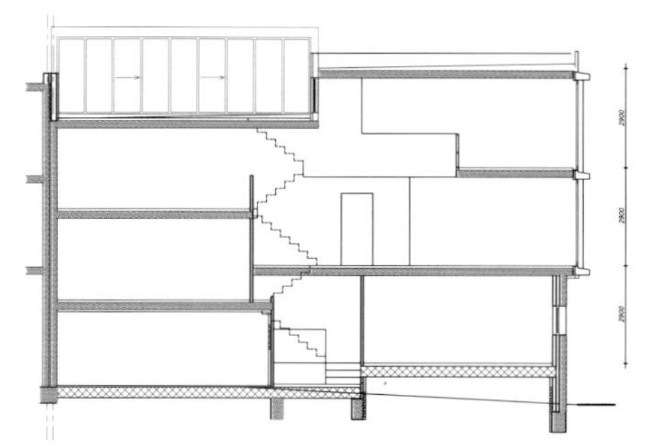

Draaisma House, Amsterdam

120
HOUSING, BEEKPARK, APELDOORN

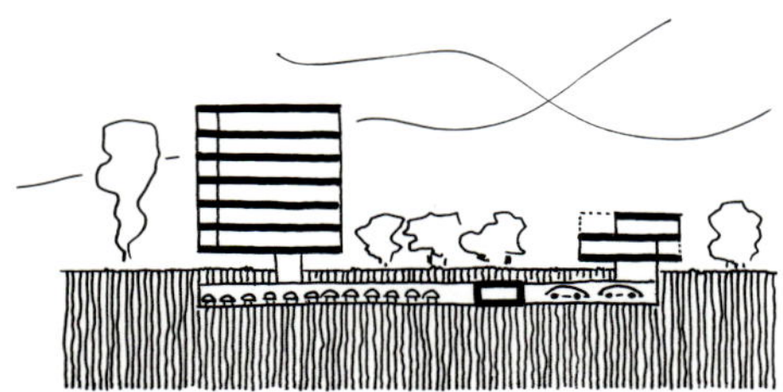

1 Beekpark, Apeldoorn
2 Erwin Heerich, pavilion, Insel Hombroich, Gut Hombroich, 1987
3 Le Corbusier, Une petite maison, Lac Léman, Switzerland, 1925

In Apeldoorn a plan was developed for an apartment tower and several small-scale blocks to be built in the grounds of Beek Park, with minimum disruption of the park landscape. To ensure the continued openness and public accessibility of the green space, there are no private gardens and parking is underground.

Each of the small blocks, which are scattered across the park like dice, contains two dwellings. They combine elements of the semi-detached house with those of the patio bungalow which here assumes a paradoxically multi-level form. The lowest level contains the sleeping quarters. Above this is the living level, with a spectacular, ten-square-metre panorama window that establishes a direct relationship with the park landscape, designed by Annemieke Diekman. On top of this again is a patio which, three metres above ground level, conjures up the easy-going ambience of the Californian bungalow. Instead
of the customary bungalow garden, each dwelling has a roof terrace.

The relaxed atmosphere of the interior is concealed behind a monolithic armour of 'mildewed' brickwork. The form is strongly articulated but not entirely congruent with the spatial configuration it contains. The arbitrariness of the geometry of the double houses returns in the apartment building in the disposition of window openings, which have been 'shuffled out of alignment'. These geometrical whimsicalities can be construed as abstract reflections of the irregularity of nature.

1

2

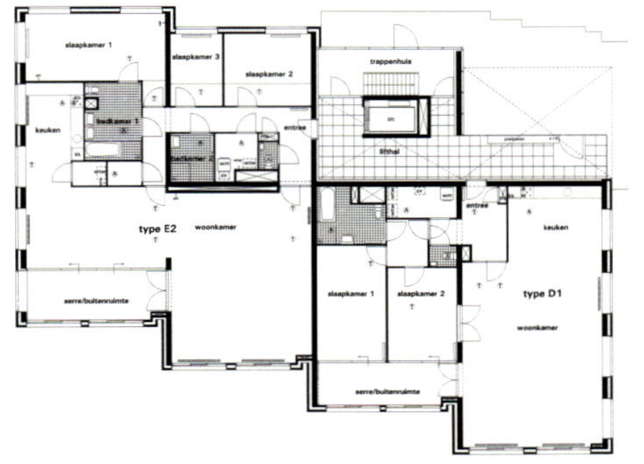

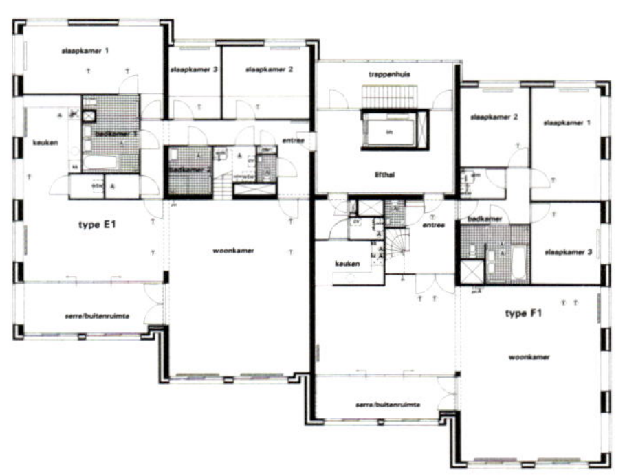

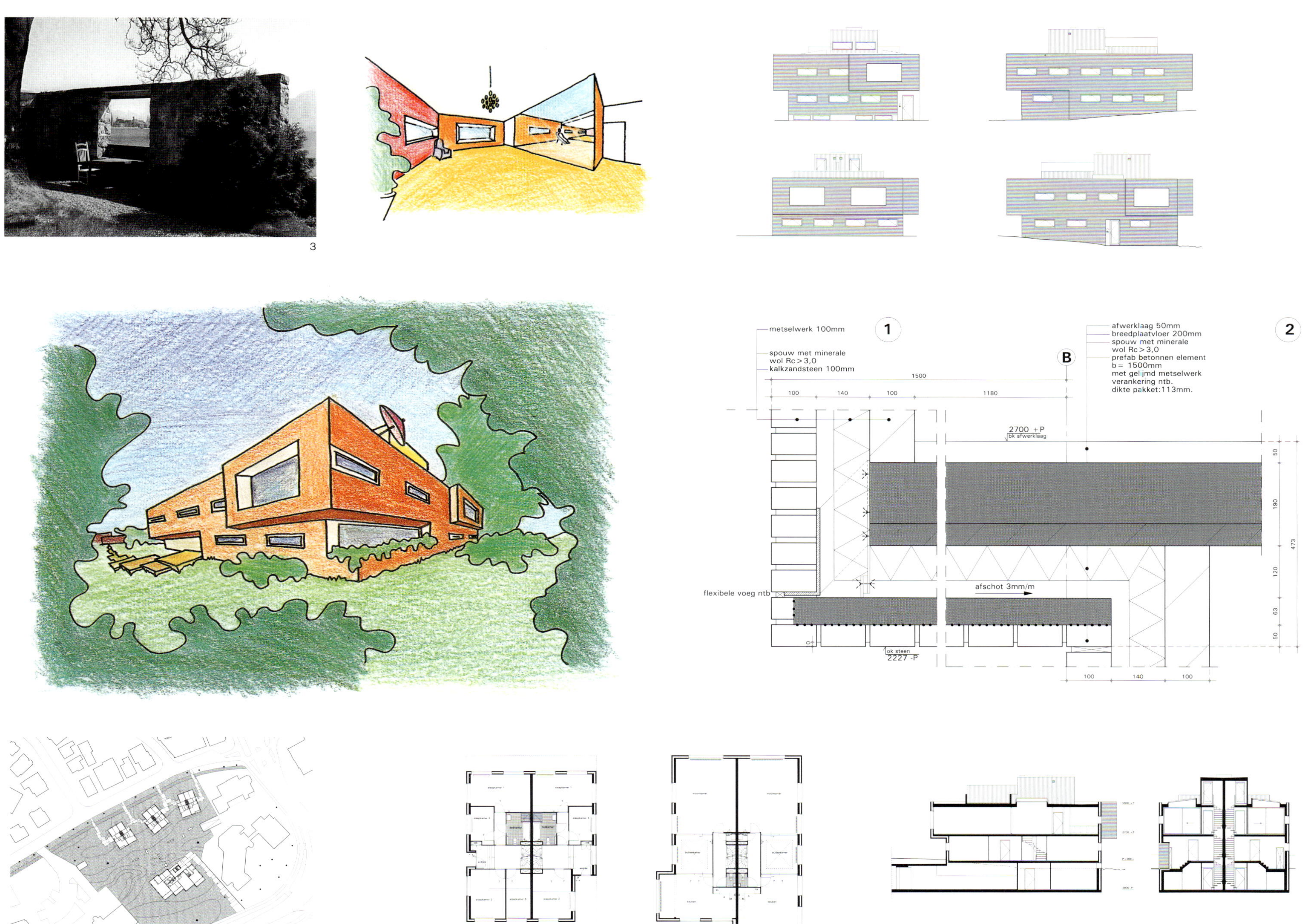
metselwerk 100mm
1
spouw met minerale
wol Rc>3,0
kalkzandsteen 100mm
B
afwerklaag 50mm
breedplaatvloer 200mm
spouw met minerale
wol Rc>3,0
prefab betonnen element
b= 1500mm
met gelijmd metselwerk
verankering ntb.
dikte pakket:113mm.
2
1500
100
140
100
1180
2700 +P
bk afwerklaag
afschot 3mm/m
flexibele voeg ntb
ok steen
2227 -P
100
140
100
50
190
120
63
50
473

3

123 HOUSING, ZENDERPARK, IJSSELSTEIN

For the huge Zenderpark expansion in IJsselstein, Claus en Kaan designed 58 dwellings on a long parcel of land only nine metres wide. The site lies on the border of the relatively urban heart of the district and the surrounding suburban sprawl. The spatial master plan for the area was made by Teun Koolhaas Associates. The entire ground plane has been developed using two interlinked and alternating dwelling types. One type has the living room and a garage on the ground floor, the other has a carport on the ground floor and the living room on the floor above. Both types have roof terraces sited with an eye to privacy, which is further enhanced by balustrades of frosted glass. The dwellings present a relatively closed face to the street but open up on the sunny side facing a canal and cycle path.

These ground-accessed dwellings without garden can be seen as a reworking of the ones the practice developed for Sporenburg and Rietlanden. The linearity of the architecture is accentuated by the facade composition. Between thick concrete bands are storey-height windows in aluminium frames and panels of light-coloured brick very close in colour to the concrete. This ton sur ton effect not only prevents the concrete bands from appearing as string courses, but also lends the architecture a reticence not demonstrated by most of the architects building in this neighbourhood. This is a deliberately neutral architecture that stands out by maintaining its distance.

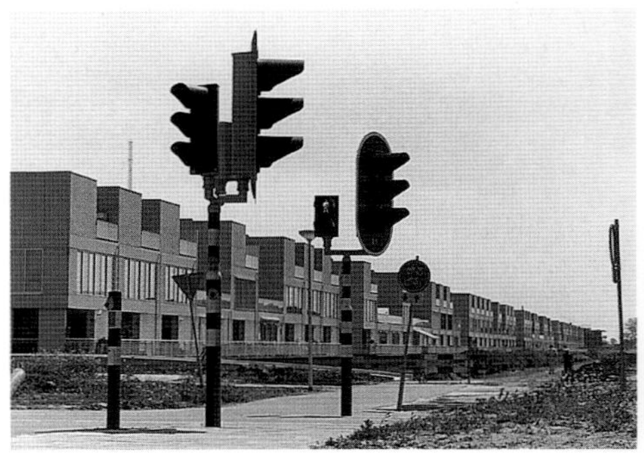

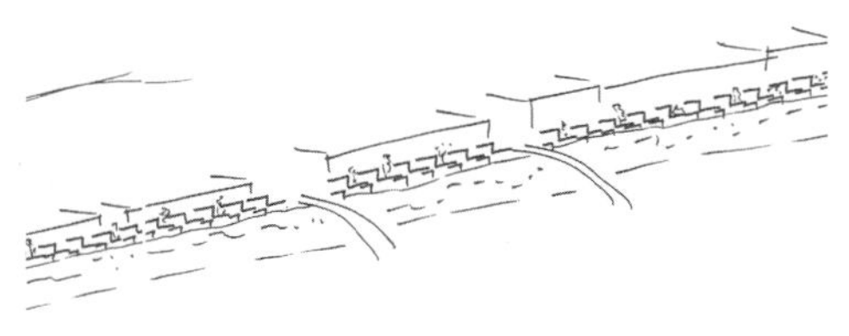

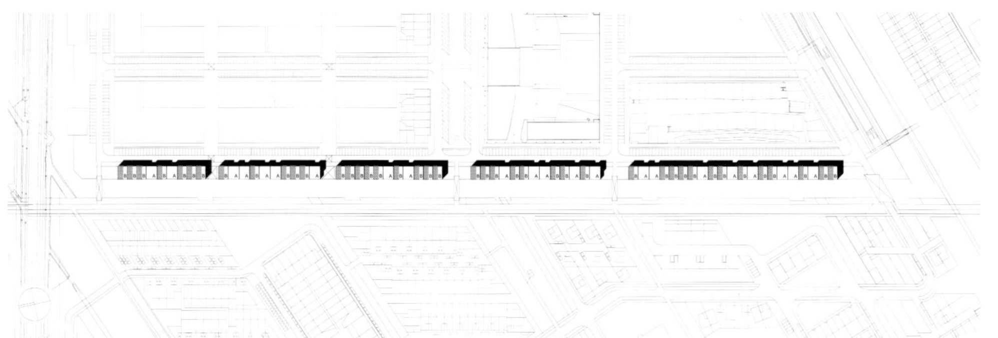

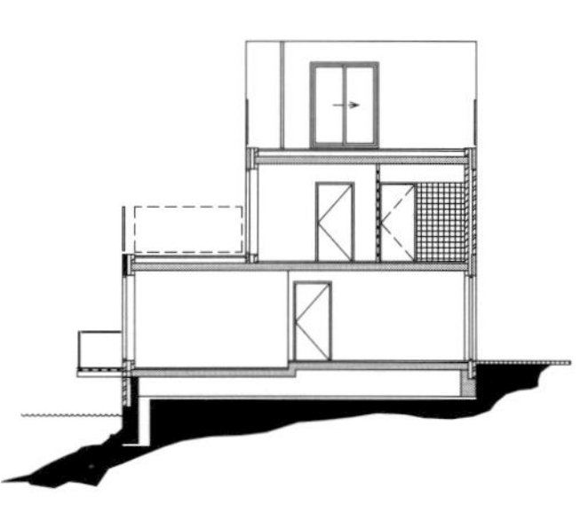

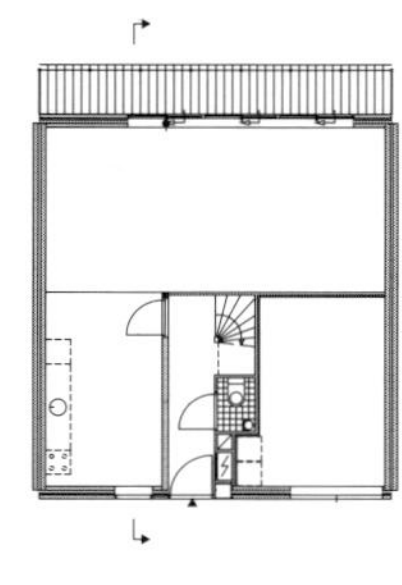

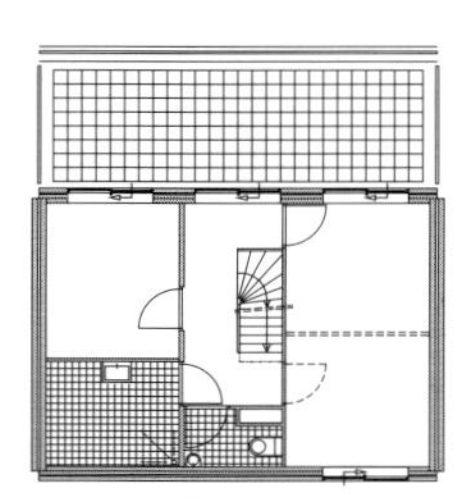

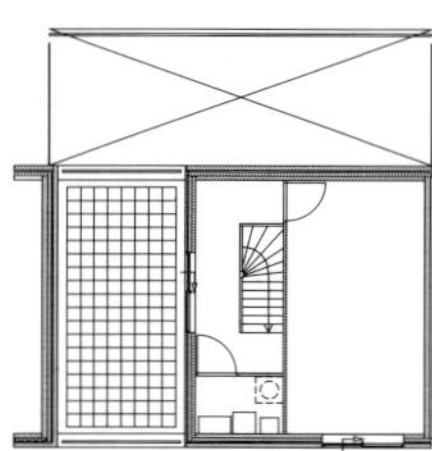

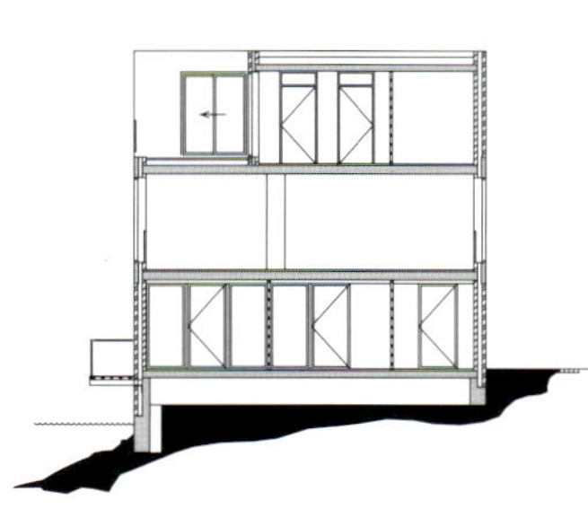

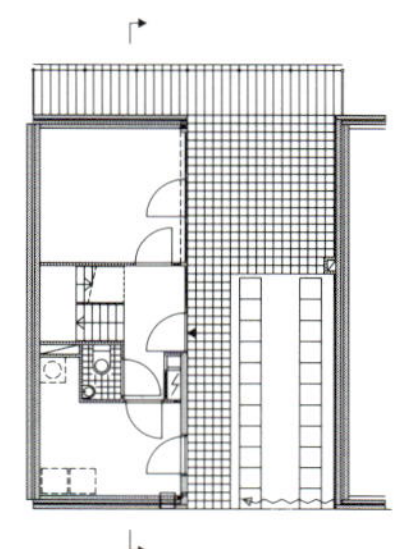

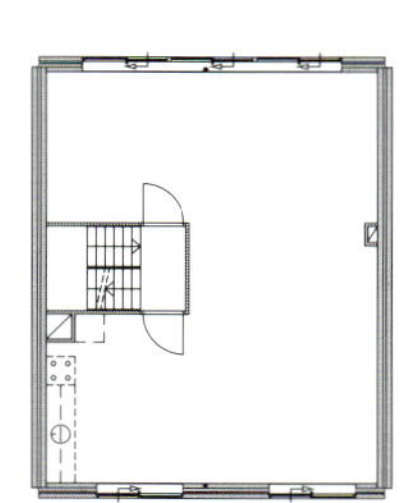

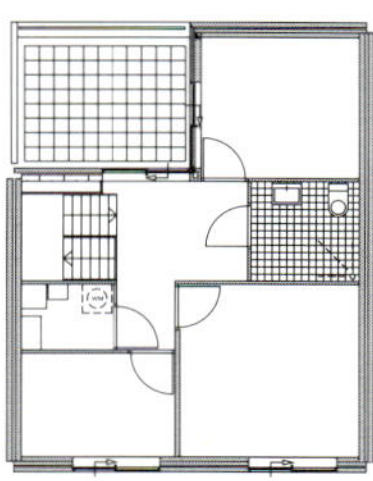

Housing, Zenderpark, IJsselstein

128 079
UNIVERSITY OF AMSTERDAM DECK, AMSTERDAM

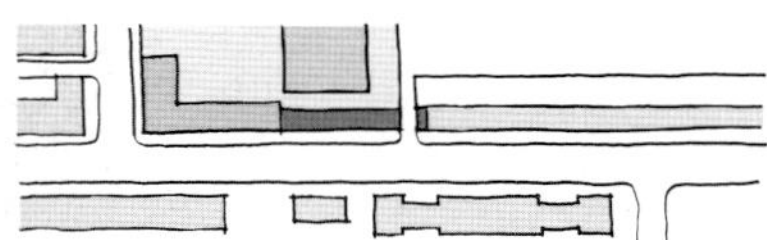

The building with 61 student flats and commercial premises in Amsterdam is part of a new street frontage that partially reverses an earlier intervention. The linear street elevations along Sarphatistraat were breached in the 1960s for a large-scale university complex designed by municipal architect N.J.J. Gawronski. The spatial master plan drawn up by Pi de Bruyn of De Architekten Cie. provides for the return of the typical Amsterdam 'street wall'. The new wall is made up of three sections. The corner was designed by De Bruyn himself, the middle section by VMX architects and the longest part by Claus en Kaan. Their original proposal envisaged a mediation with the neighbouring development built by H.P. Berlage in 1908. The corner of that section, demolished in the 1960s, was to be finished with a narrow building in the same style as the rest of the newbuild. This bridging was scrapped because the site had already been reserved by another party.

The reinstatement of the street frontage can be seen as a form of urban repair, albeit without sentimentality or nostalgia. The newbuild is quite free of blatant contextualism. The staggered windows, which break out of the grid, are a subtle, twenty-first-century variation on the decorative tremolos on windows, doors, bays and cornices characteristic of Dutch architecture at the time when Sarphatistraat was developed. This said, the regular structure of the grid is still discernible in the facade so that this architecture also pays tribute to the sober and unjustly underrated modernism of Gawronksi.

1 Location
2 Erik Gunnar Asplund, lobby of public library, Stockholm, 1920–1931

1

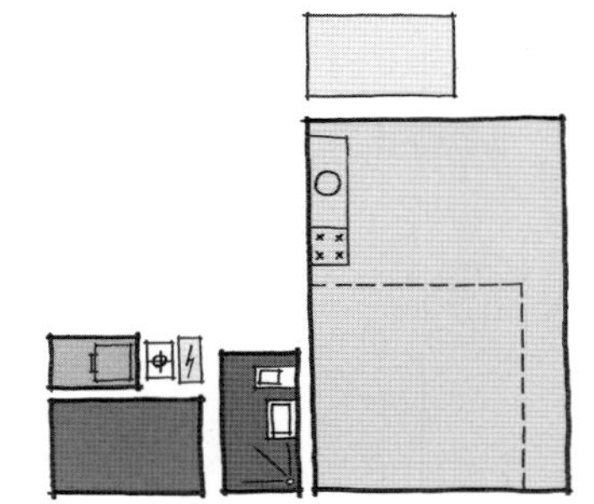

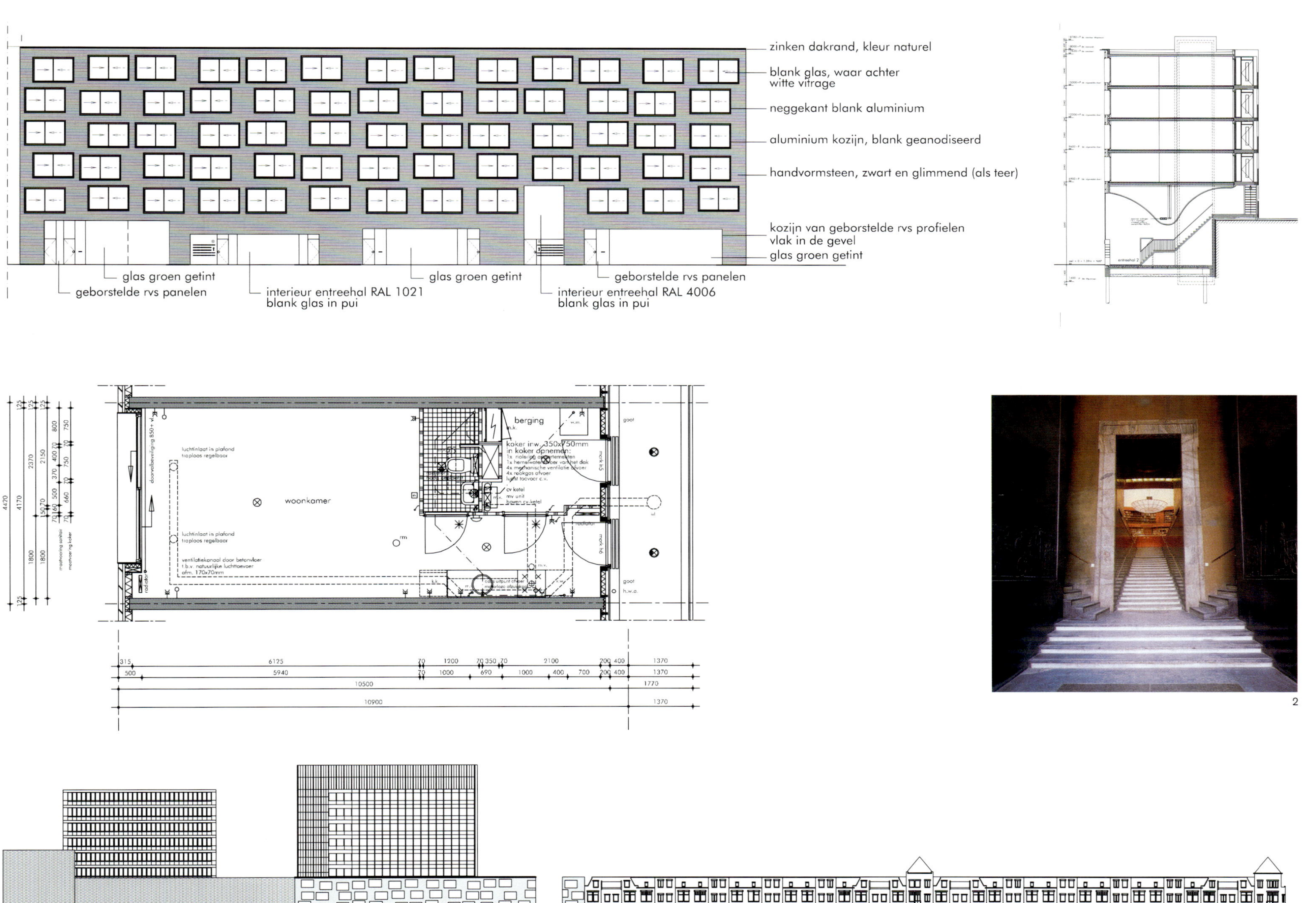

zinken dakrand, kleur naturel
blank glas, waar achter witte vitrage
neggekant blank aluminium
aluminium kozijn, blank geanodiseerd
handvormsteen, zwart en glimmend (als teer)
kozijn van geborstelde rvs profielen vlak in de gevel
glas groen getint
glas groen getint
geborstelde rvs panelen
interieur entreehal RAL 1021 blank glas in pui
glas groen getint
interieur entreehal RAL 4006 blank glas in pui
geborstelde rvs panelen
berging
woonkamer

2

133
APARTMENT TOWER, ALMERE

The tower block containing 58 apartments stands just outside Almere's town centre which, two decades after its construction, is undergoing a major transformation orchestrated by Rem Koolhaas's Office for Metropolitan Architecture. The aim of OMA's spatial master plan is to create a more concentrated, vibrant urban centre. The tower is on the edge of the planning area, directly overlooking Weerwater, the artificial lake at the heart of this sprawling, polynuclear polder town. The building has been conceived as a Dutch version of Schipporeit-Heinrich's Lake Point Tower of 1968, an autonomous object standing on the boundary of Chicago and Lake Michigan.

The meander form of the tower reinforces the logo-like singularity of this building while at the same time catering to the practical demands of the market: there are plenty of takers for the top and bottom levels of a tower, far fewer for the middle section. The middle has therefore been reduced to a minimum and the top and foot maximized. An equally rigid logic informs the distribution of windows, which is a direct reflection of the rooms they serve. Each window is positioned symmetrically vis à vis the central axis of a room and the area of glass is a fixed percentage of the floor area of the room behind. The aluminium cladding is like a tight skin that has been drawn over the building.

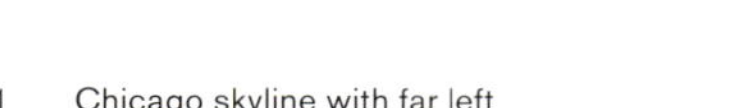

1 Chicago skyline with far left Lake Point Tower by Schipporeit-Heinrich
2 Yayoi Kusama, untitled, 1968
3 Japanese apartment building, Sendai

1

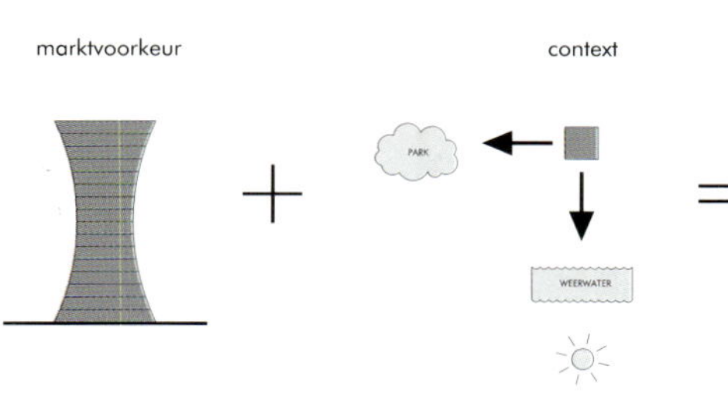

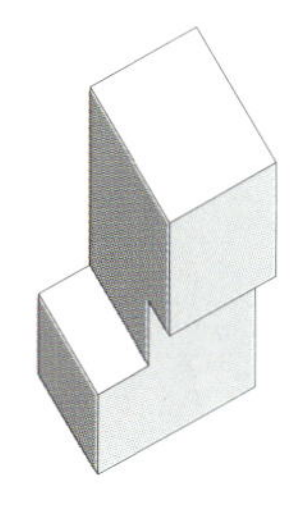

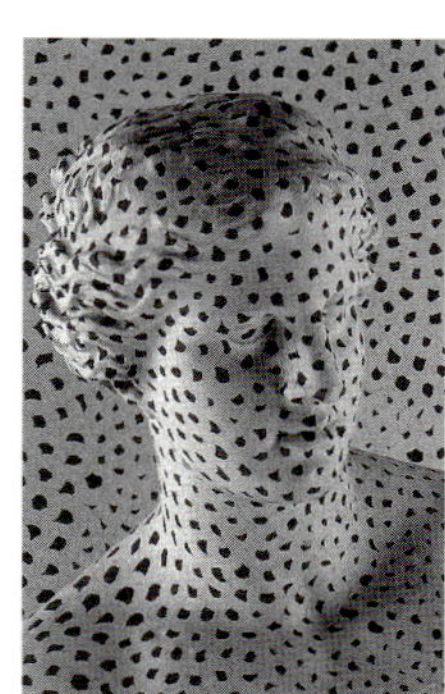

2

3

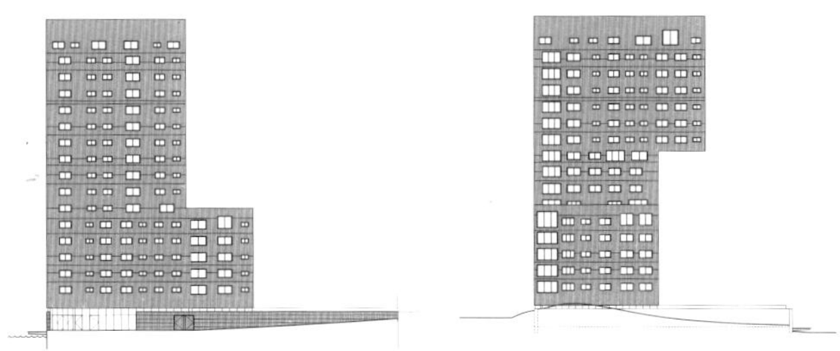

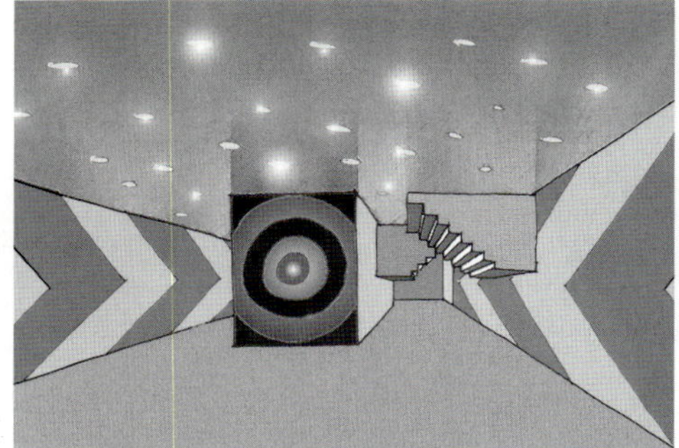

Impression of car park and hall

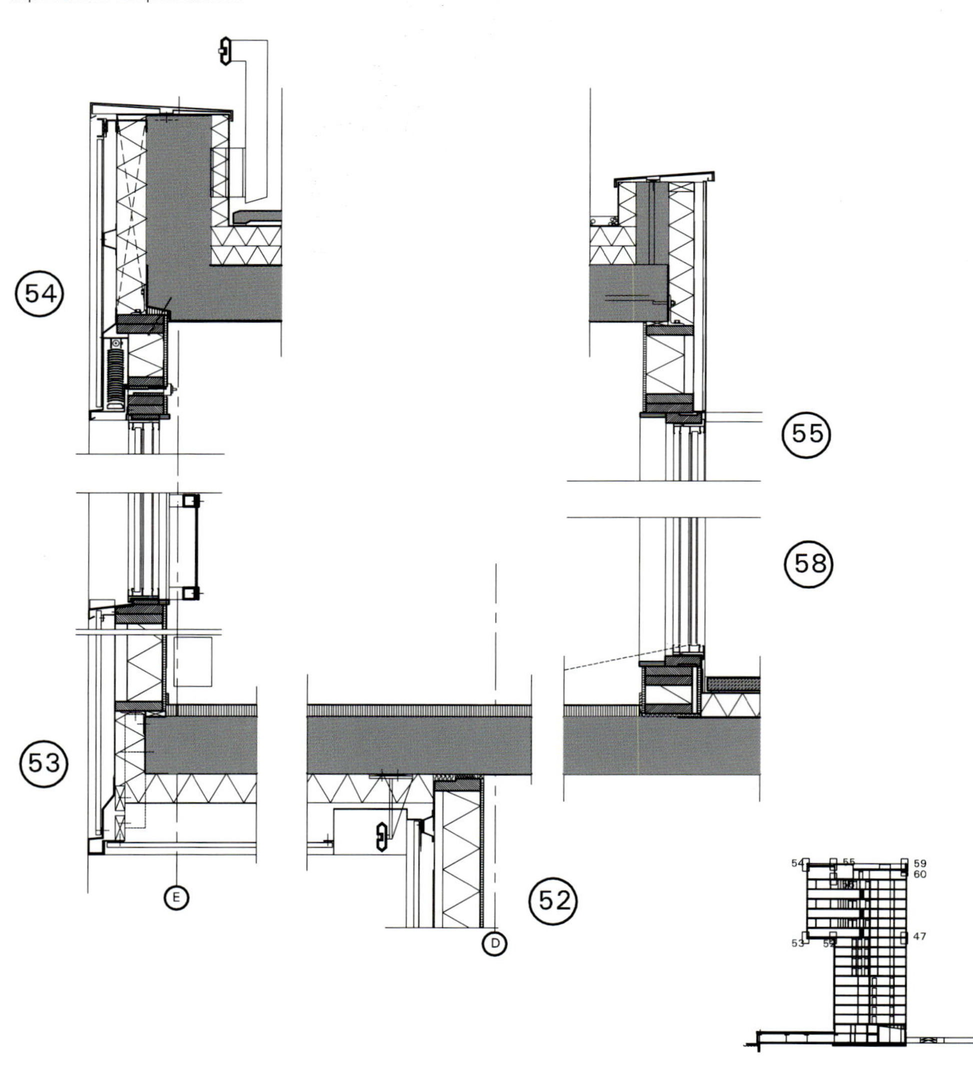

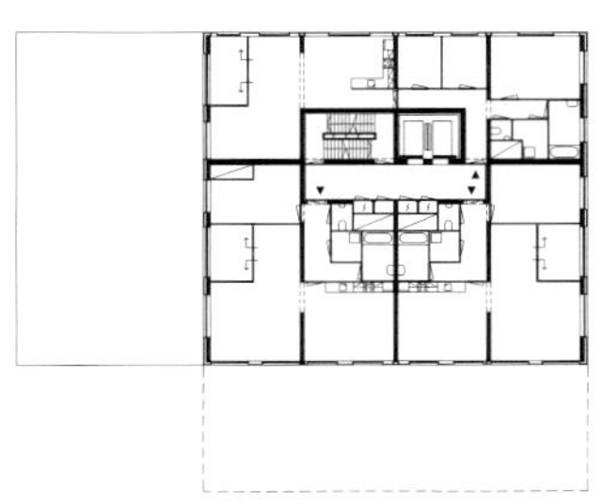

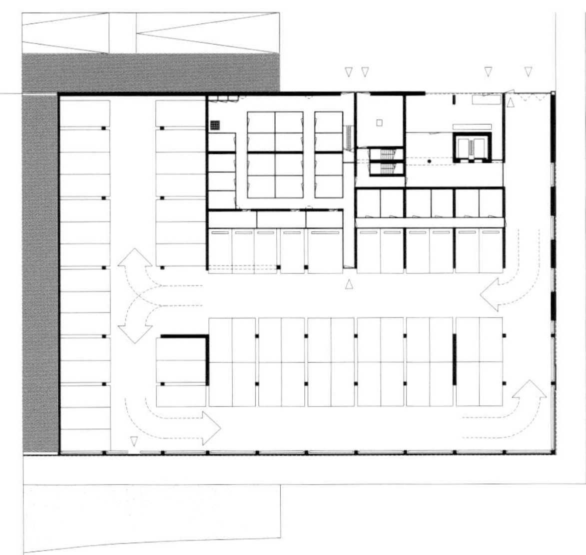
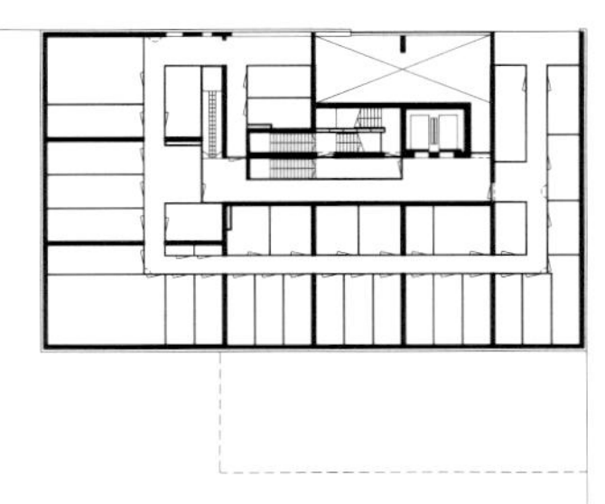

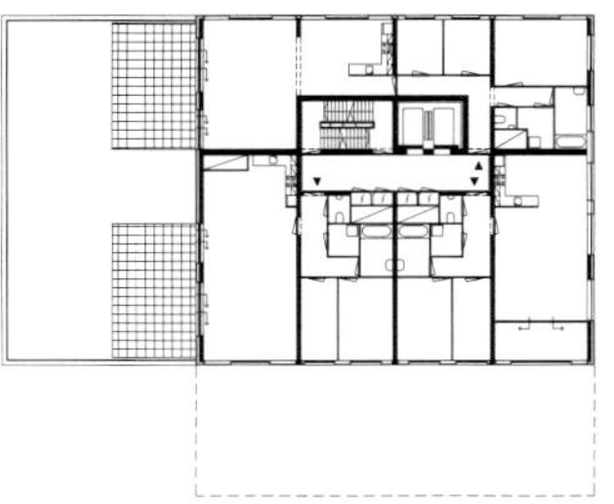

137
DUTCH EMBASSY, MAPUTO

The Dutch embassy in Mozambique is located close to the ocean and just outside the centre of the country's capital, Maputo. The building has been pushed to the edge of an orthogonal, gently sloping site so as to leave room for a walled garden. Since this is the southern hemisphere, the building opens up to the cooler south side while its north face is much more closed, designed to admit light while keeping the heat at bay. Climatological considerations, which played an important role in the design, coincided with the desire to hide the clutter behind the building from public view.

The building and the enclosing walls were conceived as a rough concrete monolith out of which a piece has been cut, allowing the building to open up on this side and leaving space for the garden. The garden wall and the short ends of the L-shaped complex are in rough concrete. Where the building has been cut open it is fronted by the filigree steel framework of a veranda – a motif borrowed from the local Portuguese colonial architecture.

The building consists of a rectangular volume with offices on the garden side, a middle zone containing the amenities and a double-height circulation zone behind the south facade.

The rough concrete of the exterior returns inside in the floor and the ceiling. In the open space of the long leg of the L is an autonomous wooden box which is the floor of the mezzanine and the ceiling of the ground floor level. This box contains the services for both floors.

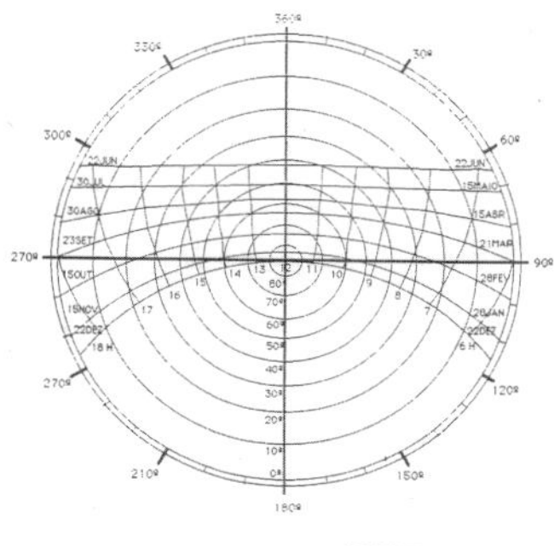

1

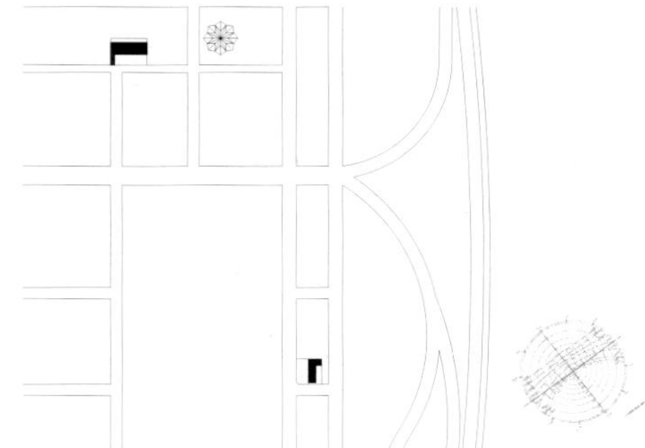

1

2

2

3

1 Street scene in Maputo
2 Study models of chancery
3 Pinto, model in aluminium, 2001

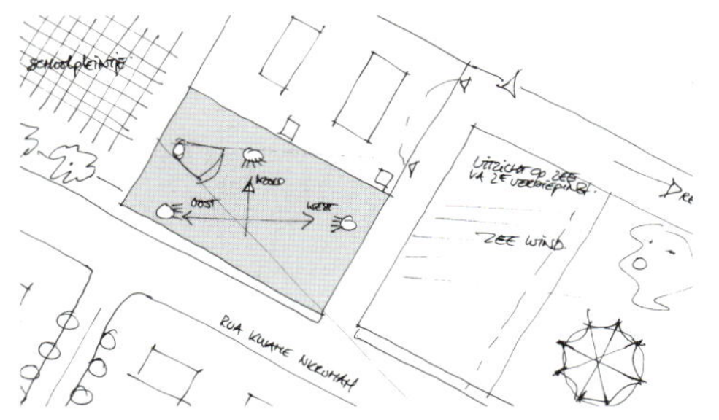

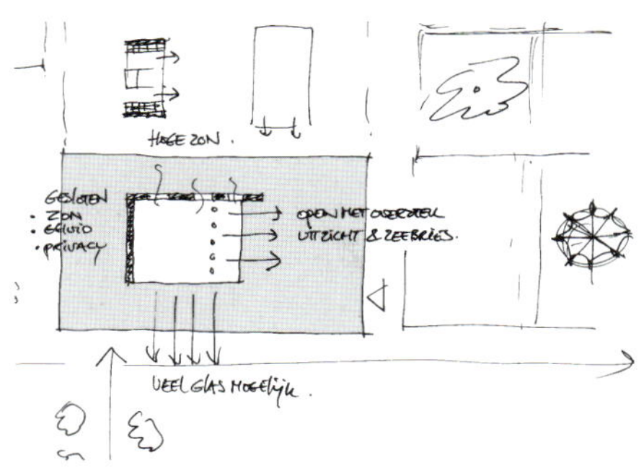

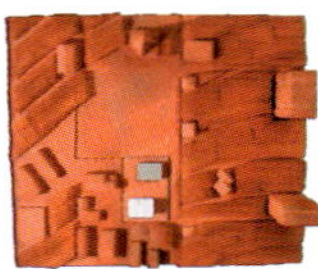

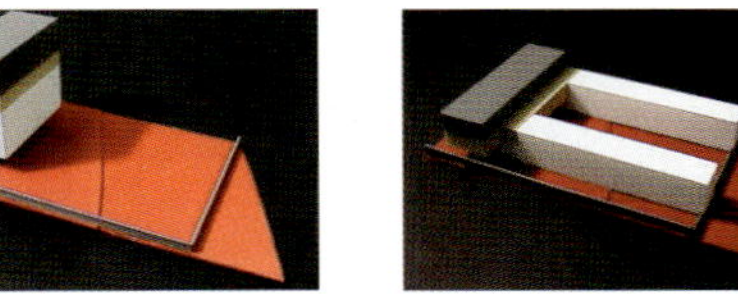

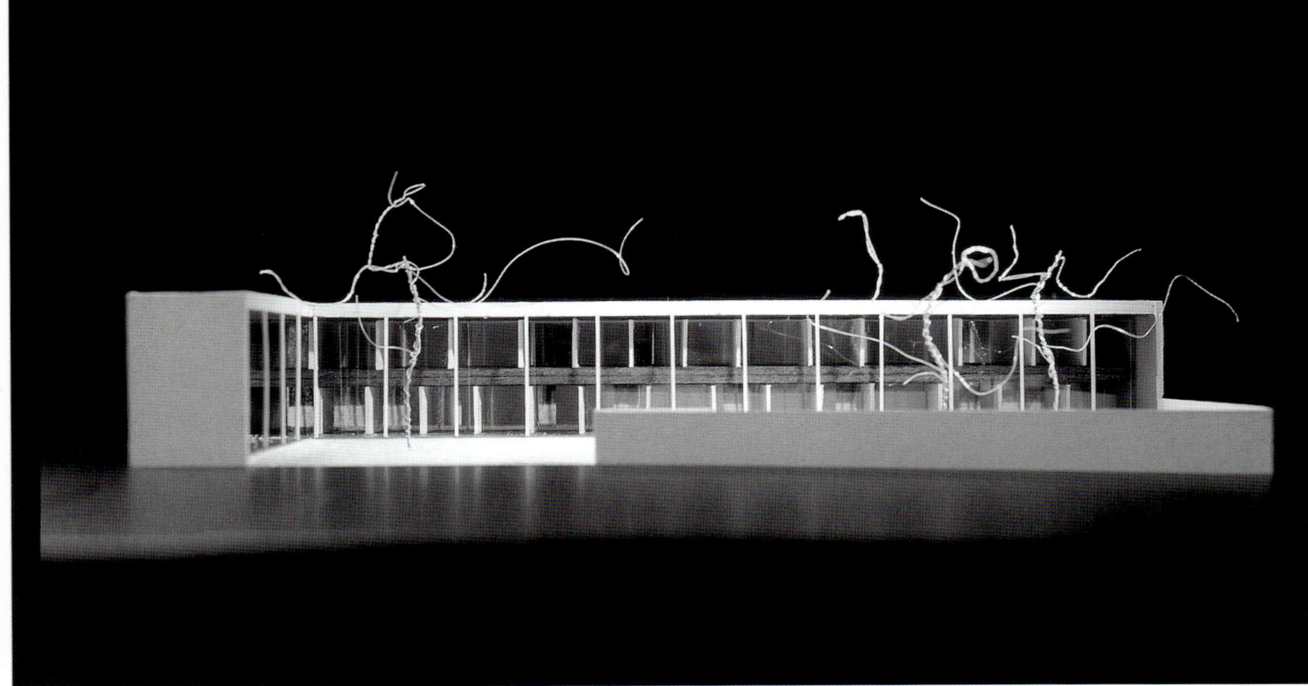

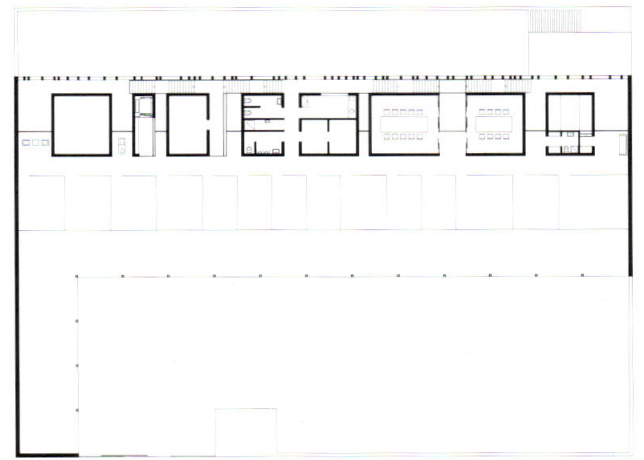

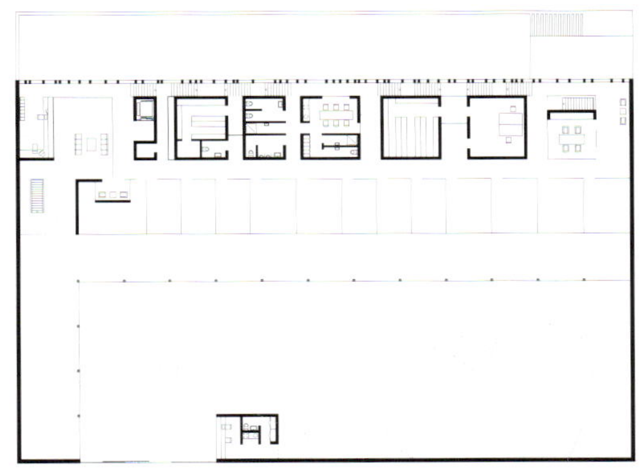

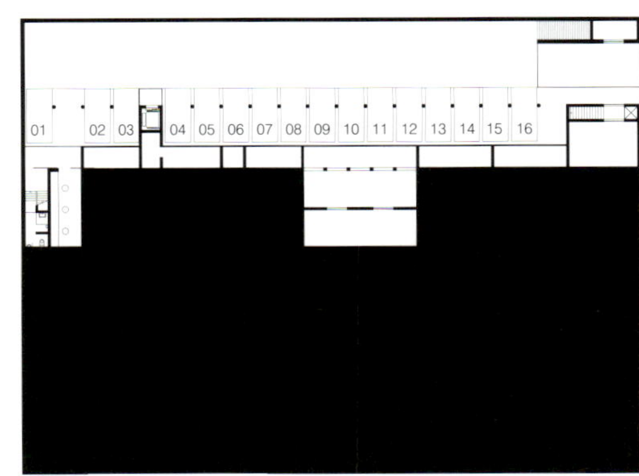
01
02
03
04
05
06
07
08
09
10
11
12
13
14
15
16

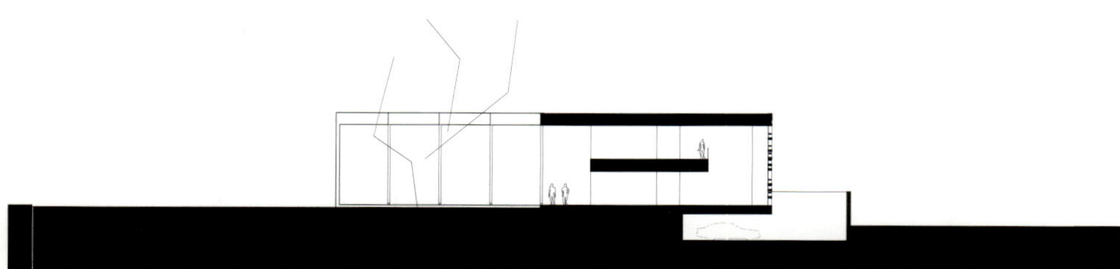

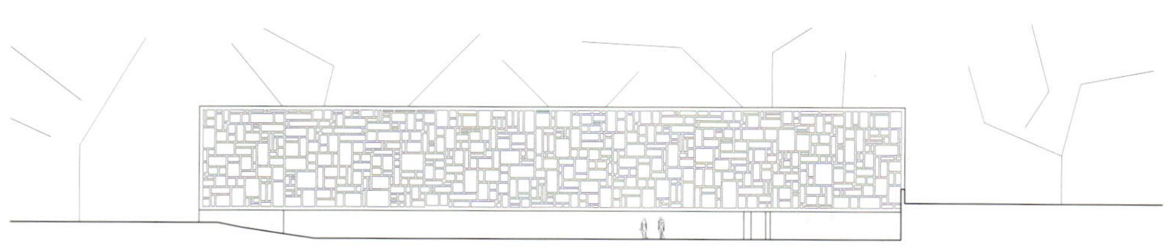

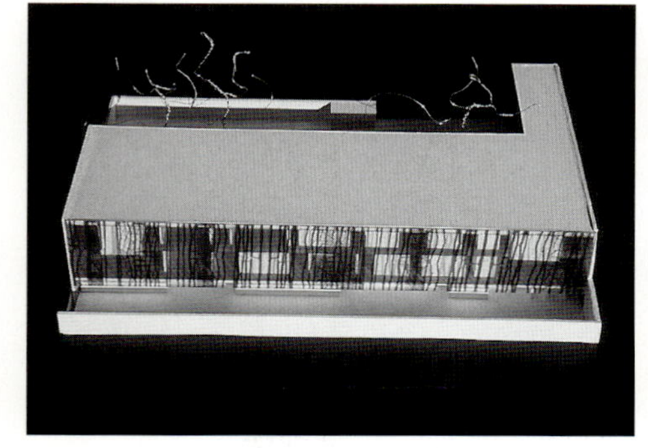

2

2

Chancery

1

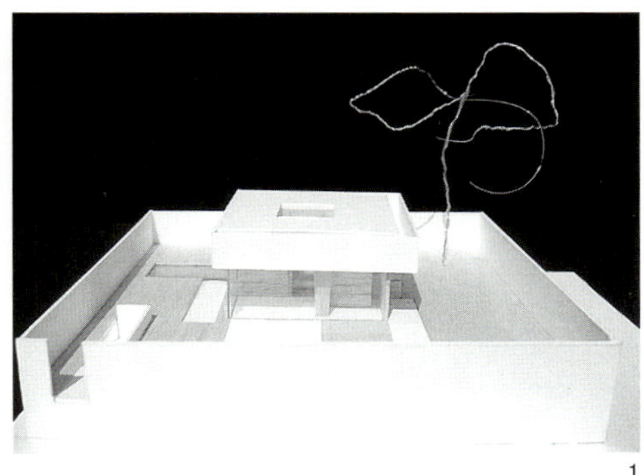

1

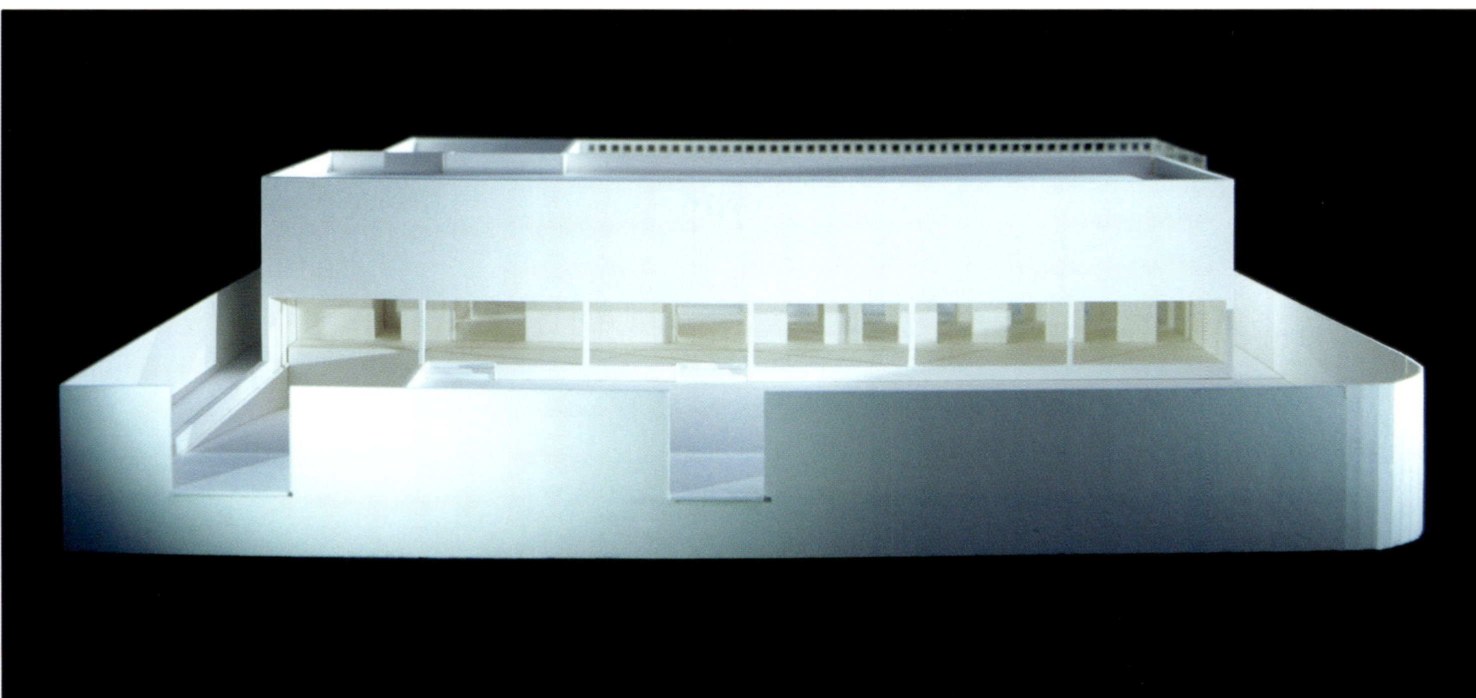

1 Study models for residence
2 Scenes from Maputo
3 Pinto in his workshop

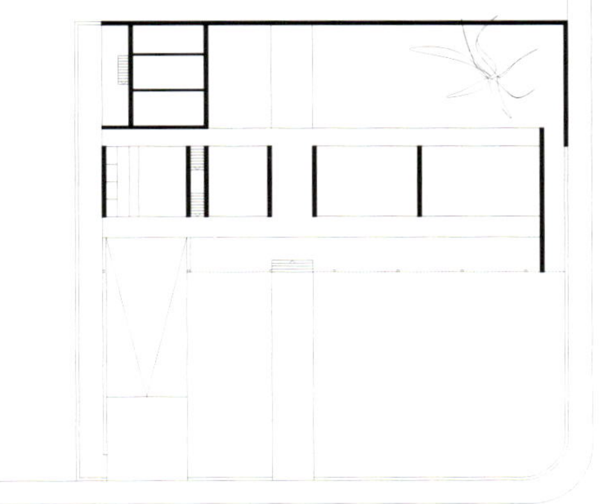

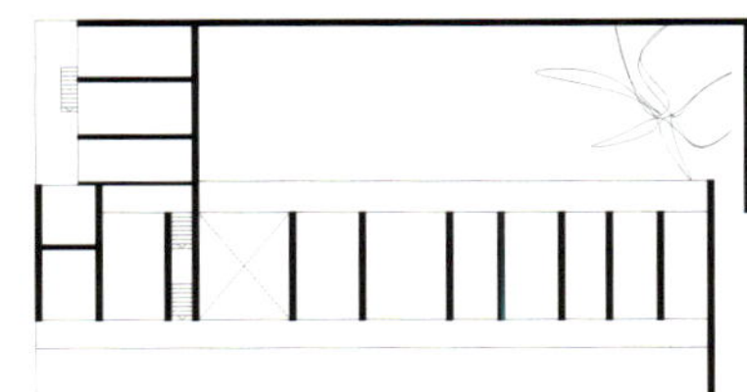

3

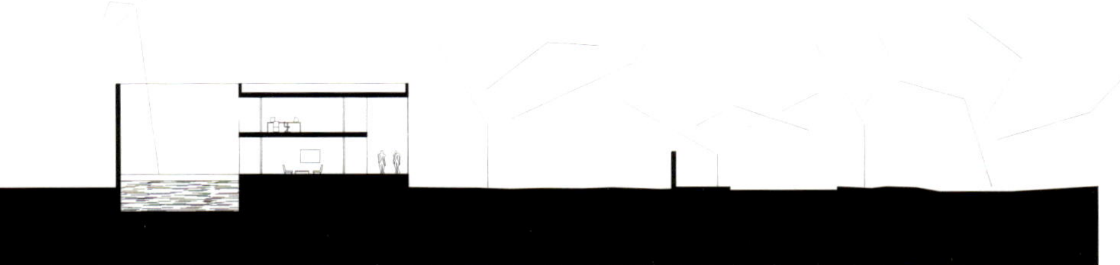

138
HOUSING, FLORIANDE ISLAND 10, HOOFDDORP

In Haarlemmermeer developers are busy constructing a new residential area consisting of twelve islands ranged along a watercourse. Each island accommodates some three hundred dwellings. For one of these islands Claus en Kaan have produced a plan that encompasses subdivision, landscaping and the architecture of the 307 dwellings.

The ratio of surface area to programme is so tight as to leave very little scope for public space on the island. To make the neighbourhood look as spacious as possible, public space has been concentrated at the entrance to the quarter where there will be an irregular planting of birch trees, as an overture to this relaxed, green neighbourhood, with landscape architecture by Annemieke Diekman. This solution can be seen as the spatial planning version of a motif that recurs in many Claus en Kaan housing projects where the architectural fireworks are usually reserved for collective entrance lobbies.

Cars are hidden away in courts so as to avoid disrupting the streetscape and more the street profile. As a result, the hedges lining the front gardens, which are part of the landscape design, are able to contribute fully to the impression of this neighbourhood as a delightful green spot, in much the same way as Jorn Utzon has done in Copenhagen.

The dwellings are spacious and efficient. The architecture is deliberately simple, the only special touches being a handsome brick and Provençal roof tiles. They strengthen the intended impression of a hedonistic lifestyle that has nothing to do with anything so arduous as running a household.

1

1

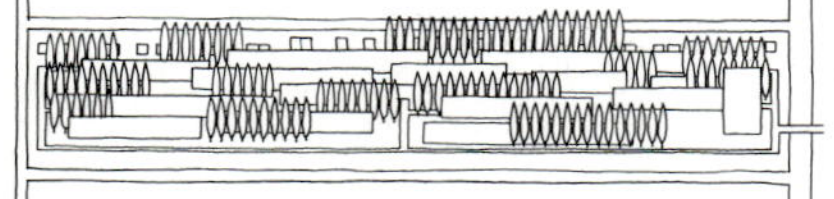

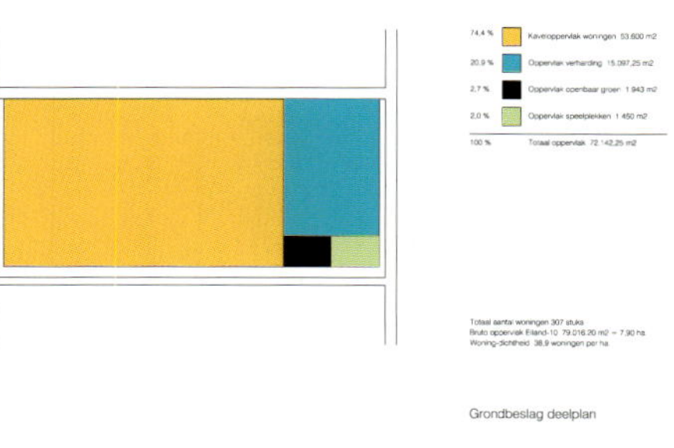
Grondbeslag deelplan

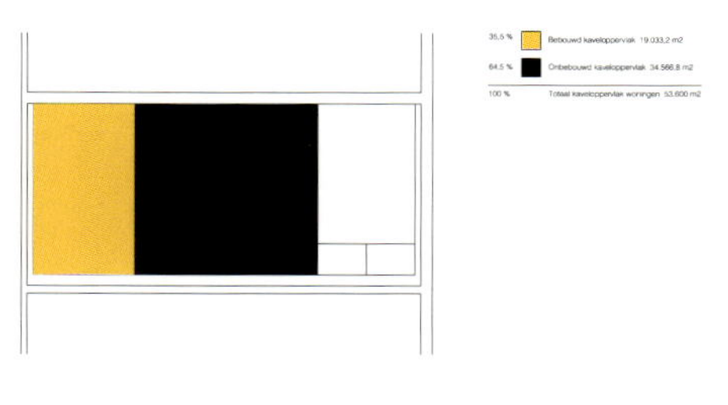

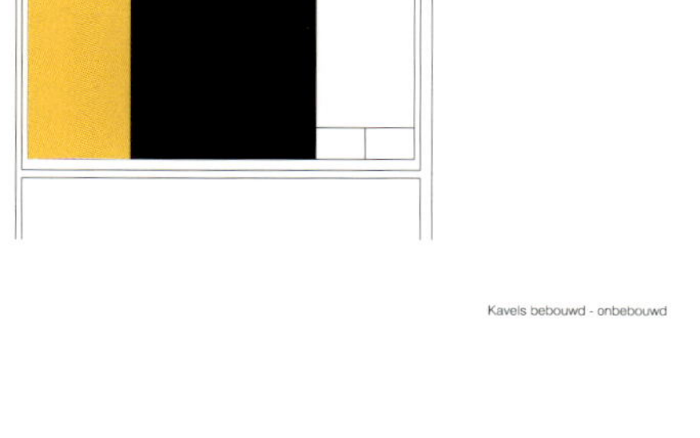
Kavels bebouwd - onbebouwd

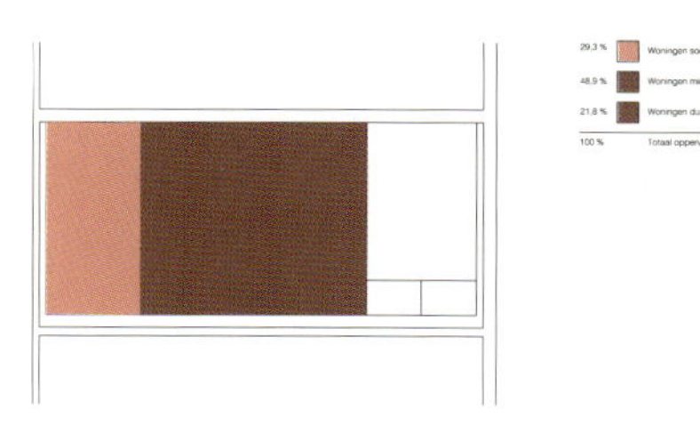
Woningcategorieën in aantallen

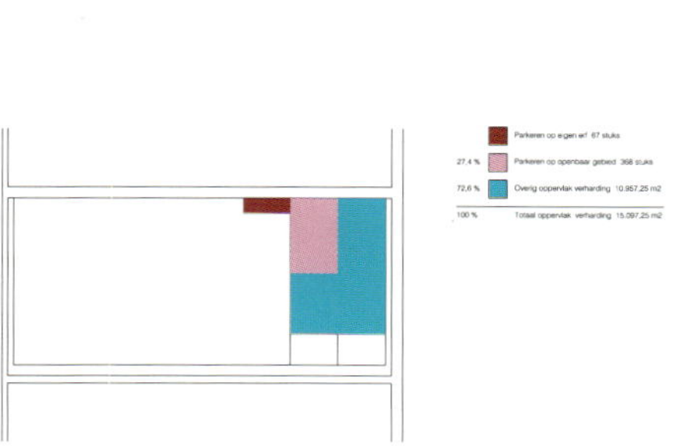
Parkeren

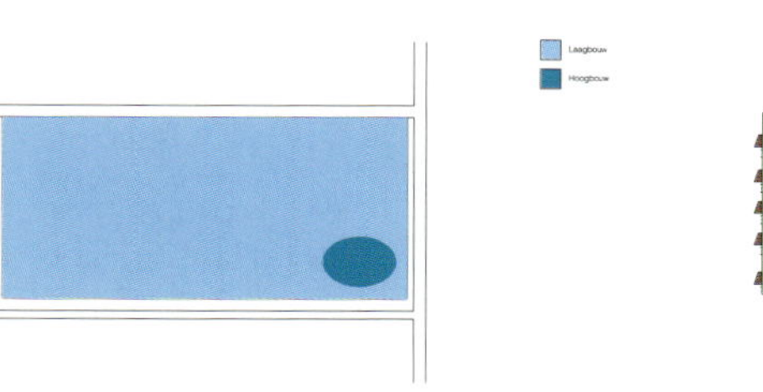
Morfologie

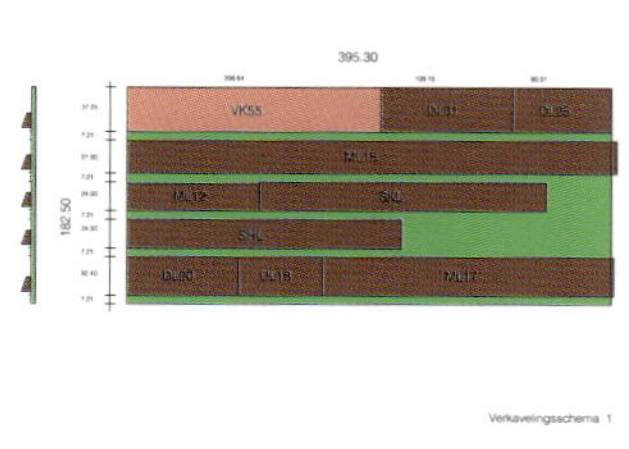
Verkavelingsschema 1

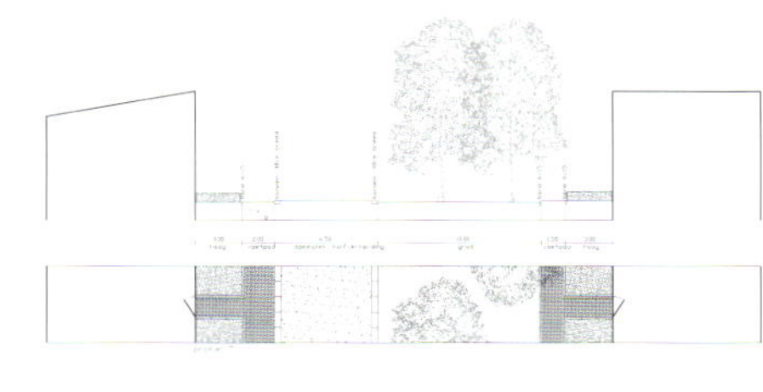

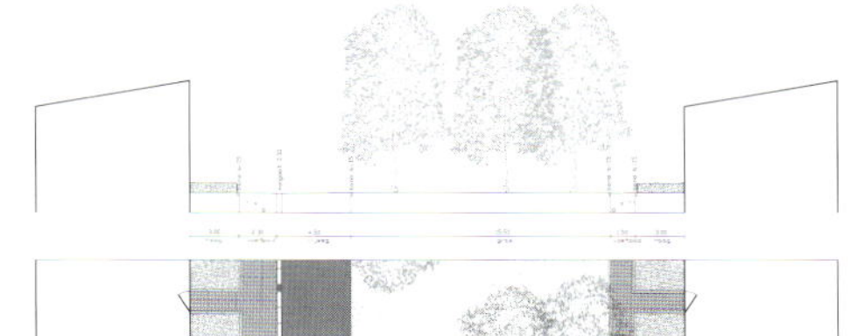

2

1 Jørn Utzon, housing scheme in Fredensborg, 1979
2 Landscape design proposals by Annemieke Diekman
3 Acer Campestre
4 Genus Betula

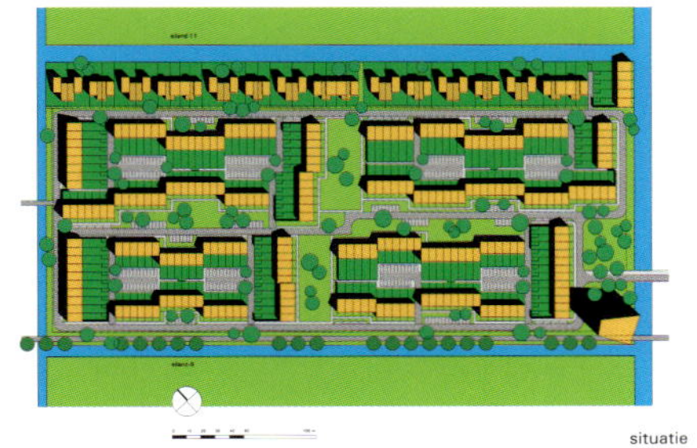

situatie

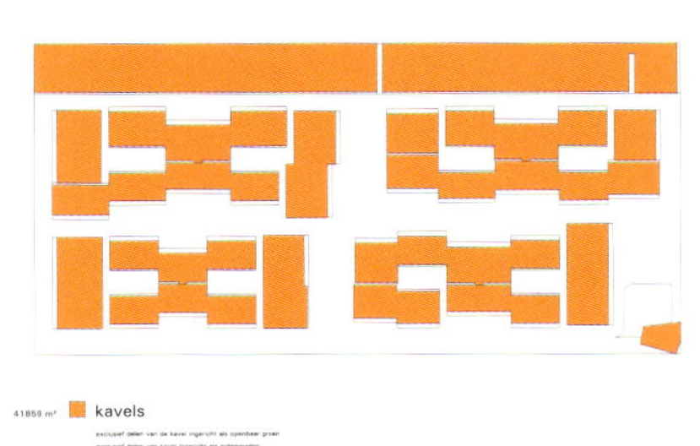

kavels

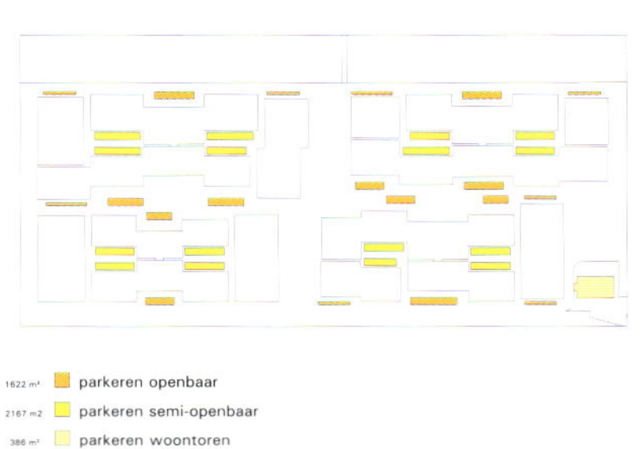

parkeren

3

groen

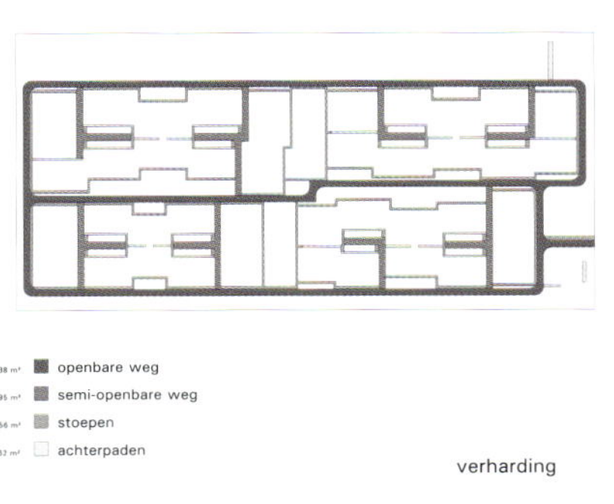

verharding

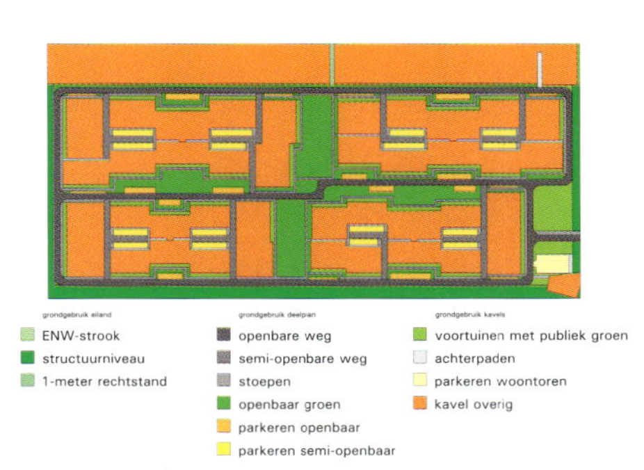

4

141
URBAN DESIGN, HAVEN-EILAND AND RIETEILANDEN, AMSTERDAM

IJburg is a development area east of Amsterdam that is being built on a cluster of artificial islands in the IJ lake. Eventually some fifty thousand people will live here. The urban design for the first phase of 3,600 dwellings was made by Claus en Kaan in collaboration with Frits van Dongen of Architekten Cie. and Ton Schaap of Schaap & Stigter. As a guard against formal caprice, the plan is based on the most neutral configuration urban design has to offer: a non-hierarchical grid.
The neutrality of the grid is matched by the freedom allowed in the elaboration of the fields. There is a programme for the blocks and there are a (limited) number of building rules, but they prescribe neither form nor typology and are little more than 'zoning laws'. The idea was to provide 'the conditions ... for a balance between order and chaos, consistency and variation'.

The rules that must be observed in the development of the fields in the grid relate chiefly to the street frontage. In the plan for IJburg, the street is the 'agent of urbanity', and density an indispensable ingredient. With sixty dwellings per hectare the density will be twice that of the average new suburban development. And the addition of a substantial programme of office space and amenities makes it potentially much more than an ordinary suburb.

An essential aspect of the grid plan is the contrast between street and block, between two worlds of inside and outside. The streets running on endlessly to the horizon and the enclosed space of the inner courts satisfy two universal human needs, to be part of the wider world and to enjoy the shelter of one's own private domain.

The main streets are 30 metres wide, the average street 22 metres. Precondition number one is a continuous street frontage. It is further stipulated that 'development along the streets is to be formal and at least three storeys high', that 'living should take place on the street side' and that dwellings abutting the street should also have their front door there. And, as in the historic canal zone, 'living on the street' is best served by placing the living room half a metre above street level. In addition, the blocks are to be bordered by a 1.20 meter wide margin to be used for a flight of steps or a small front garden that will act as a transition between public and private. The rest – how the street elevations should look, how the programme is fitted into the block and what happens in the courtyards – is not laid down, and that is unusual in the Netherlands. Nearly every block is made up of sub-projects designed by different architects under the direction of a block supervisor. The fact that the programme for each block is much too large to be accommodated in a standard perimeter block, is intended to stimulate architects to come up with innovative solutions.

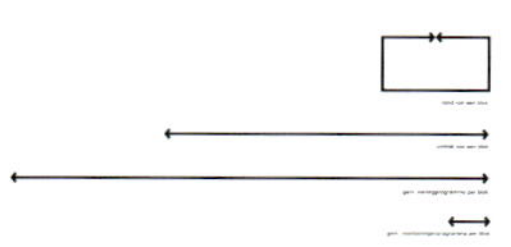

Programme in block

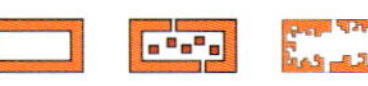

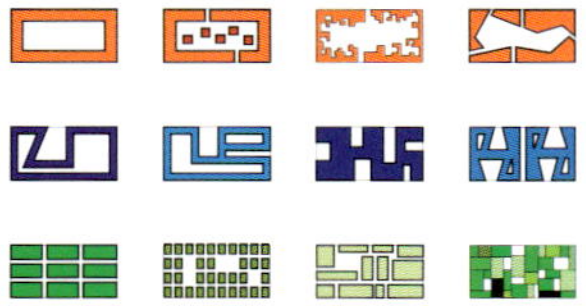

Strategies for block infills

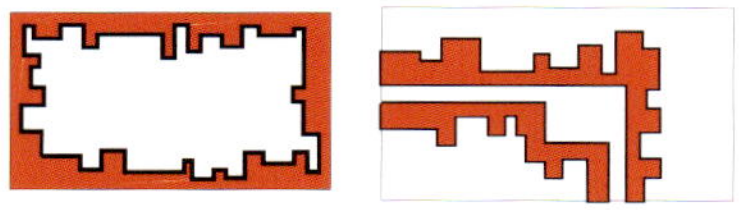

Formal perimeter, informal interior

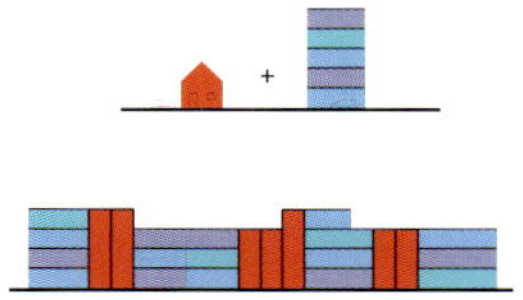

Typological mix

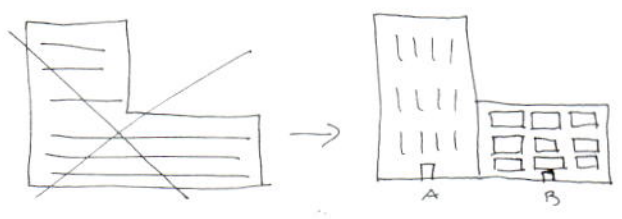

Typological mix

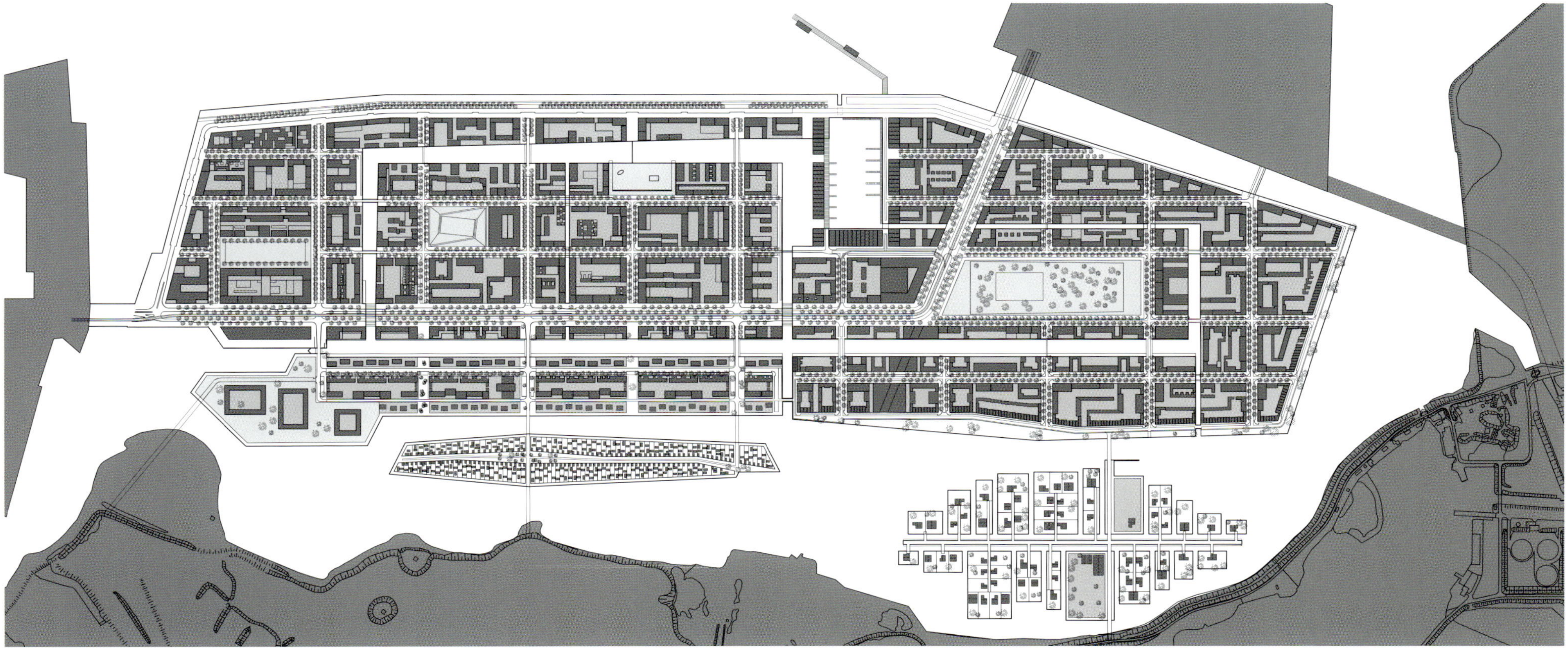

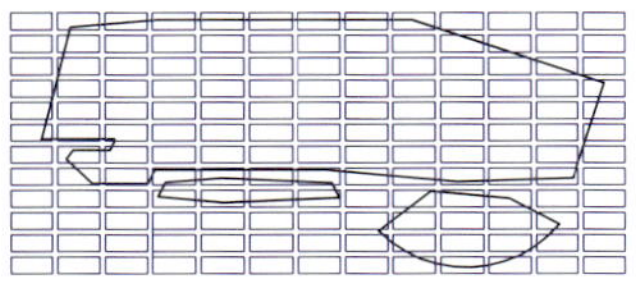

Grid

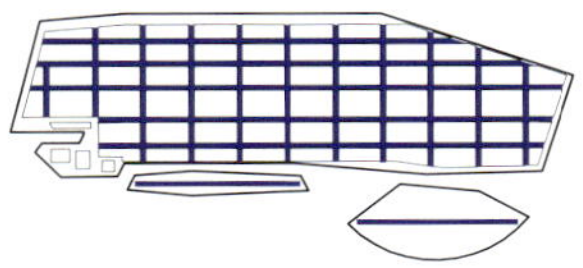

Streets

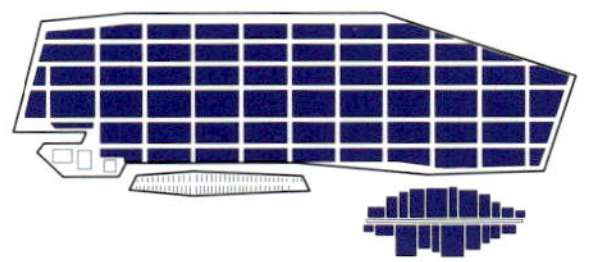

Blocks

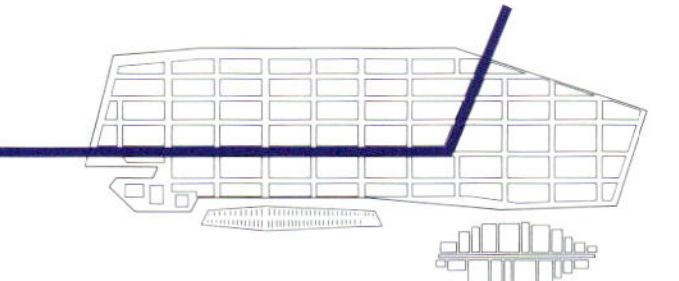

Boulevard

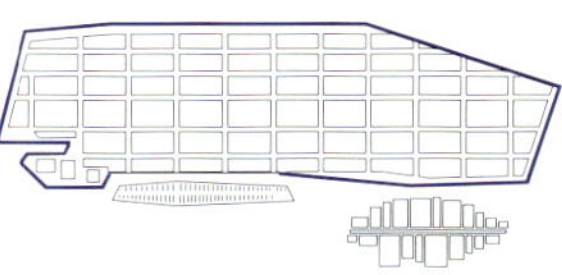

Perimeter

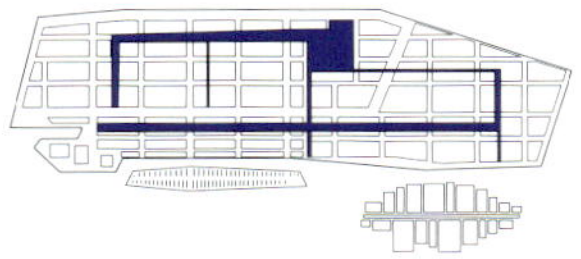

Water

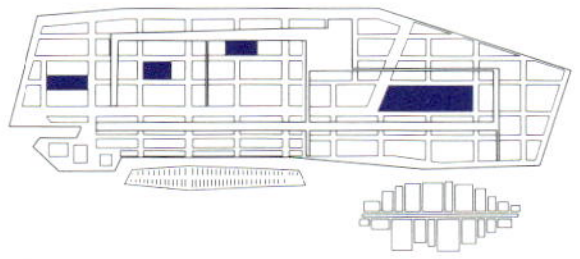

Parks

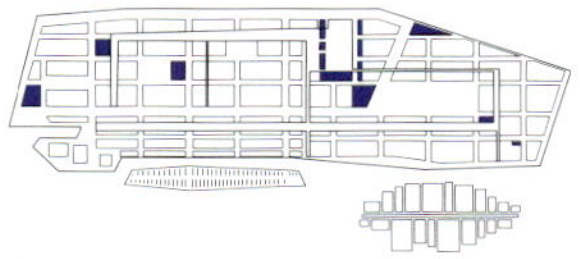

Solids

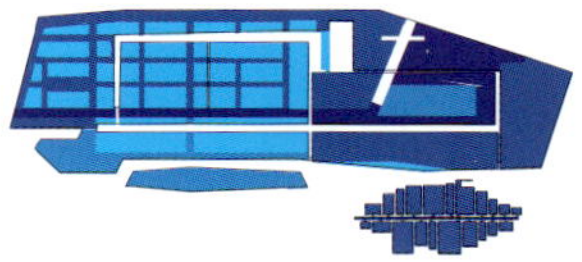

Differences in height

Urban Design, Haveneiland and Rieteilanden, Amsterdam

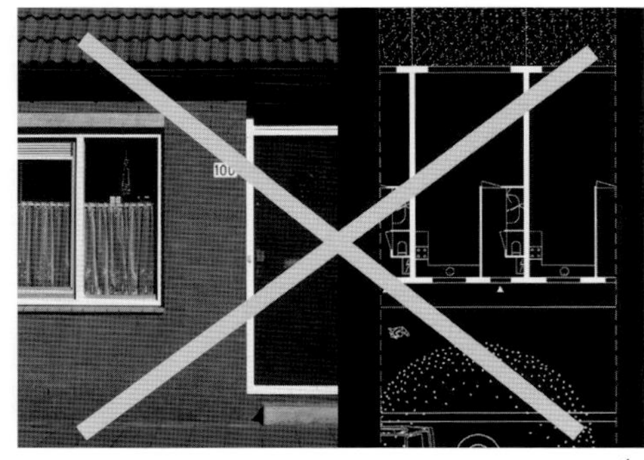

1a

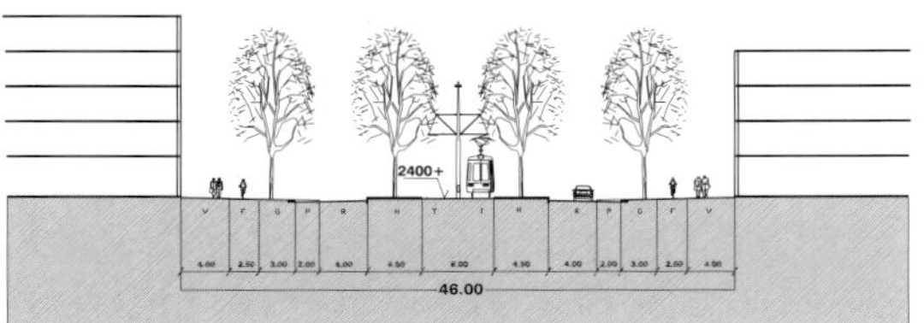

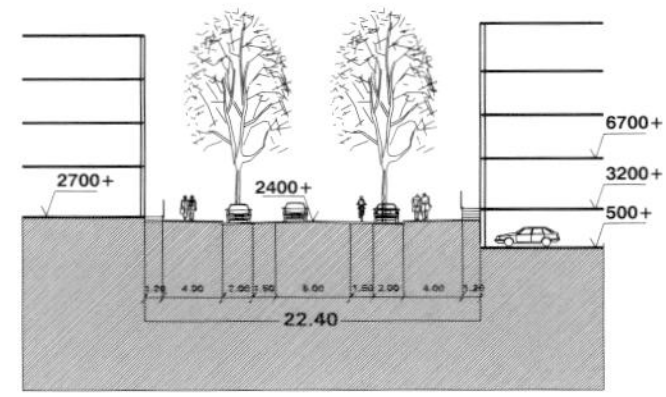

1b

1c

1 Desired streetscape: *a* no continuous street elevation, *b* 3.50 metre storey height on ground floor, *c* green spaces
2 Step-by-step consolidation of the grid to give formal street elevations and informal interior spaces
3 Berenice Abbott, Union Square, New York, 1938

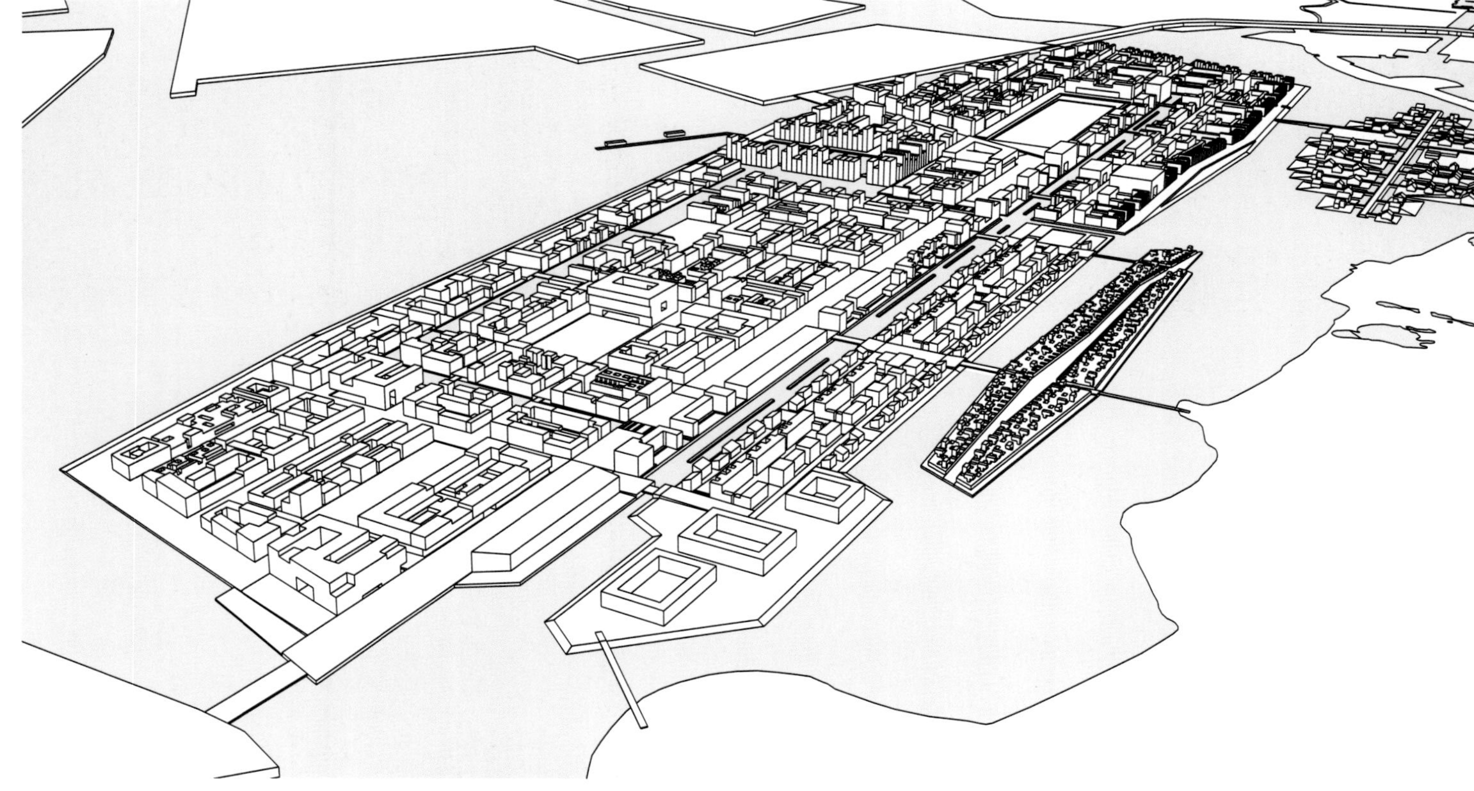

2

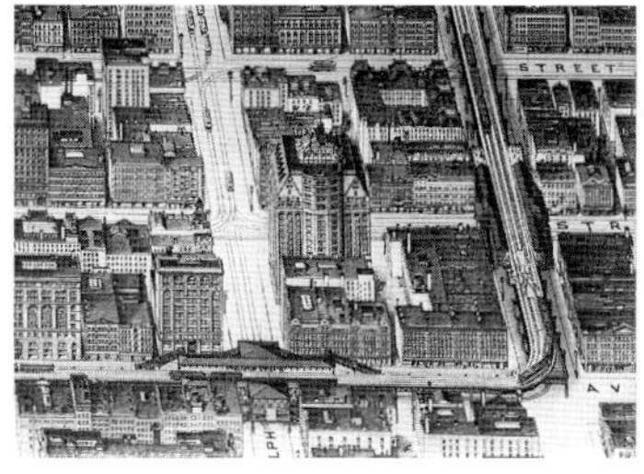

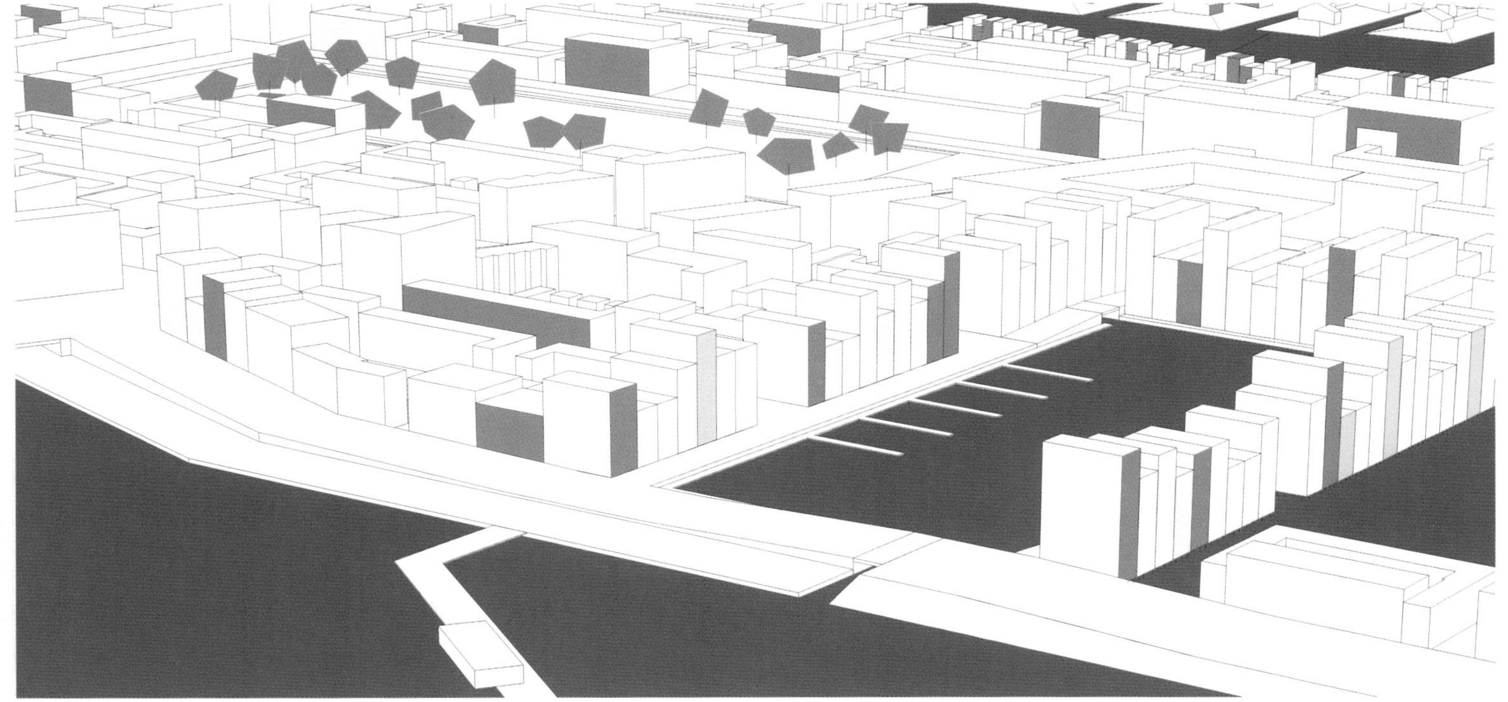

3

144
HOTEL, OOSTELIJKE HANDELSKADE, AMSTERDAM

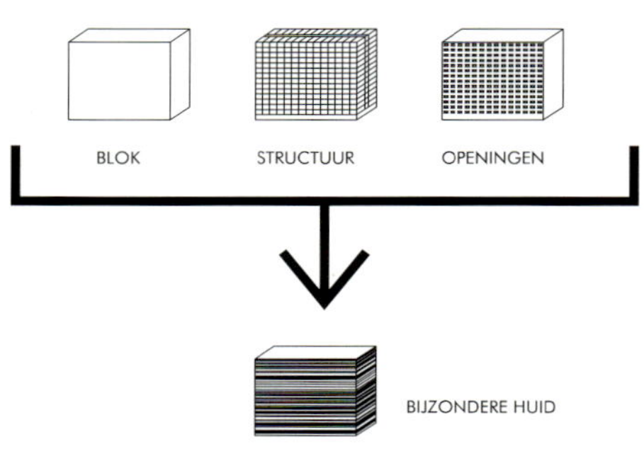

The hotel on the IJ inlet, not far from Amsterdam's Central Station, is part of a mixed development comprising a tall office tower, a cruise terminal and a music centre in addition to the hotel. The buildings share a continuous plinth out of which they rise as four autonomous volumes. These volumes, whose silhouette was laid down in the city council's spatial master plan, have nothing to do with one another except for the fact that they all demand attention.

It was not only the building's spatial envelope that was determined in advance; another given was the complex programme. The plinth contains a car park, a coach terminal and conference facilities. Out of the plinth rises the semi-public section of the five-star hotel: the lobby, which is the spatial and organizational node between the substructure and the tower with its 400 hotel rooms occupying the sixth to the nineteenth floors.

The skin of the hotel tower consists of horizontal bands of green granite, white marble, glass and white concrete. Their effect is to deprive the facade of legibility since they express neither the concatenation of cells of which the hotel is composed nor the standard floor height. In this respect the hotel is related the tower block in Groningen with the illusory disruption of scale in one of the head elevations. In addition, the imperviousness of the cool, stony skin explicitly insulates the building from its visually busy surroundings.

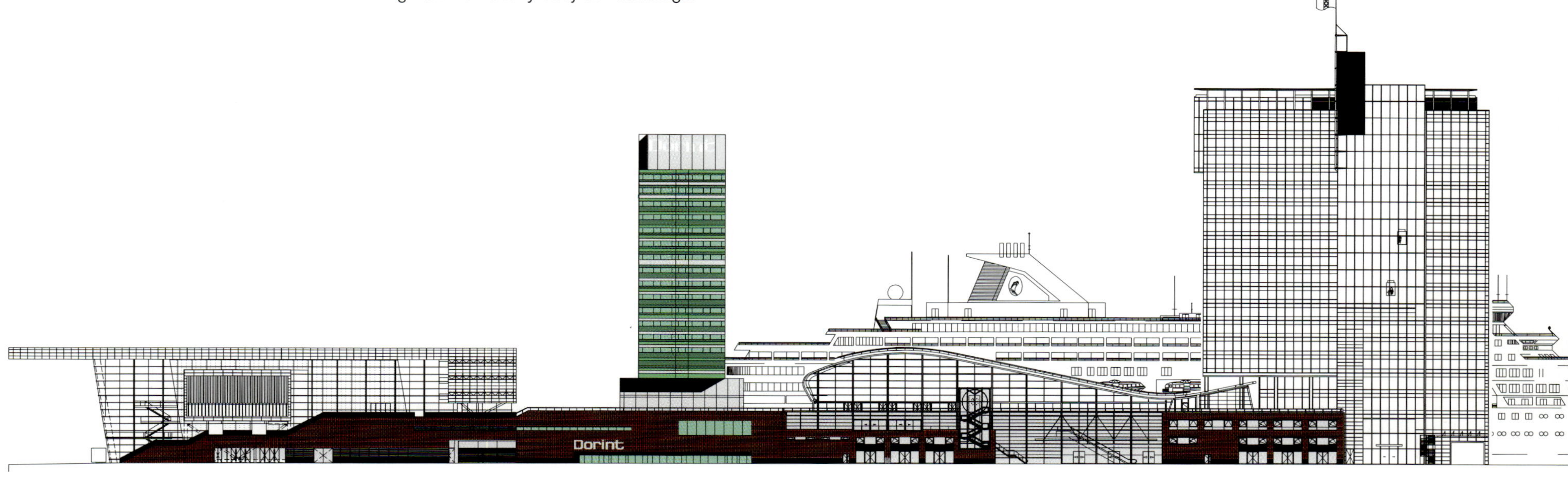

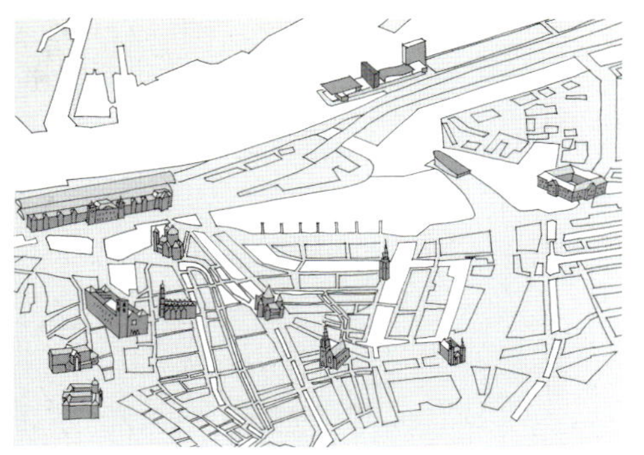

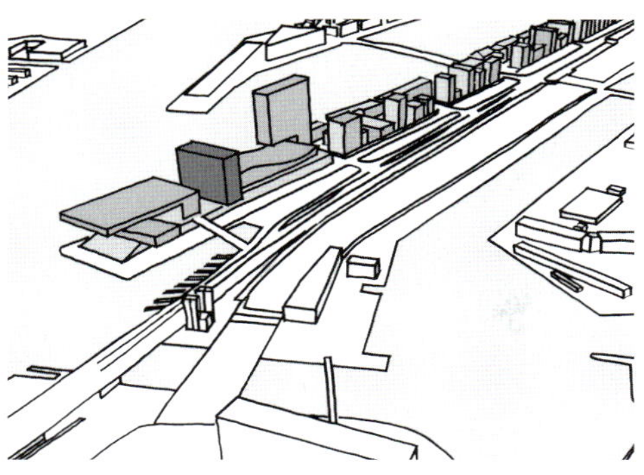

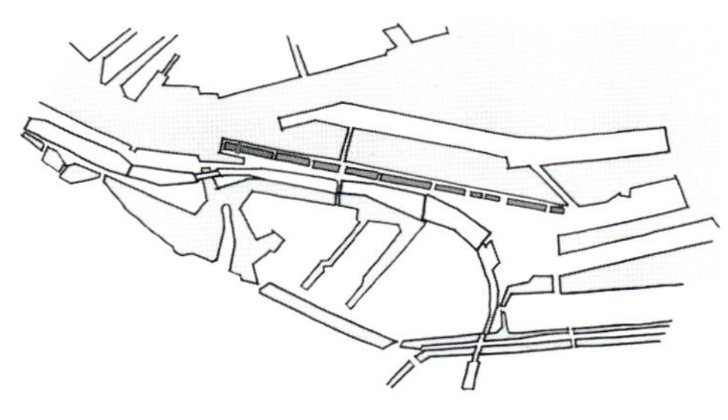

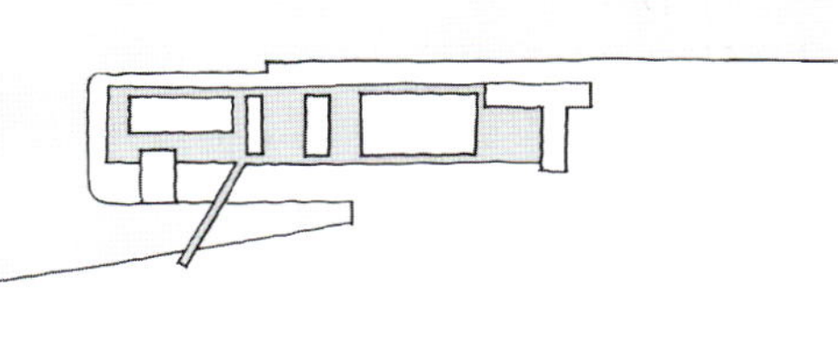

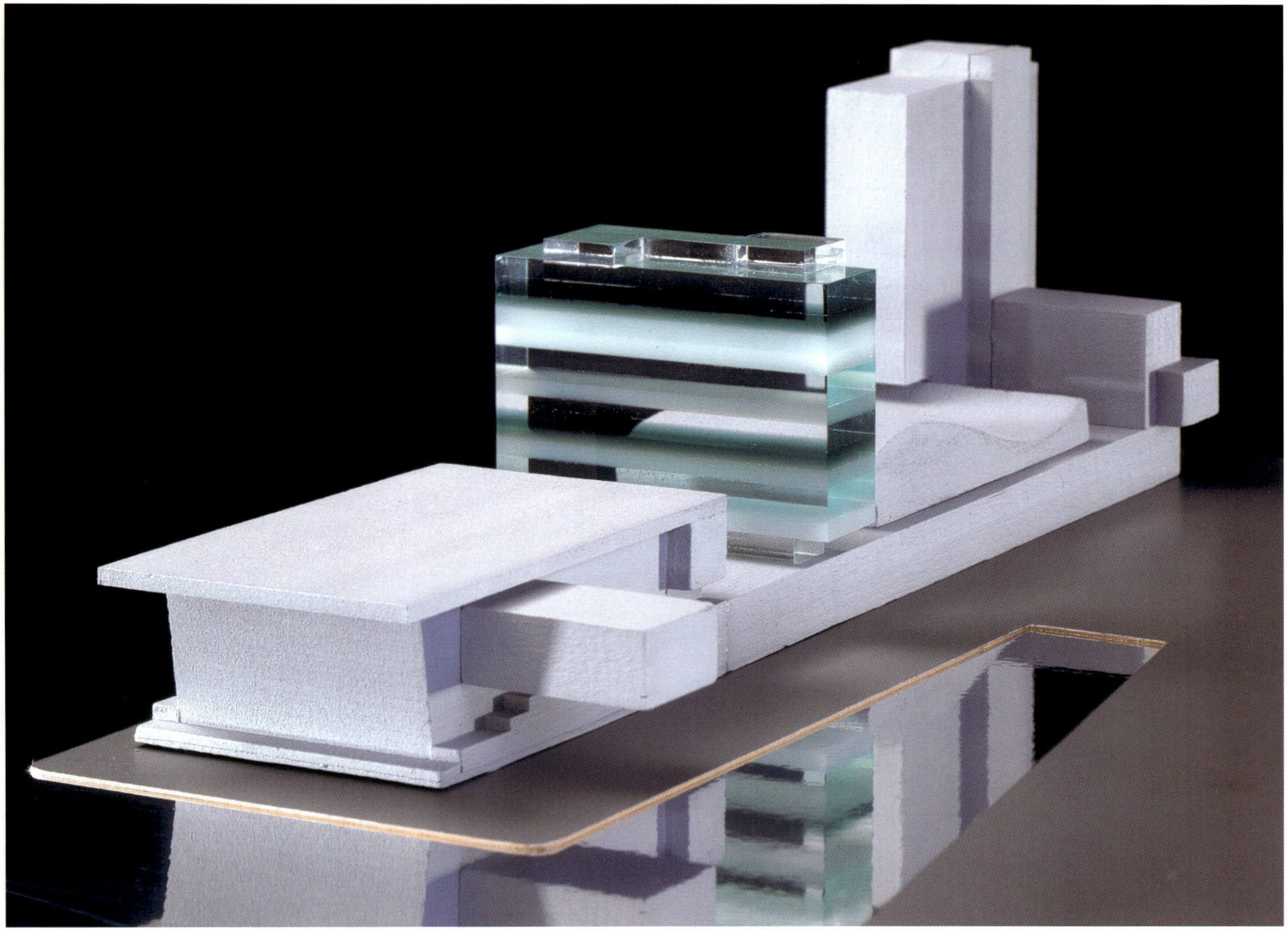

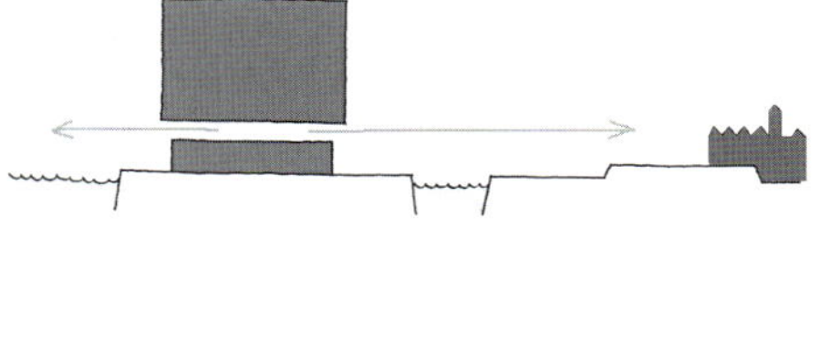

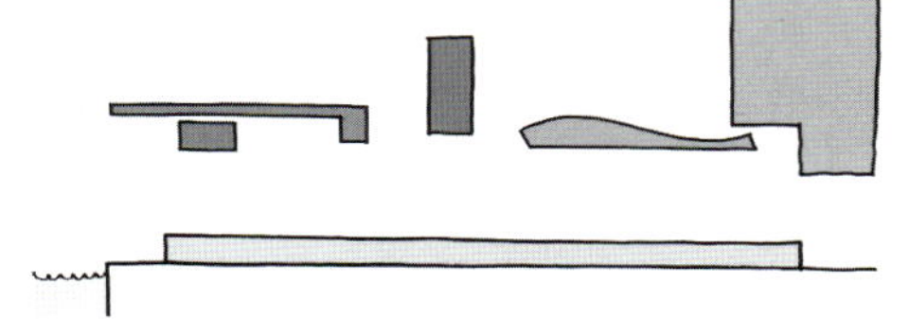

Hotel, Oostelijke Handelskade, Amsterdam

Luigi Moretti, office building with apartments, Milaan, 1951–1953

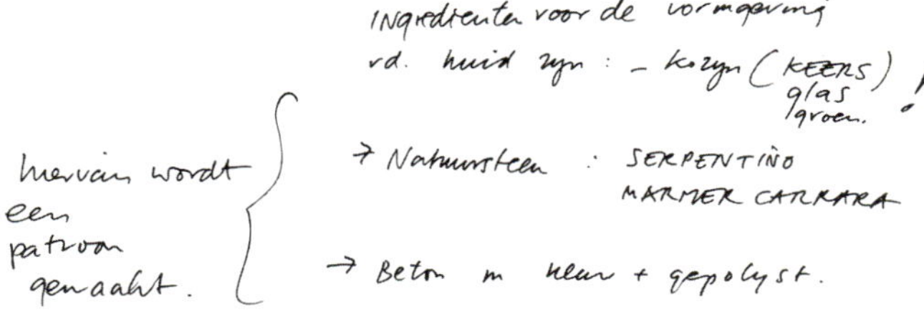

PATROON

Niet "Superimposed" als bij Peter Struycken.
(geen oppervlakte behandeling door iets toe te voegen)

Maar als "textiel weefsel" om de huid te verbijzonderen : vergelijk metselwerk
is er iets beters?

en moet het wel, want het gaat slechts om abstrahering vh oppervlak en vermijden van de "optelling"

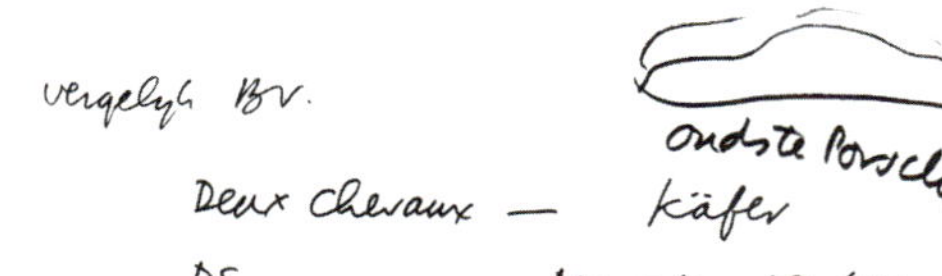

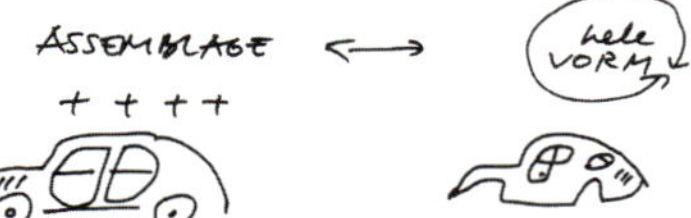

En daarmee vergelijkbaar met

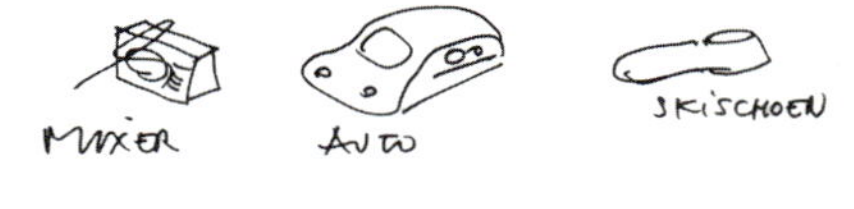

Het is een Ding — vergl Auto (Porsche of Mercedes)

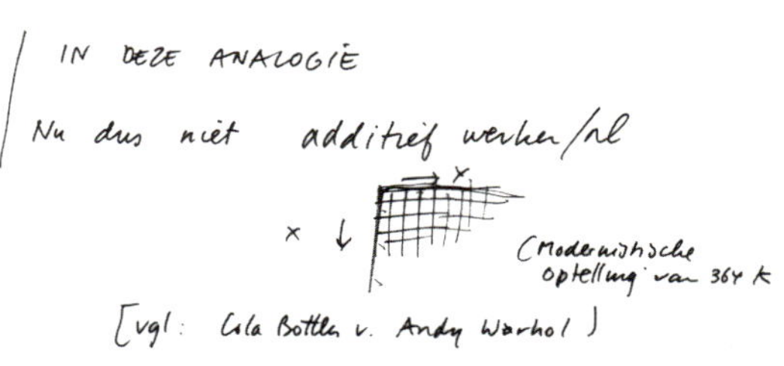

Maar de hele vorm maken.

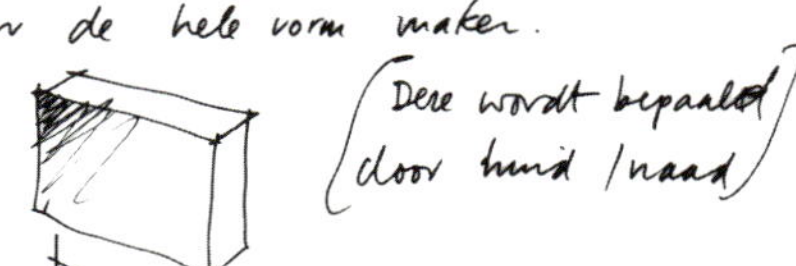

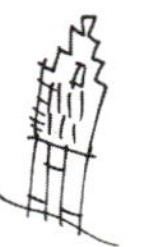

→ Niet verbonden met de aarde.

Lili Schultz, Tea caddies, c. 1928

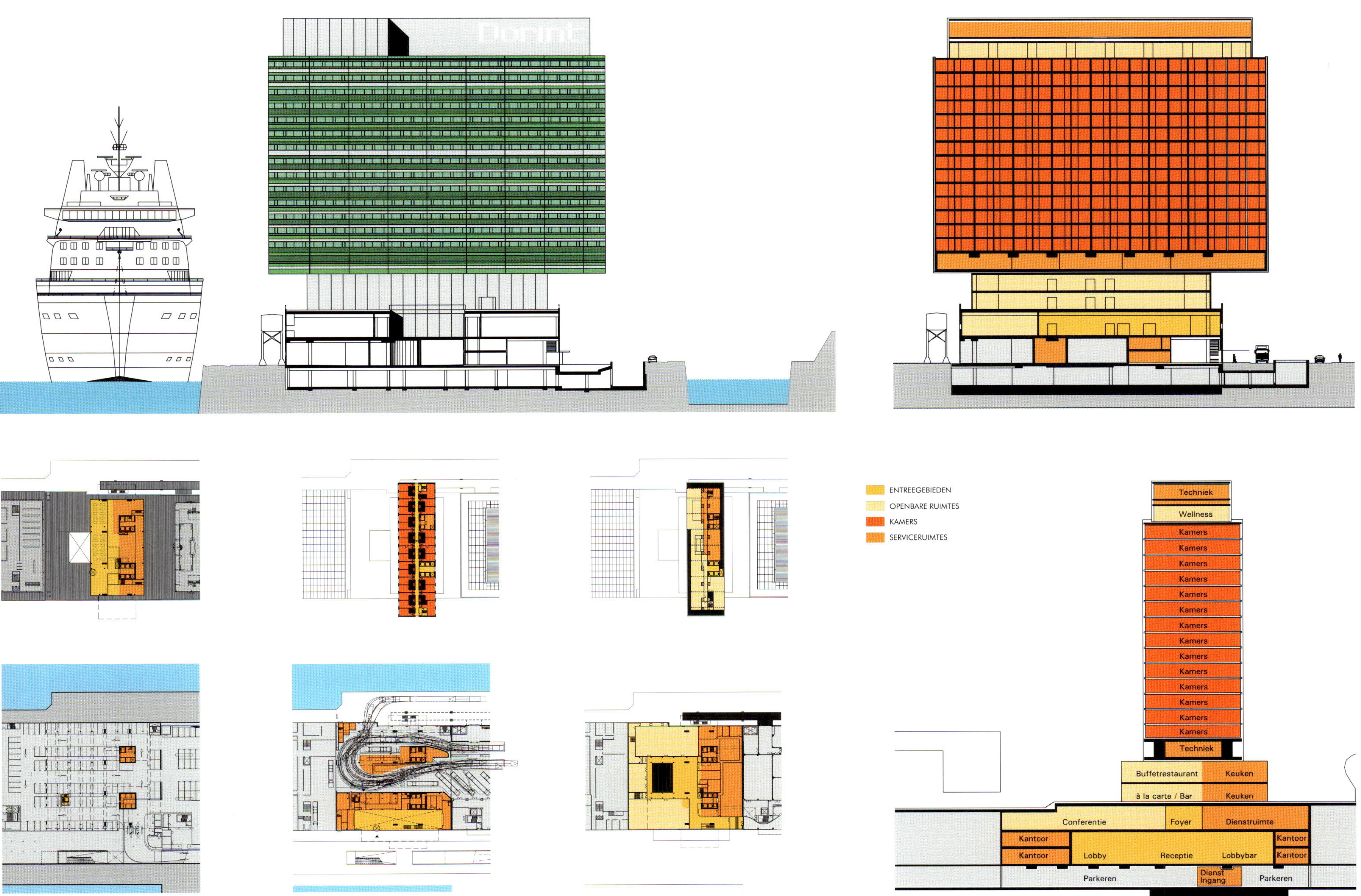

Hotel, Oostelijke Handelskade, Amsterdam

149 186 203
NETHERLANDS FORENSIC INSTITUTE, RIJSWIJK

1

Commissioned to design a new headquarters for the Netherlands Forensic Institute (NFI) on a site on the edge of the Ypenburg residential district and within sight of a spaghetti of motorways, Claus en Kaan produced a boxy structure reminiscent of a civil engineering work in the way it rises up out of a grassy earthwork. Because the NFI wanted to allow for future expansion, the site is a large one and the present structure luxuriates in an extensive landscape. The building is at one and the same time a tightly guarded stronghold and – in response to the client's stated wish – an eye-catching object. Expressed diagrammatically, the NFI programme yielded a corridor almost 1100 metres long, lined on one side by cellular offices and on the other by laboratories. This 'corridor' was then folded to produce a building on four levels, one of which is underground. The programme is arranged around six patios and in such a way that the size and position of the individual laboratories can be adapted to changing circumstances. Symbolic of the completely generic nature of this complex is the spinal void at the centre of the building: an empty hall seventy metres long and seven metres wide and high. It is flanked on either side by three patios lined by offices. The laboratories are located along the outer perimeter of the building.

The complex as a whole is a steel box, with Miesian undertones, that has been cut open to reveal the glazed volume concealed within. The steel box acts as the building's solar shading. Because solar access differs from one elevation to the next, the depth of the steel bands around the building varies, too, with the result that the glass box is not exactly in the centre of the steel box. A comparable subtlety on a bigger scale are the walls of the building, which become progressively thinner as one moves from inside to outside: the patios are surrounded by heavy brick walls punctured by sturdy frames, the innermost corridor wall is of concrete, the outer one of frosted glass and the external wall is of clear glass. The overall effect is a progressive evaporation of the building's mass.

Inside the building the architectural expression and spatial experience are almost entirely determined by material and colour, and by their lustre and tactility. For the rest, form and space are pretty well generic in the interior, except in the section immediately beside the entrance where auditorium, library and conference centre are stacked one above the other. The exterior, in its Donald Judd-like abstraction, is almost nothing but form.

1 Staff of SOM, Knoll, Turner Construction and Connecticut General
2 Durand, assembly of portals, *Précis des leçons d'Architecture. Partie graphique*, Paris, 1821

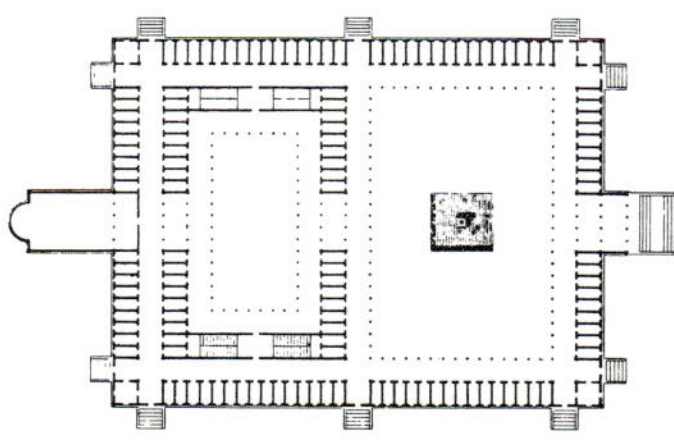
2

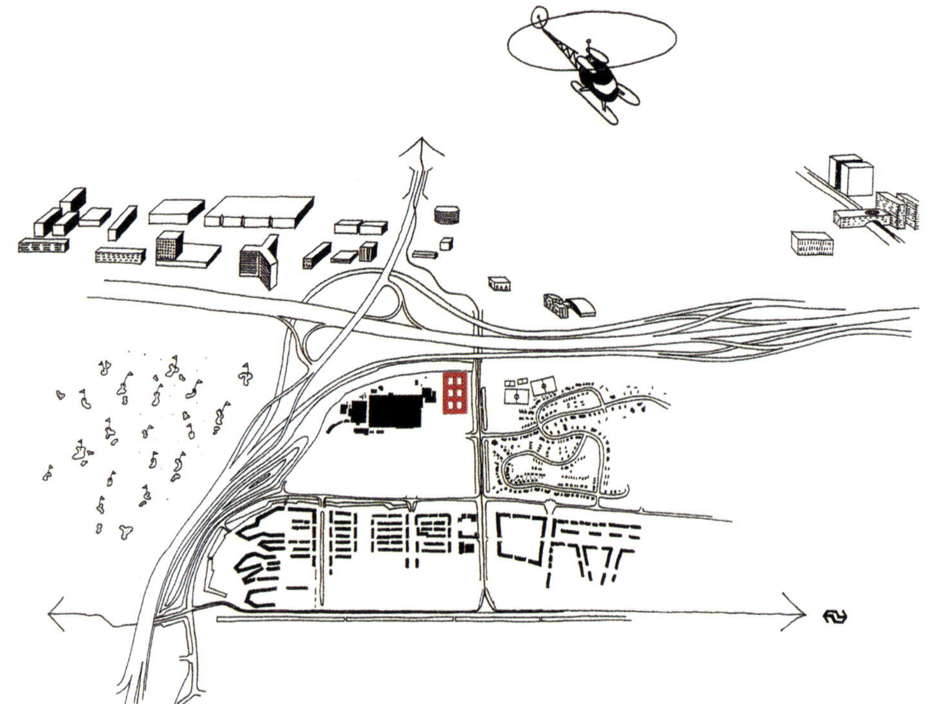

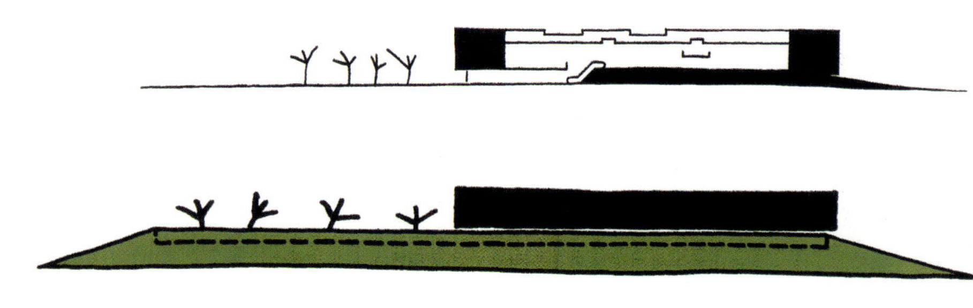

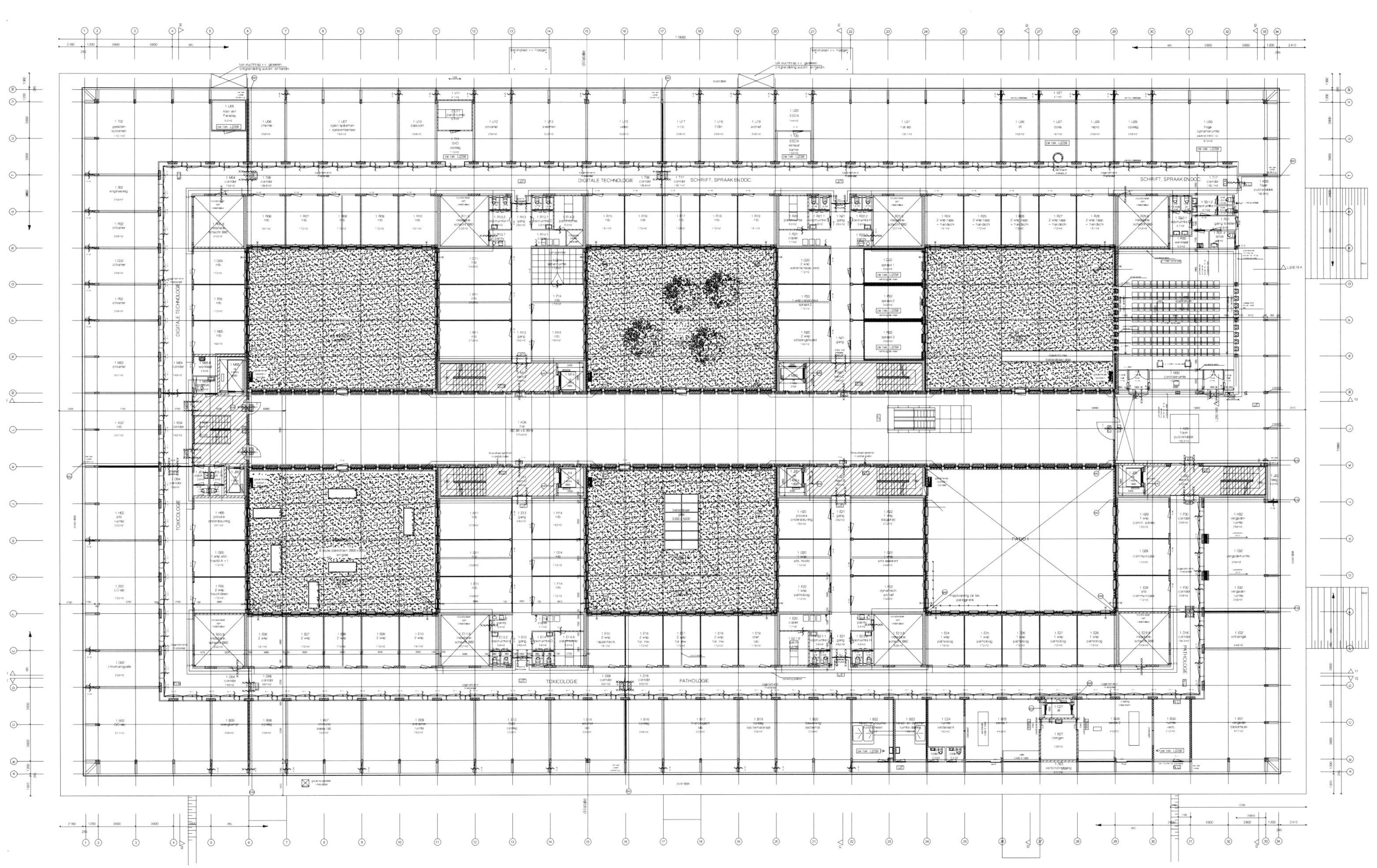

Netherlands Forensic Institute, Rijswijk

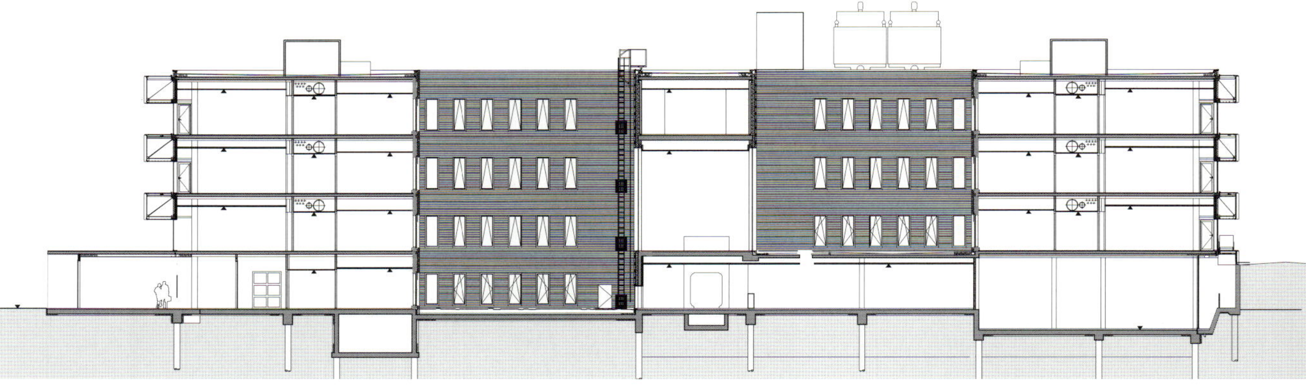

Louis Kahn, Salk Institute for Biological Studies, La Jolla, San Diego, 1959–1967

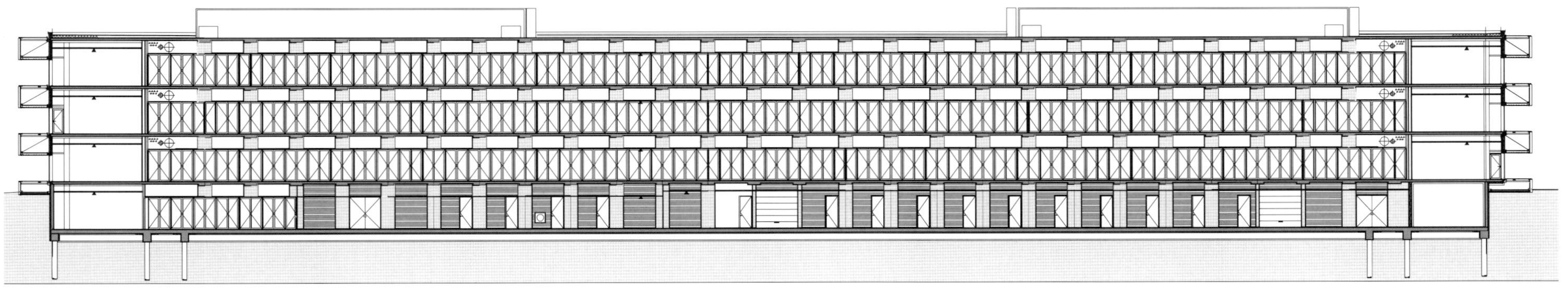

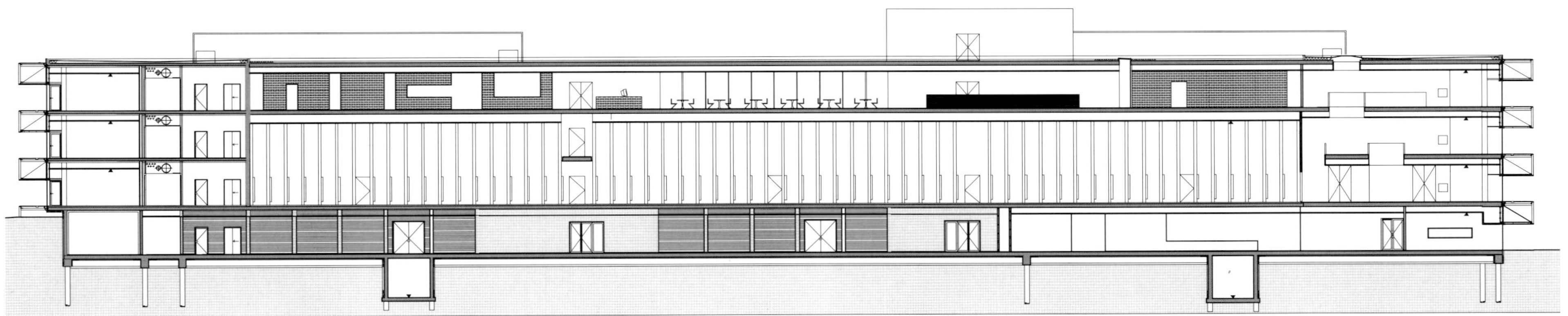

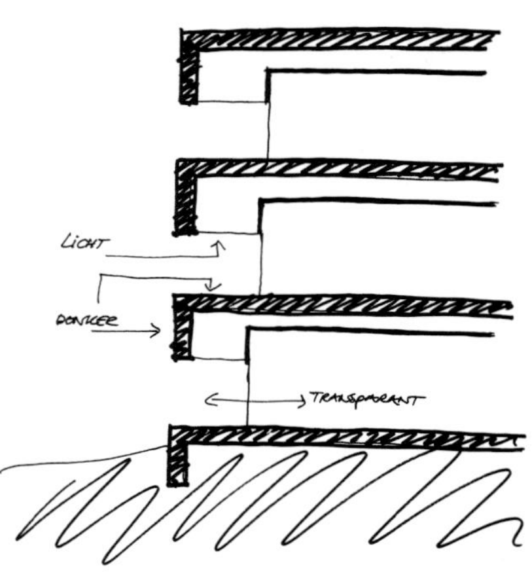

1 Variable dimension of facade bands
2 Donald Judd, untitled, 1968

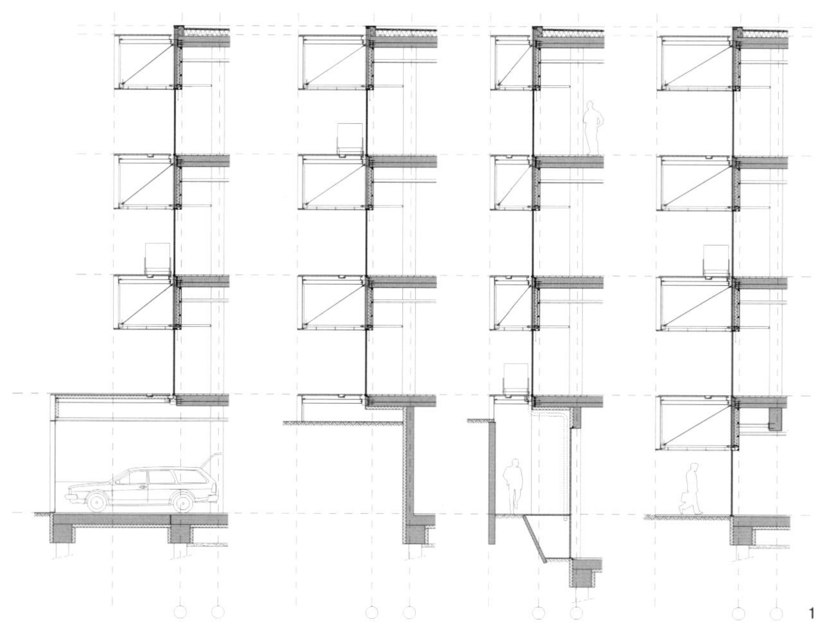

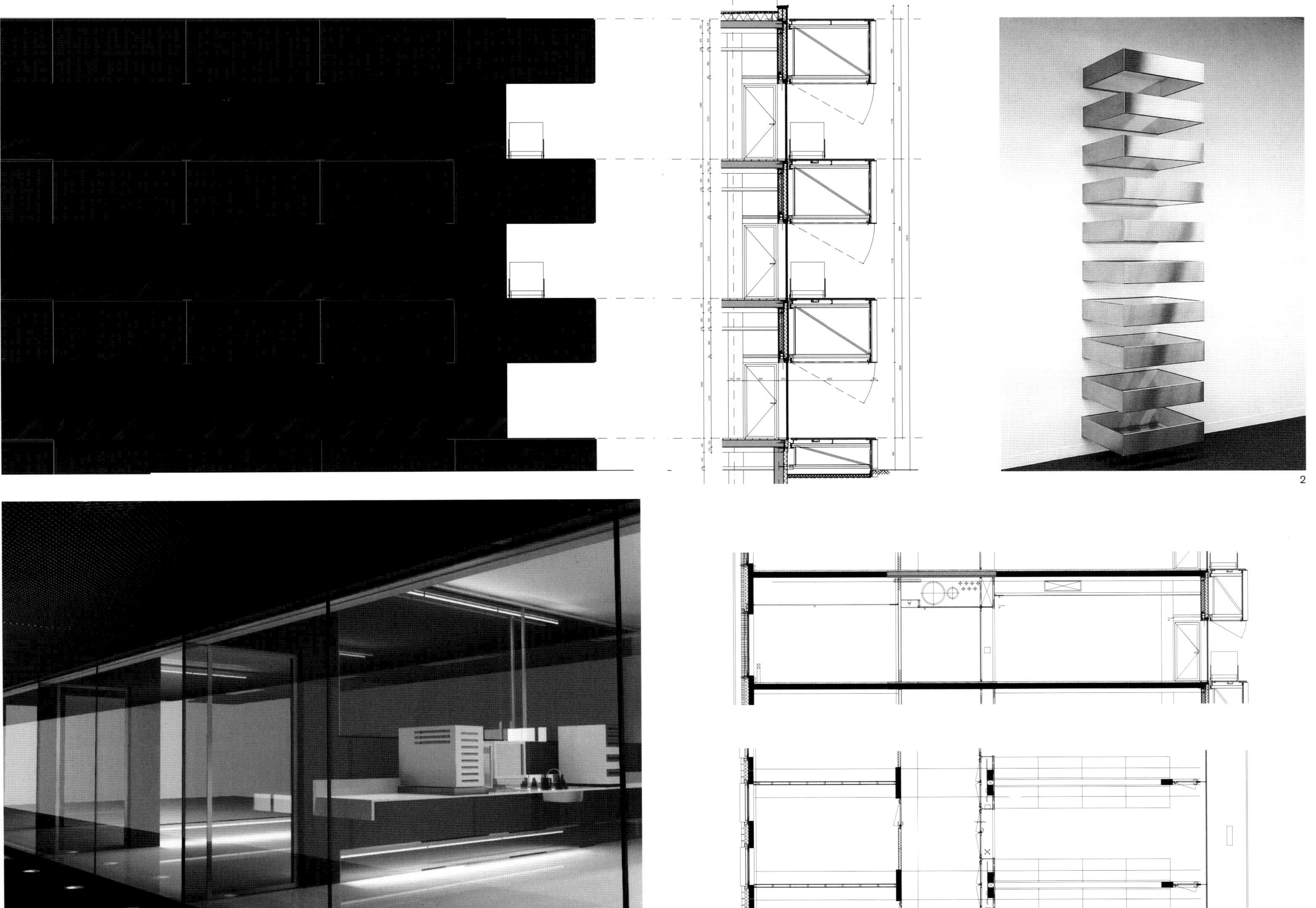

2

151
HOUSING, OOSTELIJKE HANDELSKADE, AMSTERDAM

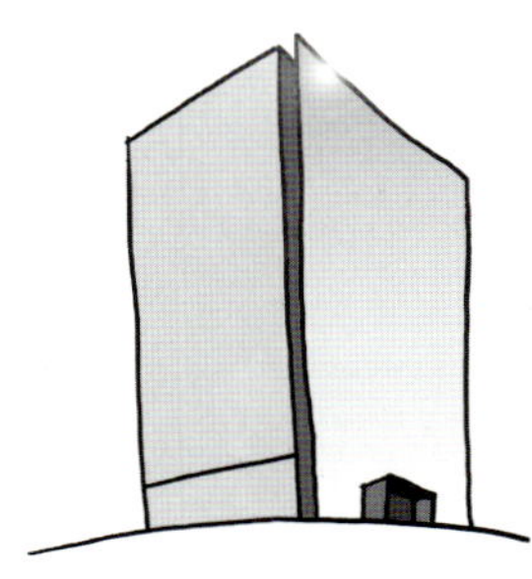

1 Lake Shore Park, Chicago
2 I.M. Pei, King's Bay Plaza, New York, 1962
3 Andy Warhol, Green Coca-Cola Bottles, 1962
4 Auguste Perret, Rue Franklin, Paris, 1904

The robust architecture of Claus en Kaan's apartment building on the Oostelijke Handelskade in Amsterdam appears to be a clear example of 'what you see is what you get'. The grid of concrete frames makes no attempt to conceal the true nature of the object: an assemblage of housing units. By the same token, the very monotony of the concrete frames serves to conceal the variation in the floor plans.

The building, containing 66 subsidized rental units, lies a little further along from the five-star hotel, on a site that was once occupied by a contiguous development of warehouses and industrial buildings. Most of these have since been demolished and what remains of the docklands architecture is now being subsumed in a redevelopment scheme designed by Kees Christiaanse Architects and Planners. By Amsterdam standards, the scheme represents a considerable densification of what was previously a peripheral zone. Claus en Kaan's apartment block, which is essentially an ordinary galleried apartment block, conjures up at least two other images. While the rationalistic simplicity gives it the appearance of an industrial building, the refinement of the grid-facade betrays a family resemblance to American high-rise buildings of the 1960s designed by the likes of I.M. Pei. Where the grid-facade ends, these similarities disappear and the building abruptly changes character. Here the shell has burst open to reveal a softer, and, thanks to the colours, warmer side.

1

2

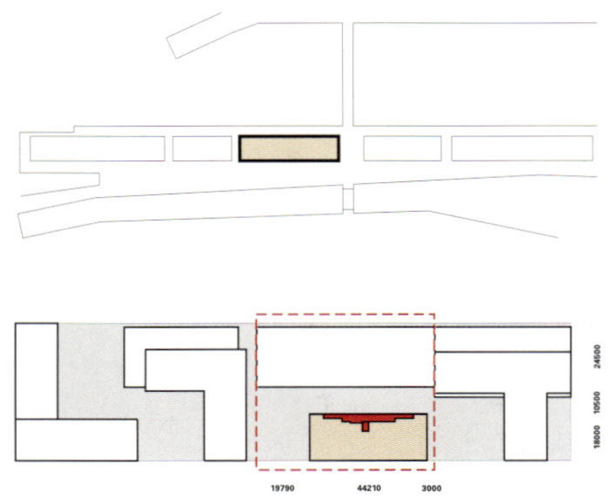

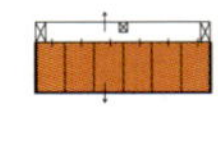

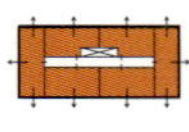

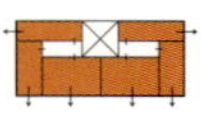

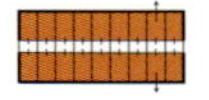

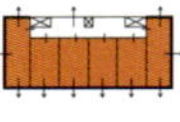

3

4

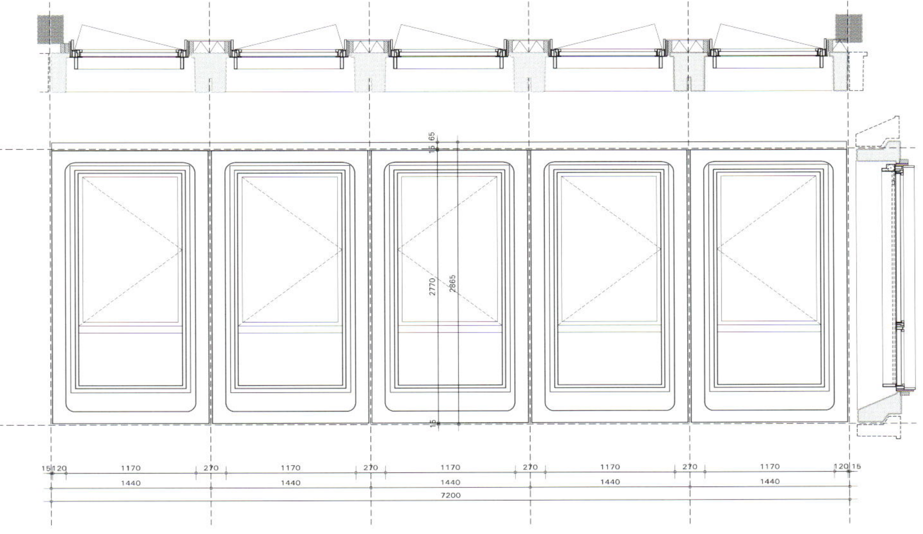

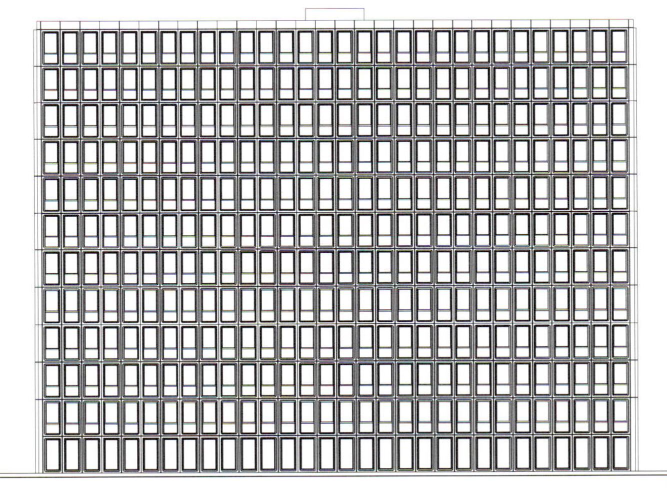

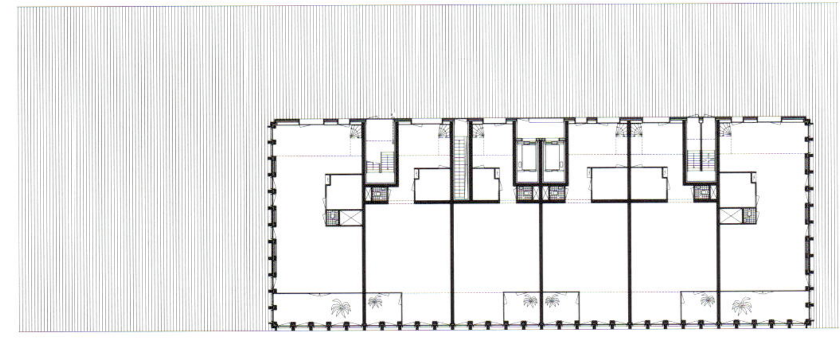

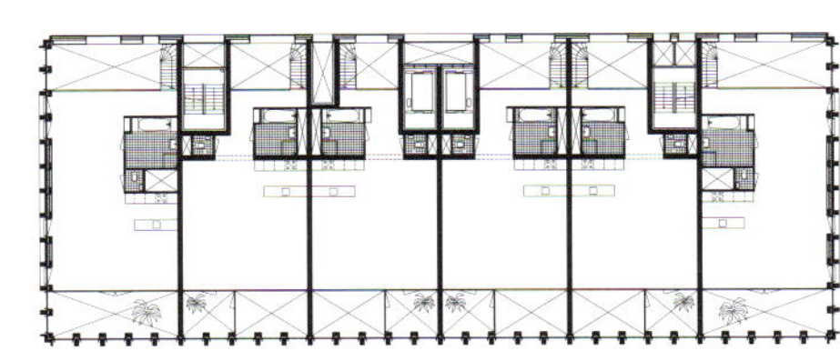

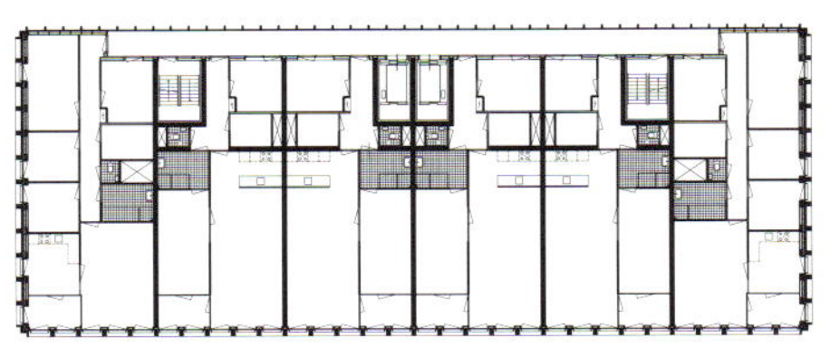

Housing, Oostelijke Handelskade, Amsterdam

165
MUNICIPAL OFFICES, BREDA

The extension to the building for local government officials is part of the redevelopment of the Chassé site in the centre of Breda to a master plan drawn up by Rem Koolhaas's Office for Metropolitan Architecture. Both the programme (office space) and the envelope (a long box) were laid down in the brief.

Taking the box as given, the architects then sought the optimal depth required for a layout with a central corridor with one- and two-desk offices along one side and large office spaces on the other. The construction, too, was influenced by the brief. The decision to place the building on columns, for example, was a response to the requirement that delivery vans serving the Chassé theatre should have room to turn and that cars should be able to reach the entrance to the underground car park.

Another requirement was that the building should be visible between all the other development on the site from the square on top of the basement car park. This led the architects to emphasize the building's horizontality still further with horizontal lines. The south elevation consists of alternating bands of steel and glass. The north facade has large windows that become smaller with each floor in a rational response to changing levels of light penetration. A gently canted facade allows civil servants working on this side a view of the ground below rather than the older building to which the box is tied by two footbridges.

The new building is a black box on a light and open base. Frosted glass volumes beneath the building light up at night like lanterns. The white soffit enhances the lightness of the space between the columns, briefly erasing awareness of the weight of the black mass above.

1

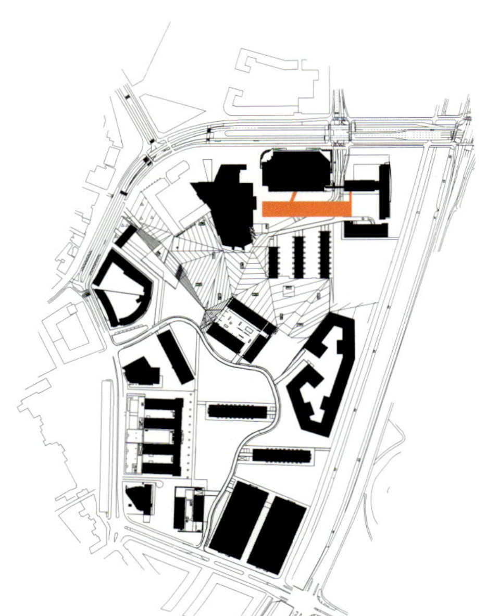

2

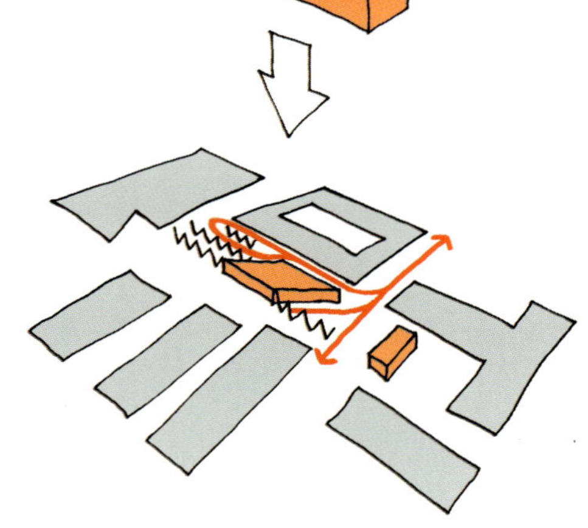

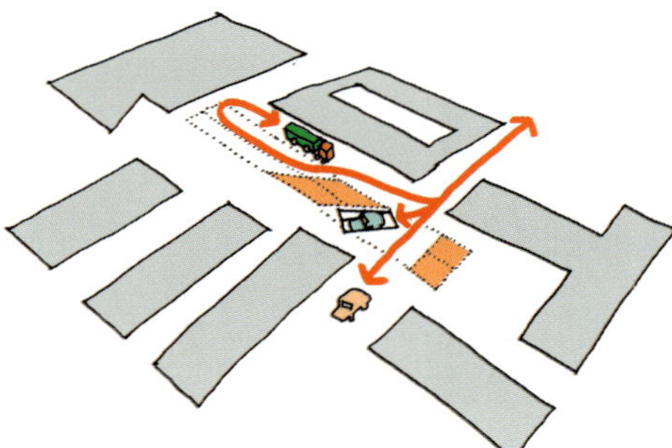

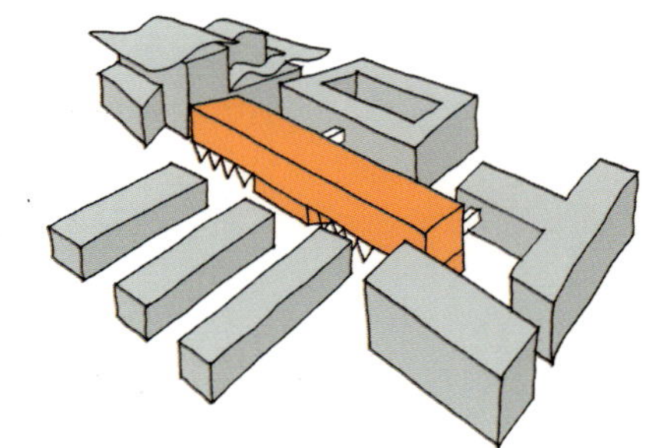

1 Edward Durell Stone and Perkins & Will Partnership, Amoco Building, Chicago, 1974
2 Site
3 Oscar Niemeyer, Brasilia Palace Hotel, Brasilia, 1957
4 Oscar Niemeyer, Museum of the City of Brasilia, Brasilia, 1958–1960

3

4

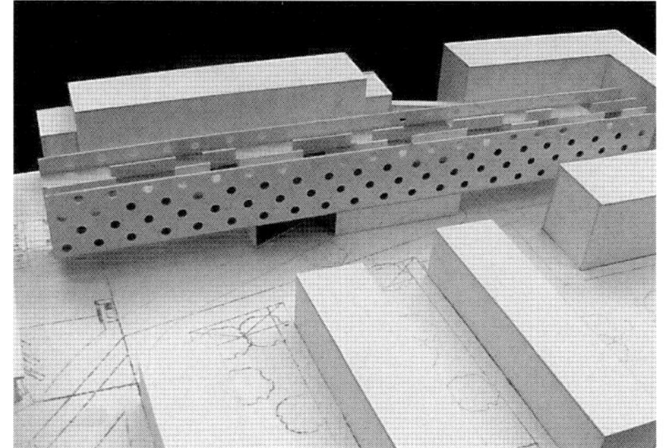

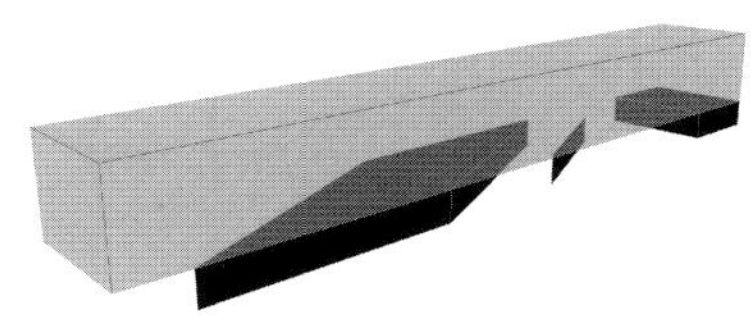

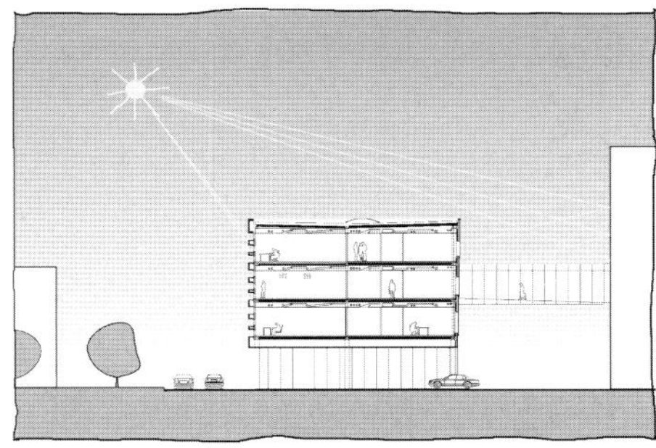

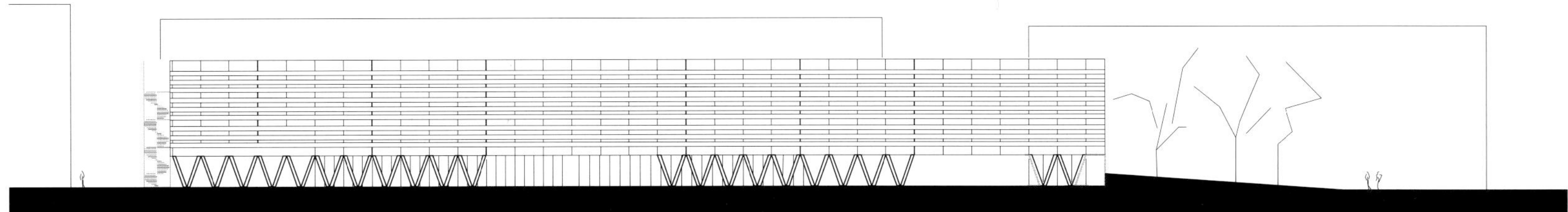

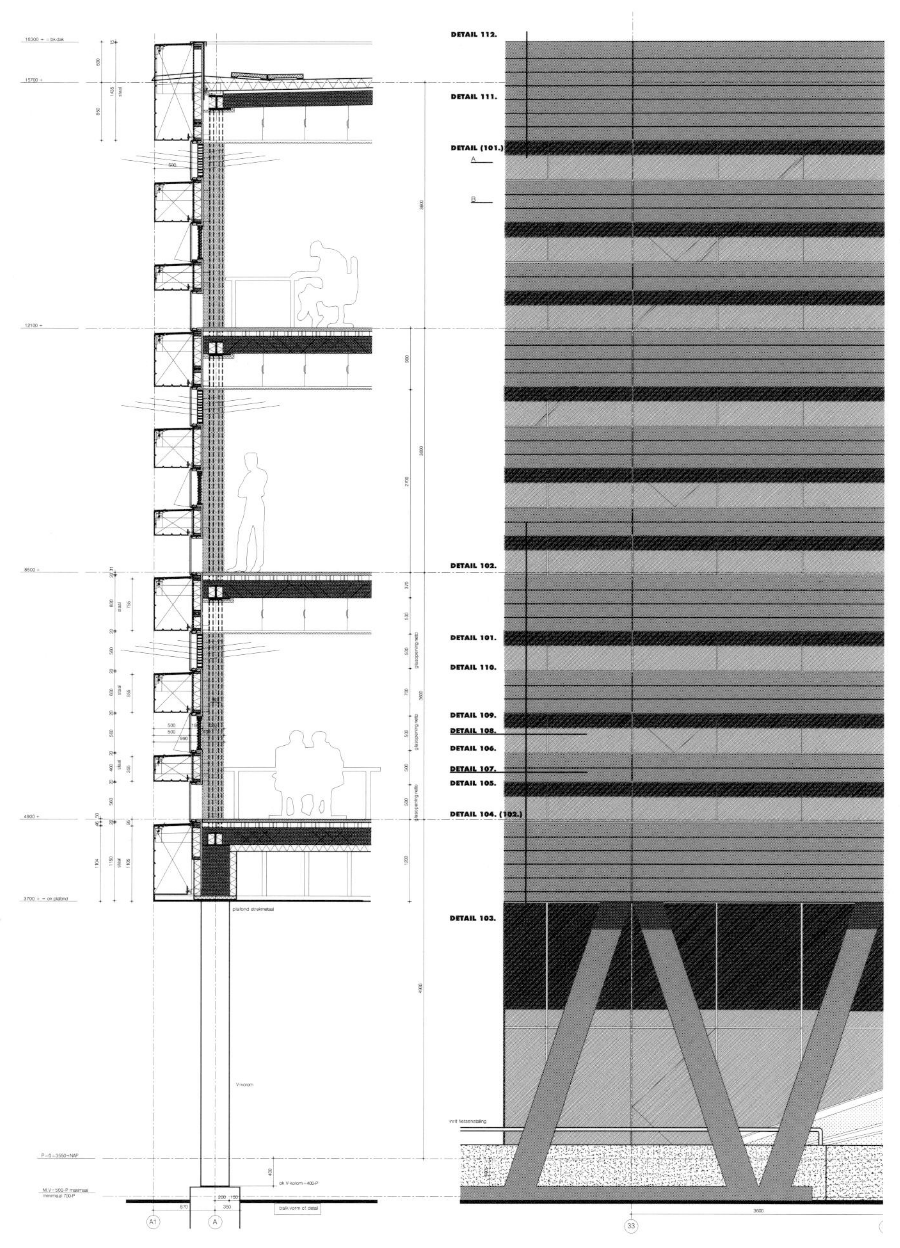
DETAIL 112.
DETAIL 111.
DETAIL (101.)
DETAIL 102.
DETAIL 101.
DETAIL 110.
DETAIL 109.
DETAIL 108.
DETAIL 106.
DETAIL 107.
DETAIL 105.
DETAIL 104. (102.)
DETAIL 103.

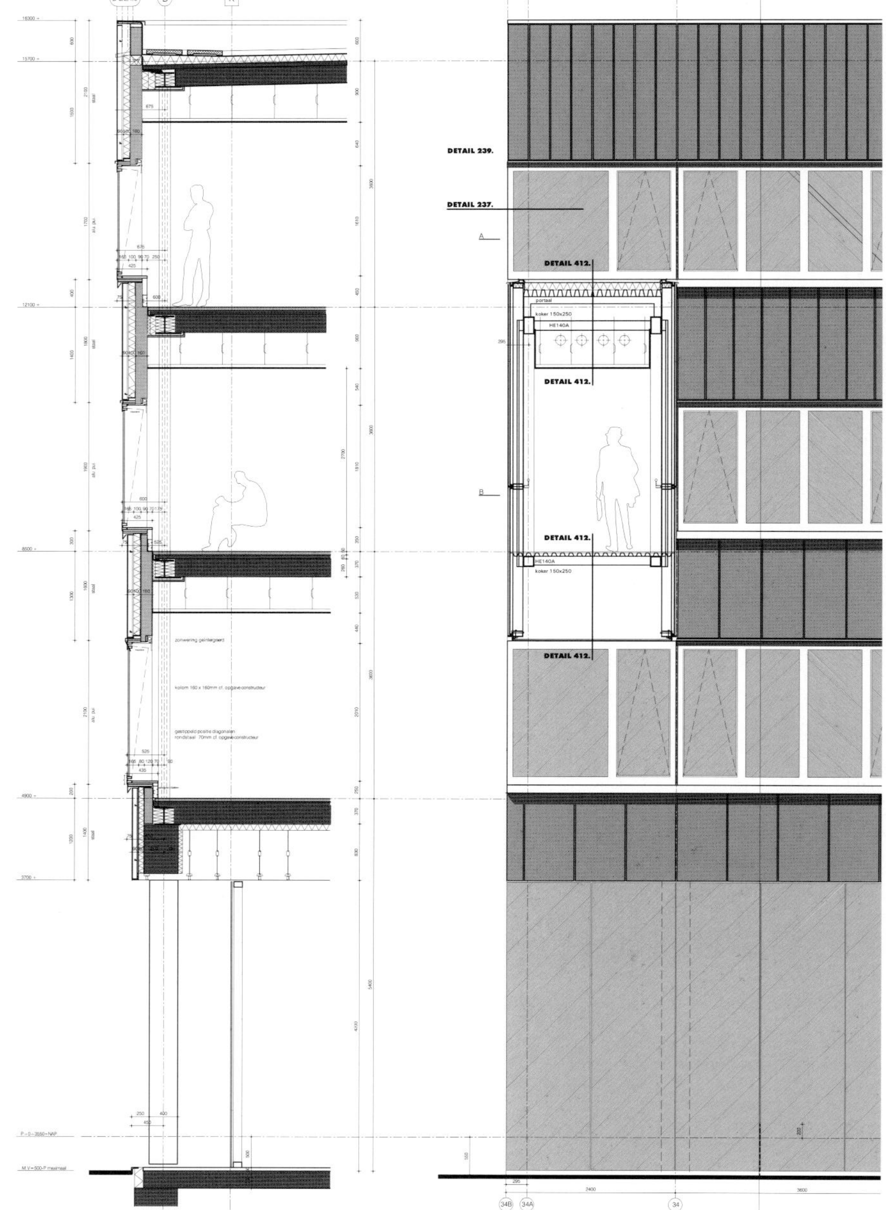
DETAIL 239.
DETAIL 237.
DETAIL 412.
DETAIL 412.
DETAIL 412.
DETAIL 412.

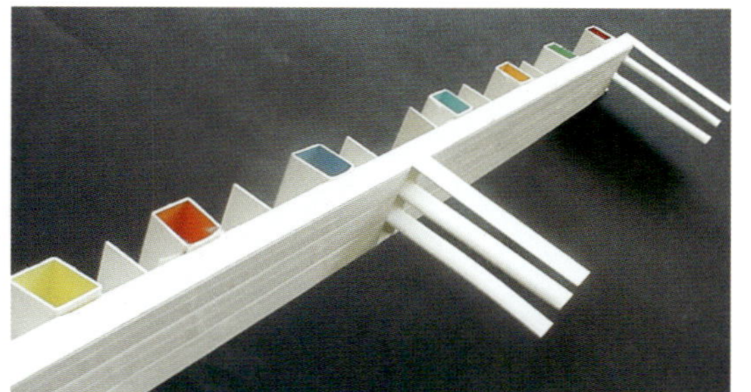

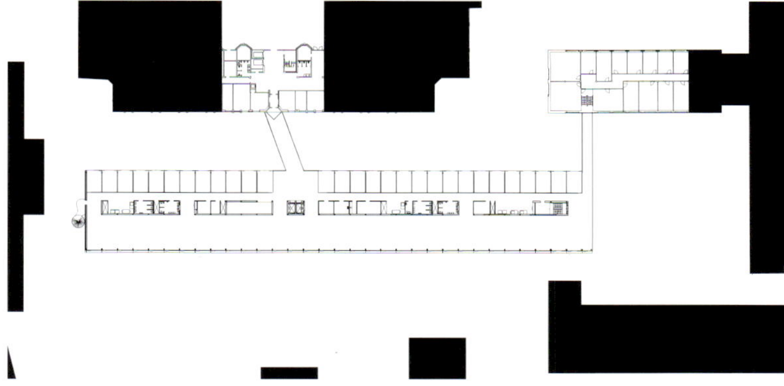

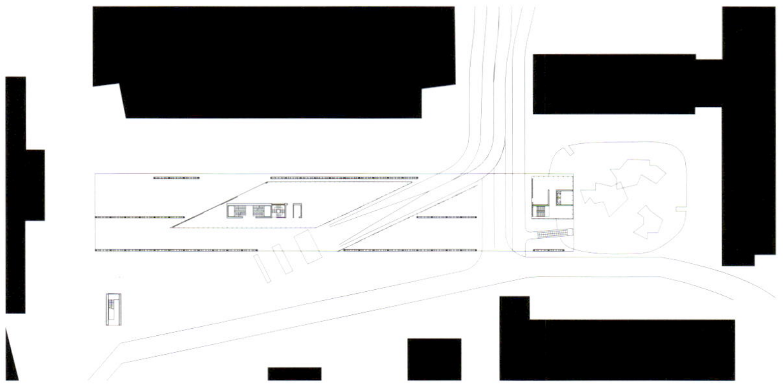
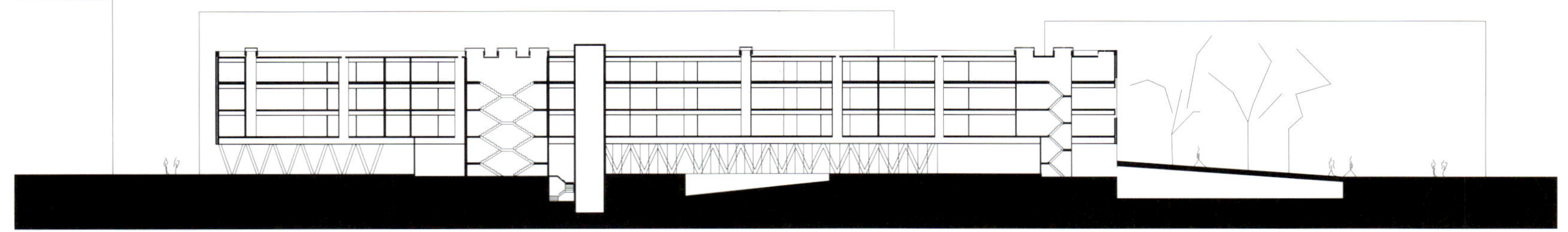

178
NATIONAL MUSEUM OF MODERN ART, ROME

This design was produced by Claus en Kaan in response to an invited competition for an extension to the museum of modern art in Rome, an early twentieth-century neo-classical building by Cesare Bazzani. The museum had already been extended once before in the 1960s when a flat, L-shaped, two-storey volume designed by Luigi Cosenza was added on behind the existing building.

This neglected 1965 addition forms the starting point for Claus en Kaan's proposal. The structure is accepted as is and the facades encased in a second skin of terracotta Roman tiles that renders the architecture monolithic and in so doing underscores the object quality of the building.

Inside, the semi-sunken ground floor is disencumbered as much as possible of all incidental functions in order to allow it to be what, in essence, it is supposed to be: an exhibition space that fills the building as a continuum. Necessary amenities, such as rest rooms, are accommodated in free-standing boxes.

Patios and large skylights were inserted to allow daylight to penetrate the building. The upper floor is largely taken up by offices. The remaining functions, such as the auditorium and utility room are located beside the building in a new underground structure. The roof of this addition is a sculpture garden.

The end result of all these interventions is a two-way radicalization of the original pavilion. The exterior has been simplified, the interior made more complex. The architects' proven strategy of allowing old and new to exist side by side was impossible here because the building allowed no scope for anything but a far-reaching appropriation. The outcome of this appropriation is typical Claus en Kaan, however. The original building was predicated on a homogeneity of inside and outside. This design, which was not selected for further elaboration, transforms it into an architecture in which inside and outside are two different worlds. Moreover, the terracotta carapace heightens the contrast with the white classicism of Bazzani such that in spite of its physical proximity, the extension distances itself even further from the main building.

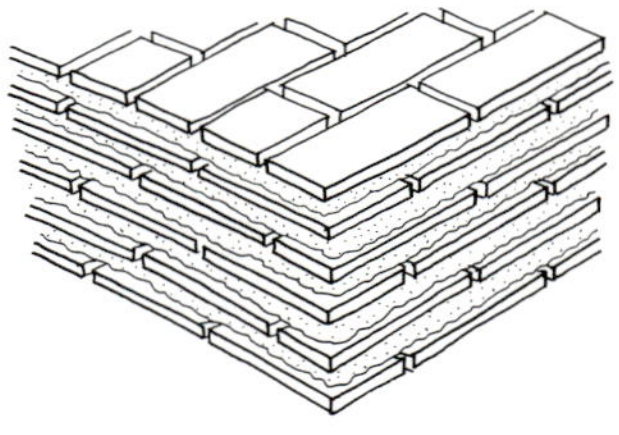

1

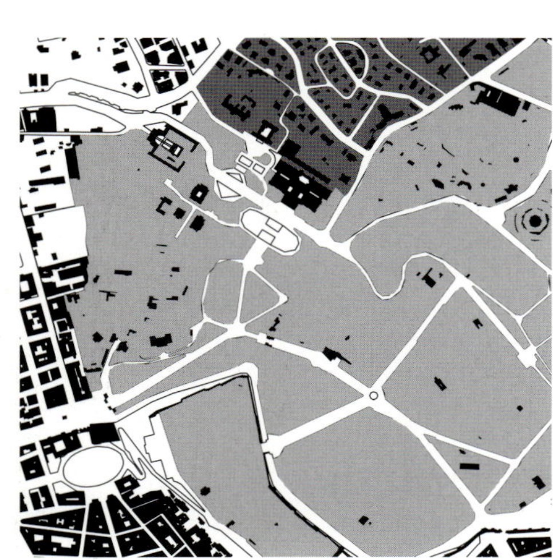

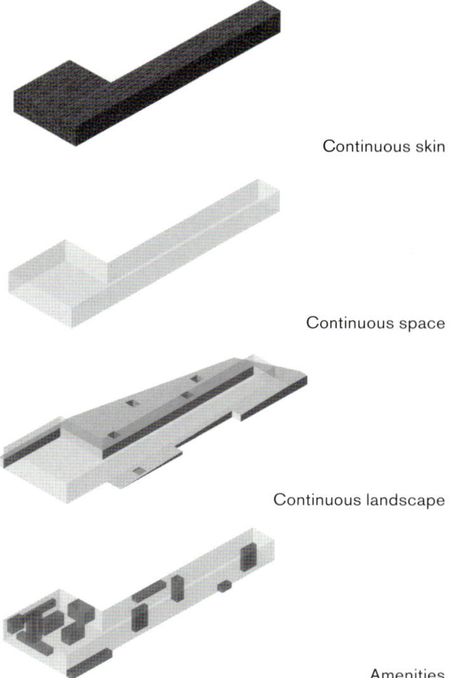

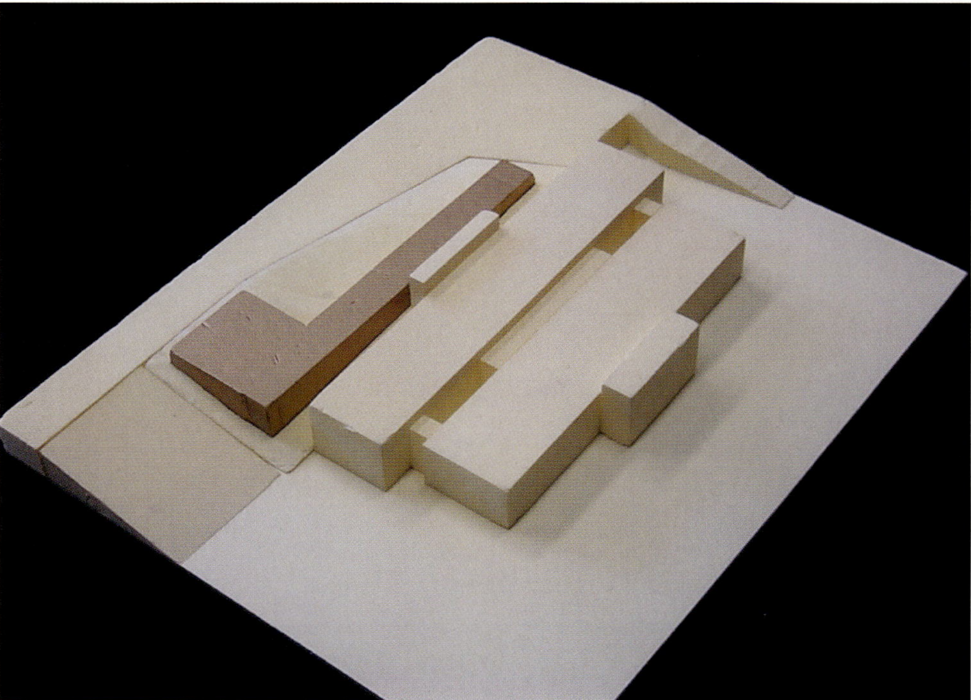

1 Opus incertum
2 Museum of Modern Art and surroundings Villa Borghese, Rome, c.1959
3 Gordon Bunshaft, Albright-Knox Art Gallery, Buffalo, New York, 1962

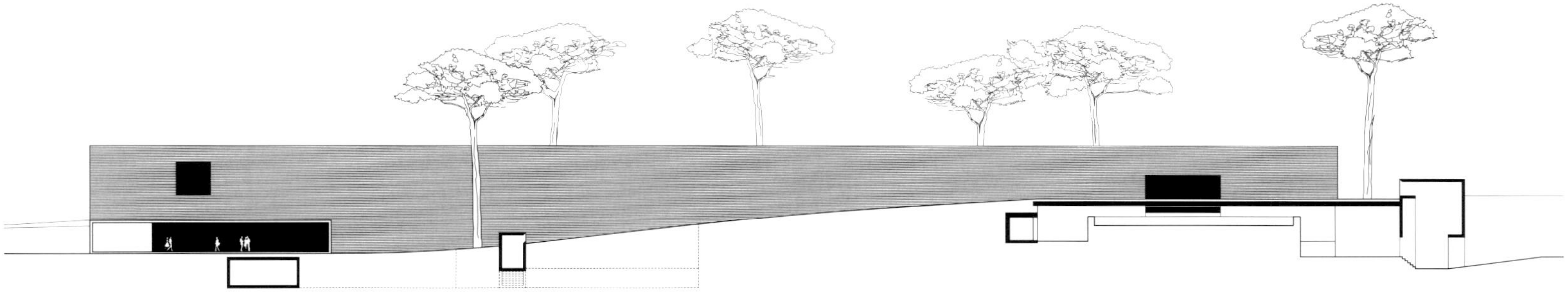

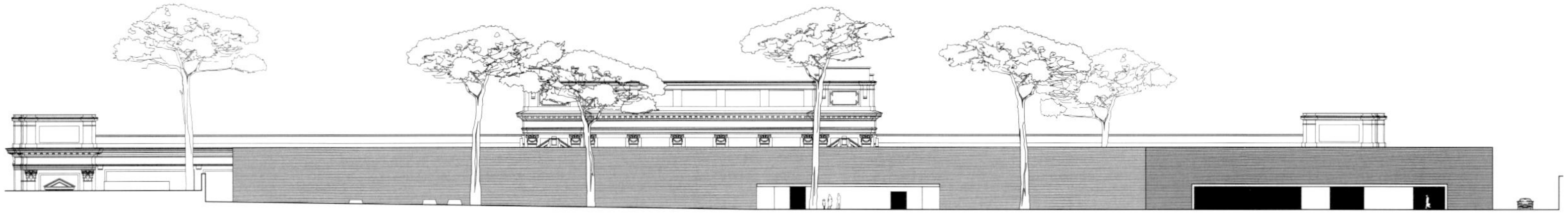

2

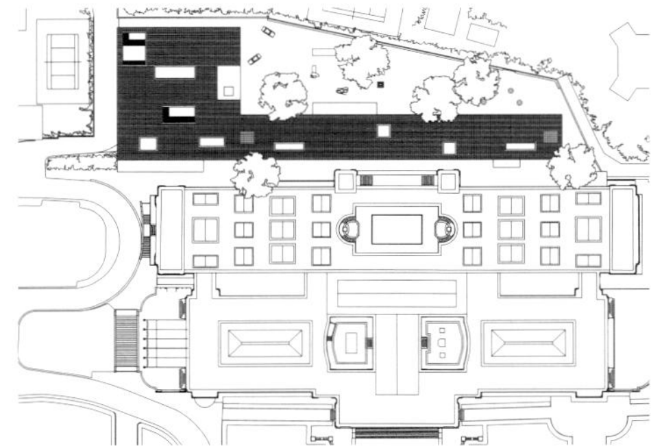

3

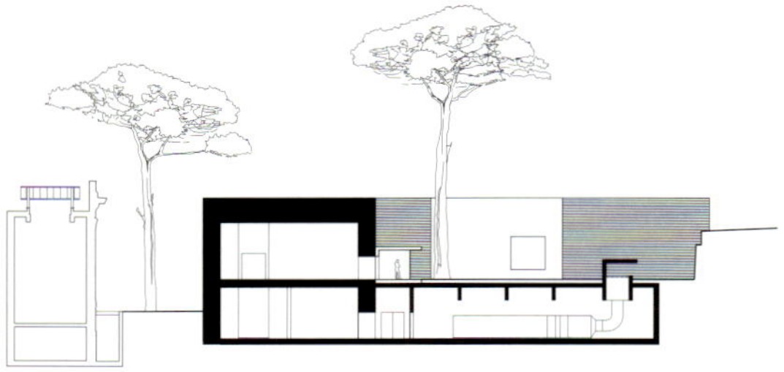

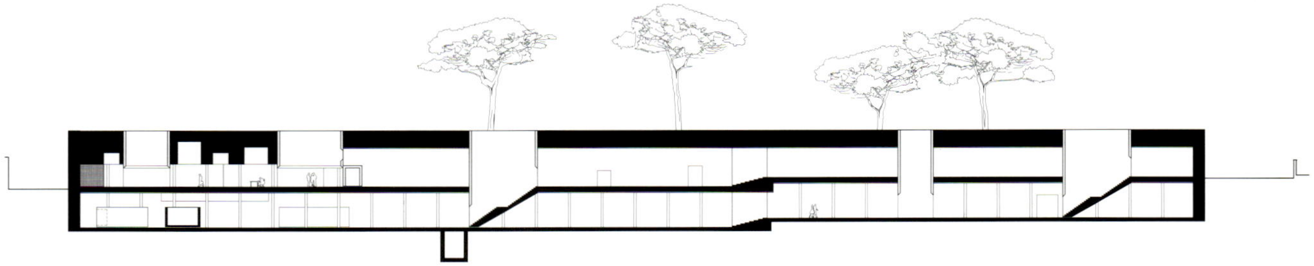

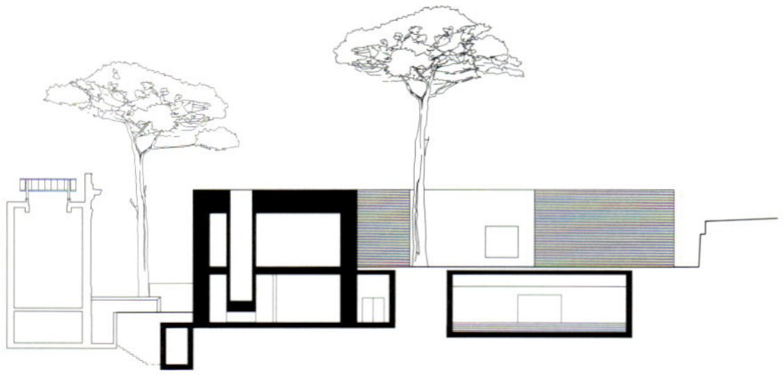

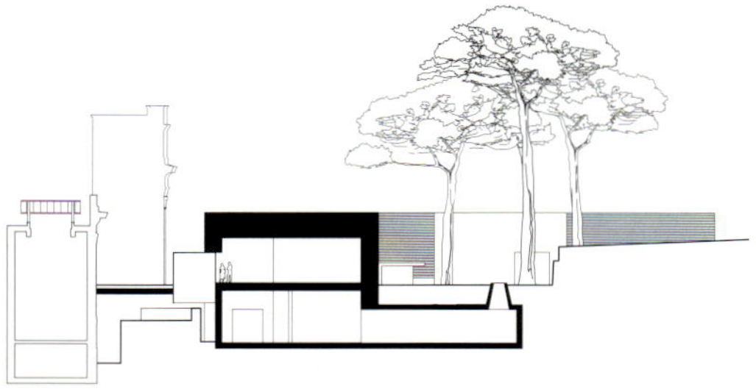

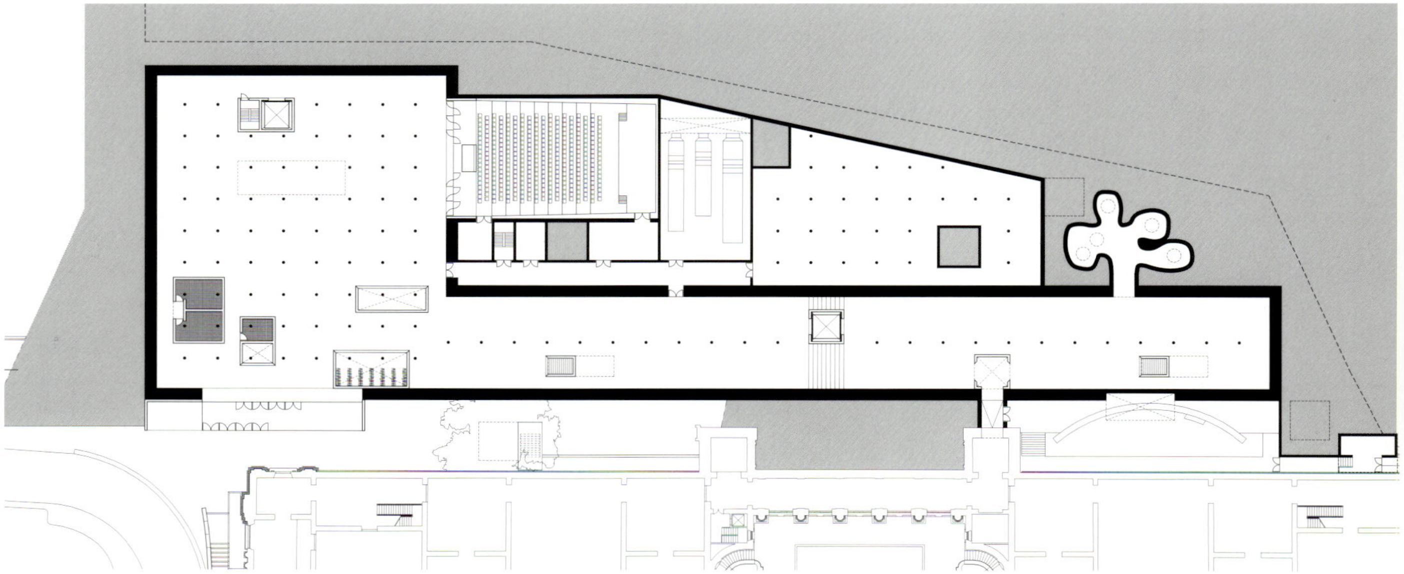

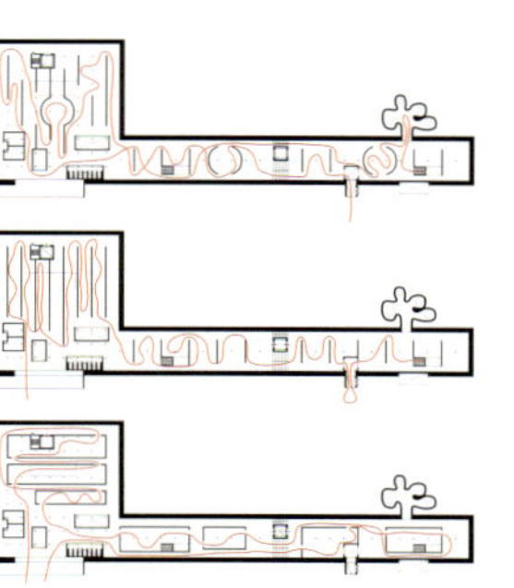

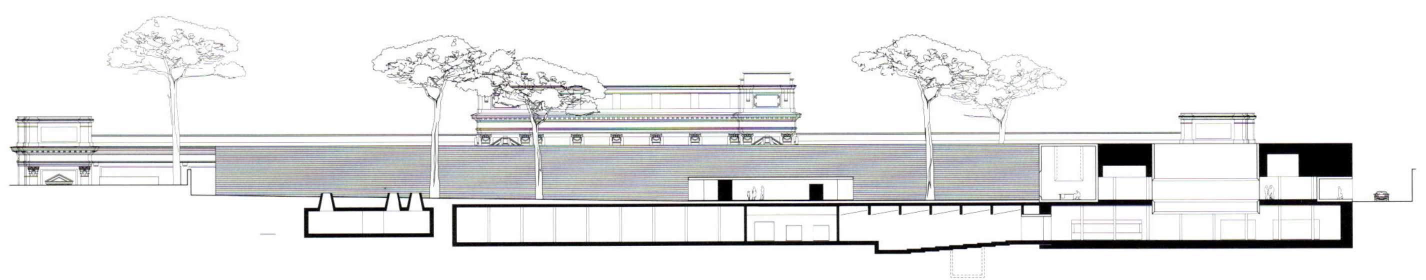

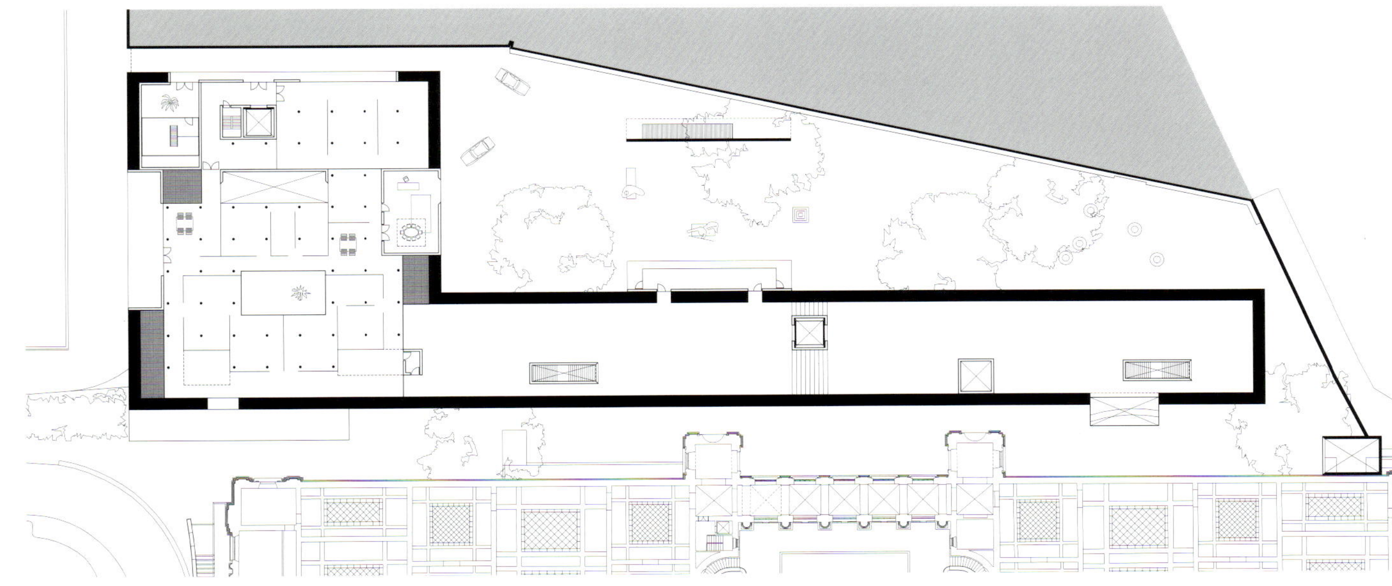

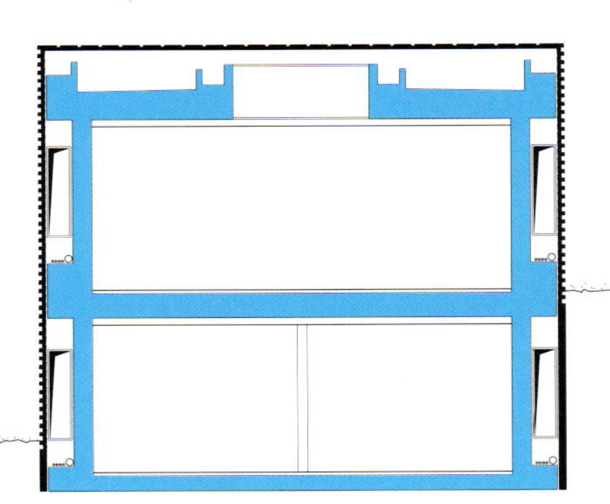

The ergonomics of the building

In this design the galleries are climate-controlled by a combination of a six-fold balanced ventilation system with radiation cooling and heating in the floor. This solution is environmentally friendly, produces a very stable indoor climate and is effective with a hard floor finish. The conditioned fresh air is piped in via horizontal shafts incorporated in the double skin of the museum. Introducing the fresh air close to the museum objects makes for a stable indoor climate with little risk of disturbance from public entrances. Moreover, the same climatological conditions obtain on both sides of the museum walls which is ideal for the exhibition of paintings or photographs.

National Museum of Modern Art, Rome

188
MUNICIPAL ARCHIVES, AMSTERDAM

The extension and partial renovation of the municipal records office in Amsterdam is a complex of volumes that is largely invisible from the street. It fills most of the courtyard beside and behind the former Nieuwer-Amstel town hall, previously the entrance to the records office. The new main entrance is in a glazed volume that forms the public face of this municipal service. Below is the public lobby, above that a floor of offices and right at the top reading rooms and a restaurant that pierces the glazed volume and affords a view of the Amstel.

Behind this public face lies a large torso that encompasses a former diamond cutting establishment in Tolstraat. These works are to be adapted to the new use. In the complex as a whole, which is first of all a spatial solution to the complicated logistics and organization of the records office, are five gardens, each with a different character and function.

Apart from the addition of a new building and the renovation of three existing buildings, the design also entails the repair of the city block of which the record office is part. Two nondescript, hermetic buildings which belong to the records office are to make way for a new structure that will make a more meaningful contribution to the urban fabric. In addition, at the presentation of the plan, it was suggested that the river bank might be cleaned up in order to reinstate the Amstel, now all but invisible behind trees and houseboats, in the streetscape.

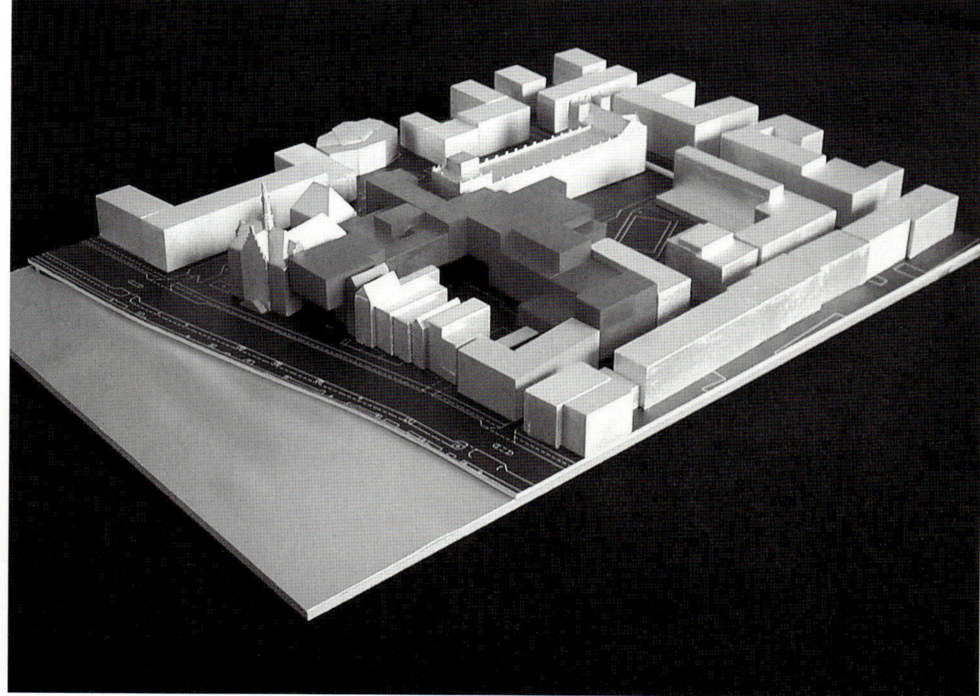

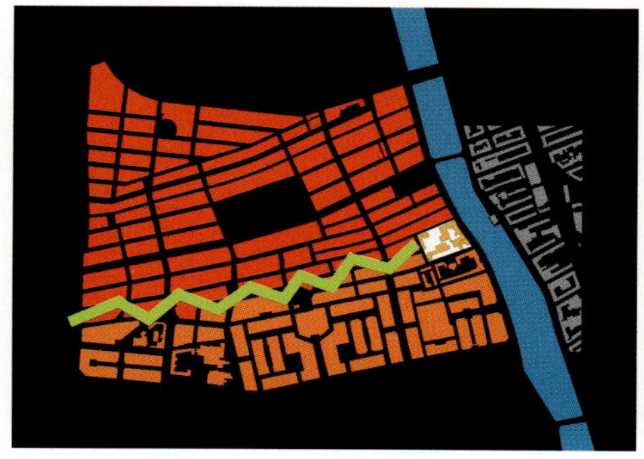

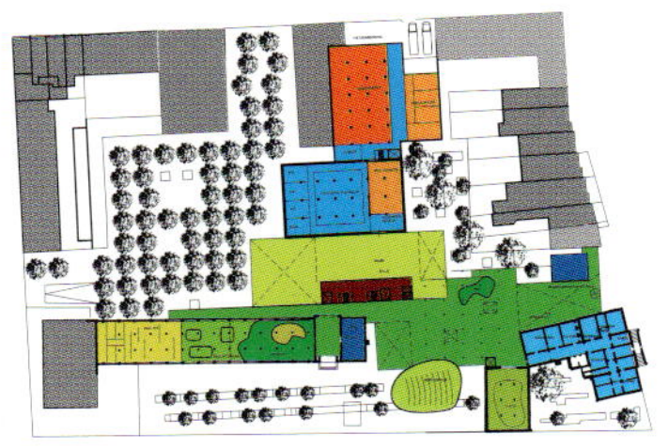

DEPOT
BEWERKINGSRUIMTE
VERKEERSRUIMTE
STIJGKERN
STUDIEZALEN
HAL/INFOCENTRUM/MULTIFUNCTIONELRUIMTE
AUDITORIUM
TENTOONSTELLING
WINKEL
RESTAURANT
EDUCATIE
INFORMATIECENTRUM IRA
DIENST/WC/OPSLAG
RESTAURATIE
TUSSENDEPOT
DIENST/WERKPLAATSEN/CENTRAAL MAGAZIJN/KANTOREN
BEVEILIGING/ALGEMEEN BEHEER/DIENST/PERSONEELSRESTAURANT
KANTOREN BIBLIOTHEEK
TENTOONSTELLING
PRESENTATIE EDUCATIE EN VOORLICHTING
VERGADERRUIMTEN EN SPREEKKAMERS
BESTAANDE WONINGBOUW
NIEUWE WONINGBOUW
BESTAANDE KANTOREN ASSCHER

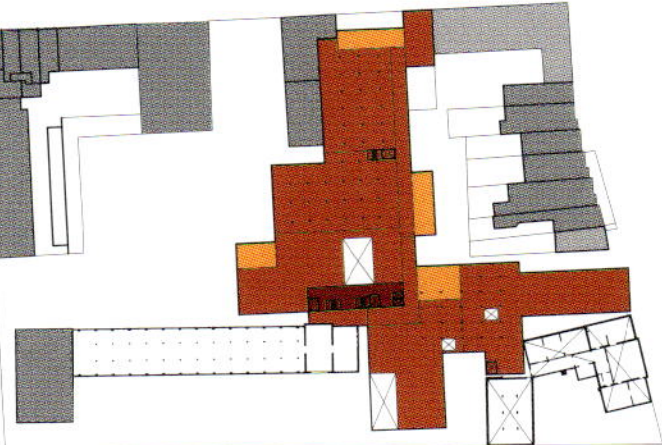

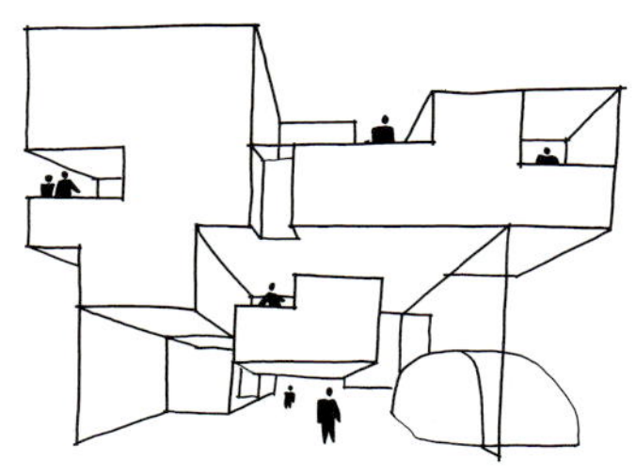

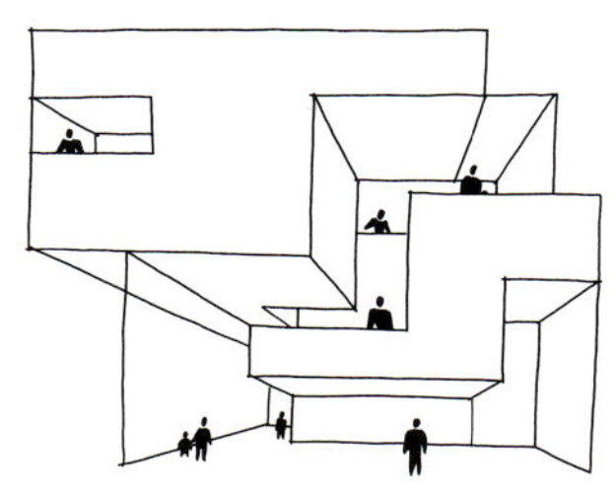

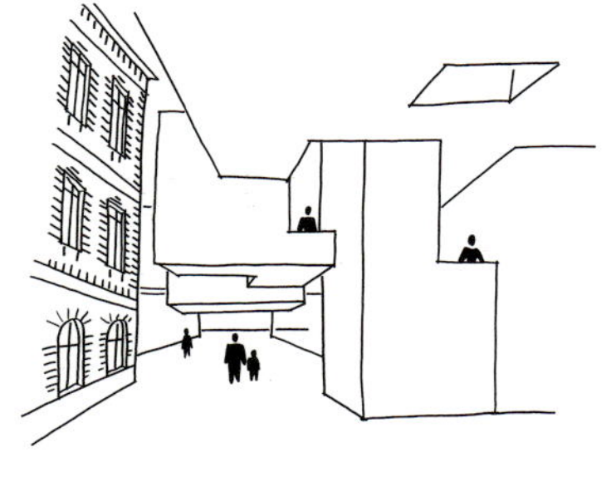

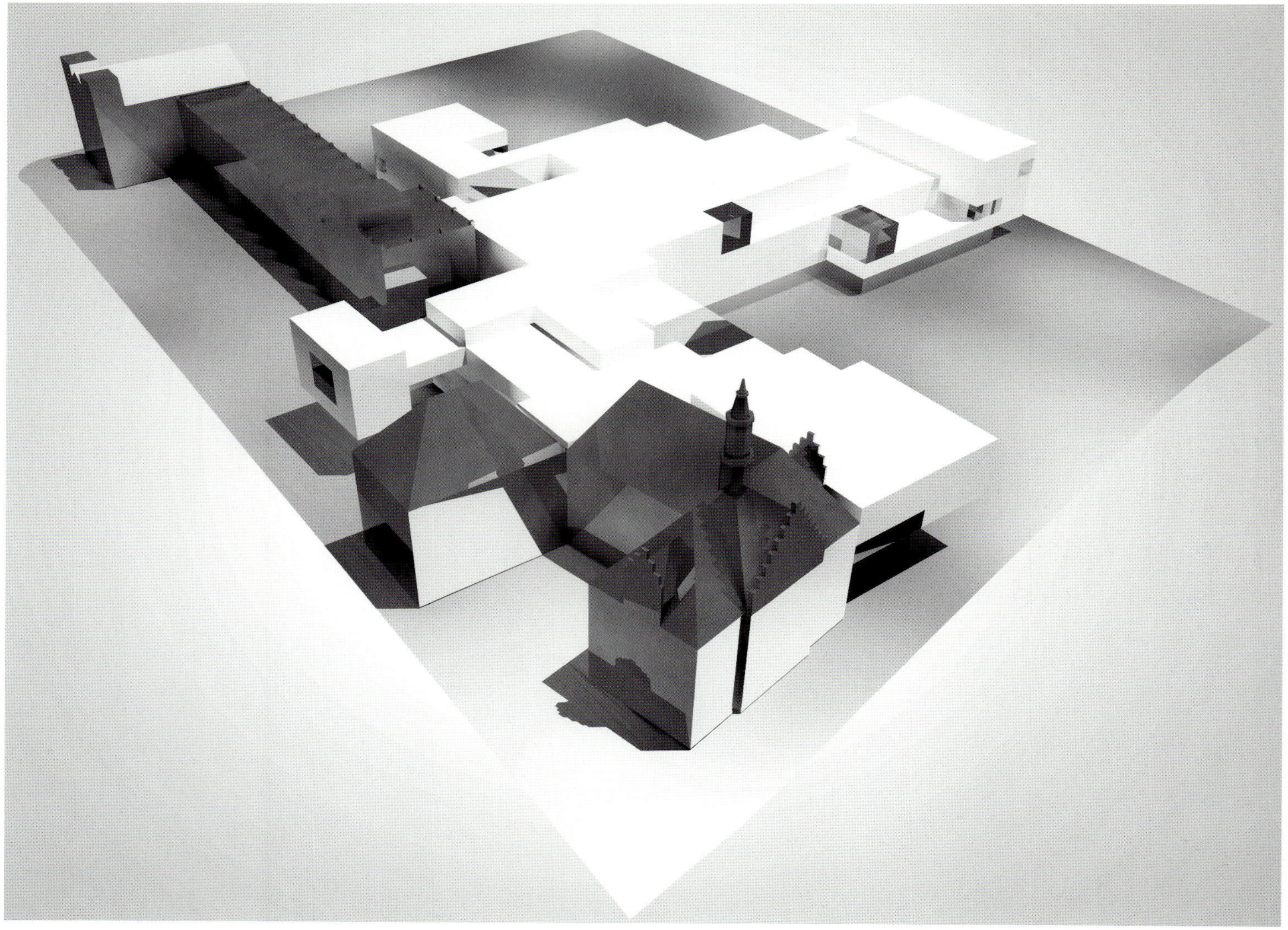

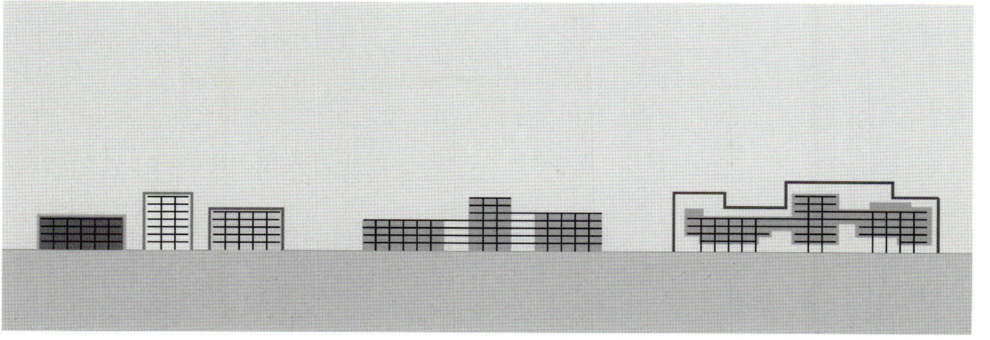

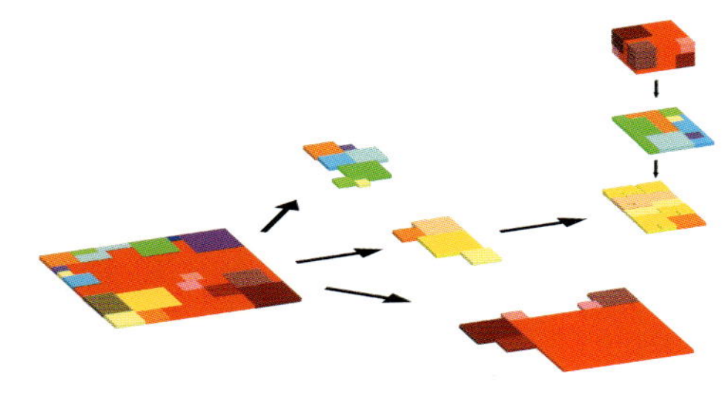

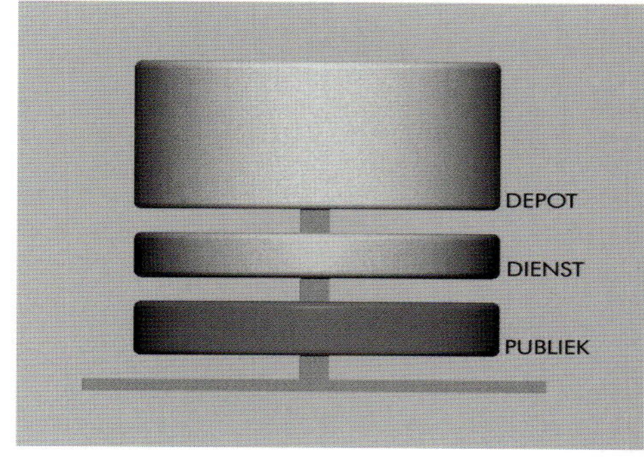
DEPOT
DIENST
PUBLIEK

JACOB
OLIE

196
MUSEUM NATIONAAL MONUMENT KAMP VUGHT, VUGHT

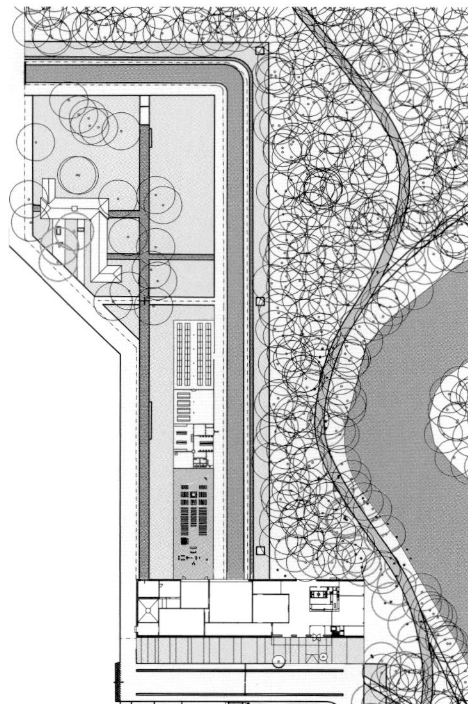

Not much is left of the Vught concentration camp but a small piece of ground with the remains of the crematorium. These remnants stand more or less in the shadow of the maximum security prison built in the grounds of the former camp. The foundation responsible for the camp's upkeep, Nationaal Monument Kamp Vught, commissioned Michael van Gessel to design a new layout. Claus en Kaan were subsequently asked to design an entrance pavilion. The building, which contains exhibition space and offices for the foundation marks the entrance to the camp in the form of a screen.

The Roman tiles used in the design for the extension to the museum of modern art in Rome return here. Bands of this thin terracotta material alternate with heavy bricks laid set back so that the space between the terracotta tiles can be filled to look like a thick joint.

There are two routes through the building, one that visitors follow upon entering and the other as they leave the site. The exhibition rooms, which follow a pre-modern organizational principle, consist of an enfilade of rooms without any connecting corridor. The individual exhibition rooms are tailored in length, breadth and height to their particular function, a principle that Adolf Loos applied in his domestic architecture in order to give each room proportions appropriate to its use. It is yet another illustration of the distinction between the indoor and outdoor world that plays such an important role in the architecture of Claus en Kaan.

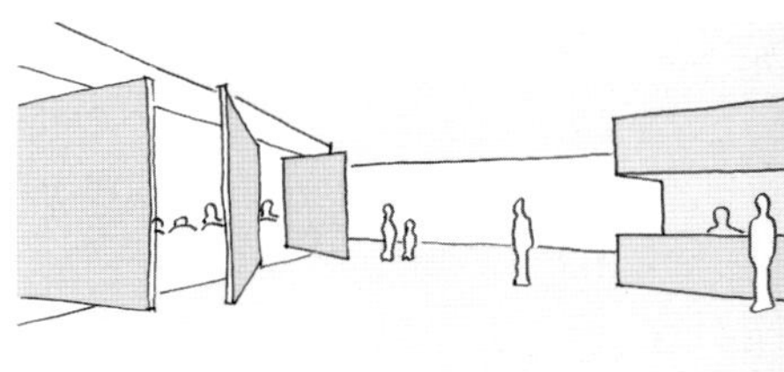

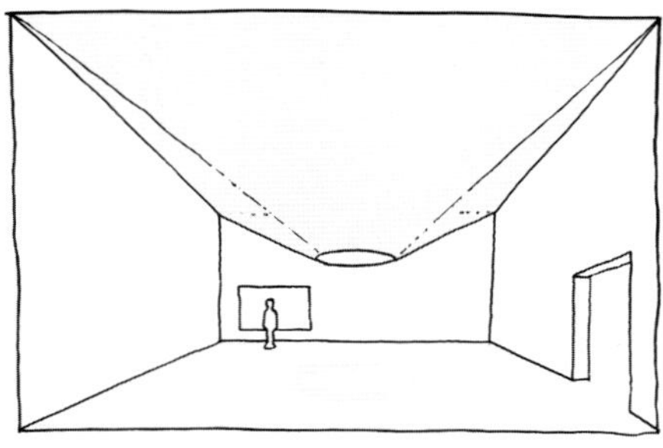

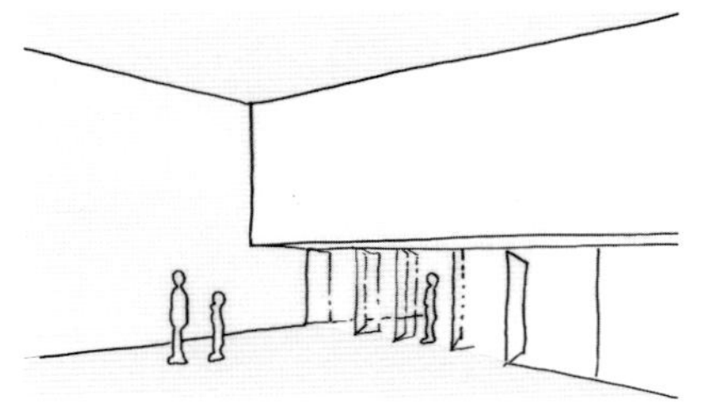

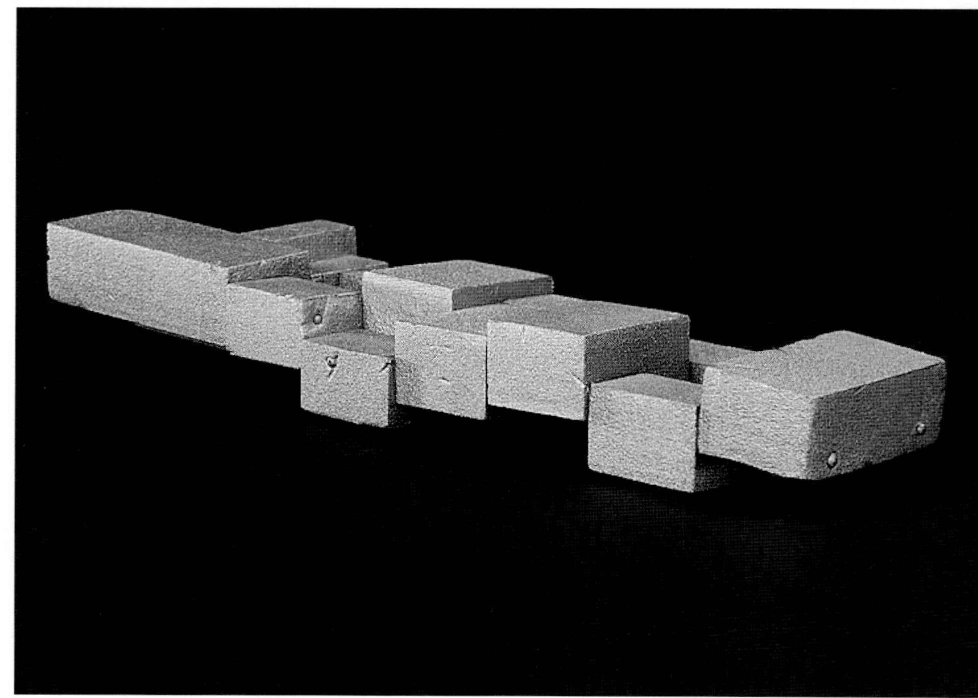

Frank Lloyd Wright, Taliesin West, Scottsdale, Arizona, 1937

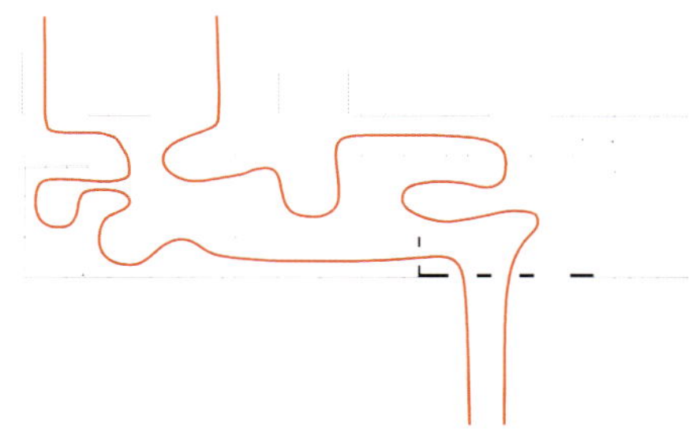

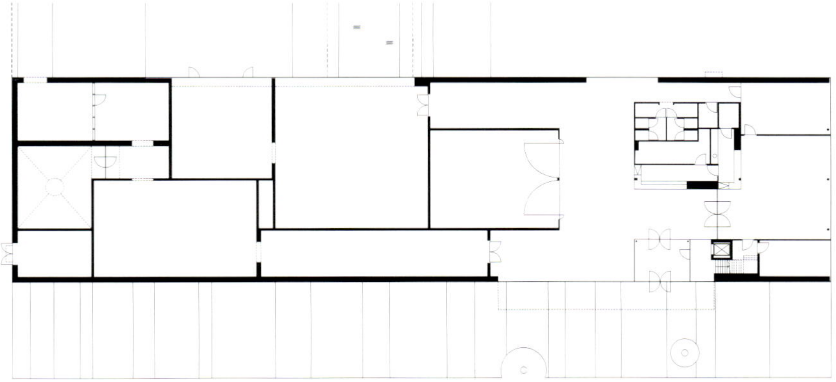

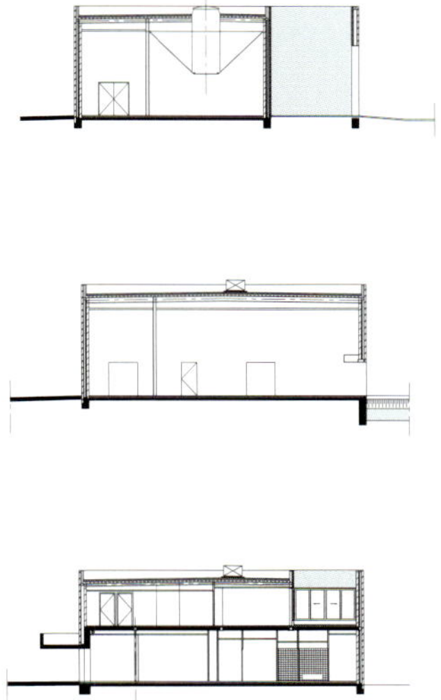

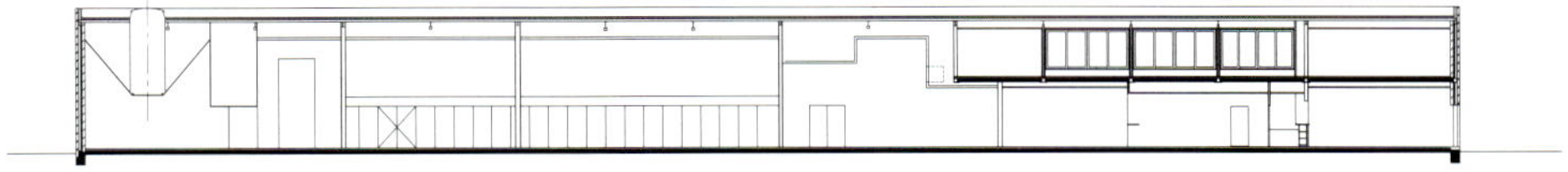

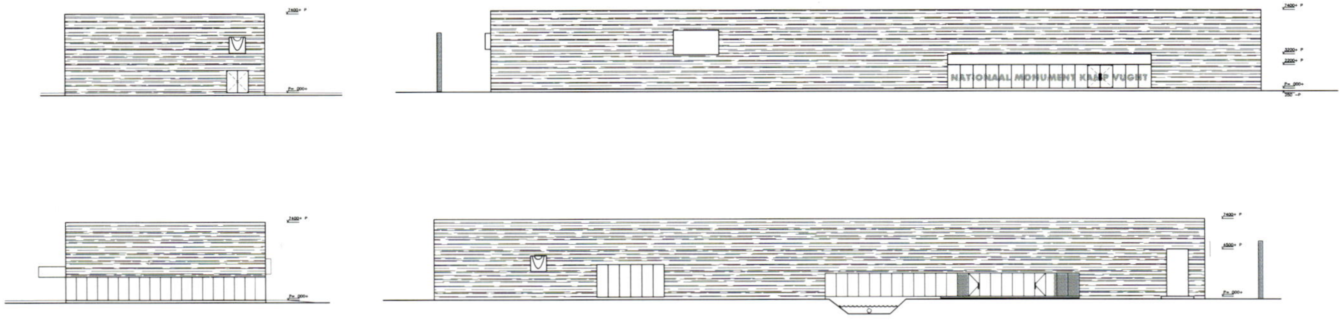

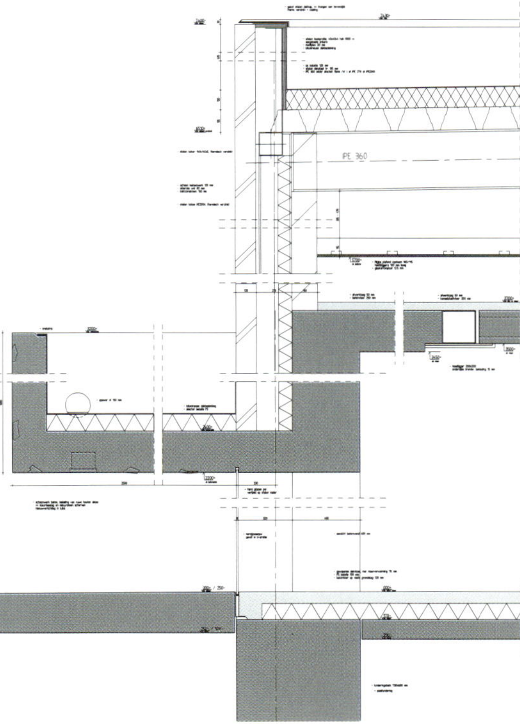

198
TOWN HALL, TYNAARLO

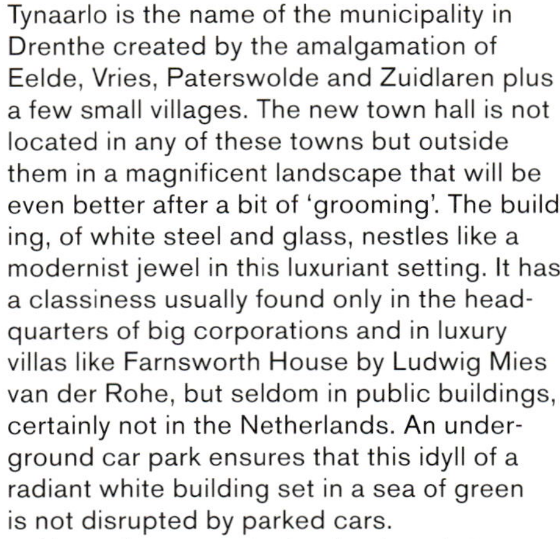

Tynaarlo is the name of the municipality in Drenthe created by the amalgamation of Eelde, Vries, Paterswolde and Zuidlaren plus a few small villages. The new town hall is not located in any of these towns but outside them in a magnificent landscape that will be even better after a bit of 'grooming'. The building, of white steel and glass, nestles like a modernist jewel in this luxuriant setting. It has a classiness usually found only in the headquarters of big corporations and in luxury villas like Farnsworth House by Ludwig Mies van der Rohe, but seldom in public buildings, certainly not in the Netherlands. An underground car park ensures that this idyll of a radiant white building set in a sea of green is not disrupted by parked cars.

Above the car park stands a largely transparent building in which the council chamber is on the ground floor, general offices on the floor above while the top floor is reserved for the grander offices for council members, but also for the staff canteen so that the view, too, is democratically shared.

In its siting, architectural expression, crisp detailing and the addition of monumental art, the building is a celebration of public administration such as has seldom been seen in the Netherlands since the days of H.A. Maaskant.

1

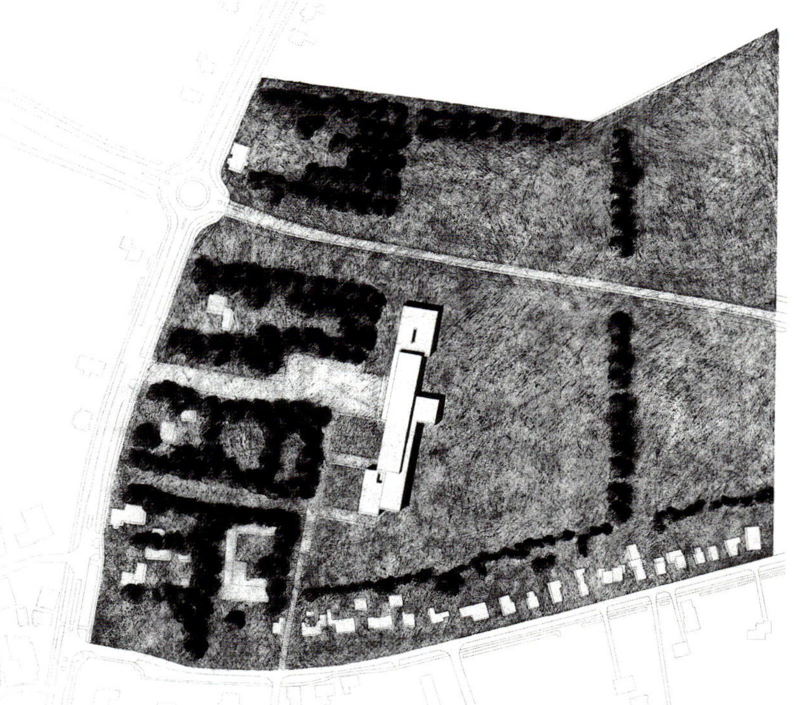

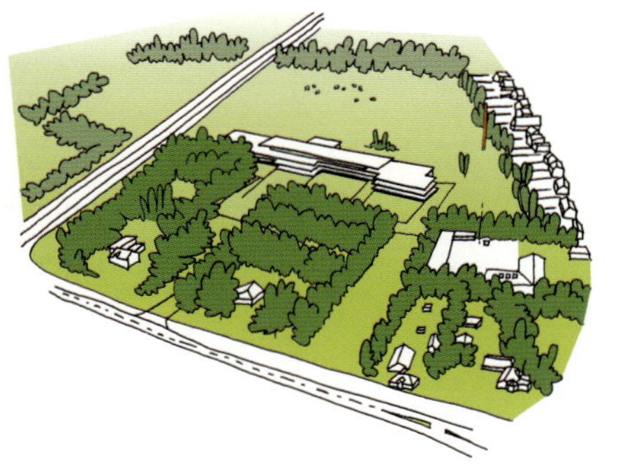

1 Paul Rudolph, Bass residence, Fort Worth, Texas, 1972
2 Site
3 Arne Jacobsen, Rodøvre town hall, Copenhagen, 1954–1956
4 Tea house, Yoyogi Park, Tokyo
5 Ludwig Mies van der Rohe, design for Stanley Resor House, Jackson Hole, Wyoming, 1937–1938
6 Le Corbusier, Villa Savoie, Poissy, 1929–1931

2

3

4

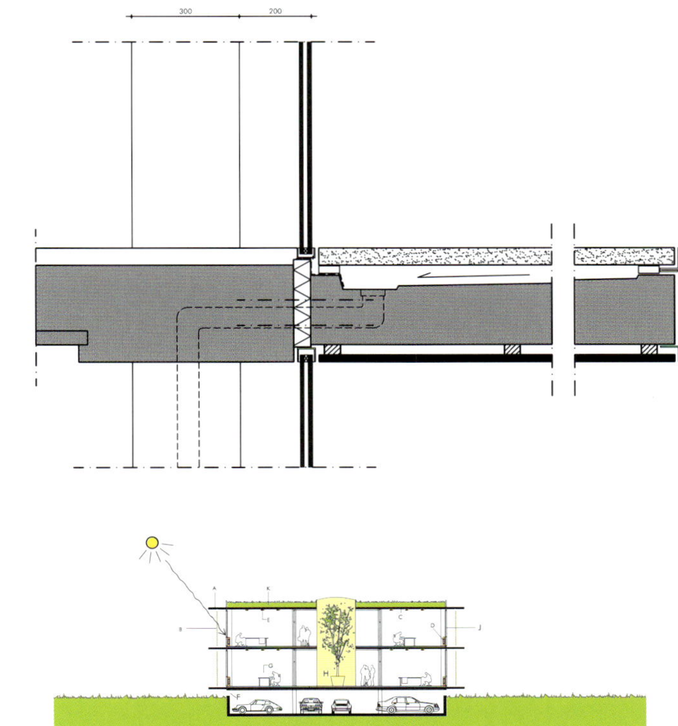

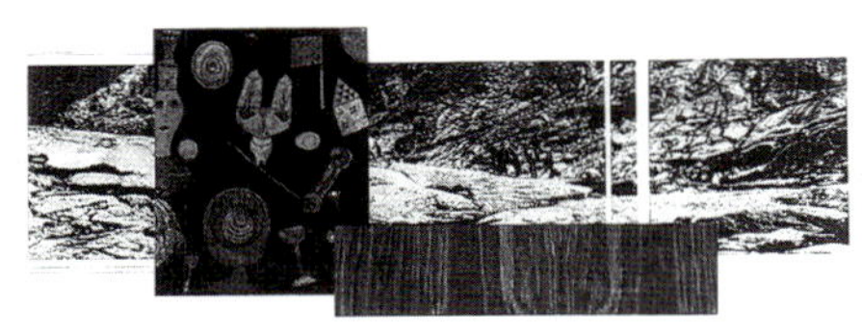

5

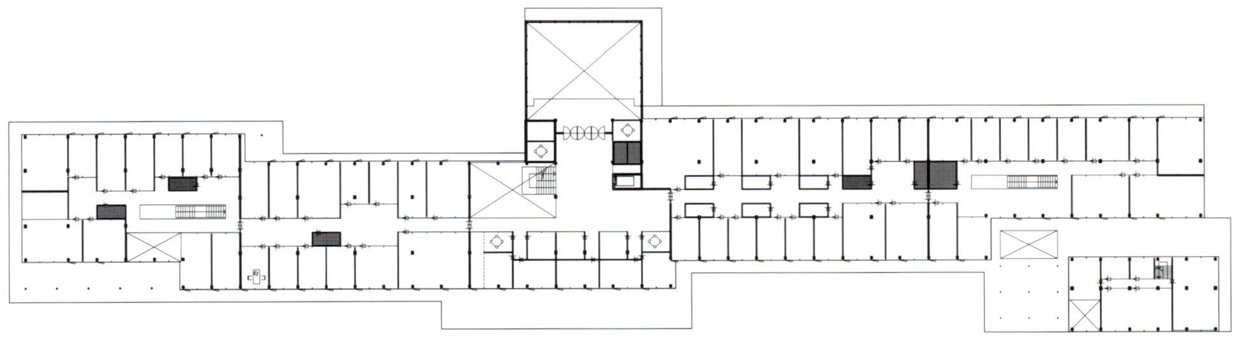

6

In der vorigen Woche war ich Preisrichter für das Landestheater in Darmstadt: Mir standen die Haare zu Berge. Was so bedeutende Persönlichkeiten wie Aalto, Scharoun und ähnliche Individualisten bei der heranwachsenden Generation für Schaden anrichten, ist kaum noch gut zu machen.

Man kann nicht laut genug die Stimme erheben gegen den unverstandenen Gebrauch der Formsprache dieser Männer, die sich ja bei ihren dichterischen Räumen – deren Schönheit nicht abgestritten werden soll – eben diese Schönheit durch Vernachlässigung aller notwendigen und guten Konstruktionen erkaufen müssen.

Da kann ich – und ich weiss auch Sie – nicht mehr mit. Natürlich ist man etwas neidisch auf die Freiheit und Vielfalt der Gedanken, die sich da in Bauwerke umsetzen, und man ist in den berühmten kritischen Stunden, die man – wie oben gesagt – in ratloser Einsamkeit mit sich verbringt, geneigt, die eigenen Arbeit wirklich für unvollkommen zu halten, und der Verzweiflung nahe, aber ich kann aus meiner Haut nicht heraus.

Fragment: letter by Egon Eiermann to F.W. Kraemer on May 6th 1953
Egon Eiermann, *Briefe des Architekten 1946–1970*, Stuttgart 1994

SERIOUS AND ROMANTIC

David Chipperfield

The built work of Claus en Kaan is a testament to their modest and unpretentious approach. Quietly they have accumulated an oeuvre that demonstrates the power of their serious, careful and considerate method.
At a time when architects are encouraged to make bold and spectacular architectural demonstrations it is refreshing to observe their straightforward style. They have made explicit through their writings that they regard themselves as honest professionals. In their own words they 'design in order to build'. Phrases and words recur: 'down to earth', 'craft', 'act normally'. The basis of their practice is clearly set out. They are not interested in complex intellectual narrative, or in celebration of the unusual. Architecture is to be found where it has always been found, in the careful and critical elaboration of normal tasks. The fact that so much of their work has been housing confirms their interest in architectural development.

Their buildings are not monuments to a new architectural order or genius, but rather critical experiments in the continuum of architectural development. Their intellectual and formal context is the Modern Movement. Their architectural language enjoys the compositional tendencies of abstraction and simplification. This language has developed in recent projects and tends to rely less on compositional variation and asymmetry and more on repetition and reduction. In all cases the buildings are elegantly resolved, their careful and intelligent detailing avoids gesture and succeeds in achieving coherence and consistency in the project.

What can we describe as their achievement at a time when they are no longer to be classified as emerging talent, but are entering a more critical phase of architectural development and expectation?
Firstly we must acknowledge their extensive work in housing. Operating within restricted budgets and difficult physical situations they have built a large number of housing projects of the highest standards. These projects operate successfully and coherently at all levels, with early projects such as the Landsteinerlaan Apartments in Groningen demonstrating a quality of project that was to be repeated many times. The equivalence given to the humane interpretation of the programme, the urbanistic response and the faultless architectural execution defines the sophistication of these projects.

Three housing projects establish the credentials of their approach; the above-mentioned Landsteinerlaan Apartments, the Amstelveenseweg Housing in Amsterdam and finally the Rietlanden Housing in Sporenburg, Amsterdam. All of these projects are sophisticated, articulated and above all humane. The architectural elaborations are always in check, never disproportionate to the straightforward ambitions of the scheme. Even gestures that may be seen as formalistic – the manipulated placement of windows or the compositional use of timber cladding – are carried out with a restraint and precision that maintains the stability of the project.

In my opinion the Rietlanden project is the most rigorous in conceptual and physical terms. Here the architects' established skill is used to make a seemingly effortless composition, relying on proportion, repetition and scale. Within the architectural variety of the Sporenburg complex the Claus en Kaan project asserts its calm and sophisticated maturity.

On visiting the buildings, even a low cost and semi-industrial project such as the Business Centre Papaverweg in Amsterdam, one is always impressed by the attention to detailing, not from any conceptual virtuosity, but as a part of the precision, elegance and proportion of the project. Much of the charm of these 'innocent' projects lies in the proportions; the relationship between solid and void, the slightly too thin windows, the overlarge openings, the window that goes around the corner, etc. These are not grand architectural gestures but manipulations, articulations made possible for these architects because they are totally in control of the elements, materials and techniques of their craft.

Claus en Kaan have worked their way towards architectural solutions by way of their 'skill', as opposed to starting with conceptual ideas and learning how to build them, acquiring skill and method on the way to constructing ideas. Their sophisticated agility as professionals (accumulated through their unassuming stance) allows them to work in an increasingly free method.

Claus en Kaan concern themselves with simplicity. They do not work to achieve this ambition by omission or reduction, but through clarity and purposefulness. It is necessary to discuss this ambition, as in many ways it seems to disguise another tendency. That tendency can be identified as a sort of romanticism. In some projects it is manifested by the choice of materials (i.e. the Buitenveldert Depot, Amsterdam), in other projects colour is introduced as a vibrant expression, occasionally (as in the Police Post and Social Services, Amsterdam) the windows take on a rather overstated importance. It seems to me therefore that underneath this restrained body of work there is continuously bubbling under the surface a romantic and less objective tendency. This I suspect is what gives charm to their projects. An example: the Reception Pavilion at Zorgvlied Cemetery in Amsterdam is a beautiful and well-placed object. The designers intelligently rejected the idea of extending the existing building, but instead placed a separate building. This move was careful, simple and precise. The building itself is, let us say, 'minimal'. A simple white volume with an 'over-heavy', cantilevered porch. The simplicity of this building seems to have been achieved by simplification and reduction, the sense of 'restraint' that comes through in other projects is missing. It doesn't feel as if simplicity has been achieved by holding back other ideas, by stopping at the right time as it were, but by outright omission.

I instance this building not in order to criticize it, for in fact I found its placement and general demeanour very convincing, but to try to identify something that I find difficult to describe, that is, 'What is simplicity in the work of Claus en Kaan?'. Looking at the projects in the process of formulating opinions, not about an individual work but about the body of work, the term simplicity (which is continuously used by the architects and by critics describing their work) seems less and less relevant.

I enjoy the constant characteristics of their projects. Firstly, an ability to put a building together, to use the constructive components as a sort of discipline and to give this 'cleanliness' and orderliness an apparent ease. For this ability to put a building together in a faultless manner is a sort of formalistic freedom, like a writer able to use words with such ease that simple statements seem convincing beyond their meaning. Secondly, an absence of whimsy and fashionable folly that would in their opinion invalidate the seriousness of their ambition to achieve the straightforward, to avoid the pitfall of the spectacular. Thirdly, an underlying romantic tendency, which is continuously at odds with the first two characteristics; an attraction to the expressive qualities of form, material, colour and a desire always to include sufficient 'romantic spice' to prevent the idea from remaining flat, absent, empty.

Claus en Kaan are not interested in simplicity for its own sake. They are interested in that vague boundary where subjective, romantic, intuitive prejudices can give identity and direction to a project while at the same time restricting and constraining these ideas within a discipline and rigour that gives singularity to their work. Their success in achieving this status is all the more admirable given their prodigious output and their willingness to search for new ideas.

Claus en Kaan are part of a generation of European architects who have re-established confidence in modern architecture. They have achieved this not by building spectacular objects, nor by establishing an ideological agenda. Unlike the previous generation, they have fulfilled the tasks they set for themselves. It is apparent from their recent work that their ambitions are evolving, but we can be assured that these architects will maintain the essential relationship that is consistent throughout their built work: the relationship between the idea and its resolution.

LES EXTRÈMES SE TOUCHENT

VISITING CLAUS EN KAAN

Andrea Deplazes

1 Moving mountains 'Dutch style'

During my last visit to Rotterdam, Kees Kaan took me to a building site somewhere outside The Hague. Five or six firms of architects were busy at various locations on a vast plain, apparently working together in harmony on a sort of 'patchwork quilt in the making', working to a master plan for the construction of over a thousand apartments and terraced houses. Blocks of terraced houses, which differed greatly from each other and were inexplicably close together in my view (the distance between the plots being no more than five to seven metres) alternated with large plots which, for some equally unfathomable reason, were undeveloped and did not seem particularly well suited for bringing unity into the heterogeneous buildings of this embryonic suburb. The spatial scale chosen for the homes seemed completely at odds with that of the residential area as a whole. But then, with a casual gesture, Kees showed me the solution to the puzzle: water glistening in a drainage ditch. The water level was half a metre below ground level. Suddenly the penny dropped and it became clear to me that there were still 'mountains to be moved' here. A man-made landscape would come into being, with leafy trees lining extensive lakes, canals, dams, ponds and islands, water being the binding and characteristic element. In a reversal of the usual process, this man-made landscape was not being reclaimed from the sea, rather water was being allowed to flow into the topography, as if it had always been like this, so that the ratio between the site as a whole and actual building density all at once seemed self-evident and natural. Suddenly, the incredibly narrow spaces between the terraced houses (unacceptable by Swiss standards) became inevitable and it even seemed that the planners had made the most of the little islands or narrow strips of land that were available. The enormous amount of earth still to be excavated around the edges of the new housing estate was being used to build dams and embankments to shield the estate, not from the sea but fromthe noise of the traffic speeding along the adjacent motorway.

2 City landscape or landscaped city

I am not aware of any other country in Europe, not even Switzerland, where such intrusive encroachments into the topography are made as a matter of course as in the Netherlands. In Switzerland, which is slightly smaller in area than the Netherlands, the topography looms large, in the form of the enormous, unchanging mountain ranges, which occupy around a third of Switzerland's territory and make it necessary for residential areas to be laid out efficiently. This leads not only to all sorts of national myths and topoi (comparable with the Netherlands' famous dikes and polders) but also affects the economic and resulting cultural conditions. Alpine tourism relentlessly consumes the landscape as a non-renewable resource but must also, at all costs, preserve it as a marketable sanctuary for physical and mental relaxation. Meanwhile, in the country's central region, compensation must be provided for the highly concentrated urban life of industrial and service centres in the lowlands. In this game of reciprocal projections, the traditional dichotomy between town and country is being abandoned. In Switzerland, the linking together of various autonomous centres has led to the growth of a cross-shaped 'network city'; its Dutch equivalent is the Randstad, the urban agglomeration of the western Netherlands.

Space has been created within it for, amongst other things, the above-mentioned areas for recreation, the overspill areas for the cities, a sort of 'urban expansion tanks' (regardless of whether we describe them as suburb, agglomeration, region, landscape or whatever else), which are, however, riddled with exclusively (albeit different) urban characteristics: autonomous residential areas, 'networks' and 'satellites', the private waterside home with its own landing stage, streets and infrastructure, waterside cycle paths, characterized in part by an idyllic nature that can scarcely be outdone – endless Sunday afternoons, the sun beating down on the cooling water, leafy trees providing shade, city landscape or a landscaped city...

3 Strategies and 'pictoconcepts'

In this connection, I recall a drawing by the Dutch artist Joep van Lieshout. At the ETH (Eidgenössisch Technischen Hochschule) in Zurich, he displayed a plan for an autonomous mini-state in Rotterdam, led by his atelier. The plan was drawn with a felt-tip pen and might have been done by a child. In a direct and somewhat naive style it showed self-built homes, a pigsty, tractors and machines for cultivating agricultural produce, a factory for processing those products and so on. The project could have been dismissed as a collection of childhood dreams or a fanciful vision of a rural paradise, were it not for the fact that the seriousness of the undertaking was explicitly underlined by the presence of watchtowers, fences, a bomb factory and armed residents. That evoked the whole complex of political, ocial, cultural and historical experiences, expressed in a staggeringly pithy fashion and taken to its logical extremes. Little of this enigmatic, complex dualism of human coexistence is in evidence in the new housing estate in The Hague. Instead, the pronounced 'individualism' that is tangible in Van Lieshout's free state (Van Lieshout built himself a home that he dubbed 'autocrat') and now more than ever characterizes European society (together with a strong leaning towards 'consumerism') has been transferred to the architectural programme: the pursuit of total 'self realization'.

In Lieshout's graphic language, the message about the appropriation of personal, free space in the sense of self-realization and personal input (key word: artistic authorship), reduced to a pictogram, is immediately clear. It is a graphic system aimed at instant recognition and the lightning-fast transfer of information, using the devices of the advertisement, comic strip and an 'innocent child's drawing' in order to recast the most complex information into 'architectural concepts' by way of vignettes and logos. The important thing is that it concerns easy-to-digest arguments that are not connected to deep and densely layered or interconnected networks, but that remain spontaneous, sporadic and specific so that they are able to link up in an 'unforced' and 'playful' way to preconditioned patterns of social conventions. In this way a new arsenal of design strategies is created that makes use of a non-architectural language, thereby responding to the insecurities of a clientele that can no longer be communicated with on a personal basis (building consortiums, investors and managers). In this respect, the current 'information society' differs essentially from the old 'knowledge society'. The latter was ultimately concerned with a value system that was applicable for use in daily life and consistently understood humanistic knowledge as a synthesis of prior knowledge processes, derived from similar, mutually influencing variables. On the other hand, the flow of information and the pluralism of value systems do not permit a predetermined hierarchical subdivision, unless it is an arbitrary, personal and specific subdivision that can only be justified on a case to case basis via the axiom of the architectural concept. This form of architectural argumentation may be extremely entertaining and liberating now and then, but the architectural products that arise from it are to all intents and purposes inert when measured against pure architectural criteria such as 'materiality' and 'structurality' in the tectonic and structural sense. The phenomenon of advertising and the pressure of economics on the construction market have probably contributed to the invention of 'architectural marketing' in the Netherlands and given rise to concepts that are sold as open action strategies, process-oriented, in the form of pictograms – a not unimportant fact when one conceives the reality of architecture as a question not just of the art of building, but also of the marketing of, and the market for, buildings – a reality that forces architectural firms engaged in the daily competitive struggle to adopt survival strategies. Against such a background, one should really speak of a concentrated architecture that scarcely reflects the density of information in its 'pictoconcepts'.

4 Extremes without contradictions?

There are therefore no contradictions involved in the adoption of extreme architectural positions, such as is occurring on the various building sites in that housing estate in The Hague. They all have their origins in the primary architectural basis of the artificially staged topography as recreation space and in the social concept of a 'leisure landscape' that runs parallel to it, two sides of the same coin. All other conceivable conflicts in social interaction are concealed or at least invisible. All individual freedoms, by contrast, are maximized and architecturalized. Occasionally such antics give rise to an idiosyncratic, 'interesting shape'. In one instance, the theme of a 'residential landscape' has been translated, uncontested, into a colourful collection of houses like the ones children are apt to draw – a red house, a blue house, a silver one, a wooden one and so on. In another, as if in a sort of reverse process, one giant house has been created by piling and sticking a number of single family homes together, collage-wise. Compared with these, the project by Felix Claus and Kees Kaan, at the entrance to this estate, makes a remarkably taciturn and intractable impression.

Four cubes with five storeys of varying lengths, which by their very dimensions make an oddly urban impression in this village-like, rural suburb, stand in a row. Here, contrary to the usual practice, the 'tunnel formwork principle' which forms the basis for the construction of all modern flats and terraced housing, has been applied along the length of the volume rather that across it, so that there are always two flats back-to-back facing in opposite wind directions, one facing inwards towards the new development and the other facing outwards towards the existing suburb. As Kees explained to me, they fulfil the urban role of 'gatehouses' as described in the master plan. This surprised me greatly, as I had not expected to encounter such a classic urban planning theme here, in this architectural 'game reserve' with its strategic stamp, where every action seems to be aimed at 'flying low to evade the radar of unfavourable circumstances'.

At the moment, tall frames of reinforced concrete can be seen, partially clad with clinker bricks (fair-faced brickwork). The structural openings at the front of the concrete skeleton are linked by bonded brick walls, while the purely decorative rows of clinkers at the sides do not interlock but are laid directly one on top of another. The two layers meet, without merging into a single whole, at the ribs of the cubes. What appears from close-up to be evidence of Claus en Kaan's interest in the material and its stacking and shaping potential, reveals itself at a distance to be a strict proportioning of socially balanced, three-dimensionally and homogeneously situated buildings: 'boulders in the field' as Kees Kaan puts it. Nevertheless, those cubes are not at all clear representations of boulders and, unlike pictoconcepts, they do not tell a 'story'.

5 A condensed concentrate

The extreme reduction of these structures seems to want to stimulate a discourse on classic architectural themes (e.g. the placing of structures or the determination of their location in the topography, their 'specific gravity' etc.) strictly within the tradition of the profession, without calling upon 'outside' effects. This reductive process is oddly enough aimed at creating complexity, not through a complicated toying with building parts or exploding constructions, but in the densely layered nature of the observation of the built environment and the intellectual understanding derived from it. In chemistry, 'reduction' amounts to boiling something down (letting the excess moisture evaporate) until one is left with a strong concentrate. What remains is the essence (from the Latin 'esse', to be). It is a question of transcending the individual and specific of a task and penetrating to that which is real and exemplary, and crystallizing and articulating precisely that, without however entertaining the illusion that it will be possible to give a 'genuine' value judgement. This is underlined by the taut, extremely regular punch pattern of the window openings in the houses in The Hague which leaves open the question of whether the spaces behind are homes, offices or studios. The absence of differentiation should not be confused with a lack of clarity or decisiveness. It is ultimately a question of what can be formulated most generally, what in terms of giving ultimate shape to the architectural aspects is the most extreme consequence of a specific problem; (a procedure that can also lead to 'breaches', as we shall see below). In this respect, Claus en Kaan's projects (and not only this one in The Hague) differ from what other contemporary architects in the Netherlands are building and publishing. Despite the adverse effects of the construction industry and the necessary survival strategies, they pay a lot of attention to execution and detail, to sensuous material (time and again they opt for good old-fashioned brick), and to added architectural value that goes beyond the brute building construction and service to which Claus en Kaan, just like their fellow architects, are subject. They do in fact regard architectural products as cultural objects, even if the half-life of their life expectancy is short. Nevertheless, I would not wish to argue that the duo designs 'beautiful buildings' or pursues 'beauty', something that could perhaps be said of early works like the Business Centre or the Buitenveldert Depot in Amsterdam which at least maintained the illusion with their superior wood types and rust-coloured slate slabs.

Observations of this kind are all too quickly laid aside and 'frozen' into categories, which is what happened five to ten years ago in Swiss architecture whose architectural canon had very little to offer other than craftsmanlike accuracy in detailing, a sophisticated use of materials and the geometric, orthogonal form of buildings, in 'Schweizer Kisten' (Swiss boxes). Such reductive observations came not so much from the architects themselves as from the press, particularly the German-language section of it. They led to the widespread misunderstanding that the 'reduction' related to the geometric form of simple cubes or to superficial aesthetics, or even to instant understanding or the simple self-evidence of 'minimalism'. The projects by Claus en Kaan described above do indeed display a certain intellectual kinship and affinity with certain areas of interest in Swiss architecture. Although the motivations on either side do not always originate from the same source or share the same honourable aims, they do both show evidence of extremely pragmatic influences such as the economy or the construction process. And that is still the case.

6 Abstract or concrete?

It is clear that there are also observational differences in the case of Claus en Kaan, or even contradictions or 'breaches', but that may be more to do with my 'conditioning' as an observer than with anything else. At Almere, in the Flevopolder, I encountered a situation that seemed to me to be comparable to that in The Hague. Here the man-made landscape, with small lakes and a lot foliage along the water, is already in place. A tower, or rather the towerlike form of a structure clad in silvery profiled metal, rises into the noonday sky. Its top projects perilously above the lead-coloured lake, while its base widens its grip on the ground. Obviously the classic theme of mass and weight, of instability and stability was being played out here, I decided. When asked, Felix Claus confirmed that according to the original plan the tower was to have been constructed of brick. However, due to the intervention of Rem Koolhaas, designer of the master plan for Almere, and on the grounds that, in any case, the brickwork would only have formed a facing wall, it was finally decided to use a light-weight facade cladding of profiled aluminium. This avoided a visual analogy, while at the same time observation focuses not on the material scale, that of the chase bonding of the brickwork, but rather on the raw, overall form of the tower, whose only articulation is a few horizontal seams. The industrial character of the metal panels disappears into the background, together with every specific material pretension. The tower-like building 'persists', as it were, in the abstract, or better still, according to the definition of Max Bill, in the concrete. In his manifesto, *Konkrete Gestaltung* (1936/1949), he wrote: 'Concrete artworks are works of art that do not originate through abstraction, but rather through their own resources and regularities, without relying on natural phenomena or a transformation thereof.' Although a 'reverse effect' is used – light aluminium cladding instead of heavy brickwork – the fundamental theme or concept of the design survives (a displacement of the conceptual centre of gravity, just like the gatehouses in The Hague, I now realize with hindsight). Indeed, the rigid layout of the windows also forms a dominant presence on the tower, which finally no longer needs to conform, for example, to the inner logic of a brickwork module – something that, in the case of the structures in The Hague can still be regarded as an ordering imposed 'from outside', even if the placement of the windows went against the logic of the brickwork.

7 Routine construction work and windows

Around 80% of buildings constructed in Switzerland each year are 'run-of-the-mill'; only a small proportion of them are designed by contracted architects. It is therefore very remarkable indeed that in the Netherlands, social housing is the 'admission ticket' for new firms of architects. It is also fairly unique in Europe as a whole. From an architectural perspective, it is a difficult field to work in, requiring a great deal of discipline from the architect. There is little glory to be had and there are strict limits upon freedom, because of the numerous parameters the architect has to work within. Often it is dominated by fairly gratuitous whims and fashions, by compulsive or contrived escape attempts by architects or their clients, who are unwilling or unable to pose the inherent, mostly unexciting, questions. Claus en Kaan do not seem to allow themselves to be scared off by such doubts and fears. With 'Miesian obstinacy', or rather in the firm belief that they are on the trail of a binding architectural canon, they present their work as the classical masters did, with themes that do not at all fit into the present Dutch architectural spectrum. I was strangely touched, for example, by the way their projects for filling gaps in Amsterdam's inner city repeatedly, in countless variations, address the same theme: the window and its relationship to the structure. How few resources are required to evoke a picture of an entire architectural universe – and without striking personal attitudes or cutting any capers! And – I gladly stress this again – without that obvious pursuit of design, of 'beautiful architecture'. In contrast to the quotation from St. Augustine that Mies van der Rohe was fond of citing, 'beauty' for Claus en Kaan lies not in 'the shine of truth' but, translated into our own context, in the 'light of clarity' – that is to say, conceptual clarity, minimal resources, complex stratification. Clarity is always related to order, to following hierarchical relationships and rules, using tools of reference that may include the specific case, but tend more towards the exemplary. It is all the more striking that we sometimes experience our own daily living environment as chaotic and incomprehensible, as an unmanageable muddle that is beyond our personal influence – an observation that from other perspectives would be regarded as simply wrong. Although entropy affects chaotic processes, chaos may itself be a complex form of order. Or to put it the other way round: order is a component of chaos, a chosen fragment that is deliberately kept so small that the rules remain clear and in balance within the entire complex, thereby becoming exemplary.

Without getting caught up in contradictions, we are aware that although order may be underpinned axiomatically, it subsequently develops or repeats itself logically and regularly. That could give rise to a design technique.

8 Keeping the secret

Are Claus en Kaan in pursuit of something hopelessly outdated? Perhaps, if one considers only formal questions, classical ideas and unchanging dogmas. But not if it is a question of an almost archaeological process of penetrating to the essence of a particular assignment, of 'fieldwork' on the borders of an intellectual *terra incognita*, of exploratory drilling in an apparently all too familiar *locus amoenus*. Time and again, this study brings us back to the necessity of continually facing a choice between numerous vague or highly personal preferences, each of which drags in its wake an endless jumble of continuing, uncertain choices. As a reaction to and consequence of that, essential clarity and procedural logic become ideals worth pursuing.

Quite apart from all of that, the work of Claus en Kaan emits sparks of an indefinable secret, something inexpressible, an inner tension that may cause friction, and in which the classic themes of architecture distinguish themselves from every hasty attempt at a picto-concept that must reveal all immediately – and there are no second chances.

Paul Valéry expressed this unstable, open state or process very clearly and concisely when he wrote: 'What we don't hold on to is nothing. What we do hold onto is dead'.

URBANE ARCHITECTURES

Christoph Grafe

The two buildings in Amsterdam reveal their full splendour around seven o'clock in the morning when the early morning light brushes rosily over the smooth brickwork leaving behind thin, oddly glowing lines in the delicate network of pointing that is traced across the facade. The framework retains its silvery sheen, as though seeking to match the indeterminate colour of the Amsterdam sky reflected in the glass of the window panes. The refractions of light, that show up every edge, every irregularity, give the facade the appearance of a single thin, sharply defined plane, standing flush with the building line. And then there are the winged hinges by which the windows latch onto the frames – the kind of constructional ingenuity one is familiar with from industrial machinery, originating not from the primitive repertoire of brick and mortar construction, but from the much more precise world of the mechanical engineer. They suit the window frames and yet, in their three-dimensionality they are an alien presence on this facade, rather like a series of sharply cut ornamental gems that have grown out of the flat surface.

The facades on Laagte Kadijk, in a neighbourhood that twenty years ago consisted of a few down-at-heel almshouses, factories and warehouses, but which is now a popular residential area tucked away in the middle of Amsterdam, are by no means spectacular. The composition of the elevation (if composition is the right word) – three rows of casement windows, the lowest of which is interrupted by a shallow recess – has the decorous regularity we know from the eighteenth- or early nineteenth-century facades that line the Amsterdam canals or the streets of middle-class neighbourhoods in London and many another northern European mercantile city. This one differs only in that it is a little wider and lacks the addition of classical elements, and while the repetition of windows is not quite sufficient to form a grid, it is just enough to sustain the alternating pattern of open and closed of the existing street elevation.

The facades on Laagte Kadijk are no isolated occurrence. Indeed, in the work of Claus en Kaan nothing is an isolated occurrence. A succession of jutting narrow towers and receding niches is a continuation of the existing ribbon development along the main road of an Amsterdam suburb. Small blocks in the middle of the Bijlmer, the Netherlands' largest and most heroic public housing experiment of the 1960s and '70s, are literally adaptors between the existing flat buildings and the new brick town houses that are supposed to rehabilitate the Bijlmer. In the urban design plan for IJburg, where there is no question of any pre-existing context, a sense of continuity is evoked by giving the new district the appearance of a compact, but nonetheless semi-urban, suburb such as might have sprung up a hundred years ago. This architecture makes use of elements whose appearance and meaning can both be assumed to be familiar. The notion of invention takes on a qualified meaning here, becoming an answer to the question inherent in a given situation. Just what is new remains somewhat elusive, and would not seem to matter either, were it not that it is the addition itself that opens one's eyes to the physical qualities and the meaning of what was already there. Only now does the ribbon development truly become an endless reiteration of small houses lining a main road. The open landscape with tall blocks of flats that is the Bijlmer, finally becomes the green polder garden dotted with houses envisaged by its planners. And the IJburg layout finally raises the possibility of Amsterdam becoming the great compact, polycentric city it might have become a hundred years ago had it not been for the puritanical fear of the anonymity of the metropolis which led instead to the establishment of diverse centres of urban development in a concretization of the ideal of the Netherlands as a collection of small villages and towns. As such, one could characterize the projects of Claus en Kaan as 'corrections', in the sense that they transform a latent quality into something visible. The notion of correction refers here not to a reactive attitude but rather to a tactical position.

Just because the architects have been rather reticent about presenting a theoretical interpretation of their work, does not mean that they have no considered views on designing. Their ideas have crystallized out over the course of a long period of submitting to the forces that dominate the development, production and use of the city. All too obviously a priori theories would only hamper a process that calls for openness and flexibility in thinking. Their position is the outcome of a cumulative process in which previously hidden motivations manifest themselves gradually and theory is the result of reflection rather than a hypothesis to be confirmed retrospectively by practice.

In the context of Dutch architecture, with its tendency to look for 'innovation' – much of it fairly unmotivated – the steady consolidation of a design approach that characterizes the work of Claus en Kaan in the 1990s, is to say the least exceptional. The architects seem keen to point out the need for a number of clear but also negotiable agreements capable of regulating the way the individual building functions in the context of the city. It is a matter of rediscovering a flexible architectural etiquette. In the succession of projects wrought by Claus en Kaan, the accumulation of knowledge also assumes a concrete form. There is an explicit recurrence of typologies and technical solutions in buildings that are specific and unique, but at the same part of a series. In the built work, therefore, it is possible to read and in time to identify, what was initially no more than an intuitive presence: an argument about the role of architecture as discipline, about its place in the radically changing landscape of the Netherlands, and about the tumultuous cultural shifts that started to make themselves felt here in the last three or four decades of the twentieth century and that so swiftly became reality around the turn of the present century that the new *embarras des richesses* evokes a much older kind of uneasiness.

The language of an urban architecture

In the 1980s, the period when Claus en Kaan embarked on their architectural career, the ideas and methodology of Italian architects like Giorgio Grassi and Aldo Rossi were starting to filter into the urban design debate in the Netherlands.[1] Fuelled by a critical historical analysis of (prewar) modern urbanism and the traditional European city, Grassi and Rossi sought to redefine the relation between the individual building and its physical and psychological context. The extensive Internationale Bauausstellung held in Berlin in 1987 can be seen as the moment when this approach became visible on a large scale and with the participation of a great many architects. West Berlin, with its still gaping war wounds and a crude modernist postwar planning history, was the ideal site for an investigation into how insertions at the scale of the individual building could be used to re-establish the city as a spatially and functionally coherent system. In the Netherlands it was a group of architects attached to Delft University of Technology and active mainly in Rotterdam, who attempted to revise the tradition of housing from the perspective of these 'international' ideas. It was the first time since Bakema's megalomaniac proposals in the 1970s that a reasoned pronouncement had been made on the relation between the territory of the individual and the public urban domain, a relation that was to be given architectural form by construing design as the redefinition of familiar models. According to this view, a design derives its meaning not from the original gesture, the architect's inspiration, but from the way architectural concepts – street, urban block, court or passage – are interpreted, and from the inevitable shift between tradition and the new reading of that tradition.

In Berlin, as earlier on in southern Europe, this approach was instrumental in the formulation of an architectural language for 'the' European city eventually mutating into dogma after political reunification in the new German capital. In the Netherlands, the quest for continuity with the nineteenth-century model of the large city (or: *Großstadt*) was more problematic in that despite metropolitan impulses in both Amsterdam and Rotterdam around 1900, a distinct Dutch model of such a city had failed to evolve. But the negligible influence of Grassi and Rossi, and of the debate they had initiated, also had its origins in the repudiation of their approach as historicizing. Moreover, the occasional historical quotation in Rossi's work formed a pretext for dismissing the architect as a postmodernist. Aldo van Eyck's tirade against the 'Rats, Posts and other Pests' at the Royal Institute of British Architects in 1981, in which the Italian architects were lumped together with Robert Venturi and Charles Moore, testifies not only to a subtle rhetorical misconception, but also to a wilful refusal to recognize the relevance of an international architectural debate to the Netherlands.[2] The fact that the opposite and prevailing model of urban renewal, with its emphasis on the small scale and the expression of the individual dwelling, though it might have be practical in a period of economic stagnation and urban consolidation, offered few starting points for a more dynamic development, was completely overlooked.

The lack of a broad debate about the role that architecture should play in its urban context, given that a city is not merely a physical datum but a collective cultural product, became painfully apparent twenty years later in the formalistic dressing-up of highly conventional terrace houses in the new urban development schemes of the 1990s. In the absence of any concept of a contemporary urban or suburban form, or of how this form might be translated into an idea of suburban living, it was mostly the cardboard images of the project developers that were realized in the liberalized mass housing market. The repetition of the standardized, two-storey single-family dwelling, which the Victorians had translated into anonymous, and therefore urban, residential areas, is now hidden behind over-designed facades that have been subjected to the full force of the architect's formal repertoire. The essentially repetitive character of the suburb is thereby categorically denied by masking techniques in the form of ever-gaudier brick facades or decorous white rendering. Just what risible forms the fear of banality can take, was equally apparent in the invention of that wonderful, untranslatable term 'beeldkwaliteit' (literally, 'visual quality') which subsequently required the invention of an elaborate planning mechanism known as the 'visual quality plan'.

It is precisely in these outer suburbs that many of Claus en Kaan's projects are located. It is in Zaandam, Spijkenisse, Haarlemmermeer, Amstelveen – middle-Holland in other words – that a conception of designing as a meticulous reading of the underlying laws of a standardized programme, is being thought through to its most essential consequences. The results of this research are appallingly clear: a house in the Netherlands is the outcome of a prevailing building method, a conventional notion of living that has been laid down in regulations and standards, clear notions as to how private territory should be defined vis à vis street and neighbours, and a planning tradition that persists in coupling the individual dwelling to an expression of collective control. In the absence of a client capable of influencing the details of the programme, any suggestion of individual identity must be imposed by the designer, something Claus en Kaan can only reject as inappropriate. By deliberately eschewing architectural gestures that might distract from the fundamental given of the programme, they create the space in which the shaping of these details can take place.

The task of determining the basic elements of a dwelling demands an effort that is only made possible by approaching it systematically. A decision about the profile of the front door or the colour of the letter box, is not a resultant of a design process that seeks refinement in architectural detail, rather it creates the condition for the understanding of the design as a whole. The profile determines whether the door stands in a shallow recess or flush with the street; the letter box may, by its colour, manifest itself as a rudimentary expression of an address and its occupant, or explicitly refrain from making any such declaration. The moments of decision must be precisely defined, not as steps in a linear process, but as points at which a statement presents itself or is actively formulated, or arises as a consequence of fresh insight. However much a solution to a design problem may be determined by pre-established conditions and by the project's position in a series, a new design always goes beyond these con-

1 On the occasion of the first Architecture International Rotterdam (AIR) in 1982, Aldo Rossi was invited to present his proposals for the revitalization of the docks area on the left bank of the Maas.

2 Aldo van Eyck, 'R.P.P. (Rats, Posts and other Pests). The RIBA annual discourse', *AD News Supplement*, 1981/7 and *RIBA Journal* April 1981, pp. 47–50.

fines by subjecting a clearly defined aspect to further investigation. In Amstelveen, it is the relation between the repeating articulation and a surrounding expanse of brick; in Zaandam it is about the balance between the broad brick grid and the horizontal windows as a device for making a heavy building with large openings, while the Amsterdam projects on Borneo-Sporenburg and Laagte Kadijk, express window and wall as two conditions of the same razor-sharp plane. Through the explicit choices that are made between the general and the particular, and the fundamental decision to present the building both as a distinct object and as an echo of its context, the projects refer back to their designers who reveal themselves by their handwriting. Deliberately stripped of any expression of individuality, this handwriting becomes a language capable of expressing the general. Because of this, the projects, despite their limited physical range, make a statement about the generic quality of the their street, their neighbourhood, their city. The handwriting suddenly becomes a vernacular idiom. The projects of Claus en Kaan could be described as natural embodiments of generally accepted agreements. But this is to overlook the fact that the restriction to an architectural language that expresses the non-specific, is an exception in Dutch architectural production at the beginning of the 21st century.

Public and private

The position taken by Claus en Kaan could be called conservative. After all, their buildings evince not the slightest interest in challenging the laws they obey. Yet this approach is a logical reaction to the realities that have been created in the Netherlands during the past ten years; realities whose implications are as yet only intuitively recognized. In a country whose entire planning system has been geared to the preservation of decentralized, autonomous communities, the intensity of the consolidation now taking place is bound to sow confusion and unease. The flexible and ultimately ambivalent position of public opinion regarding physical and social change, must seem puzzling to an outsider and, depending on the observer's viewpoint, it elicits aversion, respect or admiration. International interest in the Netherlands centres on social and cultural experiments, such as the euthanasia legislation or the liberalization of the welfare state. International amazement is greatest, however, when it comes to the architectural experiments of young Dutch architects. The combination of a pragmatic rhetoric, an unorthodox interpretation of the programme and a highly developed feeling for architectonic spectacle, operates with enviable dexterity and precision in the circles in which international architectural production is discussed and processed into consumable images. The ironic, at any rate unbiased, attitude to ostensibly immutable laws, not only spawns an entertaining kind of architecture, but the stunning gestures, displayed with boyish nonchalance, are perceived as crystallizations of the transition to a mature information society.

The reinterpretation of the notion of the Netherlands as a socio-economic trailblazer in light of a decade of prosperity – the polder as one big laboratory for what is referred to as the 'second modernity' – has a muddying effect on the perception of the reality of the processes that are manifesting themselves in the urbanization of the countryside.[3] Granted, the increase in scale of the existing urban cores disrupts the continuity of the controlled lines of development of spatial planning and heralds the end of the conceptualization of the Netherlands as a collection of small cities, but compared with the spatial and social explosions that urban regions elsewhere in Europe were subjected to at the beginning of the industrial age, this is more in the nature of a long postponed catch-up exercise.[4] The question is whether the Netherlands can really be said to have had a full-blown 'first modernity'. The earlier clinging to the concept of a well-organized and self-regulating small-town society in which social differences were channelled into a vertical organization (the famous socio-political 'pillars') certainly did nothing to promote the development of an anonymous metropolitan society. Behind the exceptionally prominent role of Dutch architects in classic modern architecture, and behind the forcefulness with which modern architecture entered the scene immediately after the Second World War, lies another reality – one in which varying coalitions of religious political groupings dominated both public and private life until well into the 1960s. Their success in preserving the norms and values of close-knit communities in the face of ongoing economic and technological development was in itself an obstacle to the cultural levelling that characterizes industrial society. Instead of developing into a secularized, civil society, the Netherlands underwent a civilized form of religious tribalization and mutual exclusion that effectively postponed the development of an everyday modernity. As a frame of reference for architecture, the experience of the anonymous, rootless metropolitan masses that looms so large in the literary work of Charles Baudelaire or Alfred Döblin, or the blasé attitude of inhabitants of the modern metropolis that Georg Simmel diagnosed as a reaction to living cheek by jowl,[5] and the translation of this experience into an aesthetic of the *Großstadt*, is consequently limited in the Netherlands.[6] Perhaps it is the very absence of the model of the classic nineteenth-century metropolis and of the modernity it exacts from its inhabitants that prompts an explicit search for architectural forms that articulate the modern rather than being an outcome of it.

The work of Claus en Kaan is devoid of any trace of partiality for a social reality in the sense that this should be expressed in the form of the architectural object. The stern reticence that characterizes the demeanour of these buildings, and the sharp line the envelope draws between the interior and the public realm, must seem regressive to those who are opposed to any distinction between the personal and the public statement. The affirmation of that distinction is after all carried to extremes in this work through the formulation of an architectural idiom derived in the first instance from the everyday and the commonplace. The neutrality of the architectural gesture that is so precisely and so consciously evoked here that the naturalness in turn makes way for an heightened perception, implies a view about the distance the private realm should observe with respect to the street. The demarcation of the individual's sphere of influence and the refusal to allow the street (read: the public realm) to be taken over by manifestations of individuality, is the outcome of a mature definition of the public sphere. The neutrality gives expression to the civility that is the precondition for the development of urbanity. The privileging of the shell and the emphasis on the treatment of the facade as a shallow plane behind which an inner world may hide, is a logical architectural rendering of this neutrality that makes intimacy possible precisely by restricting it. The result of such elucidation is an interior that not only evades the influence of a long-since anonymous collective, but is also the very place where the individual can leave his or her mark.

3 See: Bart Lootsma, *Super Dutch. New architecture in the Netherlands*, London 2000.

4 For the crucial period of 1800 to 1850, Rob van Engelsdorp Gastelaars even speaks of de-urbanization and blames the lack of a dominant big city capable of spawning a metropolitan culture on the relatively late industrialization that facilitated decentralized development in small and medium-sized towns. 'Verstedelijking van Nederland tussen 1800 en 1940', in: Ed Taverne and Irman Visser (eds), *Stedebouw: de geschiedenis van de stad in de Nederlanden van 1500 tot heden*, Nijmegen 1993, pp. 174–179.

5 Georg Simmel, 'The Metropolis and Mental Life', in: Richard Sennett, *Classic Essays on the Culture of the Cities*, New Jersey 1968.

6 According to Ed Taverne and Cor Wagenaar the big city also plays a negligible role in Dutch literature, especially in comparison with French and German examples. 'De stad in de Nederlandstalige literatuur 1500–1950', in: Taverne/Visser 1993, pp. 335–340.

1988 2001

001 **Molenerf De Ster**
(see 003, 006, 008)
Day care centre in existing building on site of former sawmill

Utrecht
1988–1994

p. 16

002 **HoLaTuKa**
(see 071)
Feasibility study for housing on Hoogte, Laagte and Tussen Kadijken

Amsterdam
1988

p. 90

003 **Molenerf De Ster**
(see 001, 006, 008)
Two studios, freestanding volume inside existing building on site of former sawmill

Utrecht
1988–1994

p. 16

004 **Spruit House**
Flexible, open-plan house for musician on site designated for agricultural use

Huybergen
1988

005 **Kaan Assurantiën**
(see 029)
Two houses located on a main road merged to form house with office

Bergen op Zoom
1988–1991

p. 20

006 **Molenerf De Ster**
(see 001, 003, 008)
Music practice space in former workman's dwelling
Not built

Utrecht
1988

p. 16

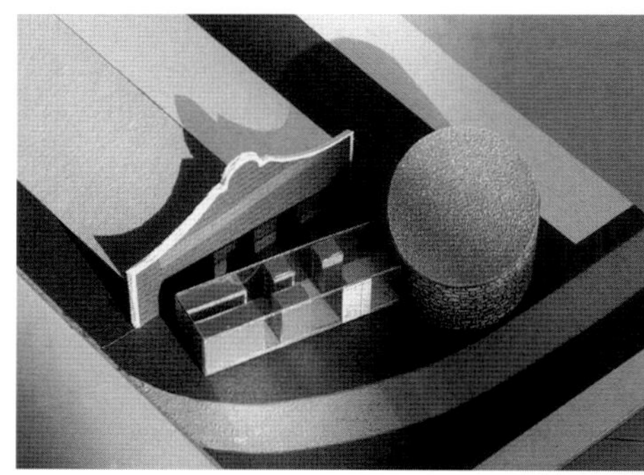

007 **Juvenaat**
Feasibility study of seminary complex

Bergen op Zoom
1988

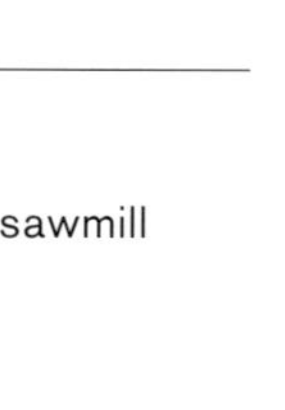

008 **Molenerf De Ster**
(see 001, 003, 006)
Adaptive reuse of former sawmill for offices

Utrecht
1988–1994

p. 16

009 **AMRO Warehouse**
Feasibility study for conversion of warehouse to residential use

Amsterdam
1989

010 **Kadijken Legal centre**
Design for office interior

Amsterdam
1989

011 **Hans Ebbing Prize for Furniture Design**

1990

012 **Health Centre**
Three consulting rooms, a waiting room, treatment room, office, kitchen and washroom

Rotterdam
1990–1992

p. 22

013 **Almere de Fantasie**
Competition

Almere
1990

Competition design for a house in Almere in which living in the landscape has acquired an extreme form. The ten by ten by three metre house is divided up into four spaces that are separated from one another by a cruciform wall unit. For the rest it consists of little more than a floor and a roof and in-between elevations made up of two by three metre pivoting glass panels.

014 **FDO**
Feasibility study for conversion of FDO building for residential use

Amsterdam
1990

015 **Plein 40-45**
Plan for reorganization of the area around Plein 40–45

Amsterdam
1990

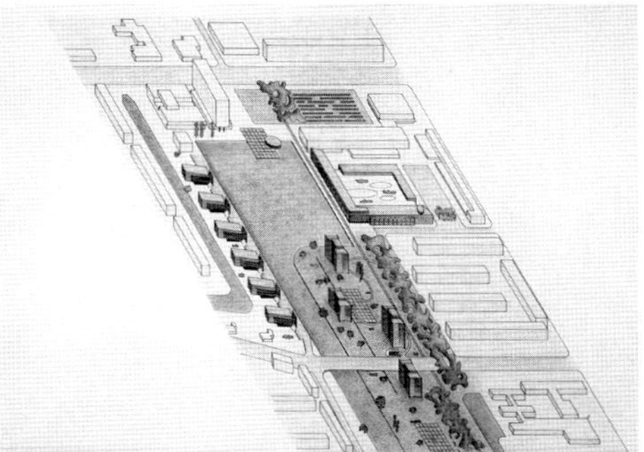

016 **Klein & Partners**
Advertising agency interior

Amsterdam
1990

017 **Brouwersgracht Schilfgaarde**
Feasibility study for conversion of warehouse to dwelling and gallery

Amsterdam
1990

018 **FDO Monumentenzorg**
Feasibility study for conversion of industrial building for residential use, preserving monumental details

Amsterdam
1990

019 **Korte Prinsengracht**
Feasibility study for conversion of warehouse for residential use

Amsterdam
1990

020 **Stichting De Ruimte**
Feasibility study for adaptive reuse of industrial buildings

Amsterdam
1990

021 **Victorieplein**
Housing study

Amsterdam
1990

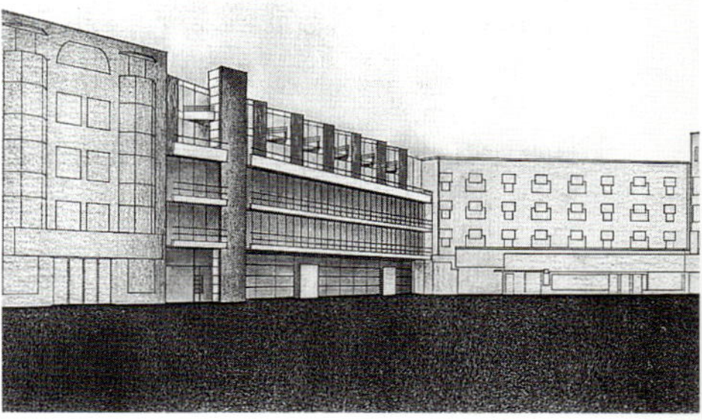

022 **Prix de Rome**
Competition: Residence for collector of doll's houses

Delft
1990

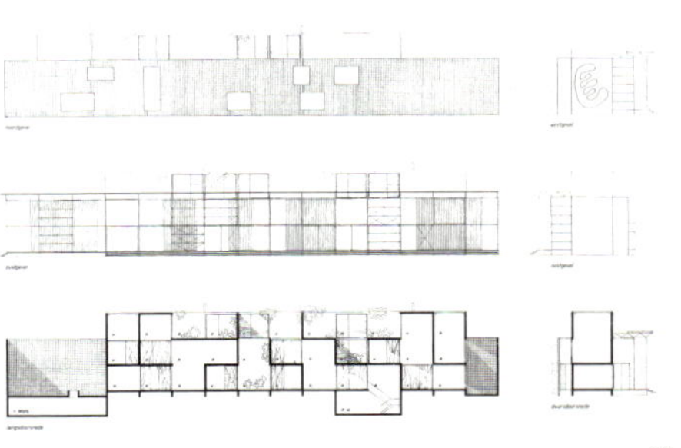

023 **Buitenveldert Depot**
Depot for three different municipal services

Amsterdam
1990–1992

p. 24

024 **'t Breed Day Care Centre**
Conversion of school to day care centre

Amsterdam
1990

025 **Korte Prinsengracht**
(see 046)
Restoration and conversion of double warehouse

Amsterdam
1989–1993

Conversion of a warehouse in the centre of Amsterdam into five apartments and a gallery. The insertion of large windows changes the 'penthouse' apartment into an airy space.

026 **Molenwijk Children's Centre**
Day care centre for babies and toddlers, a play room for pre-schoolers and after-school facilities for older children

Amsterdam
1990–1993

p. 30

027 **Molenwijk**
Study for reorganization of area around children's centre

Amsterdam
1990

028 **Housing Haarlemmerbuurt**
(see 030, 048, 059)
Sixteen dwellings and 150 m^2 commercial space at four different locations

Amsterdam
1990–1997

p. 34

029 **Kaan Assurantiën**
(see 005)
Fitting-out of apartment

Bergen op Zoom
1990–1992

p. 20

030 **Binnen Vissersstraat**
(see 028, 048, 059)
Restoration and conversion of old houses into nine apartments

Amsterdam
1989–1997

p. 34

031 **Clubhouse Plejadenplein**
Clubhouse with party room for playground association

Amsterdam
1991–1991

p. 38

032 **Corpus den Hoorn**
(see 035, 036)
Urban development study
for Maria den Hoorn site

Groningen
1991

p. 40

033 **De Boer House**
House with garage on
Nieuwe Jonkersstraat

Amsterdam
1991

Design for a house in the Nieuwmarkt quarter of Amsterdam. The focal point is the facade composition. The combination of glass and natural stone interspersed with wood, in rectangular panels and bands, lends even such a small-scale facade a graphic monumentality.

034 **Wester Gasworks**
Feasibility study for adaptive reuse
of industrial complex

Amsterdam
1991

035 **Patio Dwellings**
Corpus den Hoorn
(see 032, 036)
24 patio dwellings on Donderslaan

Groningen
1990–1993

p. 40

036 **Pensioner Apartment Building**
Corpus den Hoorn
(see 032, 035)
48 pensioner flats
on Landsteinerlaan

Groningen
1991–1993

p. 40

037 **Amsterdam School of Business (HES)**
Spatial design study for HES site

Amsterdam
1991

038 **LaKa Playground**
Design for playground
on Laagte Kadijk

Amsterdam
1991

039 Cancelled

040 **Jurg**
Glazed rooftop unit extension and kitchen refit

Rotterdam
1991

041 **Cornelis Troostplein**
Feasibility study for housing on Cornelis Troostplein

Amsterdam
1992

042 **Business Centre Papaverweg**
Commercial buildings on Papaverweg comprising 1,880 m² business units and 860 m² offices

Amsterdam
1992–1994

p. 44

043 **Bussumerstraat**
Twenty dwellings with basement car park and 420 m² business accommodation

Hilversum
1992–1995

044 **Berlage 75**
Design for housing on site of former tram depot

Amsterdam
1992

Urban development study for a site in Amsterdam South on the edge of Berlage's Plan Zuid. In this plan the tram depot makes way for mixed-typology housing that fits in with the Berlagian perimeter blocks while eschewing its hermetic quality. The new development opens up towards the Amstel, thereby raising the question of the city's flawed relationship with the river, using the same argumentation as was later to be used in the design for the Municipal Archives (188).

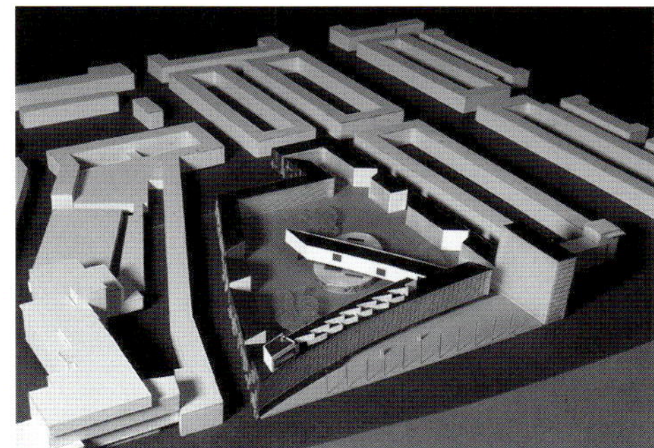

045 **Housing Amstelveenseweg**
(see 070)
31 single-family dwellings spread over four locations

Amsterdam
1992–1998

p. 48

046 **Korte Prinsengracht**
(see 025)
Studio interior

Amsterdam
1989–1993

047 **Western Canal Zone**
Inventory of new-build locations in the western canal zone

Amsterdam
1993

Design study for small infills in the western part of the centre of Amsterdam. Apart from research into mini-floor plans and compact circulation, the study included an analysis of building costs. This revealed that the facade accounted for only two per cent of the total building costs, giving the lie to the prevailing wisdom that such projects were only financially feasible with prefab facade elements. In fact, Claus en Kaan showed that a uniform technocratic image is not a sine qua non; it is perfectly feasible to develop a specific architecture for each different location.

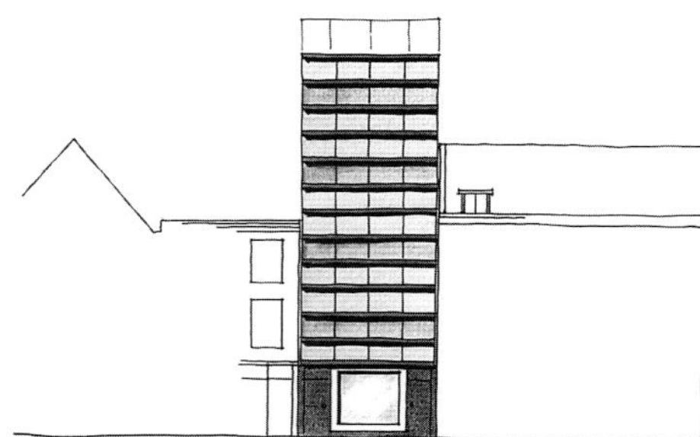

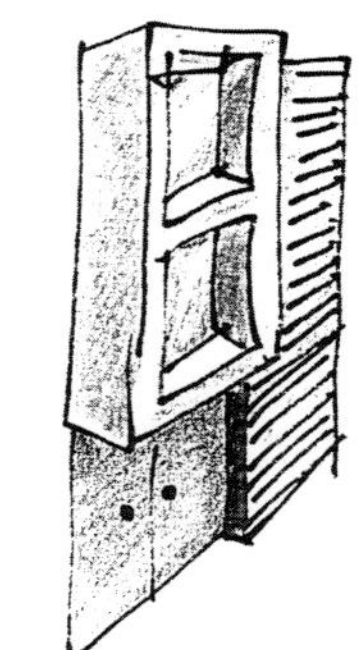

048 **Housing Haarlemmerbuurt**
(see 028, 030, 059)
Street A+

Amsterdam
1990–1997

p. 34

049 **Key Chalet**
Design for conversion of freestanding chalet on Veemarkt square into offices for the Lieven de Key Foundation

Amsterdam
1992

050 **Borneo-Sporenburg**
Urban development plan for Borneo-Sporenburg

Amsterdam
1992

051 **Sloten ZW 1**
Spatial Master Plan for Southwest Quadrant of Nieuw Sloten

Amsterdam
1992

p. 52

052 **Jacques Veltman**
Sketch design for 120 dwellings, school, community centre, business units and 120 parking spaces on Jacques Veltmanstraat

Amsterdam
1993

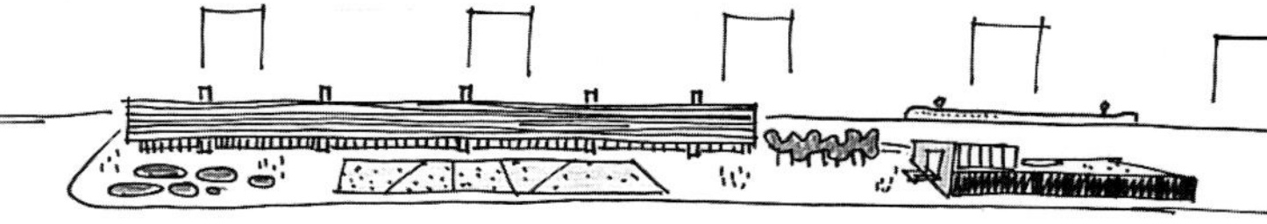

053 **International School**
Subdivision proposal for housing on former International School site

Amsterdam
1993

054 **Hoornse Heem Pensioner Apartments**
Apartment tower with 56 flats/sheltered accommodation for the elderly in close proximity to nursing home

Groningen
1993–1997

p. 56

055 **Land Registry**
Reorganization of reception area and offices for the land registry Board of Directors

Apeldoorn
1993–1994

056 **Bijlmer BeBo**
(see 058, 074, 083, 113)
Study for stacked, single-family dwellings (BeBo is a contraction of the Dutch for 'up-and-down') on Bijlmerdreef. Part of the restructuring of the Gulden Kruis housing estate.

Amsterdam
1993

p. 62

057 **PoSo**
(see 075)
Combined accommodation for police post (Po) and social services (So) district office

Amsterdam
1993–1995

p. 58

058 **Housing, Gulden Kruis**
(see 056, 074, 083, 113)
67 BeBo (up-and-down) dwellings on Bijlmerdreef. Part of the restructuring of the Gulden Kruis housing estate.

Amsterdam
1993–1997

p. 62

059 **Housing, Haarlemmerbuurt**
(see 028, 030, 048)
66 Haarlemmerstraat, part of Street A+

Amsterdam
1990–1997

p. 34

060 **Bos en Lommer**
Study for dwellings with flexible floor plans along the Westelijk Marktkanaal. Proposal for four elongated buildings of fifteen storeys, with drive-in dwellings at ground level

Amsterdam
1994

061 **Frederikspark**
Invited competition for redevelopment of Frederikspark with housing

Haarlem
1994

Design for luxury apartments at Frederikspark in Haarlem. Massiveness is avoided by dividing the volume, with three flats per floor, into three vertical elements linked by a glazed stairwell. The slim tower blocks project over the sunken parking deck. Because the building does not look like housing, the public character of the park is maintained. The individuality of the domestic interiors is hidden behind an abstract fenestration.

062 **Ronald McDonald House and Apartments**
(see 069)
Thirty apartments with car park for temporary occupancy by relatives of sick children being treated at the nearby VU Hospital.

Amsterdam
1994–2000

p. 70

063 **Wibautplein**
(see 101)
Restructuring of postwar Nieuwland district. 94 single-family dwellings with gardens on an inner courtyard and a five-storey apartment building at the short end.

Schiedam
1994–1996

064 **Housing, Marvelo**
Elaboration of master plan by Concko and Gautier with high-rise at tip of island 1, quayside high-rise on island 3, and several low-rise blocks

Zaandam
1995–1999

p. 74

065 **Housing, Sporenburg**
(see 098, 106, 109, 118)
Sporenburg 2 and 7

Amsterdam
1994–1997

p. 80

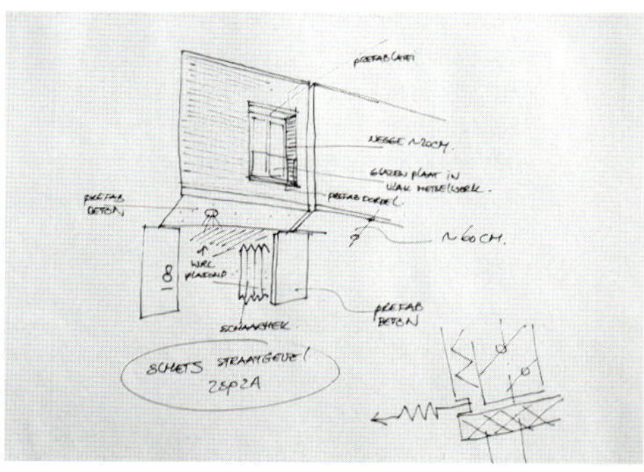

066 **Communal Amenities, Dierdonk**
Competition: Urban design for the centre of Dierdonk in collaboration with Michael van Gessel and Fortuyn/O'Brien

Helmond
1995

p. 86

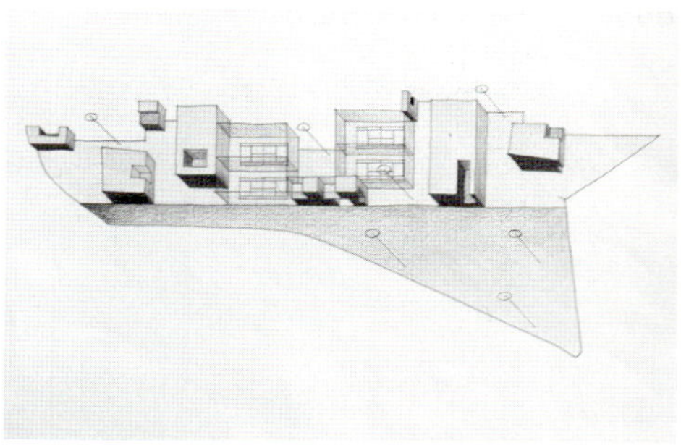

067 **Van Schaik Company Premises**
Design of warehouse and offices for construction company

Breukelen
1994–2000

p. 88

068 **Houthavens**
Design study for transformation of Houthavens to residential area

Amsterdam
1995

Design study for the transformation of a former docks area (Houthavens) in Amsterdam into a residential district. The harbour character is preserved in the form of jetties at which houseboats are moored, reminiscent of Sausalito-style living. In a programme dominated by single-family dwellings, the architects' concern was to strike a balance between the scale of the individual dwelling and the size of the area.

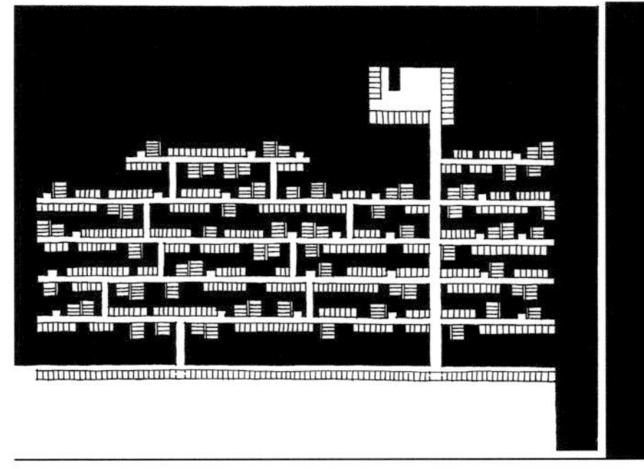

069 **Apartments Amstelveenseweg**
(see 062)
Apartments beside Ronald McDonald House

Amsterdam
1994–2000

p. 70

070 **Housing Amstelveenseweg**
(see 045)
Interior

Amsterdam
1992–1998

p. 48

071 **HoLaTuKa**
(see 002)
Housing on Hoogte Kadijk and Laagte Kadijk: 26 urban dwellings for subsidized rental and owner-occupied sector

Amsterdam
1994–1998

p. 90

072 **De Held**
(see 076)
135 single-family dwelling in various types for urban development (Vinex) location

Groningen
1995–1997

073 **Smallest Dwelling**
(see 128)
Detailed study of minimum dwelling

Amsterdam
1995

Study of the minimum dwelling under the (then) new Bouwbesluit (Buildings Decree 1991). Adherence to all the rules laid down in this act results in a statutory Existenz-minimum dwelling of 33.60 square metres. The study was more in the nature of a mental exercise than a serious design challenge for the prosperous Netherlands where, despite the rising pressure on space, density levels do not yet call for the construction of such small dwellings. The findings from this study were later put to good use in the design of 61 student flats in Amsterdam (128).

p. 134

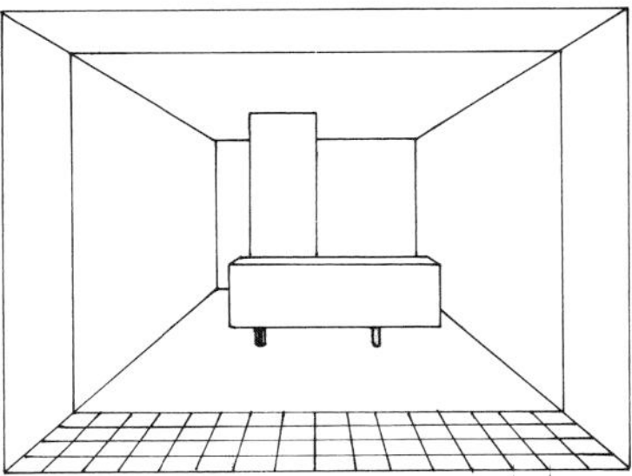

074 **Bijlmer art**
(see 056, 058, 083, 113)
27 ceramic panels for the BeBo dwellings on Bijlmerdreef by Eddy Varekamp

Amsterdam
1995

p. 62

075 **Interior of police post and social services**
(see 057)

Amsterdam
1993–1995

p. 58

076 **De Held op Zondag**
(see 072)
Part of the De Held housing scheme

Groningen
1995

077 **Vijverhof**
Refurbishment of interior of Ministry of Agriculture, Nature Management and Fisheries

Diemen
1995–1995

Remodelling of an office complex in Diemen for the Ministry of Agriculture, Nature Management and Fisheries. First of a series of renovations by Claus en Kaan in which the atmosphere of the existing building is drastically altered. In this case a rather bland building acquires an environment at odds with the classic image of a civil-service biotope. The interior could almost be called chic: functional, chaste and formal.

078 **Switching stations for PTT Telecom**
Switching stations for various locations

Amsterdam
1995–1997

p. 96

079 **Dresden**
Invited competition for exhibition site in collaboration with Bureau B+B

Dresden, Germany
1995

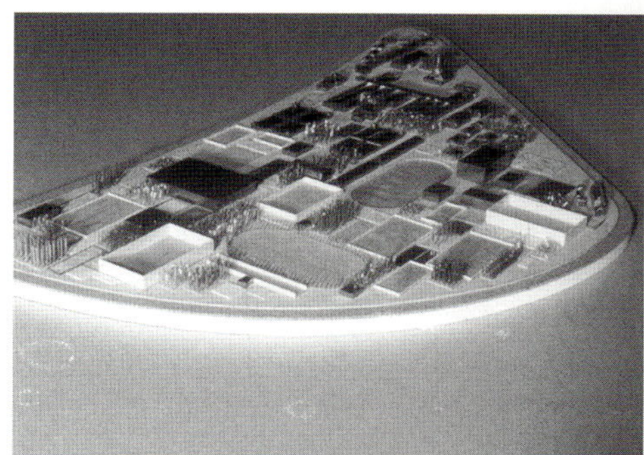

080 **De Meent**
Housing around shopping centre

Hilversum
1995–1998

081 **Housing, Vier Ambachten**
138 pensioner flats in urban development plan by DKV

Spijkenisse
1995–1997

p. 98

082 **Rietlanden**
Preparatory study for a school

Amsterdam
1995

083 **'Pawn' dwellings**
(see 056, 058, 074, 113)
24 non-subsidized owner-occupied waterside dwellings. Part of the restructuring of the Gulden Kruis housing estate

Amsterdam
1995–1997

p. 62

084 **Housing, Kalenderpanden & Lage Loodsen**
Renovation and conversion of old warehouse into 42 luxury dwellings

Amsterdam
1995–

p. 102

085 **ING Terneuzen**
Competition: New ING Bank office

Terneuzen
1995

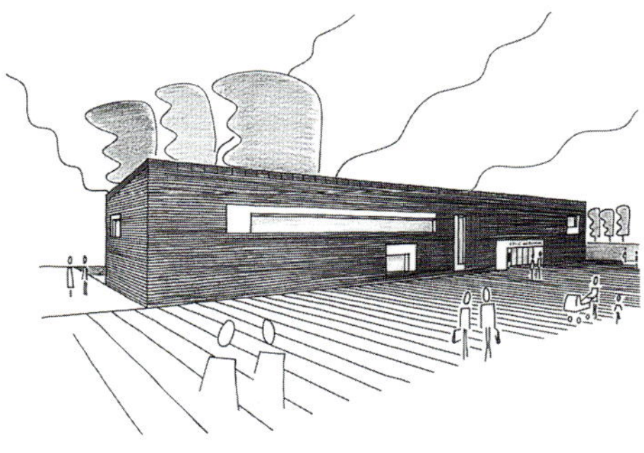

086 **Taxation Department Pavilion**
Reception building for the regional taxation office

Haarlem
1995–1998

p. 104

087 **Tilburg**
Urban development plan and design for 20 detached villas

Tilburg
1996–1999

088 **Warmelo**
Housing study

Amsterdam
1996

089 **Admiralty**
Reception room with bar, lounge and conference suite for the admiralty

The Hague
1995–1996

Interior design for the admiralty top brass in The Hague. An ordinary office space has been transformed into a lounge where the emphasis is on space, light and materials. The functions room can be construed as an autonomous volume inside the building, as a box within a box. The original idea was to create a windowless space but that ran into opposition from the users who felt that they had spent enough time in hermetic spaces on ships and submarines.

090 **Zorgvlied**
Reception pavilion beside the old funeral hall at Zorgvlied cemetery

Amsterdam
1996–1998

p. 106

091 **Housing, Rietlanden**
35 subsidized rental dwellings,
54 non-subsidized owner-occupied dwellings and 6 business units

Amsterdam
1996–2000

p. 110

092 **Housing, De Aker**
(see 100, 153, 205)
91 single-family dwellings distributed over four streets

Amsterdam
1996–1999

p. 114

093 **Parking attendants**
Competition: Design of 'attractive' huts for car park attendants

Amsterdam
1996

Recently [...] we declined the commission to make a study of suitable accommodation for traffic wardens and produce a design concept. [...] the urban public space, important though it is, is becoming the object of an excess of design, not out of necessity but out of frustration.
We have come to the conclusion that a conceptual approach, given the solution sought is undesirable. At the same time, we do not consider ourselves capable of optimizing designs for standard accommodation for the traffic wardens, since we prefer the imperfection of the makeshift shacks, which at the present moment are a blot on the cityscape, to a perfectly detailed Ford cabin.

094 **AMF Pump House Basement**
Conversion of former pump house basement into theatre space

Amsterdam
1995

095 **Kraaihoek**
Competition: No design made

Papendrecht
1996

096 Stadstimmertuin
Design for freestanding building on plot in Stadstimmertuin, with ten dwellings and 108 m² office space

Amsterdam
1996

Design for an office building with dwellings that in both form and type shuns Dutch traditions. On a mews-type street that is in itself unusual for Amsterdam, the architects designed an object-building surrounded by a garden. The front elevation is consequently not the usual hard boundary between street and interior with the front door acting as threshold. Instead it is a raised building with a set-back entrance and parking spaces below the building.

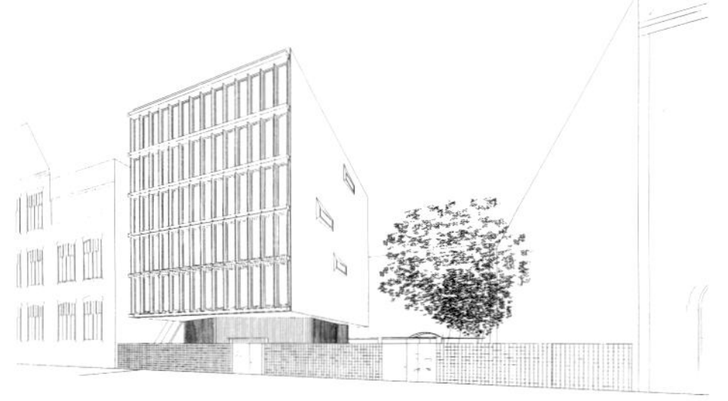

097 Housing, Eekmaat
55 non-subsidized single-family dwellings in urban development plan by Sjoerd Soeters

Enschede
1996–1997

p. 116

098 Housing, Sporenburg
(see 065, 106, 109, 118)
Sporenburg 7, head elevation
Five dwellings on Sporenburg island

Amsterdam
1996–1999

p. 80

099 Student Housing, Drienerlo
Renovation and restructuring of existing student housing at TU Twente, 119 student bedsits in 21 units

Enschede
1996–1997

p. 118

100 Housing, De Aker
(see 092, 153, 205)
Nineteen dwellings

Amsterdam
1996–1999

p. 114

101 Dalsland
(see 063)
24 subsidized rental dwellings, 32 owner-occupied dwellings and 70 owner-occupied apartments on Dr. Wibautplein and Savorin Lohmanstraat

Schiedam
1996–1999

Housing in a postwar district of Schiedam. Together with the Wibautplein scheme (063), it is a contribution to the restructuring of this terraced housing estate. The first part is a perimeter block that defines the open space and lends it substance. The second project was based, at the request of the alderman concerned, on Swedish models in which parking is banished to the edge of the site and the houses stand in rows on sloping ground. This pocket park serves as a collective area for all the dwellings which have a veranda but no private garden.

102 **Housing, Park Duijnwijk**
51 downstairs and 51 upstairs dwellings and 29 apartments

Zandvoort
1996–2001

p. 122

103 **Housing on the Hill**
Seven hill villas and 25 park houses (one detached, six semi-detached and the rest linked)

Amersfoort
1996–1999

There are two types of dwellings, hill villas and park houses. The latter are suburban cousins of the town house with living concentrated on the upper floors. The villas are a mixture of dike house, drive-in home and bungalow, with the main and largest level on the top floor.

104 **Nieuwland**
153 dwellings in sustainable building scheme

Amersfoort
1996–1999

The design encompasses the spatial master plan, the landscaping and the architecture. The prescribed use of solar panels formed the rationale for both the architectural design (the sloping roof) and the spatial subdivision in which nearly all the rows of housing are lined up facing the same way. Apart from the solar panels, which are not yet an everyday phenomenon in the Netherlands, this is a pretty ordinary neighbourhood. At each level, the architects have sought the essence of Dutch suburban tradition. That's the reason their work is a clear testimony to their cheerful acceptance of the ordinariness of the task.

105 **ENECO**
Competition: Transformer kiosks

In and around Rotterdam
1996

106 **Housing Sporenburg**
(see 065, 098, 109, 118)
Sporenburg 15 and 16
187 dwellings, subsidized owner-occupied, medium-priced owner-occupied and market sector

Amsterdam
1994–1999

p. 80

107 **De Velden**
(see 110, 129)
70 market sector dwellings in De Velden district

Leidscheveen
1996–1998

108 **Sheltered Housing for the Elderly, Stadshagen**
60 pensioner dwellings, district service centre, day care centre and car park

Zwolle
1997–2000

p. 124

109 **Draaisma House**
(see 065, 098, 106, 148)
Interior of dwelling in end elevation of Sporenburg 7

Amsterdam
1999–2000

p. 128

110 **Catholic Housing Association, Leidschendam**
(see 107, 129)
84 rental dwellings in De Velden housing estate

Leidscheveen
1997–1998

111 **Kennedystrook**
Urban design plan for the Kennedystrook with proposal for apartment blocks of varying heights with a maximum of three apartments per floor

Amsterdam
1996

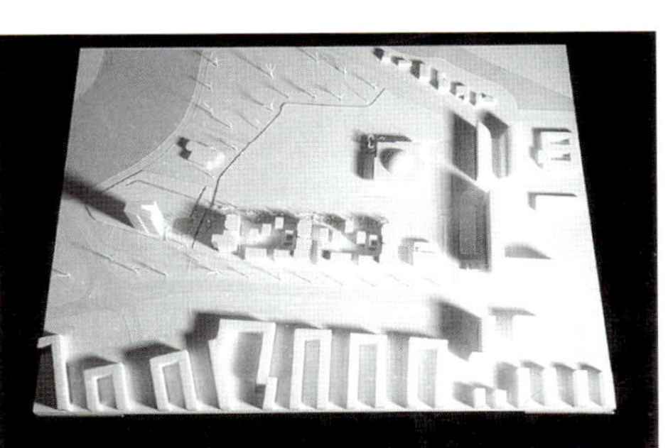

112 Cancelled

113 **Housing Blocks Nieuw Gerenstein**
(see 056, 058, 074, 083)
148 dwellings in twelve tower blocks that mediate in height between the adjoining low- and high-rise. Part of the restructuring of the Gulden Kruis housing estate

Amsterdam
1997–1999

p. 62

114 **Stramanweg**
Study of development options along the north side of Stramanweg;
200 dwellings and car park

Amsterdam
1999–

115 **Schwerin**
Invited competition: 400 dwellings, 125 apartments, hotel, offices and car park

Schwerin, Germany
1997

116 **Plant 26**
Competition: Assembly plant, store rooms, truck yard and dock units, offices and 900 parking spaces

Heerenveen
1998

117 **Müller Pier**
Spatial infill in collaboration with BGSV, Buro Stedenbouw Rotterdam, Ooms Makelaars voor Müllerpier, Lloydpier and Westzeedijk. A total of 845 up-down dwellings, town houses, tower blocks, villas and patio dwellings

Rotterdam
1998

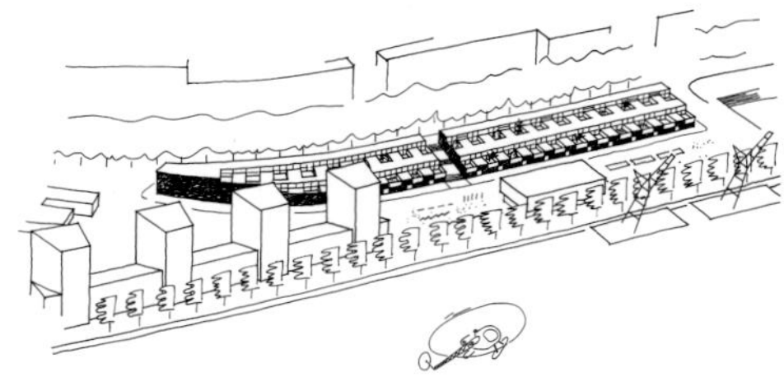

118 **Housing, Sporenburg**
(see 065, 098, 106, 109)
Sporenburg 13

Amsterdam
1996–1999

p. 80

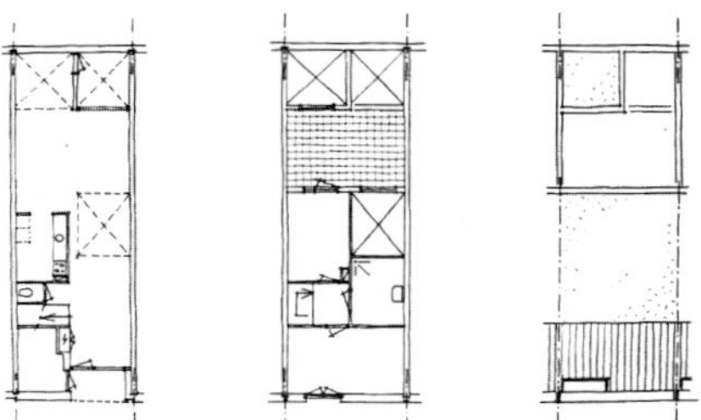

119 **Admiraliteitskade**
Development planning advice for Admiraliteitskade

Rotterdam
1999

120 **Housing, Beekpark**
Tower block with nineteen apartments and three double villas

Apeldoorn
1999–2001

p. 130

121 **San Francisco Verkade**
Feasibility study for housing on former site of Verkade biscuit factory

Zaandam
1997

122 **Lepelkruisstraat**
Study for one-room flats

Amsterdam
1998

123 **Housing, Zenderpark**
64 drive-in dwellings on Praagsingel

IJsselstein
1997–2000

p. 132

124 **Van Hasseltweg**
Supervision of urban development plan

Amsterdam
1997

125 **Warmenhuizen**
Fifty owner-occupied apartments with garage in two building volumes

Warmenhuizen
1998–2001

126 **Naarderstraat**
Capacity study for 24 dwellings and basement car park in three volumes of three to five storeys

Hilversum
1997

127 **Fisherstraat**
Re-structuralization Transvaal district, 74 single-family dwellings and 34 apartments

The Hague
1997–

Urban renewal in the Transvaal district of The Hague. The building line of the old block was maintained, as was the closed form. The typological diversity is hidden behind a uniform skin with large window openings. The long sides consist of single-family dwellings with street-side storage spaces on the ground floor. One short end consists of apartments, the other of four-storey town houses with roof terrace and garaging for eighteen cars underneath. Another, semi-sunken, parking area is located in the narrow courtyard (the block as a whole is only 36 metres deep) behind the gardens belonging to the single-family dwellings. Thus, with a bit of juggling, the architects managed to satisfy the demand for a measure of off-street parking.

128 **University of Amsterdam Deck**
(see 073)
61 student flats and commercial premises on Sarphatistraat

Amsterdam
1998–

p. 134

129 **Apartments Leidscheveen**
(see 107, 110)
32 apartments and four penthouses distributed over four housing blocks in the De Korenbloem district

Leidscheveen
1998–2001

130 **Station Square Leiden**
Redevelopment of offices on Station Square

Leiden
1998

131 **Burgemeester Kootpark**
Urban development and landscape design comprising single-family dwellings, apartment blocks and villas. Visual quality plan for single-family dwellings and detached and linked villas.

Uithoorn
1998–2000

High-density housing scheme on the site of a former sports park in Uithoorn. The outer zone of the estate has a park-like layout. In the centre is a perimeter block that in form, materials and details is reminiscent of provincial architecture of the inter-war years. The perimeter block is a scaled-down version of the mega-block. Inside it are three smaller blocks enclosing green squares.

132 **Scrap**
Sketch design for multi-occupancy building for BSO/Piet Hein and Scrap

Rotterdam
1998

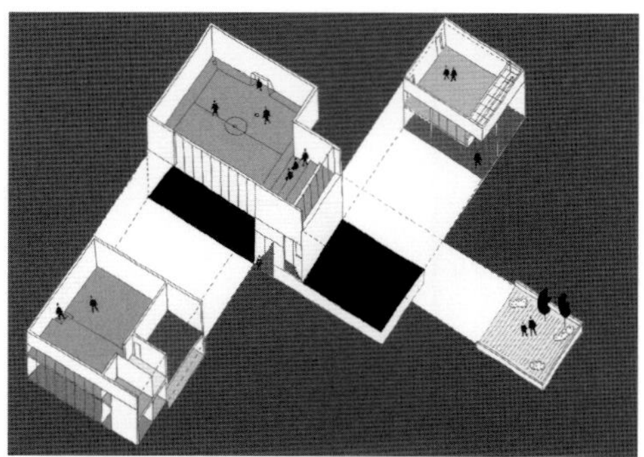

133 **Apartment Tower**
Tower block with 58 dwellings in spatial master plan by OMA

Almere
1998–2001

p. 136

134 **Katendrecht Workshop**
Workshop on urban development plan for Katendrecht

Rotterdam
1998

135 **Grote Kerk**
Invited competition for tourist information office next to church

Arnhem
1998

136 **Almere Low-Rise**
Three rows of single-family dwellings including 140 owner-occupied

Almere
1998–

137 **Dutch Embassy**
Design of chancery and residence for the Netherlands Embassy

Maputo, Mozambique
1999–

p. 140

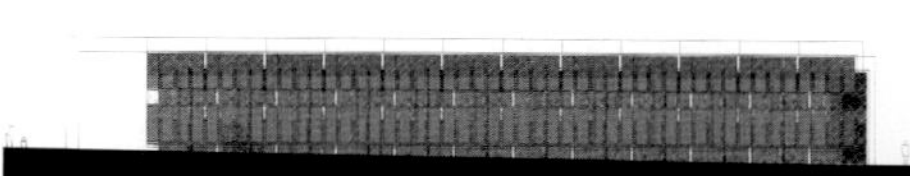

138 **Housing, Floriande Island 10**
Spatial layout and landscape design with 307 low-rise dwellings and tower blocks

Haarlemmermeer
1998–

p. 144

139 **Leo Polakhuis**
Geriatric nursing home. Residential home for the elderly with general spaces, day care, day treatment, service centre and apartments

Amsterdam
1998–

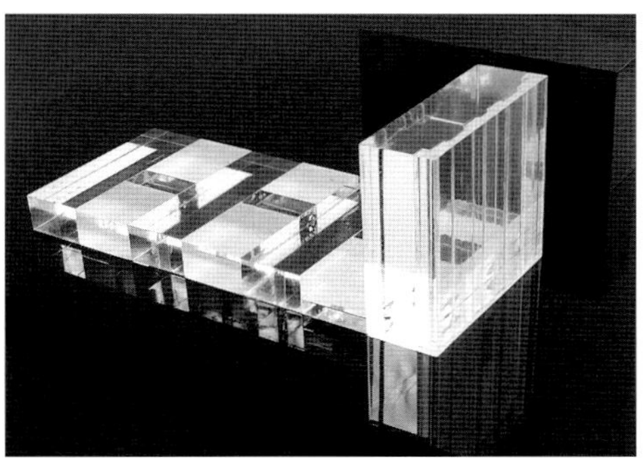

140 **Ypenburg plot 16**
458 dwellings, 209 in a courtyard block, in an urban development plan by Kraaijvanger Urbis

Ypenburg
1998–

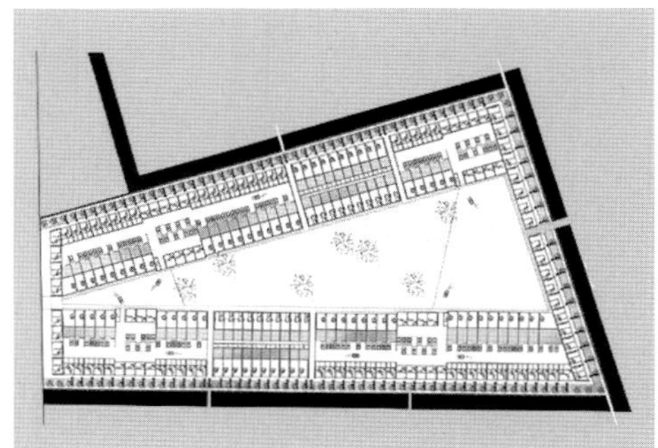

141 **Urban Design**
Urban design for Haveneiland and Rieteilanden comprising 7000 dwellings, 260,000 m^2 amenities, various schools, infrastructure and public space at IJburg
with de Architekten Cie. and Schaap & Stigter

Amsterdam
1998–

p. 146

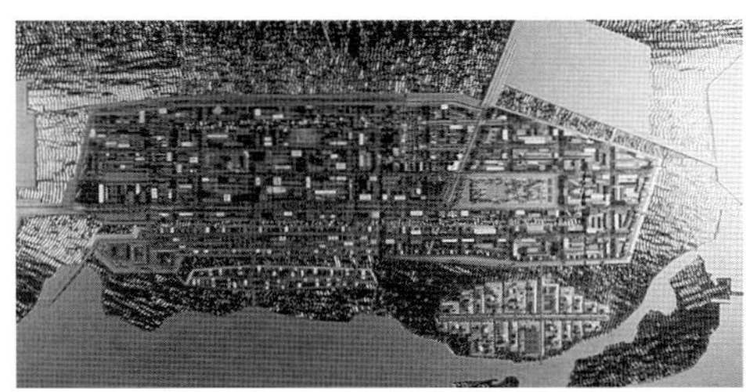

142 **Mayersloot West**
Competition: Spatial master plan for site in rural surroundings facing water; 25 single-family dwellings, 36 apartments (twelve for pensioners), eleven detached houses

Langendijk
1998

143 **Jurg**
Renovation of private home

Rotterdam
1999

144 **Hotel, Oostelijke Handelskade**
Conference hotel with 400 rooms, bus terminal, car park

Amsterdam
2000–

p. 150

145 **Noorderhelling**
Subdivision models for the redevelopment of the Noorderhelling site

Rotterdam
1998

146 **Plot 10**
(see 183)
Housing in Rietvelden and Landingslaan

Ypenburg
1998–

Two housing schemes in a subarea of the Ypenburg urban development scheme. The original spatial master plan drawn up by MVRDV envisaged fully built-on jetties with housing either side of streets no more than six metres wide. Apart from the water, the only 'breathing space' was provided by the parking lots. In the built alternative the parking lots have been scrapped and the rows of housing moved further apart. Each dwelling now has a balcony overlooking the water at the rear and at the front a garden on the other side of the street. Cars are parked in the garden. The character of the street and neighbourhood has consequently changed from a strict sequence of zones, from public to private, to a hybrid in which the private domains of house and garden are separated by the public domain of the street. The second project is an apartment complex that forms a wall between this section of the district and the next. It stands to left and right of the bridge giving entry to the estate. The complex is a smooth, rectangular sculpture of brickwork in 'offset tile bond'. The apartments, instead of lying perpendicular to the long side of the block in the usual way, are arranged in twos or fours in the longitudinal direction.

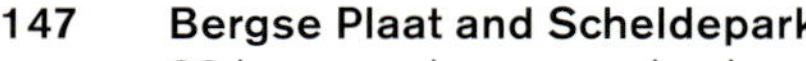

147 **Bergse Plaat and Scheldepark**
33 in a row along an embankment, 18 detached, and twelve 'energy' dwellings

Bergen op Zoom
1999–2001

148 **De Laantjes**
Part of new-build site with 60 apartments with car park and 60 low-rise dwellings

Zwolle
1998

149 **Netherlands Forensic Institute**
(see 186, 203)
Building and landscape design comprising laboratories, offices and car park

Rijswijk
1999–

p. 154

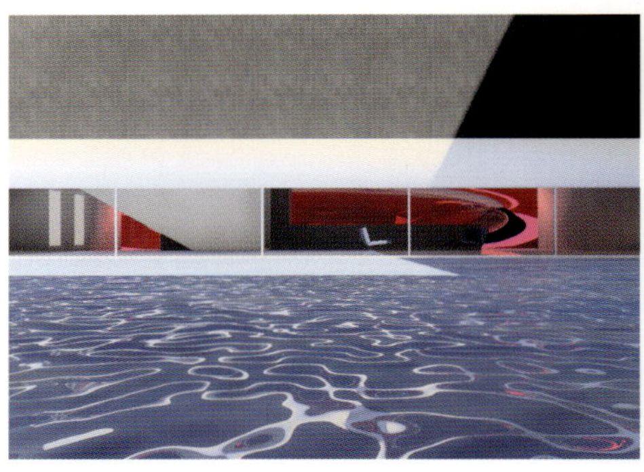

150 **Twiske Zuid**
Competition: 174 dwellings on two locations in Het Twiske recreation/nature reserve

Amsterdam
1998–

The architects looked for ways of using the rustic clutter of ribbon development and discrete objects as a starting point for the new development. The chosen subdivision can be construed as a modern interpretation of that older contiguous development of individual houses with staggered building and roof lines. The only large-scale element in the plan is a three-storey apartment block projected onto a peninsula at the edge of the estate, which it shares with a scattering of a dozen or so plots earmarked for private development.

151 **Housing, Oostelijke Handelskade**
60 gallery-access apartments and six live/work units at street level

Amsterdam
1999–

p. 160

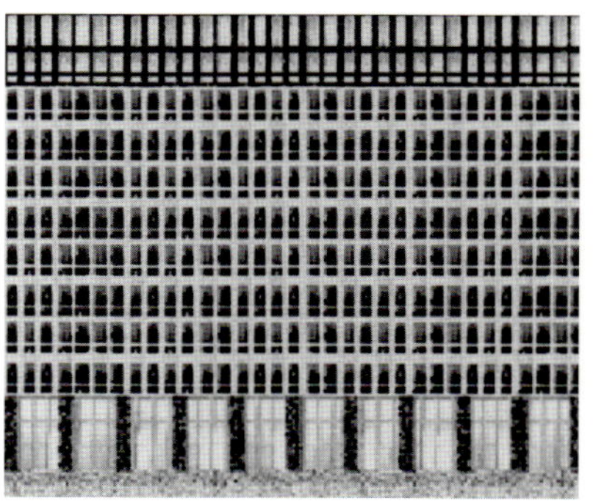

152 **Dromelot**
Redevelopment of plot for day care centre near Vondel Park

Amsterdam
1999

153 **De Aker Housing Scheme**
(see 092, 100, 205)
104 owner-occupied dwellings

Amsterdam
1999–

p. 114

154 **Het Leger**
Apartment complex with thirty flats and basement car park on Amsterdamseweg

Amstelveen
1999–

155 **Cruise-Inn**
Apartment complex comprising forty flats, commercial space and car park on Zeeburgerdijk

Amsterdam
2000–

156 **Olympic Stadium Redevelopment**
Urban redevelopment plan for 130 non-subsidized rental units with superior facilities

Amsterdam
1999

157 **Middenmeer**
Urban design study for pensioner dwellings on an open space in the middle of a residential area

Middenmeer
2000–

158 **Almere Expo**
Competition: 43 single-family dwellings with highly flexible floor plans and a day care centre

Almere
1999–2001

159 **Town Centre Plan**
Urban design plan developed in collaboration with Kraaijvanger Urbis; includes shopping centre, offices, housing and 1000 parking spaces

Etten-Leur
1999

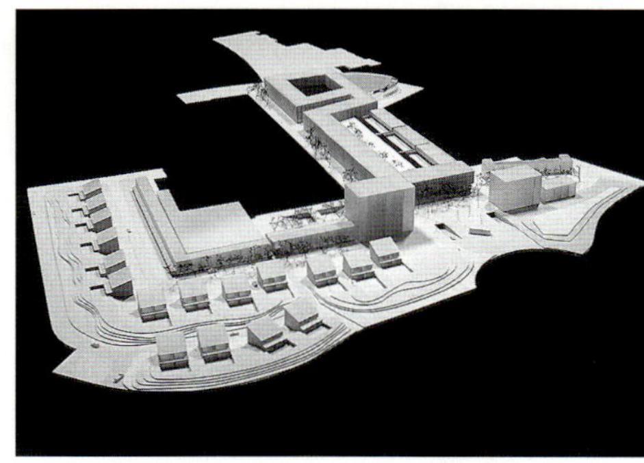

160 **Tussen de Vaarten**
37 pensioner units

Almere
2000–

161 **Boerhavelaan**
Feasibility study for a variety of housing types

Leiden
1999

162 **Oosterheem**
94 non-subsidized dwellings including 21 villas, 62 street-access dwellings and 22 apartments

Oosterheem
1999–

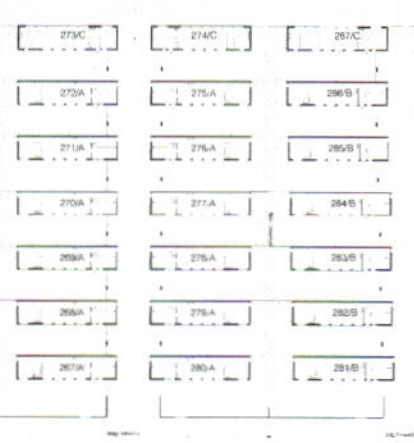

163 **Diependaalselaan**
Sixty dwellings

Hilversum
1999–

164 **Stompetoren**
Competition: Twelve rental units, 118 owner-occupied dwellings

Stompetoren
1999

165 **Municipal Offices**
Extension of municipal office complex to accommodate internal operations and offices of Breda's various district councils

Breda
1999–

p. 162

166 **Analysis urban structure inner town Goes**

Goes
2000–

167 **Het Funen**
Apartment building with 22 dwellings in urban development plan by Frits van Dongen and de Architecten Cie.

Amsterdam
2000–

Block of flats on a former industrial site in Amsterdam. It is one of several free-standing buildings in a park-like setting in the lee of a continuous wall of development separating the estate from the neighbouring railway tracks. The rounded contour of the building with aluminium facades departs from the angularity laid down in the urban development plan by Frits van Dongen of de Architecten Cie. The entrance is a glazed slot almost the full height of the block. Behind it, from ground floor to roof, is an atrium that changes shape with each floor.

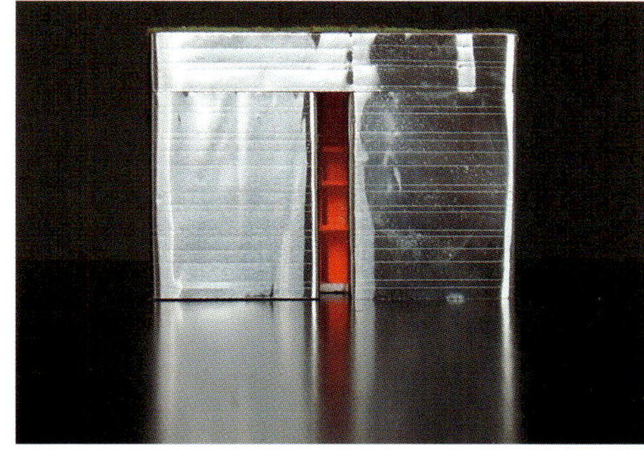

169 **Driebergenbuurt**
(see 187)
Restructuring of early twentieth-century district: urban development plan, landscape design, supervision and 230 dwellings

Deventer
2000–

The basic premise was an increase in social and architectural diversity. At the architectural level this is achieved externally by the succession of clearly differentiated houses and internally by typological variation. This multi-formity caters in turn for a wide spectrum of tastes and purses.

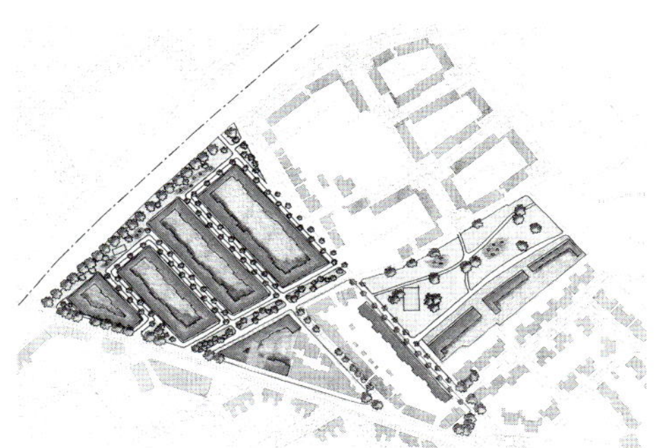

168 **Buikslotermeerplein**
Interior of head office of Wilma Bouw/Amstelland Vastgoed

Amsterdam
1999

Conversion of the former Amsterdam North district office into offices for a developer. In the semi-public space where potential house buyers are received, the birch floor merges seamlessly with the rectangular sculpture of the reception desk. The walls are clad with carpet that not only adds colour to the area but also serves as acoustic insulation. The interview
areas are enclosed by low, circular walls finished in the roughcast 'pizzeria' render that was all the rage in the 1970s.

170 **Saendelft**
Study for Mediterranean-style living in Zaandam

Zaandam
1999–

171 **Droste Site**
Design of office building on former Droste factory site

Haarlem
2000

172 **200+**
Study for innovative housing that would contribute to the redevelopment and revitalization of urban areas

1999

Architectural proposal in the context of the *Wonen in de stad* (Living in the city) manifesto published by the Eurowoningen construction company at the beginning of 2000. It is a concept for the kind of residences that are lacking in Dutch cities: high-specification stacked dwellings of two to five hundred square metres and with high ceilings. The proposal identifies two possibilities for such luxury housing developments – one in Rotterdam overlooking the Maas, the other in Amsterdam beside the Amstel – featuring ample underground parking, an elegant street-level lobby with above that a mansion, followed by a loft apartment and at the very top a penthouse.

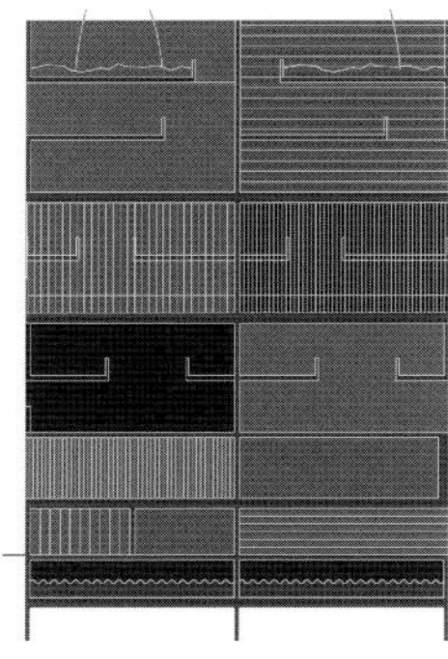

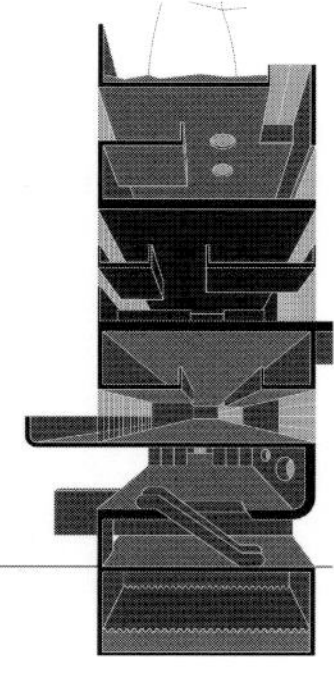

173 **Solid 18**
Leisure centre, hostel, long-stay hotel, commercial space, NOCNSF sports hall on IJburg

Amsterdam
2001–

174 **Hoefkade**
Competition: Design of 24 downstairs and 25 upstairs dwellings

The Hague
1999–

Urban renewal housing in The Hague, consisting of stacked single-family dwellings. Originally made for an invited competition, the design has been extended into a uniform, continuous street frontage some four hundred metres long. The only disruption to this horizontality – the soaring church – pre-dates the new-build. Apart from up and down dwellings, the scheme encompasses a number of shops and premises that will initially be used as a school but will in future be suitable for residential use. The formality of the front elevation is determined by the regular pattern of large windows that reduce the brickwork from a plane to a grid. The rear elevation is informal. The lucid regularity of this architecture, with its formal front and informal back, calls to mind several other Claus en Kaan housing schemes such as Rietlanden (091) and Stadshagen (108) while the typology is related to that of the dwellings on Bijlmerdreef (058).

175 **Assumburgweg**
32 dwellings and forty parking spaces in Moerwijk

The Hague
1999

176 **Jeurlink/Vijfhoek**
48 dwellings in urban design plan by SVP Amersfoort

Deventer
2000

177 **Onstein**
Extension of private dwelling in Buitenveldert, optionally in combination with adjacent homes

Amsterdam
1999

178 **National Museum of Modern Art**
Competition: Extension of National Museum of Modern Art

Rome, Italy
2000

p. 166

179 **Joure**
Competition: Two apartment blocks

Joure
2000–

Upmarket housing in the centre of Joure consists of a row of low houses and an apartment building with an irregular, amoeba-like shape reminiscent of Luigi Moretti's Watergate Office Building. The unusual thing about the project, which was chosen after an invited competition, is that the architects were allowed to nominate a developer rather than the other way round. This is intended to ensure that this architecture in glass and white steel will be executed with the necessary degree of refinement.

180 **Concordia**
Forty single-family dwellings, 85 apartments, basement car park

Ede
2000–

181 **Medical Association**
Competition: New-build comprising offices, reception and meeting rooms for the Berlin doctors' association

Berlin, Germany
2000

The building on Friedrichstrasse eschews the prevailing ideology of 'critical reconstruction'. Although the entire plot is built on, the set-back facade of the low-ceilinged ground floor and the modernist ribbon glazing are at odds with the rigid traditionalism of perimeter block development prescribed in this part of Berlin. The building is organized around a large hall which connects the public part, the offices and the three boardrooms. The latter are contained in three separate volumes on the roof.

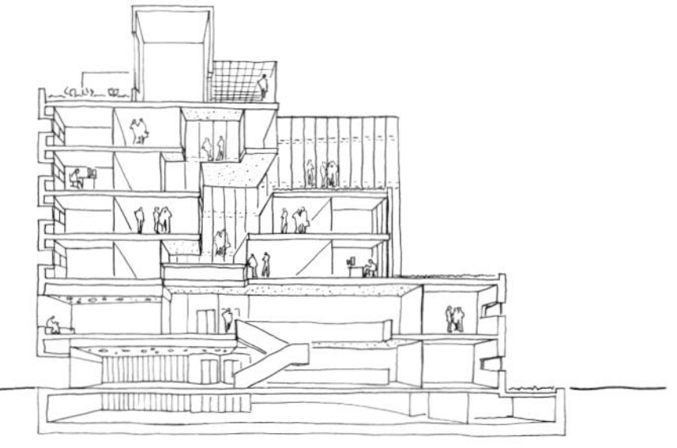

182 **Raaks Stadshoven**
(see 206)
Conversion of school to dwellings, plus new, high-specification dwellings in palazzo form, shops and car park in a master plan by Kraaivanger Urbis

Haarlem
2001–

183 **Day Care Centre**
(see 146)
Day care centre over two floors of one of the apartment blocks on Landingslaan

Ypenburg
2000–

184 **Fisherman's Cove**
Invited competition for sketch design of riverside residential area

Zaandam
2000

185 **BETA Service Stations**
Commissioned study for new service station design

2000

186 **NFI Laboratory Interior**
(see 149, 203)
Design for suspended laboratory tables

Rijswijk
2000

p. 154

187 **Burgersdijk**
(see 169)
Study for restructuring of residential area

Deventer
2000

188 **Municipal Archives**
Renovation and extension of municipal records office and design of inner courtyard

Amsterdam
2000–

p. 170

189 **Zuidwijk De Burgen**
Urban development plan and restructuring for 700 dwellings

Rotterdam
2000–

Restructuring of a neighbourhood in Zuidwijk, the earliest postwar suburban development in Rotterdam, the spatial master plan for which was made by W. van Tijen. The single-family dwellings are maintained but in a different form. Nearly all the medium-rise blocks will be demolished to make way for low-rise. In the course of this operation one thousand dwellings of roughly sixty squares will be replaced by six hundred dwellings double the size. In combination with a realistic parking ratio of two cars per dwelling, this results in a considerable increase in building density. The architects have done their best to retain and reinforce the structure of collective green space that is so characteristic of this district by concentrating the housing, building some back to back and placing the private gardens at the front.

190 **Plot 90**
Study of development possibilities for office complex

Amsterdam
2000–

191 **Monastery Garden**
Invited competition for housing scheme

Apeldoorn
2000

The brief asked for a design based on the metaphor of the monastery garden. The housing in this design, which takes it cue from the Sankt Gallen monastery in Switzerland, is grouped in small clusters around quadrangles that function as green rooms for collective use. The plan demonstrates the possibilities of a housing development layout unrelated to the traditional street.

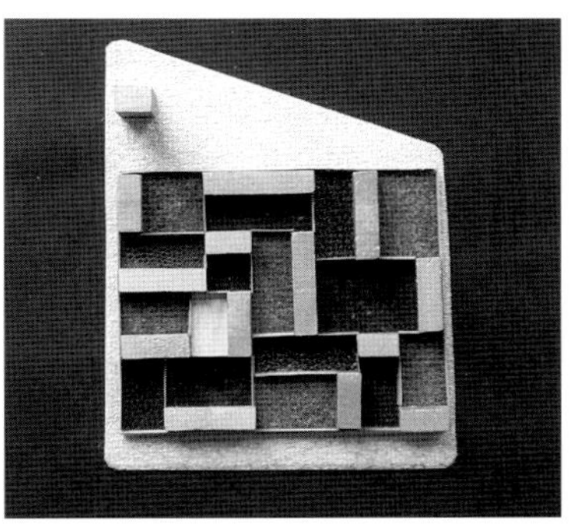

192 **Block 24 IJburg**
64 apartments (42 single-family) in block development coordinated by Meyer & Van Schooten architects

Amsterdam
2000–

193 **Block 25 IJburg**
28 apartments (8 single-family) in block development coordinated by Faro architects

Amsterdam
2000–

Two housing schemes for IJburg, in blocks 24 and 25 which were coordinated respectively by Meyer & Van Schooten and Faro. In block 24 the development is subdivided into four separate buildings. In block 25 the volume is also divided up, this time into two sections, one of which has an emphatically vertical articulation and the other an equally explicit horizontal organization. As a result of the reduction of the total volume, both infills conform to an intermediate urban scale, midway between the big block and the town house.

194 **KBB Site**
3,000 m^2 retail space, 50 dwellings and a car park

The Hague
2000–

Located behind the Bijenkorf department store in The Hague, a masterpiece of Amsterdam School architecture, this complex completes the perimeter block. It also mediates between the large scale of the department store and the smaller scale of the buildings behind it along the Gedempte Gracht. Cutting the volume up into smaller pieces not only makes this mediation possible but also allows for strategically advantageous phased development.

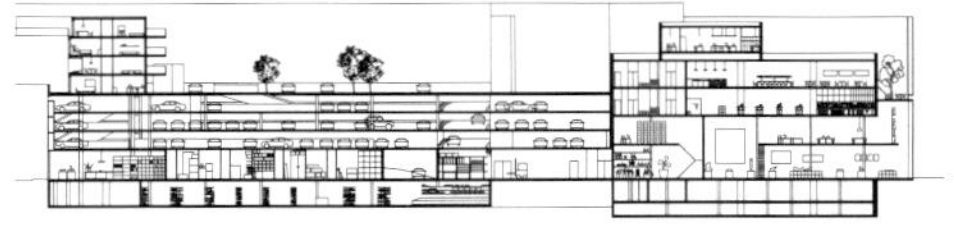

195 **Atelier Bloemendaal**
Design for three apartment blocks in dune landscape on site of former institution for the mentally handicapped

2000–

196 **Museum Nationaal Monument Kamp Vught**
Reception and exhibition building, offices

Vught
2000–

p. 174

197 **Hillegom**
Invited competition for urban design

Hillegom
2000

198 **Town Hall**
New town hall plus tourist information office, police station and basement car park

Tynaarlo
2000–

p. 176

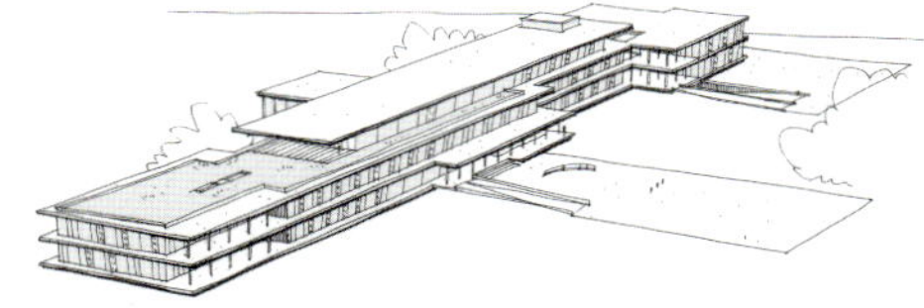

199 **Vathorst**
(see 217)
Programmatic study of Stationskwartier De Laak 1 in spatial master plan by West 8

Amersfoort
2000

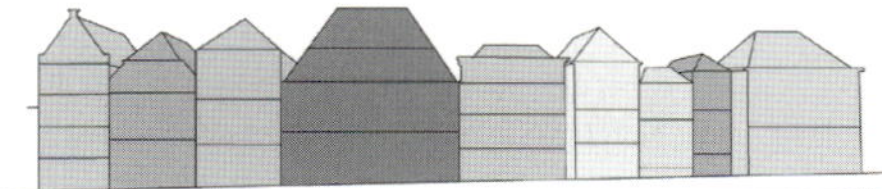

200 **Amenity Cluster**
Schools, sports hall, swimming pool, health care centre, youth clinic, activity centre for the Leidsche Rijn urban development

Utrecht
2000–

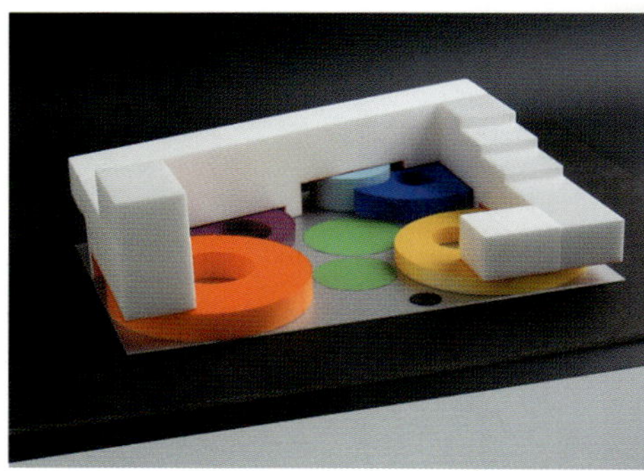

201 **Patio Dwellings**
49 patio dwellings and twelve apartments

Almere
2000–

Housing in Almere's Tussen de Vaarten district. The patio dwellings will completely cover their narrow and extremely deep plots (37.5 by 5 plus metres). Each house has a linear sequence of patios. The apartments have semicircular roofs with barrel vaulting, similar to those in Le Corbusier's Roq et Rob plan.

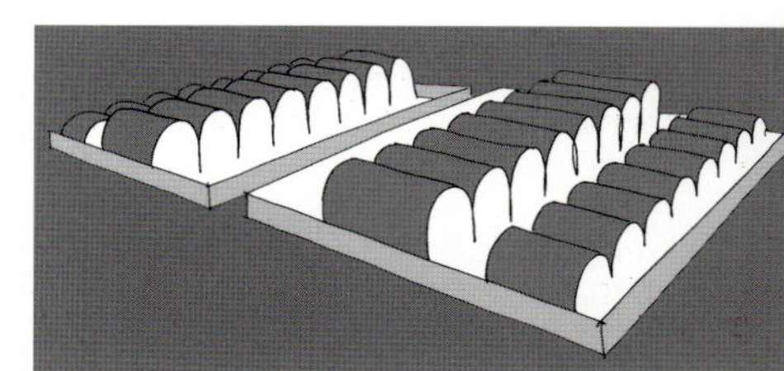

202 **IJsselmonde Centre**
Urban design concept

Rotterdam
2000

203 **NFI interior**
(see 149, 186)
Interior design for Netherlands Forensic Institute

Rijswijk
1999–

p. 154

204 **Geuzenbaan subarea 4**
Invited ideas competition for the restructuring of a postwar residential area

Amsterdam
2000

205 **De Aker Housing Scheme**
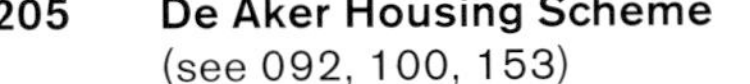
(see 092, 100, 153)
Block 6, follow-up commission

Amsterdam
2000–

Housing on the outskirts of Amsterdam, on the boundary between De Aker suburban development and a leftover strip of polder which the Amsterdam populace has voted to keep green. The building, which accommodates a complex programme, folds itself voluptuously like a mini-Chilehaus along the edges of the plot. Inside, access to the dwellings is off a spacious 'atrium-lobby' that changes character on every floor. The facades are done in a dark, L-shaped brick. The indentation in the bricks has been filled with mortar such that brick and joint form bands of equal height in the wall.

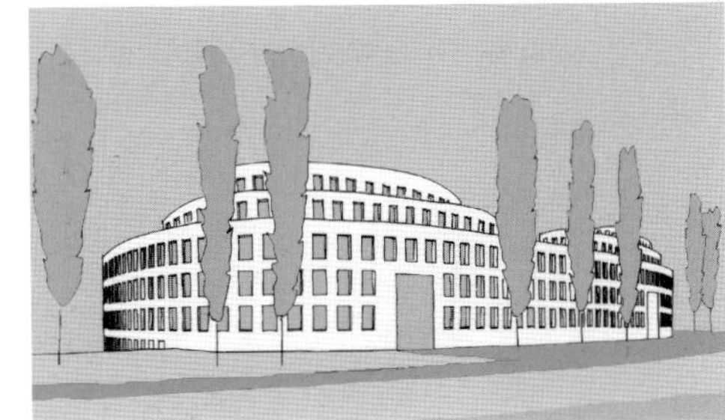

p. 114

206 **Schous**
(see 182)
Stadshoven entrance zone

Haarlem
2001

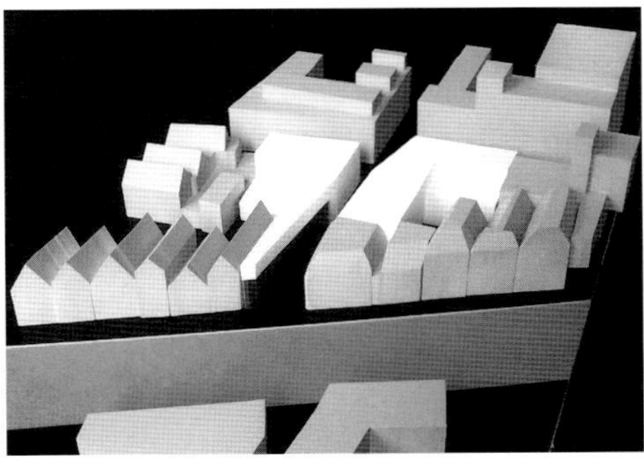

207 **Hamerstraat**
Study and coordination of filling-in of area around Hamerstraat

Amsterdam
2000–

208 **Spuimarkt Moneo**
Dutch counterpart for Rafael Moneo. Housing, restaurants, cafés, shops and offices on Spuimarkt square

The Hague
2000–

209 **Nesselande**
132 dwellings of which 51 semi-detached houses, 65 island dwellings and 16 courtyard dwellings

Rotterdam
2000–

210 **Riethof**
108 single-family owner-occupied dwellings in different types

The Hague
2000–

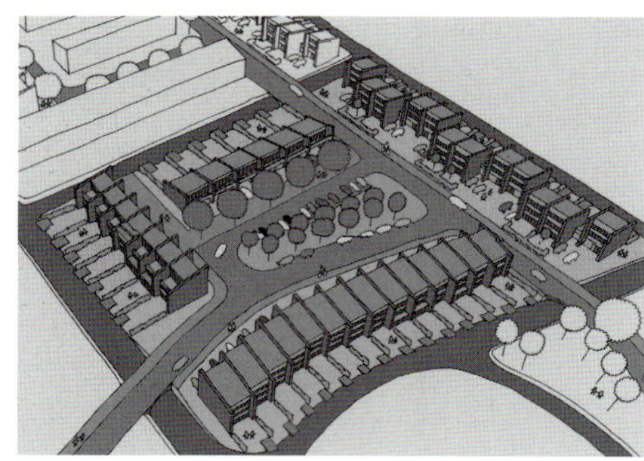

211 **Bosrijk Eindhoven**
Development study for the Bosrijk section of the Meerhoven scheme comprising 450 to 500 dwellings and adaptive reuse of existing buildings

Eindhoven
2000

On a triangular site, a former military terrain covered with meandering greenery, the architects propose a subdivision of meandering buildings. Together, the two meander patterns form introverted urban spaces. The design is premised on retention of the trees and soft landscaping. None of the buildings is visible above the trees whose root systems are protected by water-permeable paving.

212 **Blackbird**
First multi-occupancy office building on new business park site at Lelystad airport

Lelystad
2001–

213 **Citadel**
Design of office interior for housing corporation

The Hague
2001

214 **Willem van den Bergh**
120 units for mentally handicapped residents, 400 dwellings, and facilities

Noordwijk
2001–

215 **Dreef Complex**
Invited competition for extension to the offices of the North Holland provincial government

Haarlem
2001

The extension comprises two buildings, an office for provincial functionaries and a state room. The latter functions for the most part as a (commercial) conference centre, since the

provincial government makes only occasional use of the formal meeting space. The architecture, in accordance with the brief, is durable and energy-efficient; the building has no need of air conditioning.
The vertically articulated conference section represents the building's public function in a manner and with a grandeur that has ceased to be a tradition in the Netherlands; the office building is distinguished by, among other things, a storey height of almost four metres that lends the offices a palatial air seldom seen nowadays.

216 **Teleport**
Development of teleport area

Amsterdam
2001–

Master plan for the further development of the area around Sloterdijk railway station west of Amsterdam. In consultation with the Amsterdam Physical Planning Department, a concept was developed aimed at increasing the urbanity of this area by trebling the density. Instead of buildings standing in the middle of the allocated plots, as is now the case, Claus en Kaan propose that all buildings should in future toe the building line. This will eventually result in urban densities and a correspondingly city-like public space.

217 **Vathorst**
(see 199)
135 dwellings in Stationskwartier De Laak 1

Amersfoort
2001–

218 **Southwest Quadrant of Osdorp subarea C**
Subdivision proposal for 800 dwellings plus commercial premises, to replace four existing housing blocks

Amsterdam
2001–

A contribution to the restructuring of this postwar housing estate in Amsterdam West. The sheer size of the task raises the question of how to tackle such a quantity. The number is too great for a single building, nor is there any occasion for artificial variation. The architects consequently settled on repetition and uniformity in the tradition that gave rise to open housing estates like Osdorp which were based on the principle of the repetitive unit.

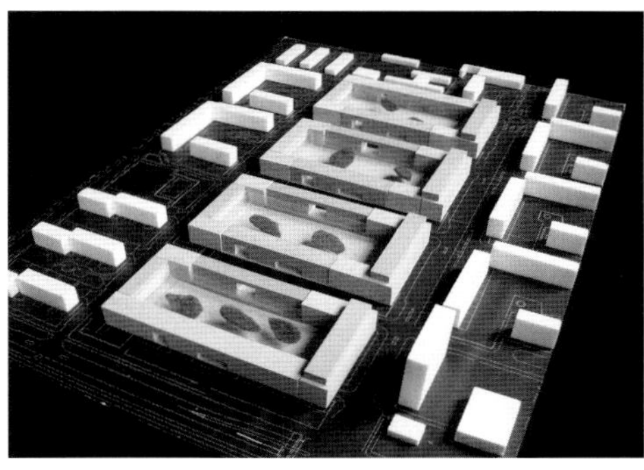

219 **Wedemeiland Development**
Twelve semi-detached dwellings and three villas on the theme of 'consumer-oriented building'

Bergen op Zoom
2001–

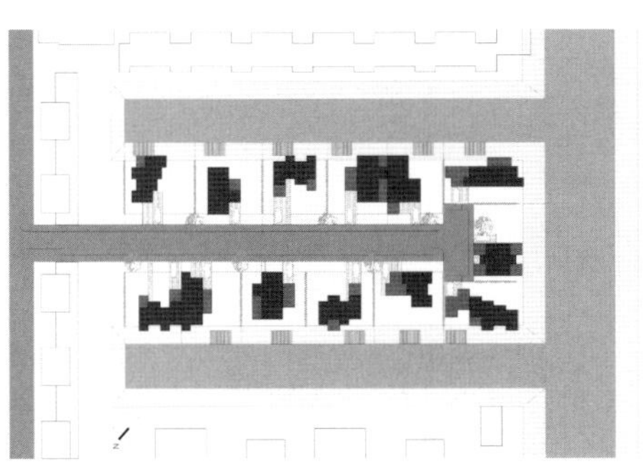

220 **Blankenstraat**
Office Building

Amsterdam
2001–

221 **Steigereiland Zuid**
Competition: Strategy for Steigereiland Zuid, IJburg

Amsterdam
2001

222 **Blocks 56, 57, 58 IJburg**
Typology study for housing and school

Amsterdam
2001

223 **Steigereiland Noord**
Competition: Strategy for Steigereiland Noord, IJburg
Amsterdam
2001

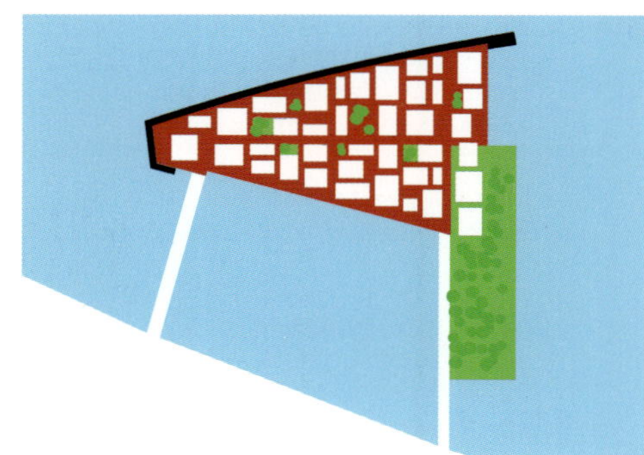

224 **Volkerak Lock**
Invited competition for a service building at the Volkerak Lock

Willemstad
2001–

The design is an undemonstrative object with a taut, prismatic form and a restrained use of colour and materials. The silvery building is incised with a glazed gash, the consequence of ergonomic requirements with respect to views out and operation. In its monolithic simplicity, the building is in stark contrast to the techno-brutalist structures usually associated with this client (Rijkswaterstaat, the government department responsible for roads and waterways). In a gesture of frivolity, the glazed slit emits light which varies in intensity according to the speed with which water is pumped into or out of the lock.

225 **Waterhof Vreeswijk**
63 ground-accessed dwellings with business premises in the Waterhof development at Vreeswijk

Nieuwegein
2001–

226 **Gouden Leeuw**
36 ground-accessed dwellings and 52 apartments on former brewery site

Venray
2001–

227 **Fascinatio**
36 apartments and 37 single-family dwellings

Capelle aan de IJssel
2001–

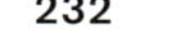

228 **Pedagogenbuurt**
Invited competition for urban design

Utrecht
2001

229 **DEO Redevelopment Scheme**
Competition: 290 dwellings, super-market, school and car park on site of former hospital

Haarlem
2001–

230 **Vossekuil**
Restructuring of Vossekuil, Molenberg

Heerlen
2001–

231 **Beekpoort**
Housing

Weert
2001–

232 **Nootdorp 's-Gravenhout**
Competition: 76 single-family dwellings around the station of 's-Gravenhout

Nootdorp
2001–

233 **Forumpark Crescent**
35 apartments, 1,000 m² commercial space and car park

Apeldoorn
2001–

234 **Zuideramstel Depot**
Study for a new public works depot combing several services in one building

Amsterdam
2001

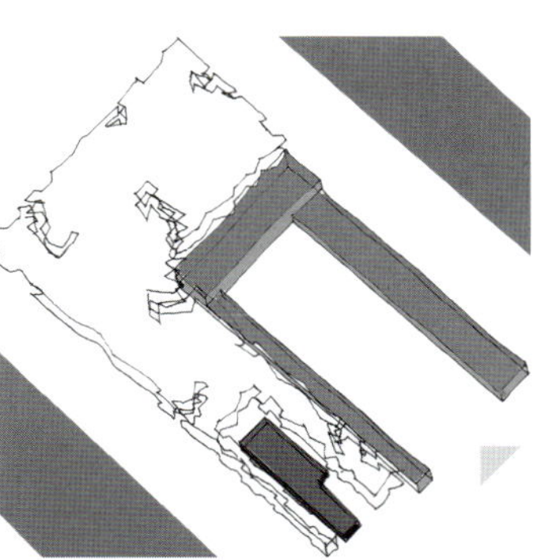

235 **Bagijnhof Dordrecht**
Housing and commercial space

Dordrecht
2001–

236 **Gershwin**
Shortlisted with Due South for the development of 250,000 m^2 dwellings and amenities on the Southern Axis

Amsterdam
2001–

237 **Kohnstamm House**
Study for extension with offices and dwellings on inner court of the Hogeschool van Amsterdam

Amsterdam
2001–

238 **Schuytgraaf**
Urban design for Veld 20, Schuytgraaf
with Moriko Kira

Arnhem
2001–

239 **Vierhavens Strip**
Urban design study for the redevelopment of part of disused marshalling yard

Rotterdam
2001

240 **KPN Building**
Study for conversion of former KPN offices to residential use

IJmuiden
2001–

241 **De Alliantie**
Design for office interior

Huizen
2001–

242 **Schuilenburg**
160 apartments in Zuidwijk
De Burgen

Rotterdam
2001–

243 **Kasteel Haverleij**
Elaboration of one of the 'castles' in Sjoerd Soeters's spatial master plan

's-Hertogenbosch
2001–

244 **Lyceum, Alkmaar**
Feasibility study for apartments

Alkmaar
2001–

245 **Southwest Quadrant Osdorp subarea D**
Subdivision proposal for 400 dwellings, 4,000 m² business premises and a car park for 600 vehicles

Amsterdam
2001–

246 **Grote Podium Accommodatie**
Plan for the integration of GPA on Noordereiland

Zwolle
2001–

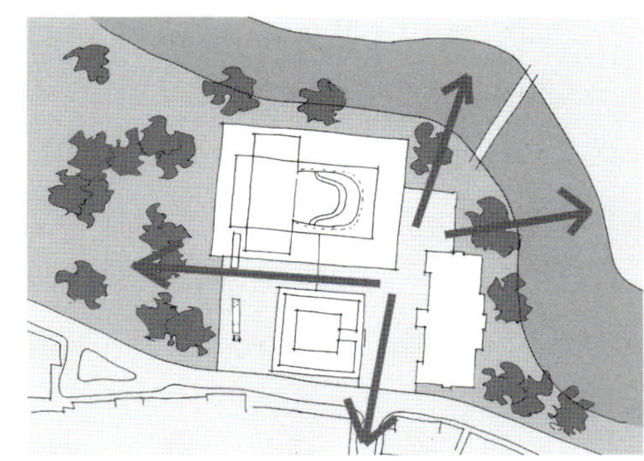

247 **Jan van Galen Pool Complex**
Invited competition for indoor and outdoor swimming pools, sunbathing lawn, restaurants and cafés, party room, fast food drive-in restaurant

Amsterdam
2001–

248 **Lockhouse**
Invited competition for a lockhouse on the Steigereiland on IJburg

Amsterdam
2001

249 **Rhijnspoorplein**
Urban design for junction Wibautstraat/Singelgracht

Amsterdam
2001

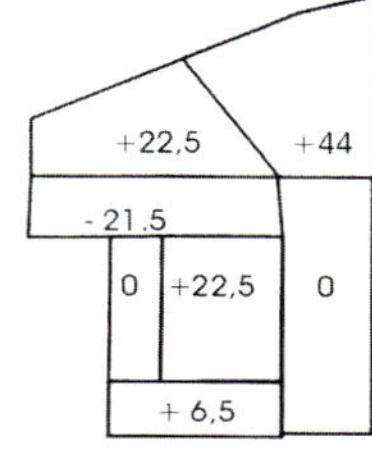

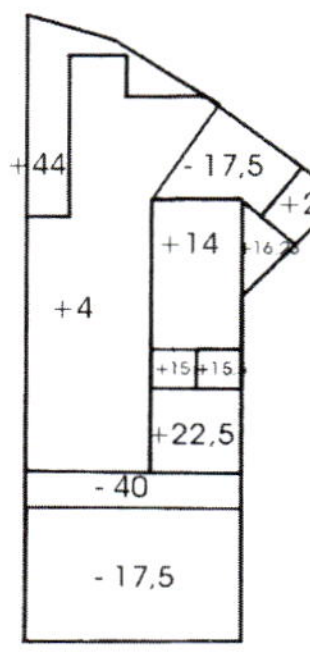

250 **Poortgebouw**
Feasibility study for restoration and conversion of the Poortgebouw at the Kop van Zuid

Rotterdam
2001

251 **Hoofddorp**
Urban design for centre Hoofddorp with Ton Schaap

Hoofddorp
2001

252 **Sloterdijk**
Development of 60.000 m² office space in Sloterdijk

Amsterdam
2001

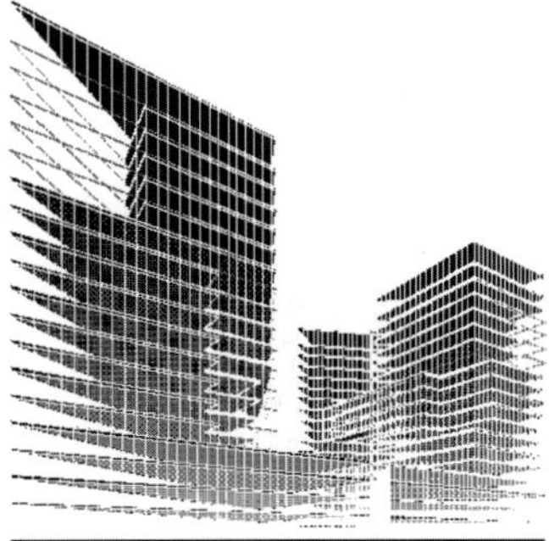

253 **Theatre Middelburg**
Regional theatre with a large and small auditorium, and a movie theatre

Middelburg
2001–

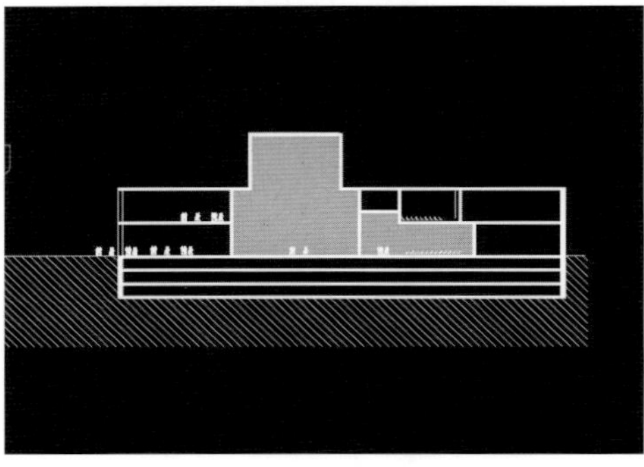

Felix Claus
Arnhem, 11 April 1956

Education
1974 Gymnasium, Arnhem
1978 German and Russian literature, University of Amsterdam
1987 Architecture, Delft University of Technology

Appointments
Guest professor of Architecture at the RWTH, Aachen
Head of atelier at Academy of Architecture, Amsterdam
Guest lecturer at Delft University of Technology, Hull School of Architecture, Berlage Institute Amsterdam/Rotterdam, IAAS Hamburg/Barcelona, Shih-chien University Taipei
Council for Culture, Committee for Architecture and Urban Planning 2001–
Netherlands Foundation for Fine Arts, Design and Architecture 1999–
Amsterdam Advisory Council for the Preservation of Historic Monuments 1998–
Committee for Aesthetic Control and Historic Monuments, Amsterdam 1996–2000
Jury Rietveld Prize, Utrecht 2001
Jury Pyramides 2000
Jury Das erste Haus, Berlin 1998–2001

Kees Kaan
Breda, 8 June 1961

Education
1979 Gymnasium, Bergen op Zoom
1987 Architecture, Delft University of Technology

Appointments
Quality Team Kop van Zuid, Rotterdam 2001–
High-rise Team, Rotterdam 2001–
Committee for Aesthetic Control and Historic Monuments, Rotterdam 2001–
Committee for Aesthetic Control, Architecture and Historic Monuments, Breda 2001–
City architect, Goes 1999–
Lecturer at the Academy of Architecture, Amsterdam/Rotterdam 1994–1998
Visiting lecturer at Delft University of Technology, Berlage Institute Amsterdam/Rotterdam, Kyoto University, Scott Sutherland School of Architecture Aberdeen, Universities of La Coruña and Madrid
Jury Rotterdam Bouwkwaliteits prize 2001
Jury Architekturpreis Rheinland Pfalz, Mainz 1998

BIBLIOGRAPHY

Journals

2001

'IJburg', *a+u* no. 228, pp. 76–79

'Redefining the Box', *Perspecta* no. 32, p. 60

'Woontoren krijgt uitkraging op dertig meter hoogte', *Bouwwereld* no. 1, pp. 26–28

Fisher, L., 'Die Insel und die Stadt', *Bauwelt* no. 21, pp. 32–37

Ibelings, H., 'Enforcing Ingenuity New Housing in Amsterdam', *Maja* no. 1, pp. 67–72

Hagendijk, K., 'Neo-modernisme en Amsterdamse School gecombineerd', *Stedenbouw* no. 576, pp. 4–7

2000

'Claus en Kaan: Ampliación de la Galeria Nacional de Arte Moderno and Roma/Claus en Kaan: Extension of National Gallery of Modern Art in Rome', *a+t* no. 16, pp. 40–47

Abrahamse, J.E., 'Van stadsrand tot stedelijk gebied. Zaanwerf van Concko-Gautier and Buyskade van Zeinstra and Van der Waals', *de Architect* no. 30, pp. 66–75

Bruijne, D., 'Centrumgebied Zuidoost. Een nieuw stadscentrum verrijst', *Plan Amsterdam* no. 1, pp. 13–15

Ector, J., 'Virtuoso self-evidence. Work by Claus and Kaan', *Archis* no. 7, pp. 8–19

Holl, C., 'Stadtplanung und Konversionsprojekte in Amsterdam. Haus, Stadt, Land', *db deutsche bauzeitung* no. 2, pp. 43–51

Lootsma, B., 'New forms of collectivity. Recent work by West 8', *Archis* no. 5, pp. 8–19

Meyhöfer, D., 'Spiel mit der Moderne', *Architektur & Wohnen* no. 4/5, pp. 158–159

Opmeer, P., 'Bouwwerk. Pauline Opmeer signaleert de nieuwste trends in Architectuur', *Elle Wonen* no. 48, p. 43

Vretblad, L., 'Sporenburg och Kop van Zuid', *MAMA* no. 27, pp. 13–14

Wendt, D., 'Niet voorbij het lint. Combinatiegebouw van Claus & Kaan Architecten Amsterdam', *de Architect* no. 5, pp. 70–73

1999

'Claus en Kaan Architecten', *Werk, Bauen + Wohnen* no. 1–2, p. 34

'Prinzip "Patiohaus". "Low-rise-high-density" Grundrisse aus Borneo und Sporenburg', *Bauwelt* no. 40, pp. 2138–2145

Assche, P. van, 'Ergänzungsübungen, Wohnungsbau von Mecanoo und Claus & Kaan in Amsterdam', *Bauwelt* no. 3, pp. 124–129

Assche, P. van, 'Er is koffie na de dood', *Bauwelt* no. 11, pp. 532–536

Englert, K., 'Jedem sein Palazzo. Alt und neu gesellt sich gern: Städtebau in Amsterdam', *Mittwoch* no. 64, p. 54

Epskamp, H., 'De Rietlanden. Het nieuwe hart van het Oostelijk Havengebied', *Plan Amsterdam* no. 9

Grafe, C., 'De jaren zestig herontdekt. Entreepaviljoen voor het belastingkantoor in Haarlem van Claus en Kaan', *de Architect* no. 10, pp. 4–85

Ibelings, H., 'An Ideal Standard. Two Recent Projects by Claus en Kaan', *a+u* no. 9, pp. 58–88

Ibelings, H., 'West 8. Borneo Sporenburg', *SD* no. 2, pp. 33–36

Melis, L., 'Aus zwei mach eins', *Bauwelt* no. 40, pp. 2450–2452

Morel-Journel, F., 'Aménagement d'un site industriel and quartier d'habitat', *Le Moniteur Architecture* no. 11, pp. 84–85

Siegele, K., 'Lückenfüller', *db Detail Buch* no. 1, pp. 69–70

1998

'Claus en Kaan', *Casabella* no. 661, pp. 20–25

'Riguroso Realismo/Rigorous Realism', *AV* no. 73, pp. 54–63

'Wärmedämmerung in Architekturgarten. Studentenhäuser der Universität Enschede umfassend saniert', *Journal* no. 3, pp. 6–7

'Woningen te Amsterdam Sporenburg. De eerste mensen', *Bouw* no. 12, pp. 20–23

Grafe, C., 'Informeel wonen in neutrale omgeving. Borneo Sporenburg in Amsterdam', *de Architect* no. 9, pp. 50–55

Grünhagen, H., 'Calslaan, Enschede. Lef op de Campus', *Aedes* no. 3, pp. 32–35

Hutton, G., 'Lessons in Architecture', *Prospect* no. 67, pp. 68–69

Klieverik, H., 'Een galerijflat met veel huiselijkheid', *Woningraad* no. 15, pp. 12–15

Schneider, S., 'Studentenwohnheim in Enschede', *Baumeister* no. 8, pp. 28–32

Stuhlmacher, M. and C. Grafe, *Oase* 49/50, pp. 182–189

1997

'Iets met ramen. Combinatiegebouw te Amsterdam', *Bouw* no. 7, pp. 12–16

Delera, A., 'Riqualificazione di un quartiere di Amsterdam', *Housing* no. 7/8, pp. 6–88

Dubbeling, D. and K. de Graaf, 'De Bijlmer bloeit op. Integratie van ruimtelijke en sociale vernieuwing', *Bouw* no. 6, pp. 47–53

Giersbergen, M. van, 'Green strips, white strips. Donald Lambert', *Archis* no. 3, pp. 32–35

Heuvel, D. van den, 'De schijn van eenvoud', *de Architect* no. 11, pp. 38–45

Lachlan, E., 'Going Dutch', *Prospect* no. 64, pp. 52–53

Niggli, D. and V, Selig, 'Holländischer Wohnungsbau, ein Perpetuum mobile?', *Archithese* no. 3, pp. 43–49

Rattray, C., 'Design. Claus en Kaan: High theory and low practice', *Arq* no. 7, pp. 26–37

Ryan, R., 'Double Dutch', *The Architectural Review* no. 1, pp. 50–53

Slawik, H., 'Wohnhaus in Amsterdam. Pioniertat', *Zeitschrift für Architekten und Bauingenieure* no. 1, pp. 51–55

1996

'Centre de negocis Landsteinerlaan/Business Centre Landsteinerlaan', *Quaderns*, pp. 26–34 and 112–115

'Wohnbauen in der Haarlemmerbuurt. Amsterdam, 1995', *Werk, Bauen + Wohnen* no. 5, p. 40–41

Dijk, H. van, 'Polizeistation und Sozialamt in einem Haus in Amsterdam', *Bauwelt* no. 4, pp. 150–154

Dijk, H. van, 'Haltung statt Kosmetik', *Bauwelt* no. 4, pp. 150–153

Hulsman, B., 'On Claus en Kaan', *a+u* no. 4, pp. 46–79

Schneider, S., 'Baulücken in Amsterdam', *Baumeister* no. 5, pp. 52–54

1995

'Claus en Kaan', *Blueprint* no. 123, p. 35

'Sozialer Wohnbau in Amsterdam', *Bauwelt* no. 34, pp. 1864–1865

'Wohnbau in Amsterdam', *Bauwelt* no. 34, pp. 1864–1866

Dijk, H. van, 'Wohnanlage in Groningen', *Bauwelt* no. 34, pp. 1860–1863

Roodbol, J. and L. Melis, 'Landschappelijk casco daagt uit tot inventiviteit. Architectonische uitwerking voor Borneo Sporenburg', *de Architect* no. 5, pp. 88–105

Vollaard, P., 'Microchirurgie in de Haarlemmerbuurt', *Architectuur & Bouwen* no. 10, pp. 16–21

Wendt, D., 'Kaveloverschrijdend creatief', *de Architect* no. 10, pp. 74–77

Westrik, J., 'Patio dwellings on Borneo and Sporenburg', *Archis* no. 2, p. 46

Wortmann, A., 'Gewerbezentrum in Amsterdam', *Baumeister* no. 10, pp. 40–43

1994

'Amsterdam. Crèche et Garderie', *Le Moniteur Architecture* no. 49, p. 33

'Business Centre, Amsterdam Noord', *Domus* no. 11, pp. 28–33

Dijk, H. van, 'Normal becomes exceptional. Housing in Groningen by Claus and Kaan', *Archis* no. 6, pp. 24–28

Duursma, J., 'Sobere elegantie in Corpus den Hoorn. Claus en Kaan realiseren woonproject in Groningen', *de Architect* no. 5, pp. 98–103

Klieverik, H., 'Het ontbrekende puzzelstuk. Corpus den Hoorn, Groningen', *Woningraad* no. 6, pp. 14–17

M., I., 'Amsterdam: Straßenbauamt vom Feinsten', *Häuser* no. 1, p. 6

1993

'Festes, Spiegelndes, Leeres', *Werk, Bauen + Wohnen* no. 10, pp. 54–56

'Public Works Department. Felix Claus and Kees Kaan', *a+u* no. 10, pp. 72–80

'Services municipaux à Amsterdam. Claus et Kaan en condition métropolitaine, *L'Architecture d'Aujourd'hui* no. 187, pp. 60–64

G., J., 'Services Amsterdam', *Le Moniteur Architecture* no. 40, p. 10

Gribling, S., 'Kindercentrum Molenwijk van Claus en Kaan Architecten', *de Architect* no. 9, pp. 96–99

Zalingen, M. van, 'Architect', *Eigen Huis & Interieur* no. 4, p. 32

1992

'Verenigingsgebouw te Amsterdam-Oostzaan', *Bouw* no. 18, pp. 40–41

Boekraad, C., 'Congres over Berlages Plan Zuid pakt uit als wervingsactie voor herstel', *Architectuur/Bouwen* no. 1, pp. 16–19

Lootsma, B., 'Onbevangen interpretatie van naoorlogse modernen. Drie gebouwen van Claus en Kaan', *de Architect* no. 7/8, pp. 34–45

1991

Melis, L., 'Aus zwei mach eins', *Bauwelt* no. 6, pp. 2450–2451

Melis, L., 'Transformatie van twee onder een kap. Verbouwing van Claus en Kaan in Bergen op Zoom', *de Architect* no. 9, pp. 140–141

1989

'Kinderdagverblijf in voormalige houtzagerij', *Bouw* no. 17, pp. 19–21

Melis, L., 'Verbouwen voor kinderen. Twee kinderdagverblijven in Utrecht', *de Architect* no. 1, pp. 37–43

Newspapers

2001

Butijn, H., 'Een sober gebouw dat recht doet aan deze plaats', *Trouw* 24 September

Hulsman, B., 'Leren van Almere', *NRC Handelsblad* 25 May

2000

'Claus en Kaan (ver)bouwen Gemeentearchief Amsterdam', *Trouw* 27 June

'El consulado griego, con el puerto', *La Voz de Galicia* 28 April

'Nieuw Stadskantoor zweeft', *Het Stadsblad* 8 March

Geist, H., 'Raaks wordt geen Disneyland', *Haarlems Dagblad* 22 March

Geist, H. and W. de Wagt, 'Studentenflat valt bij lezers in de smaak', *Haarlems Dagblad* 14 February

Ibelings, H., 'De galerijflat', *de Volkskrant* 10 February

Vries, M. de, 'Rust, Ruimte and Lotgenoten', *Het Parool* 20 April

1999

Hulsman, B., 'Almere temt Weebers wilde wonen tot gewild wonen. Zesentwintig architecten ontwerpen flexibele woningen voor tentoonstelling op ware grootte', *NRC Handelsblad* 13 July

1998

Hulsman, B., 'Rijke variatie aan lichthofwoningen. Bijzondere patiowoningen te bezichtigen op dag van de architectuur', *NRC Handelsblad*

Wagt, W. de, 'Zeer magere expositie Claus en Kaan. ABC Architectencentrum gooit reputatie te grabbel', *Haarlems Dagblad*

1996

Kähler, G., 'In der Leerformel der Moderne sind viele Wohnungen. Mit einer unangestrengten Theorie und einem Schuß Pragmatismus bauen Architecten an den neuen Niederlanden', *Frankfurter Allgemeine Zeitung* 23 October

Koster, E., 'Claus en Kaan: balanceren op de grens van banale', *Het Financieele Dagblad* 29 July

Vries, M. de, 'Gouden kiezen in een oud gebit. Nieuwbouw top 5 van de Amsterdamse binnenstad', *Het Parool* 6 January

1995

'Bijlmerdreef krijgt allure van Rooseveltlaan', *De Echo* 22 March

'Gulden Kruis basis van Nieuwe Bijlmer', *Nieuws van de Dag* 21 March

'Nieuwe wijk is Bijlmer op zijn kop. Gulden Kruis biedt bewoners eigen opgang and weinig openbare ruimte', *de Volkskrant* 21 March

Hulsman, B., 'Het beste van drie werelden in een gebouw verenigd', *NRC Handelsblad* 10 October

Hulsman, B., 'Architecten zoeken oplossing voor dicht-op-elkaar', *NRC Handelsblad* 13 November

Maastrecht, R. van, 'Vernieuwing Bijlmer breekt met begrip functionele stad', *Trouw* 21 March

Mulder, Y., 'Bijlmermeer heeft burgerlijkheid nodig. In meer opzichten "op niveau" wonen', *Weekmedia* 12 April

Velden, C. van der, 'Wethouder Reijnhout bemoeit zich in Nieuwland zelfs met de voegen. Nieuwland, Schiedams eerste naoorlogse wijk, veranderd in een grote bouwput', *Rotterdams Dagblad* 5 April

1993

'Herbestemming Molenerf de Ster wint Arcinom Paris 1993', *Stadsblad* 19 May

Haan, H. de and I. Haagsma, 'Een serene doos voor de buitendiensten. Architecten Claus en Kaan respecteren jaren '50', *de Volkskrant* 17 July

Huisman, J., 'Architectuur tussen luciferdoosje and pijpenla. De "smalle modernen" voegen zich moeiteloos in het straatbeeld', *de Volkskrant* 14 May

Other publications

2001

15 jaar Gispen Archinorm Stadsverfraaiingsprijs, Culemborg 2001

Minimalismos. Un signo de los tiempos, Madrid 2001, p. 91

Broto, C., *New Housing Concepts*, Barcelona 2001, pp. 310–315

Gool van, R., L. Herstelt, F.-B. Raith and L. Schenk, *Das Niederländische Reihenhaus*, Stuttgart/Munich 2001, pp. 56–63

Hoogewoning, A. et al. (eds), *Architectuur in Nederland. Jaarboek/Architecture in the Netherlands. Yearbook 2000–2001*, Rotterdam 2001, pp. 96–97

Pfeifer, G., *Mauerwerk Atlas*, Munich 2001, pp. 272–275

Pranlas-Descours, J.-P. and M. Velly, *Panoramas Europeens*, Paris 2001, p. 31

Schaap, P.-M. and B. Verhave, *Manifest Toolenburg-Zuid. deel 1: de voorbereiding*, Hoofddorp 2001, pp. 53–57

2000

Gewild Wonen, Almere 2000, pp. 74–77

Wonen in de stad, Rotterdam 2000

Cerver, F.A., *European Masters. Eleven recent works*, Barcelona 2000, pp. 148–155

Cerver, F.A., *Hedendaagse architectuur*, Cologne 2000, pp. 814–815

Franco, A. and A. Roman, *Por Venir. Conversaciones conveinte jovenes arquitectors europeos*, Madrid 2000, pp. 74–83

Grunßer, C., *Energiesparsiedlungen*, Munich 2000, pp. 94–98

Hoog de, M., A. Misch, *Landschaparchitectuur and stedebouw in Nederland '97-'99*, Bussum 2000, pp. 116–119

Ibelings, H. (ed.), *Architectuur in Nederland. Jaarboek/Architecture in the Netherlands. Yearbook 1999–2000*, Rotterdam 2000, pp. 148–155

Ibelings, H., *The Artificial Landscape. Contemporary Architecture, Urbanism and Landscape Architecture in the Netherlands,* Rotterdam 2000, pp. 73–75

Kloos, M. and D. Wendt, *Formats for Living. Contemporary floor plans in Amsterdam*, Amsterdam 2000, pp. 53, 94, 119, 134 and 147

Michel, H., Claus en Kaan, Amsterdam 2000

Stuurgroep Experimenten Volkshuisvesting, *Herwonnen schoonheid. Vier voorbeeldplannen in naoorlogse herontwikkelingswijken*, Rotterdam 2000, pp. 58–71

Venema, H., *Buitenplaats Ypenburg. Een bevlogen bouwlocatie*, Bussum 2000, p. 108–109

Zabalbeascoa, A. and J. Rodríguez Marcos, *Minimalismos*, Barcelona 2000, p. 106

1999

Bouwen op de ZON, Utrecht 1999, pp. 80–83

Compact wonen. Onderzoek naar waardering van grondgebonden woningen in hoge dichtheid in Amsterdam, Amsterdam 1999, pp. 32–44

De schoonheid van Amsterdam. Een kader voor het welstandsbeleid 1999, Amsterdam 1999, pp. 87, 134 and 121

International Yearbook Award Winning Architecture 1998/99, Munich/London/New York 1999, pp. 89–99

Townhouses, Barcelona 1999, pp. 172–179

Dijk, H. van, *Twentieth-Century Architecture in the Netherlands*, Rotterdam 1999, pp. 89–99

Huisman, J., M. Claus, J. Derwig and G. van der Vlugt, *100 jaar Bouwkunst in Amsterdam/ An outline of Amsterdam Architecture since 1900*, Amsterdam 1999, pp. 1993 and 1999

Maar, B. de, *Een zee van huizen. De woningen van New Deal op Borneo/Sporenburg*, Bussum 1999

Provoost, M., B. Colenbrander and F. Alkemade, *Dutchtown: A City Centre Design by OMA/Rem Koolhaas*, Rotterdam 1999, p. 113

1998

Restaureren toekomst voor verleden. Opdrachtgevers and restauratiearchitect in beeld, Amsterdam 1998, pp. 38–39

Battista, K. and F. Migsch, *The Netherlands. A guide to recent architecture*, London 1998, pp. 38–40 and 114

Bergeijk, H. van and O. Macel, *Guida all'architettura del Novecento Benelux*, Milan 1998, pp. 226–227

Dijk, H. van, *Gids voor moderne architectuur in Nederland/ Guide to modern architecture in the Netherlands*, Rotterdam 1998, pp. 42, 142, 164, 174

Gausa, M., *Housing. New alternatives, new systems*, Barcelona 1998, p. 98

Graf, A., *Einfamilienhäuser aus Backstein*, Munich 1998, pp. 124–125

Ibelings, H. (ed.), *Architectuur in Nederland. Jaarboek/Architecture in the Netherlands. Yearbook 1997–1998*, Rotterdam 1998, pp. 48–49

Kaan, K., *Entdeckungen. Architekturpreis Rheinland-Pfalz 1998*, Cologne 1998, pp. 34–35

Mostaedi, A., *Residences for the Elderly*, Barcelona 1998, pp. 206–215

Stamm-Teske, W., B. Sunder-Plassmanen, I. Kupferschmid, *Preiswerter Wohnungsbau in den Niederlanden 1993–1998 Eine Projektauswahl*, Düsseldorf 1998, pp. 18–21

1997

Lotus 92, Milan 1997, pp. 50–52

Lotus 94, Milan 1997, pp. 94–95

Ferrater, C., *Claus en Kaan*, Barcelona 1997

Furnari, M., *Progrettazione Architectonica: strategie di composizione dell'edificio contemporaneo*, Milan 1997, pp. 258, 252

Siebert, E., *Architektur in den Niederlanden. Aktuelle Tendenzen und Projekte*, Munich 1997, pp. 16–17

1996

Oosterman, A., *Woningbouw in Nederland. Voorbeeldige architectuur van de jaren negentig/ Housing in the Netherlands. Exemplary Architecture of the Nineties*, Rotterdam 1996, pp. 74–75

1995

Zoeken naar Architectuur, Groningen 1995

Brouwers, R. (ed.), *Architectuur in Nederland. Jaarboek/ Architecture in the Netherlands. Yearbook 1994–1995*, Rotterdam 1995, pp. 100, 142 and 146

Ibelings, H., *20th Century Architecture in the Netherlands,* Rotterdam 1995, p. 166

1994

Brouwers, R. (ed.), *Architectuur in Nederland. Jaarboek/ Architecture in the Netherlands. Yearbook 1993–1994*, Rotterdam 1994, pp. 90–93

Dam, C., *Voor Hedy Minister van Cultuur 1989–1994*, Amsterdam 1994, pp. 14–15

1993

Premio Internazionale di architettura Andrea Palladio 1993, Milan 1993, pp. 64–69

1992

Berlage en de Toekomst van Amsterdam Zuid, Amsterdam 1992, pp. 40–50

1990

Stichting Fonds voor beeldende kunsten, vormgeving and bouwkunst, Individuele subsidies. 1 januari 1989–1 januari 1990, Amsterdam 1990, pp. 384–385 and 386–387

CD-rom

Euroscan, an interactive database of modern European architecture, Oxford 1997

Website

www.clausenkaan.com

LECTURES

2001

Stofflichkeiten, RWTH, Achen, 8 January

Un architecte, Un bâtiment, Pavillon de l'Arsenal, Paris, 21 January

Work report, University, Kaiserslautern, 25 January

Hollandse Meesters, Academy of Architecture, Amsterdam, March + April

Building Architecture, International Architecture Festival, Mexico City, 29 March

Mies van der Rohe, Academy of Architecture, Amsterdam, 28 April

Without Client, TN Probe, Tokyo, 26 June

Lecture about own work, Colegio de Arquitectes, Málaga, 4 October

Lecture about own work, AHO Oslo School of Architecture, Oslo, 12 + 13 November

2000

Lecture about own work, Zona Architettura, Turin, 2 February

Snelle Stad, Langzame Stad, Academy of Architecture, Amsterdam, 10 February

Work report, Henry van der Velde Instituut, Antwerpen, 3 March

Housing in the Netherlands, ORTE Architekturnetzwerk, St. Pölten, 12 March

Snelle Stad, Langzame Stad, Ghent University, Ghent, 13 March

Lecture about own work, Academy of Architecture, Amsterdam, 17 April

Design themes, University of Architecture, Madrid, 26 April

Housing in the Netherlands, University of Architecture, La Coruña, 28 April

Indesem 2000 Analysegroep Housing: Comparative Reflection, Delft University of Technology, Delft, 29 November

1999

Lecture about own work, Academy of Architecture, Amsterdam, 8 February

Building, Columbia University, New York, 26 March

Building, Roger Williams University, Newport, 26 March

De schoonheid van Amsterdam, een kader voor welstands-beleid, Stedelijke Woningdienst Amsterdam, Amsterdam, 3 June

The primacy of urban planning, MACB, Barcelona, 1 July

Lecture on Architecture in the Netherlands, Seminario Internacional de arquitectura industrial, Vitoria-Gasteiz, 10 September

Flexible Re-Use of Buildings and Spaces, Taiwan Holland Festival, Taipei, 20 September

Offene Raume Leere Limit Landschaft, Staatliche Akademie der Bildenden Künste, Stuttgart, 6 October

Double Dutch, Icelandic Association of Architects, Reykjavik, 15 November

1998

Work report, Staatliche Akademie der Bildenden Künste, Stuttgart, 20 January

Contrast and Analogy, Architectural Association of Ireland, Dublin, 12 February

Concept & Detail, Delft University of Technology, 12 March

Work report, Technische Universität, Berlin, 23 April

Form, Konstruktion, Detail, Fachhochschule, Dortmund, 28 April

The Dutch Experience, The Royal Incorporation of Architects in Scotland, Aberdeen, 8 May

Jour Fixe, Staatliche Akademie der Bildenden Künste, Stuttgart, 9 June

Lecture about own work, Academy of Architecture, Arnhem, 12 June

Strategies, Centro Mediterráneo, Montril/Granada, 21 September

Rational Architecture, Royal University of Fine Arts, Stockholm, 2 November

1997

Bouwen in Nederland, Academy of Architecture, Maastricht, 14 February

Materiaal en Vorm, Delft University of Technology, 6 November

Design Strategies, Scott Sutherland School of Architecture, Aberdeen, 20 November

Architectuur en Materialiteit, Provinciaal Centrum voor Beeldende Kunsten Limburg, Hasselt, 2 December

De bruikbaarheid van het woningontwerp, Zuiderkerk, Amsterdam, 16 December

1996

Architecten op weg naar de 21e eeuw, Eindhoven University of Technology, Eindhoven, 19 January

Round-table discussion in the context of the exhibition *Zoeken naar Architectuur*, Academy of Architecture, Tilburg, 27 February

Physionomie, Berlage Institute, Amsterdam, 11 March

Thicker than Paper; On architecture and materiality, University, Kyoto, April

Lecture about own work, IAAS, Hamburg, 21 July

1995

Het Primaat van de Stedenbouw, lecture to the Association of Dutch Urban Planners, Zuiderkerk, Amsterdam, 16 March

Concept & Detail, Delft University of Technology, Delft, 22 May

Different Worlds; The border between public and private space and how this aspect effects all our work, Österreichische Gesellschaft für Architektur, Wenen, 16 June

Design Strategies, Forum Stadtpark, Graz, 19 June

Different Worlds; The border between public and private space and how this aspect effects all our work, Architekturforum Tirol, Innsbruck, 20 June

Ambiguity, Kunsthochschule Berlin Weissensee, Berlin, 27 June

Thicker than Paper; Over architectuur en materialiteit, Academy of Architecture, Amsterdam, 2 November

1994

Presentation of own work at the Eindhoven Connectie, Kovos ruimte, Eindhoven, 11 January

Lecture about own work and sources of inspiration, Academy of Architecture, Groningen, 17 May

Lecture as part of series about Dutch architecture, Universität Gesamthochschule, Kassel, 21 June

Lecture in which own work is set against prevailing architectural opinion, College of Arts, Arnhem, Arnhem, 9 December

1993

Lecture about own work, Grand Café Dulac, Amsterdam, 12 October

EXHIBITIONS

2001
'Minimalismos', Museo Reina Sophia, Madrid
10 juli–8 October

2000
'Rijnland in de Steigers', Town Hall, Leiden
4 September–15 October
'Dutchtown, Aedes East, Berlin
4 September–23 October
'Bienal International de Arquitectura', São Paulo
20 November 1999–25 January 2000

1999
'Dutchtown', Netherlands Architecture Institute, Rotterdam
27 November 1999–6 February 2000
'Wilde Wonen', Town Hall, Almere
July–August

1998
'Claus en Kaan Architecten', ABC, Architectuur and Bouwhistorisch Centrum, Haarlem
4 September–18 October
'Rheinischer Architekturpreis', Stiftung Baukultur Rheinland-Pfalz, Mainz
1–18 October

1997
'De smaak van de opdrachtgever', ARCAM Gallery, Amsterdam
15 February–23 March

1996
'Vijf jaar Vedute', ARCAM Gallery, Amsterdam
24 May–6 July
'Architektur in den Niederlanden', Haus der Architekten, Stuttgart
May

1995
'Zoeken naar Architectuur', CAS, Groningen
June

1994
'Kansen voor stad and markt', Zuiderkerk, Amsterdam
December
'Bauten junger Architekten, Deutsches Architektur Museum, Frankfurt
August–September
Fontane Haus, Berlin
October–November
'Blik op de Buitenruimte', Art Colleges in Utrecht, Delft, 's-Hertogenbosch
from May
'Bienal de Arquitectura y Urbanismo', Zaragoza
March
'5 Plannen - 5 Architecten', Zuiderkerk, Amsterdam
October–February

1993
'Premio internazionale Andrea Palladio', Basilica Palladiana, Vicenza
September–October
'De actualiteiten van Lieven de Key', ARCAM Gallery, Amsterdam
October
'Bouwkunst in Het Veem', Het Veem, Amsterdam
September
'Kleine gaten in de stad', ARCAM Gallery, Amsterdam
April–June

1992
'75 Jaar Berlage-Plan Zuid', RAI Congress Centre, Amsterdam
October
'Architectuurestafette 1992', Utrecht
June
'Bouwen in Utrecht 1989–1990', Centraal Museum, Utrecht
November 1991–January 1992

1990
'Victorieplein', Zuiderkerk, Amsterdam
September
'Verbouwen of Vervangen', Galerie Wibaut, Amsterdam
February–May

PRIZES / NOMINATIONS

2001
Nomination: Best Designed Book Foundation

2000
Haarlem Architecture Prize

1999
Model status, SEV
Plan of the month, Gelders Genootschap
Nomination: Mies van der Rohe Pavillon Award
Nomination: National Renovation Prize

1997
Grand Prix Rhénan d'Architecture

1994
Honourable Mention, Océ/BNA prize for industrial architecture
Incentive Prize, Architecture, Amsterdam Art Council
Architecture Prize, Groningen

1993
Nomination: Premio Palladio
Archinorm Urban Beautification Prize

1991
Nomination: Rietveld Prize

1989
Start-up grant from Netherlands Foundation for Fine Arts, Design and Architecture

STAFF MEMBERS CLAUS EN KAAN ARCHITECTEN

Rita Abreu
Floor Arons
Esther Aronsohn
Allard Assies
Jakob Bader
Jan Bekkering
Bart Bekooy
Kurt van Belle
Henri van Bennekom
Michiel van Bijlevelt
Inez Bisschof
Dieter Blok
Diana Boogaart
Marc van Broekhuijsen
Barbara de Bruijn
Veronique de Bruin
Leo van den Burg
Christian Burzer
Sven Ove Cordsen
Andrew Dawes
Alfonso Diaz Prats
Valery Didelon
Walter van Dijk
Pier Dijkema
Katinka Dirker
Dagmar Driebeek
Eric Drieënhuizen
Olivier Ebben
Frederik Ellens
Bart van der Ende
Mario Ferreira
Mario Flamman
Kyra Frankort
Bernardo Frontera
Sigrun Gabele
Michael Geensen
Jordi Gendrau
Marcel Gerritsen
Jaap Gräber
Danielle Hagenstein
Dorothee Haneke
Leo Harders
Mirjam de Heer
Martijn van der Heijden
Kai Hellström
Jesús Hernández Mayor
Kristine Heueck
Artsje Hijlkema
Jan Hobel
Martjan den Hoed
Geert van Hoof
Leonieke Hornsveld
Manou Huijbregts
Monique Hutschemakers
Bernhard Jaarsma
Michiel Janssen
Ronald Janssen
Jan Jonkers
Martin van Kampenhout
Rob Kanbier
Jan Kerkhoff
Monica Ketting
Markus Kilian
Daniel Kinz
Ton Kip
Ron Kleinsman
Lucy Knox-Knight
Furkan Köse
Silvia Kramer
Naomi de Kuiper
André Kwakernaak
Jan Willem Lekkerkerker
Lidewij Lenders
Ana Lobo Martins
Hanneke Lommerse
Irene Lönne
Anja Lübke
Aster Maaskant
Ralph van Mameren
Sara Martin Camara
Patricia Medina Prieto
Dick van de Merwe
Agnes van der Mey
Olivier Motte
Dirk Muller
Michel Nadorp
Jeroen van Nieuwenhuizen
Siebold Nijenhuis
Liesbeth Noorman
Seada Nourhussen
Hannes Ochmann
Derk Onnekes
Susan Otto
Vincent Panhuysen
Ulrich Pantle
Michiel van Pelt
Matthias Pfalz
Delphine Plojoux
Daniela Raab
Rinske van Ramshorst
Elianne Reijers
Remco Remijnse
Roland Rens
Jenny Rheinlander
Ronald Rientjes
Ilse Rijneveld
Lies Rollmann
Björn Scharwei
Jan Scheidewind
Karsten Schellmat
Ronald Schleurholts
Edwin Schlichter
Romy Schneider
Florian Schrage
Steven Schulze
Dikkie Scipio
Heidi Serbruyns
Dimphie Slooters
Ralph Smit
Kim Sneyders
Sarah van Sonsbeek
Nuno Sousa da Silva
Maarten Steunenberg
Lisette Stomp
Lars Straeter
Sibil Sträuli
Els Stroobants
Pasquale Talerico
Wing Tang
Urdice Tuinfort
Natalie Vanderick
Mirjam Verheul
Thierry Voellinger
Dick van Wageningen
Katrin Weber
Yuri Wemer
Janneke Wessels
Margreet van der Woude
Ellen Wybenga
Pim van Wylick
Chuck Yeager
Farina de Zeeuw
Marjanneke de Zeeuw
Hylke Zijlstra
Martin Zwinggi

ABOUT THE AUTHORS

David Chipperfield (1953) trained at the Architectural Association in London. After graduating in 1977 he worked for Richard Rogers and Norman Foster, among others, before setting up his own practice, David Chipperfield Architects, in 1984. Among his best known works are the Gotoh Museum in Tokyo, and the River and Rowing Museum at Henley-on-Thames in England. He is currently working on a number of large cultural projects including the Neues Museum on Berlin's Museum Island. Over the years he has had various visiting professorships and since 2001 he has held the Mies van der Rohe chair at the Escola Técnica Superior d'Arquitectura in Barcelona. His numerous architectural awards include the 1991 Palladia Award for the Toyota Auto Kyoto Building in Japan, and in 1999 the Tessenow Gold Medal Award.

Andrea Deplazes (1960) graduated from the ETH in Zurich in 1988 after which he set up in private practice together with Valentin Bearth. In Switzerland his built works include the Williman-Lotscher house at Sevgein, the Sunniberg bridge at Klosters, and a school at Alvaschein. Since 1995 he has been editor of the Swiss architectural magazine *Werk, Bauen + Wohnen*. In 1997 he took up a professorship at the ETH in Zurich.

Christoph Grafe (1964) is an architect and writer based in Amsterdam and London, and Associate Professor of Architectural Design and Interior at Delft University of Technology. He has published widely on European architecture and since 1994 he has been an editor of the Dutch architectural magazine *Oase*. He is currently researching European cultural buildings from the postwar period.

Hans Ibelings (1963) studied art history at the University of Amsterdam. He has designed exhibitions for the Netherlands Architecture Institute in Rotterdam and edited *the Architecture in the Netherlands Yearbook*. As architecture critic he has a great many publications to his name, including *20th Century Architecture in the Netherlands*, *Supermodernism*, and *The Artificial Landscape*.

Han Michel (1946) studied at Delft University of Technology. In 1990 he was appointed director of the Lieven de Key housing association and in 1996 director of Woonstichting De Key, a housing corporation resulting from the merger of Lieven de Key, De Doelen and Onze Woning. Since 1 July 2000 he has been director of De Principaal BV, an Amsterdam property developer specializing in complex building programmes in urban settings.

Rafael Moneo (1937) graduated in 1961 from the School of Architecture in Madrid, after which he worked in the Denmark office of Jørn Utzon for two years. After a further two years attached to the Spanish Academy in Rome, he set up in private practice in Madrid in 1965. His major works include the Bankinter Bank in Madrid, the conversion of the historic Villahermosa Palace in the same city into a museum that now houses the Thyssen-Bornemisza collection, the Houston Museum of Fine Arts, the Stockholm Museum of Modern Art and Architecture, and the Potzdamer Platz Hotel in Berlin. In tandem with numerous professorships throughout Europe and the United States, Rafael Moneo has produced an extensive body of work as architectural critic and theoretician. In 1996 he was awarded the prestigious Pritzker Prize for Architecture.

PICTURE CREDITS

Pictures are numbered per page,
from left to right, and from top to bottom

Abbot, Berenice/Museum of the City of New York 149.3
Aldershoff, R. 92.1 93.1 115.1
Aprahamian, P. 156
Archiv Michael Fasshauer 47.2
Bernadó, J. 176.3
Blonk, A. 40.3 41.1 41.3 56.1 57.1 199.2
Boyer, M.146 148.4
Broek & Bakema, Van den 53.1
Casals, L. 25.2
Chillida, E./C. Roca 104.2
Christiaanse Architects & Planners, Kees 212.6
Claus, F. 8 18.2 19 24.2 27.5 45.1 58.1 62.1 106.1-2 109.1-2 128.2 137.5 148.5 148.7 160.1 166.2 175.1 176.4 179 192.5 193.1
Claus, M. 18.3 25.4 27.1-4 28 30.1-2 31 32.1-3 33.1-3 44.6 46.3 47.1 49.3 57.2-3 59.1-4 60 61.1-3 64.1 66.2 69.1-4 84 88.1-3 89.1-4 89.6 91.3 94.3 102.3 103.1 134.4 136.5 160.3-4 161.3 192.6 194.3 195.3 195.5 197.2 199.1 199.4-5 200.7 202.3 217.2
Croes, T. 140.2-3 143.2 149.1-2 162.3 163.4 210.5 211.6 222.4
Derwig, J. 120.1
Diekman, A. 130.1 145.2-3
DKV Architecten 215.6
Donald Judd Estate/5x7 Studio 159
Dormolen, H. van 36.1-4 195.6
DRO Vormgeving/Fotografie 58.4
Estes, Richard/Museum Thyssen-Bornemisza 94.2
Fondation Le Corbusier 131.1 177.3 179
Frank, Robert/National Gallery of Modern Art 80.2
Frattini 151.2
Frederiksen, J. 144.1-2
Fundação Oscar Niemeyer 163.1-2
Gargiani, R. 161.2
Gemeentearchief Amsterdam 52.1 63.1 170.2
Haags Gemeentemuseum 58.3
Hopper, Edward/Smithsonian American Art Museum 86.1
Hubers, W. 16.2
Jaeger, G. 17.2 17.4 192.1
Jones, Inigo/A.C. Cooper 240
Jorgensen, V. 154.1
Kaan, K. 20.1 21.1 56.2 76.1-2 140.1 140.4 142.3-4 143.5 162.2
Kerkhof, M./Studio Retina 75.1-3 151.1 174.2
KLM Aerocarto 34.2 40.1 118.2
Kramer, L. 81.1 85.2 102.1 103.2 111.1-6 112.1-6 113.1-5 122 123.1-4 136.3 137.1 137.6 138 139.1-3 162.1 203.6 204.4 205.3 206.1 206.4 209.1 209.3 210.1 210.3-4 212.1
Koenig, F.C. 190
Mollino, C. 14
Muciaccia 166.1
Musch, J. 128.1 205.4
Nacasa & Partners 44.1
Nederlands Architectuurinstituut 34.1 62.2 64.2
New York Public Library 116.1
Ouwerkerk, E.J. 114.1 115.2 115.4 134.1 134.3-4 137.2 137.4
Rembrandt/Rijksmuseum Amsterdam 12
Richters, C. 49.2 50.1-3 57.4 66.1 66.3 67.5-7 68 69.5 70 71.1 71.3-4 72.1-3 73 75.4-5 76.4-5 77 78.2-3 79.2 82.2 82.4 83.1-2 85.1 91.5 94.1 95 98.1 99.1 100.1 101.3 104.1 104.3 105.1-5 106.3-4 107 108.1-3 109.3-4 114.2 117.1-4 118.1 119.1-2 120.2-3 120.5 121 126 127.1 127.3-4 129.1-5 133.1-5 197.1 200.2 200.4 201.2-3 202.4 203.4 204.2-3 205.2 205.5 206.2-3 206.6 207.2-3 208.5
Riehle, T. 130.2
Rijksmuseum Amsterdam/Collectie KOG 82.1
Scagliola, D. & S. Brakkee 116.2
Schaap, T. 148.2-3
Schmitz, A. 215.4-5
Shulman, J. 25.1
Stern, P. 24.1
Stoller, E./ESTO 26.2 167.3
Street-Porter, T. 20.4
Suermondt, R. 120.4
Swart, S. 67.4
Sweering, M. 86.3 87.1
Ueno, N. 136.6
Vlugt & Claus, Van der 22.1-4 23 41.2
Vlugt, G. van der 25.3 25.5 26.1 29 35.1-3 37.1-3 38.1-4 39.1-2 42 43.1-4 44.2 45.3 46.1 52.2 63.2 64.3 65.1-2 76.3 80.1 82.3 90 91.1-2 91.4 92.2 93.2-3 96.1-3 97.1-5 99.2-3 100.2 101.1-2 195.1 196.3 198.3 199.3 200.6 202.1 203.1
Voeten, S. 20.3 22.2-1 195.4
Warhol, Andy/Whitney Museum of American Art, New York 161.1
Zeitveld, J. van 177.1
Zwarts, K. 20.2 45.2 46.2-3 47.3 49.1 51 71.2 78.1 79.1 89.5 125 145.1 197.3-4

This publication, and the preceding research, was made possible, in part, by the Netherlands Architecture Fund.

Picture editing
Leo van den Burg

Picture research
Christel Leenen, Ingrid Oosterheerd

Translation
Robyn de Jong-Dalziel (*Dutch-English*)
Paul Hammond (*Spanish-English*)
Bookmakers (*German-English*)

Copy editing
Robyn de Jong-Dalziel

Graphic design
Patrick Coppens and Karel Martens

Lithography and printing
Drukkerij Mart.Spruijt bv

Final editing and production
Caroline Gautier

Publisher
Simon Franke

Available in North, South and Central America through D.A.P./Distributed Art Publishers Inc, 155 Sixth Avenue 2nd Floor, New York, NY 10013-1507, United States. T: +1 212 6271999, F: +1 212 6279484

Available in the United Kingdom and Ireland through Art Data, 12 Bell Industrial Estate, 50 Cunnington Street, London W4 5HB, United Kingdom. T: +44 181 7471061, F: +44 181 742231

Printed and bound in the Netherlands

ISBN 90-5662-228-5

Approached to write an afterword for this monograph, I was asked if I would place Claus en Kaan in the Dutch tradition. It is the kind of question that steers a writer inescapably in the direction of the anecdotal approach so despised by theorists.

What exactly is the Dutch tradition? How are architects influenced by it? In the Golden Age, for example, when everyone's radius of action was restricted and the rest of the world existed purely for the spice trade, influences were relatively easy to identify. But today, when the world is a village where information is concerned, connections and influences have become totally chaotic.

Some would contend that cultural identity – what constitutes Dutchness – is no longer based on an absolute imperative but is first and foremost a matter of personal inclination. People have to decide for themselves what binds them to their surroundings, and that applies to architects, too. Individuals are free to invoke the Dutch tradition if they so wish. Once, at the opening of an exhibition of work by Claus en Kaan, I placed their work in the tradition of Dutch Classicism. This theme may have seemed at the time to have been based on thorough research, but had actually fallen into my lap because the show was held in Haarlem, the city of Jacob van Campen, the chief exponent of Classicism in the Netherlands.
For all that, it is true that Claus en Kaan are happy to be seen as continuing the line of Dutch Classicism. Their designs, in common with those of Jacob van Campen, Pieter Post and Philips Vingboons have a mathematical basis. Ornamentation is restrained and stylistically correct, decorations are perfectly in keeping with the structure of the building.
The 17th-century Dutch Classicists, with their harmonious proportions, pursued an absolute beauty. In this they were following in the footsteps of the Italian humanists, with Rome, the pinnacle of human civilization, as reference point.

Contemporary architects, who consume huge and haphazard quantities of theories and im ages, cannot be so clearly categorized. But the architectural tasks that Claus en Kaan take upon themselves often bear a strong resemblance to those of their predecessors. The plasticity of the wall, for example, is a favourite theme of Claus en Kaan, just as it was of the Dutch Classicists. That plasticity is accentuated by means of the ordering of the window frames: in their projects on Hoogte Kadijk in Amsterdam they used the Dutch sash window, with its characteristic spa tial effect, in caricatural fashion. This deliberate exaggeration is readily explained. Those earlier

architects were able to use sophisticated craftsmanship to emphasize the plasticity of a facade, heightening the spatial effect of window frames, for example, with high quality masonry and delicate pointing. Claus en Kaan are obliged to overdo things because their projects, especially the standardized housing schemes, are realized with modern industrialized building techniques. A keen eye for expediency, a spirit of enterprise and pragmatism are without question the enduring hallmarks of Dutch culture. They probably explain why, in spite of an impressive architectural practice, there is so little theorizing in the Netherlands. Claus en Kaan, too, are content to express themselves in their buildings rather than in writing. They manage the production of designs in their offices in Amsterdam and Rotterdam as businessmen.
They are architect–entrepreneurs.

With quiet self-confidence they analyse the programmes required by the commission and the strengths of the physical context. They concentrate on the irrefutable concept. The materialization is deferred; it will presently be a problem for the expert. First the structure, according to Dutch tradition. Which is why professional clients like working with Claus en Kaan.
One characteristic of Felix Claus and Kees Kaan that is difficult to place in the Dutch tradition, is their well-known admiration for the big personalities, the 'celebrities' of the architectural world. The Dutch predilection for moderation and reasonableness is not exactly sympathetic to compelling biographies in the making.

Claus en Kaan are now at a crossroads. They can follow the course taken by Van Campen: we know a lot about his buildings, little about his life. Except that there is no longer any tradition that imposes restrictions. Felix and Kees can also opt for a carefully orchestrated and transmitted picture of their lives as architects. Either way, they must continue to make fine buildings if they are to go down in history.

Han Michel